WILEY

MW01679749

GAAP for Employee Benefits Plans

Randi L. Starr
Patty Miller
Karen Caprio
Phyllis Dunn

JOHN WILEY & SONS, INC.
New York • Chichester • Weinheim • Brisbane • Singapore • Toronto

This text is printed on acid-free paper. ♾

Library of Congress Cataloging-in-Publication Data:

August 2000
GAAP for employee benefits plans
ISSN 1530-6461

ISBN 0-471-37961-1

Printed in the United States of America
10 9 8 7 6 5 4 3 2 1

CONTENTS

ABOUT THE AUTHORS

Karen T. Caprio is a senior manager in the Pittsburgh office of Deloitte & Touche LLP. She has over eight years of experience in public accounting, including four years as a manager. Karen has a wide range of experience in managing audits of SEC clients and employee benefits plans. Karen assists the National Industry Director of Employee Benefits and the National Audit Partner, Employee Benefits. In her role, Karen serves as one of the firm's national resources and provides consultation services regarding employee benefit matters to the various practice offices. Karen has also worked on various firm initiatives in the Employee Benefits Industry, such as organizing and serving as an instructor at the firm's annual National Employee Benefit Seminars and creating audit support software for our employee benefit plan engagements.

Phyllis Dunn is a senior manager with Deloitte & Touche LLP. She has over twelve years of public accounting experience and leads the assurance and advisory services employee benefits practice for the North Texas, Little Rock, and Tulsa offices. In this role she serves as a technical resource for employee benefit accounting and auditing matters for these offices, as well as prepares and presents training seminars in various areas of employee benefit plan accounting, financial reporting, and auditing. She holds a BA in Accounting from Texas Tech University.

Patty Miller is a manager in the Pittsburgh office of Deloitte & Touche LLP. Patty has over eight years of experience in public accounting and two years of internal audit experience with a Fortune 100 manufacturer. She has managed the audits of many of the firm's not-for-profit and healthcare clients and specializes in employee benefits plans. Patty assists the firm's National Industry Director of Employee Benefits and National Audit Partner, Employee Benefits. In her role, Patty serves as one of the firm's national resources and provides consultation services regarding employee benefits matters to various practice offices. She has presented on the topic of audit efficiency for employee benefits plans and is an active participant in the national implementation of the firm's audit support software, AS/2. Ms. Miller holds a B.S. degree in Business Administration and Information Systems from Xavier University.

Randi Starr is a national audit partner and the National Industry Director of Employee Benefits in the Pittsburgh office of Deloitte & Touche LLP. Randi has over twenty years of experience in public accounting, including ten years as a partner. She has a wide range of experience in directing and managing SEC and other audits of multilocation corporations. She has specialized in manufacturing and public utility clients. Randi serves as a national resource and is responsible for coordinating our accounting and auditing, tax, and management consulting services in the employee benefits area. She also develops the firm's policies with respect to the audits of employee benefits programs and is the firm's representative on the AICPA employee benefits committee. She has served a three-year appointment advising the Secretary of Labor as the Accounting Representative on the ERISA Advisory Council and has devoted substantial time to responding to Department of Labor employee benefit concerns and proposed regulations as they relate to the accounting profession. Randi is currently serving a year appointment as the Chairperson of the AICPA Employee Benefit Plans Committee. She holds a B.S. in Mathematics and graduated with honors from Grove City College.

PREFACE

Employee benefit plans have changed dramatically over the past twenty to twenty-five years. These plans provide many of the most popular fringe benefits that are offered to employees by employers. Often, when given a choice, an employee will choose greater pension benefits or postretirement medical coverage over wage increases. Consistent with this trend, the accounting and reporting requirements for employee benefit plans have rapidly evolved to keep pace. Most prominently, the Employee Retirement Income Security Act (ERISA) of 1974 was enacted to protect the interests of employees who participate in certain employee benefit plans and to establish the basic accounting and reporting requirements for these plans.

Since the enactment of ERISA, there have been numerous accounting, auditing, and regulatory pronouncements that have changed the structure and accounting for employee benefit plans. As a result, plan administrators, accountants, and auditors need a technical resource that covers the many accounting, reporting, and regulatory requirements that are applicable to employee benefit plans. The objective of this guide is to provide the reader with a comprehensive reference source for employee benefit plans.

Wiley's GAAP for Employee Benefits covers each type of plan--defined benefit pension plans, defined contribution pension plans, and health and welfare plans. It covers plans that are sponsored by single employers, multiple employers, and multiemployers. This guide provides a background and discussion of the various types of employee benefit plans and a practical summary of ERISA. It provides plan auditors with some useful planning and internal control considerations for audits of employee benefit plans. The guide also provides readers with detailed information regarding investments held by employee benefit plans as well as the accounting, auditing, and reporting requirements for defined benefit pension plans, defined contribution pension plans, and health and welfare plans. In addition, this guide provides a discussion of the revised Form 5500, *Annual Return/Report of Employee Benefit Plan*, and examples of employee benefit plan financial statements and disclosures, and various auditors' reports that should be issued on the financial statements for the plans.

The concepts covered in this guide do not include the accounting pronouncements issued by the Governmental Accounting Standards Board, although many of the auditing concepts and theories would be applicable to governmental plans.

This book would not exist without the hard work and dedication of a number of contributing authors. These individuals include most significantly Patty Miller, Phyllis Dunn, Alice Wunderlich, Catrina Blackwell, Juliana Casey, Beth Panza, and Mary-Beth Rigg. They helped significantly in the development of the content and were instrumental in the writing of this book. Thank you all for your contributions!

Randi L. Starr
Karen T. Caprio

June 2000

ABOUT THE CONTRIBUTORS

Catrina Blackwell is an audit manager and employee benefit plan specialist for Deloitte & Touche LLP in the Los Angeles office. Catrina has over nine years of experience in auditing employee benefits plans. She is a graduate of Woodbury University in Los Angeles.

Juliana Casey is a manager with Deloitte & Touche LLP. She has over six years of accounting experience and has worked with employee benefit plans during those years.

Beth Panza is a manager at Deloitte & Touche LLP. Her areas of specialization include employee benefits, manufacturing, and hospitals.

Mary-Beth Rigg is a senior manager with Deloitte & Touche LLP, where she manages approximately fifty employee benefit plan audits. Mary-Beth has ten years of public accounting experience and spends approximately 50% of her time in employee benefit matters. She is a graduate of Mount Holyoke College.

Alice A. Wunderlich is a director with Deloitte & Touche LLP, where she is a leader of the Chicago area employee benefit plan audit practice, which audits over 250 plans. As an employee benefit specialist, she has developed local and national training and resource materials and acts as a technical resource for quality control. Ms. Wunderlich has an undergraduate degree from Illinois State University and an MBA from the University of Michigan.

1 BACKGROUND OF EMPLOYEE BENEFIT PLANS

INTRODUCTION

Employee benefit plans, which are offered by employers throughout the United States and other parts of the world, provide employees with a wide range of fringe benefits. Such benefits are offered over and above the employee's salary or wages and can include, among many options, a benefit for the accumulation of retirement monies, payment of medical and dental expenses, adoption assistance, and payment of childcare costs. The popularity of these plans has continued to grow such that in the United States, in 1999, there were more than 9 million benefit plans covering more than 150 million people, with assets approaching 2 trillion dollars.

TYPES OF PLANS

Types of employee benefit plans include defined benefit pension plans, defined contribution pension plans, and defined benefit and defined contribution health and welfare benefit plans.

A defined benefit pension plan is one that provides a determinable benefit to each vested participant upon retirement. For plans that cover salaried employees, that benefit is often determined by the participant's age, the number of years of service with the company, and the participant's salary or rate of pay. For defined benefit pension plans that cover hourly employees, that benefit is often determined by a specified contractual amount (or benefit unit multiplier), multiplied by the years of service the participant gave to the employer. Similarly, a defined benefit health and welfare benefit plan provides for a specific benefit. That benefit may be paid directly to the participant to reimburse him or her for eligible expenses or the benefit may be paid directly to the provider or to a third-party insurer for payment of eligible services.

A defined contribution pension and health and welfare plan establishes an individual account for each participant. These plans specify how contributions are made to the participant's account and by whom, rather than defining the amount of benefit each participant is eligible to receive. An individual account increases or decreases based on

- Contributions made by the participant or the plan sponsor
- Gains or losses on the investments
- Forfeitures or withdrawals (distributions or loans)
- Investment and administrative expenses charged against the plan which are paid by the participant or by the plan

Examples of a health and welfare benefit plan, as described in the American Institute of Certified Public Accountants' (AICPA) audit and accounting guide, *Audits of Employee Benefit Plans,* include plans that provide (1) medical, dental, visual, psychiatric, or long-term health care; severance benefits; life insurance; accidental death or dismemberment benefits; (2) unemployment, disability, vacation or holiday benefits; and (3) apprenticeships, tuition assistance, day care, housing subsidies, or legal services benefits. A health and welfare plan may offer one or more of the aforementioned benefits and is either a defined benefit or a defined contribution plan.

Employee benefit plans may be sponsored by either a single-employer, multiple-employers, or a plan may be a multiemployer plan. A single-employer sponsored plan is established by the management of one employer (or a group that is controlled by one employer). A plan sponsored by multiple-employers is one sponsored by the management of more than one employer. A multiemployer plan is one that is established subject to a collective bargaining arrangement between a related group of employees and the union that represents the employees.

Benefit plans can be either contributory or noncontributory. Contributory plans permit contributions from both the plan sponsor and the plan participants or from the participants only. Noncontributory plans permit contributions only from the plan sponsor. Noncontributory plans may allow contributions from a plan participant during times when the participant is unemployed and wishes to maintain benefit coverage.

Employee benefit plans are usually established and maintained by plan sponsors according to the provisions set forth in the plan document. The plan document will detail who is eligible to participate in the plan, funding of the plan, vesting provisions, when benefit payments may begin, and identifies the fiduciary(ies) of the plan along with other pertinent provisions.

The named fiduciary, as identified within the plan document, is the individual(s) who is(are) responsible for the general operation and administration of the plan and includes the plan administrator. In a single-employer or multiple-employer sponsored plan, the plan administrator is usually an officer or other employee of the plan sponsor, or a benefit committee, and typically reports to the plan sponsor's board of directors or management. In a multiemployer sponsored plan, the named fiduciary is a trustee and a union representative. The named fiduciary has responsibility to ensure that the plan is operating in accordance with the terms of the plan document, trust instrument (required for a defined benefit pension plan), and all applicable government rules and regulations. In general, the fiduciary makes decisions regarding the interpretation of rights of the participants under the plan, how investments are managed, and the performance or the delegation of responsibilities for operating and administering the plan.

All of the concepts discussed in this introduction will be covered in greater detail throughout this chapter.

REPORTING AND DISCLOSURE REQUIREMENTS

Prior to the enactment of the Employee Retirement Income Security Act of 1974 (ERISA), there was very little regulation over employee benefit plans. Plans were not always adequately funded, benefits were often very discretionary in their focus, and there were many abuses of the plans by fiduciaries. Congressional investigations were held and disclosed several instances in which plans had terminated without sufficient assets to meet pension obligations.

After much debate, Congress finally enacted ERISA in 1974. The primary purpose of the Act is to protect the interests of employees who participate in employee benefit plans, as well as to protect their beneficiaries. ERISA, in pursuit of this objective, requires financial reporting to government agencies and disclosure to participants (and their beneficiaries) and establishes appropriate codes of conduct for plan fiduciaries. It also sets forth appropriate remedies, penalties, and access to federal courts when necessitated.

ERISA was also enacted to improve the soundness of employee benefit pension plans, primarily defined benefit pension plans. This is accomplished in three ways, by requiring plans to

- Vest the accrued benefits of employees with significant periods of service
- Meet minimum standards of funding for defined benefit pension plans
- Subscribe to plan termination insurance through the Pension Benefit Guaranty Corporation (PBGC) for defined benefit pension plans

ERISA replaced the Welfare and Pension Plans Disclosure Act of 1958, amended certain sections of the Internal Revenue Code, and generally replaced state laws that related to employee benefit plans.

ERISA gives the Department of Labor (DOL) the authority to regulate reporting and disclosure requirements and certain administrative and fiduciary responsibilities. Most plans are required to file an annual report using Form 5500. (For plan years beginning in 1999, there is only one Form 5500.) Certain plans, however, are not required to file an annual report. These include governmental plans, church plans, unfunded excess benefit plans, plans maintained outside the United States primarily established to cover nonresident aliens, and plans established only to conform to workers' compensation, unemployment, or disability insurance laws.

Title I of ERISA also requires that certain information be made available to all plan participants and beneficiaries who are receiving, or are entitled to receive, benefits under the plan as discussed under the Governmental Regulations section of this chapter.

Substantial penalties may be assessed by the DOL and by the IRS for failure to comply with the established reporting and disclosure requirements. Section 502(c)(2) of ERISA describes penalties that the DOL and IRS can assess for (1) failure or refusal to file a report (up to $1,000 per day), (2) deficient filings, namely, a missing auditor's report or missing required supplemental schedules (from $100 to $150 a day, or $36,500 to $50,000 per annual report), (3) missing required information on the Form 5500 ($10 per day up to $3,650 per annual report), and (4) late filings, that is, filed past the due date ($50 per day). Various voluntary compliance programs, sponsored by the DOL and IRS, such as the PWBA (Pension and Welfare Benefits Administration) Delinquent Filer Voluntary Compliance Program, and the Employee Plans Compliance Resolution System (sponsored by the IRS alone), are available to plan administrators to mitigate penalties assessed for ERISA violations, provided that such plan operating and reporting deficiencies are appropriately corrected. For further discussion of Title I of ERISA, including a more detailed description of penalties and the various voluntary compliance programs, see Chapter 3, Employee Retirement Income Security Act of 1974.

Generally Accepted Accounting Principles (GAAP)

Financial accounting rules for the preparation of a plan's financial statements come from various accounting literature: statements of accounting standards issued by the Financial Accounting Standards Board (FASB), AICPA Statements of Position (SOPs), AICPA Practice Bulletins, and the AICPA audit and accounting guide, *Audits of Employee Benefit Plans*.

The FASB has approved two statements directly related to employee benefit plans. The first, Statement of Financial Accounting Standards (SFAS) 35, *Accounting and Reporting by Defined Benefit Pension Plans,* was issued in March 1980. The second, SFAS 110, *Reporting by Defined Benefit Pension Plans of Investment Contracts*, which amends SFAS 35, was issued in August 1992. These two statements do not specifically apply to defined contribution pension plans or to health and welfare benefit plans but rather apply to employee benefit plans in general.

SFAS 35, *Accounting and Reporting by Defined Benefit Pension Plans,* sets accounting and reporting standards for a defined benefit pension plan. Plans that fall into this category include those that primarily provide pension benefits but may also include pension plans that provide benefits for death, disability, or termination of employment. SFAS 35 pertains to ongoing plans that provide pension benefits to participants of single-employer, multiple-employer or multiemployer sponsored plans. The plan may be funded through one or several trust funds, one or more insurance contracts, or a combination thereof. This statement applies to those plans covered by ERISA as well as those that are not subject to ERISA. It should not be applied to plans that are expecting to terminate, nor to government-sponsored plans. SFAS 35 states that

> *the primary objective of a pension plan's financial statements is to provide financial information that is useful in assessing the plan's present and future ability to pay benefits when due. To accomplish that objective, a plan's financial statements should provide information about*
>
> 1. *Plan resources and how the stewardship responsibility for those resources has been discharged*
> 2. *The accumulated plan benefits of participants*
> 3. *The results of transactions and events that affect the information regarding those resources and benefits*
> 4. *Other factors necessary for users to understand the information provided.*

Statements of Position

The following presents a brief discussion of various AICPA Statements of Position (SOP) that have been issued by the AICPA and that directly involve employee benefit plan matters.

Issued in August 1992, SOP 92-6, *Accounting and Reporting by Health and Welfare Benefit Plans*, sets accounting and reporting requirements for single-employer, multiple-employer and multiemployer health and welfare plans. SOP 92-6 requires health and welfare plans to present information regarding the plan's benefit obligations, including benefit claims payable, accumulated eligibility credits, claims incurred but not yet reported, and postretirement benefit obligations within the plan's financial statements as follows:

- A comparative statement of benefit obligations listing the various benefit obligations of the plan as previously described is to be prepared as of the end of the current and prior plan year-end.
- A statement of changes in benefit obligations, summarizing the changes in the benefit obligation components during the plan year, is to be presented for the current plan year.

This SOP was effective for single-employer plans for plan years which began after December 15, 1992, except for plans with less than 500 participants whose effective application date was extended to plan years which began after December 15, 1994. This SOP was effective for multiemployer plans for plan years which began after December 15, 1995. Following SOP 92-6, the DOL has issued nonenforcement policies for multiemployer plans waiving the requirement to file Form 5500. This nonenforcement policy, the types of reports issued by independent auditors in accordance with SOP 92-6 in these situations, as well as the provisions of SOP 92-6, will be explained in further detail in Chapter 9, Accounting, Auditing, and Reporting for Health and Welfare Plans.

SOP 94-4, *Reporting of Investment Contracts Held by Health and Welfare Benefit Plans and Defined Contribution Pension Plans,* was issued in September 1994 in response to SFAS 110, which addressed the reporting of investment contracts for defined benefit pension plans. This SOP requires defined contribution health and welfare and defined contribution pension plans to report fully benefit-responsive investment contracts held by the plan at contract value, which may or may not equal fair market value. Investment contracts that are not fully benefit-responsive must be reported at fair value. This SOP was effective for plan years which began after December 15, 1994, except that application of the SOP to investment contracts entered into before December 31, 1993, was delayed to plan years which began after December 15, 1995. SOP 94-4 and SFAS 110 will be more fully discussed in Chapter 6, Investments.

During July 1999, the AICPA issued SOP 99-2, *Accounting for and Reporting of Postretirement Medical Benefit (401(h)) Features of Defined Benefit Pension Plans*. This SOP specifies the accounting for and disclosure of 401(h) features of defined benefit pension plans from the perspective of both defined benefit pension plans and health and welfare plans. In general, this SOP covers accounting and reporting requirements for situations whereby a defined benefit pension plan provides a postretirement medical benefit component in addition to the normal retirement benefits of the plan, pursuant to Section 401(h) of the Internal Revenue Code. This SOP is effective for plan years which began after December 15, 1998. See Chapter 8, Accounting, Auditing, and Reporting for Defined Benefit Pension Plans, and Chapter 9, Accounting, Auditing, and Reporting for Health and Welfare Plans, for additional information regarding SOP 99-2.

SOP 99-3, *Accounting for and Reporting of Certain Defined Contribution Plan Investments and Other Disclosure Matters*, issued in September 1999, simplifies disclosures for certain investments. It supersedes AICPA Practice Bulletin 12, *Reporting Separate Investment Fund Option Information of Defined Contribution Pension Plans*. The SOP is effective for plan years ending after December 15, 1999. Essentially, SOP 99-3 eliminated the requirement for defined contribution pension plans to present by-fund information for participant-directed investment funds. Prior to the issuance of SOP 99-3, AICPA Practice Bulletin 12 required that information regarding each investment fund option, including the investment balance at the end of the year and significant components of the change in the investment balance during the year (attributable to contributions, investment income, distributions, and other activity), be disclosed either within the plan's financial statements or within the footnotes to the plan's financial statements. The by-fund information continues to be required for any non-participant-directed investment funds that are part of the defined contribution pension plan. In addition, SOP 99-3 substantially reduced the disclosures required for describing the types of investments held by an employee benefit plan. Note also that SOP 99-3 amended a portion of SOP 94-4, as according to the provisions of SOP 99-3, stating that disclosures regarding investment contracts held by defined contribution pension plans and defined contribution health and welfare plans are not required to be presented by the individual participant's funds but rather in total. See Chapter 6, Investments, for the additional discussion regarding the provisions of SOP 99-3.

The accounting and auditing concepts covered throughout this book include the provisions of Statements of Financial Accounting Standards issued through December 31, 1999, Statements on Auditing Standards issued through December 31, 1999, and AICPA Statements of Position issued through December 31, 1999. As mentioned in the preface, the accounting and auditing concepts covered throughout this book do not include statements issued by the Governmental Accounting Standards Board.

GOVERNMENTAL REGULATIONS

Employee benefit plans are impacted by various governmental entities. Some of these entities include the Internal Revenue Service (IRS), the Department of Labor (DOL), the Pension Benefit Guaranty Corporation (PBGC, which is part of the DOL), the Pension and Welfare Benefits Administration (PWBA, which is part of the DOL), and the Securities and Exchange Commission (SEC).

On an annual basis, employee benefit plans that are subject to ERISA requirements are required to report information to the IRS, the DOL, and, for defined benefit and some defined contribution pension plans, information is also reported to the PBGC. The information for most plans that is reported to these governmental entities is done on Form 5500, Annual Return/Report of Employee Benefit Plan. The Form 5500 is generally used to file an annual report for plans with 100 or more participants. Plans with fewer than 100 participants generally file the Form 5500-C/R. The Form 5500-C is filed at least every third year and the Form 5500-R, an abbreviated report, in the other two years. See further discussion regarding the Form 5500 in Chapter 11, Form 5500.

The Form 5500 includes financial statements generally prepared in conformity with generally accepted accounting principles and other information concerning the operation of the plan. Note that a plan's financial statements are permitted to be prepared using other comprehensive bases of accounting. See Chapter 10, Other Accounting and Auditing Considerations, for additional information. The financial statements also include certain supplemental schedules (e.g., Assets Held for Investment Purposes, Schedule of Reportable Transactions, etc.)

For plan years beginning after December 31, 1998, the Form 5500 has been revised. The new Form 5500 is similar to the individual taxpayer's Form 1040, whereby general summary information is provided directly on the face of the Form 5500, and schedules are attached as required and applicable to that particular plan. If a schedule is not applicable to that plan, that schedule is not required to be filed. The new Form 5500 is discussed in greater detail in Chapter 11, Form 5500.

ERISA

ERISA does not cover plans established or maintained by governmental entities or churches for their employees. It also does not cover plans that are maintained solely to comply with applicable worker's compensation, unemployment, or disability laws. Additionally, ERISA does not apply to unfunded excess benefit plans or plans maintained outside the United States primarily for the benefit of nonresident aliens.

Title I of ERISA requires that plan administrators make available, on an annual basis, summarized information for all plan participants as well as those receiving retirement benefits. This information includes a copy of the summary plan description (SPD), amendments to the SPD, a summary annual report, and individual reports detailing each participant's total vested and nonvested accrued benefits.

NOTE: This last item regarding individual participants' benefits is not required to be provided to participants of multiemployer sponsored plans.

The SPD and summary annual report must describe the employee benefit plan in understandable terms, including the participant's rights, benefits, and responsibilities under the plan. For defined benefit pension plans (except for multiemployer sponsored plans), this information also will indicate the earliest date on which the participant will become fully vested in the benefits provided by the plan. Copies of these documents are not required to be automatically filed with the Department of Labor, but they must be furnished to the DOL on request.

Minimum standards for participation are also specified by ERISA (Section 202), which generally provide that an employee who is at least twenty-one years old and has completed 1 year of service (more than 1000 hours) must be included as a participant of the pension plan. However, an employee may be required to have reached age twenty-one and have **two** years of service, if benefits are fully vested thereafter. ERISA also states that an individual may not be denied participation in a benefit plan based on having reached a specific age.

ERISA requires defined benefit pension plans and some defined contribution pension plans to meet minimum funding standards to help ensure the viability of the plan. Minimum funding standards are usually determined using the assistance of an actuary who performs a valuation of the plan based on the plan provisions and applicable law. This valuation is used to determine how much money should be contributed currently to the plan to ensure adequate funds in the future to satisfy benefit payments for those participants who retire from the plan or terminate after becoming vested. In short, the plan's actuary determines the minimum amount required to adequately fund the plan.

ERISA requires that defined benefit pension plans and certain defined contribution pension plans purchase plan termination insurance through the PBGC. The Act requires that the insurance be purchased to help ensure that there will be adequate resources to pay basic pension benefits to qualified participants; it helps to ensure that the benefits promised to retiring or terminating employees are available when the retirement or termination occurs. In certain circumstances, the PBGC will manage the distribution of assets in underfunded plans that have been terminated. Termination insurance does not generally apply to defined contribution pension plans as these plans establish a separate account for each individual, and the amount of the benefit is equal to that individual's account balance upon retirement or termination less any sponsor contributions that are not fully vested. In a defined benefit pension plan, the money for the retirement benefits of a participant are not specifically earmarked for that participant alone; rather the money for the benefit of all the eligible employees is combined into one large pool which is then available to pay out the benefits of each of the employees when their termination or retirement occurs. For additional information regarding plan termination insurance, see Chapter 3, Employee Retirement Income Security Act of 1974.

It is the sponsor's obligation to ensure that adequate funds exist to pay defined benefit pension benefits when a termination or retirement occurs. At the time of the payout, the monies may remain in the investment vehicle that the sponsor had selected and participants may receive monthly payouts from that fund, or the monies may be placed in an insurance contract, or an annuity may be purchased for the participant. For an annuity, the participant's benefit is calculated and the monies necessary to purchase the annuity are transferred from the sponsor's plan to the insurance company which will pay out the annuity. In a defined benefit pension plan, the money may also be distributed to the participant in one lump sum, if the plan provides for this option.

The Multiemployer Pension Plan Amendments Act of 1980 (MPPAA) imposes a liability on employers who withdraw from multiemployer defined benefit pension plans with unfunded vested benefits. For multiemployer plans, any employer withdrawing from a plan that has unfunded vested benefits is liable for its proportionate share of the benefits (regardless of whether or not the plan itself has been (terminated). The liability (i.e., the withdrawal liability) must be paid over a period not to exceed twenty years, which provides that the remaining employers participating in the multiemployer plan will not be liable for the payment of vested benefits earned by employees of employers who opt out of the plan.

VESTING OF BENEFITS

Defined contribution and defined benefit pension plans generally must have provisions that vest the accrued benefits of employer contributions (if required by the plan document) over a specified period of time. Note that participants are always fully vested in their own contributions and the related earnings thereon. These standards must vest the contributions made by the employer in such a way that, at a minimum, one of the following two options is met or exceeded (as prescribed by ERISA, Section 203(a)):

- Graded vesting of accrued benefits, with at least 20% vesting after three years of service, at least 20% each year thereafter for four years, so that the employee's accrued benefit would be 100% vested after seven years, and

- 100% vesting of accrued benefits after five years of service, with no vesting required before the end of the five-year period.

Tax-qualified plans require more stringent vesting if there is a termination, partial termination, or discontinuance of contributions to the plan, or if the plan is top-heavy. (Top-heavy means the plan unfairly gives advantage to those employees who are more highly compensated than to those participants who receive a lower compensation.) If a defined contribution pension plan is top-heavy, the minimum-graded vesting requirements previously stated are accelerated by two years. In other words, if vesting is incremental, 20% vesting after ***two*** years of service must occur, with at least 20% each year for the next four years, so that the participant's accrued benefit would now be vested after only **six** years. If 100% vesting previously occurred after five years, for a top-heavy plan, vesting must now occur before the end of a three-year period.

If a tax-qualified defined benefit or defined contribution pension plan is terminated, all participants immediately become fully vested as to plan sponsor contributions and the related investment earnings thereon. If a tax-qualified defined benefit or defined contribution pension plan has a partial termination (i.e., the plan freezes benefits for a particular group of participants), the participants affected by the partial termination immediately become fully vested. All other participants not affected by the partial termination continue with the vesting schedule previously defined for the plan in the plan document.

For money purchase plans (described in Chapter 7, Accounting, Auditing, and Reporting for Defined Contribution Pension Plans), if a plan sponsor decides to discontinue its contributions to a plan, again, all participants become fully vested as to plan sponsor contributions.

SECURITIES AND EXCHANGE COMMISSION (SEC)

Certain plans and related entities may be subject to the requirements of the Securities and Exchange Act of 1933 (1933 Act). These requirements mandate registration, usually on Form S-8 for plan securities and require annual reporting on Form 11-K under the Securities and Exchange Act of 1934 (1934 Act). Section 3(a)(2) of the 1933 Act permits an exemption from this reporting requirement for defined contribution pension plans that do not offer, as an investment option, the purchase of employer securities with employee contributions. All other 401(k) plans that offer a publicly traded employer stock investment option to participants on a voluntary and contributory basis are subject to the 1933 Act. For a plan to be both voluntary and contributory, the employees must be given the option to contribute their own funds to the plan **and,** in doing so, the participants must know that these contributions could be used to acquire employer securities. The plan sponsor and the plan's legal counsel should be consulted to determine whether the plan is subject to such reporting requirements.

Instead of requiring plans to file under Regulation S-X, Article 6A, the SEC has amended its rules for Form 11-K to permit plans subject to ERISA to instead elect to file financial statements in accordance with ERISA guidelines. For plans with less than 100 participants, if a Form 5500 (versus the current Form 5500 C/R) is not filed, the plan would be required to file under Regulation S-X.

In addition, all plans requiring a Form 11-K must be audited, regardless of the number of participants. Plans that file reports on Form 11-K in connection with the 1934 Act must do so within ninety days after the end of the plan's fiscal year. A plan that files under the ERISA guidelines must file the Form 11-K within 180 days after the plan's fiscal year-end.

INTERNAL REVENUE SERVICE

The Internal Revenue Code (IRC) has many provisions that affect employee benefit plans. If the plan qualifies under Section 401(a) of the IRC, certain tax benefits are available to the plan sponsor. These include (1) current tax deductions by plan sponsors for contributions, subject to certain limitations; (2) deferment of income to participants until the benefits are distributed; (3) exemption of the plan's trust from income taxes, other than tax on unrelated business income (unrelated business income is income derived from business activity that is not substantially related to the normal operations of the employee benefit plan); and (4) favorable tax treatment of certain benefit distributions to participants or their estates. Non-qualifed plans and trusts have special rules that apply depending on whether the plan is funded or unfunded. Generally speaking, qualified plans provide benefits to relatively large groups of employees, whereas unqualified plans provide benefits to only a few select key employees and may not be funded on a current basis.

PENSION AND WELFARE BENEFITS ADMINISTRATION (PWBA)

The PWBA, a division of the Department of Labor, protects the integrity of pension plans, health plans, and other employee benefits for more than 150 million people. The PWBA's mission is to assist workers in getting the information they need to protect their benefit rights, to assist plan officers to understand the requirements of the relevant statutes in order to meet their legal responsibilities, to develop policies and laws that encourage the growth of employment-based benefits, and to deter and correct violations of the relevant statutes.

The PWBA is charged with the responsibility to administer and enforce the fiduciary, reporting, and disclosure provisions of Title I of ERISA. In this regard, one of the functions of the PWBA is to review employee benefit plan audits. This role came about as the result of the DOL's Office of the Inspector General's (IG) initial review of approximately 300 employee benefit plan audits for the 1987 plan year in order to determine the compliance with ERISA and the requirements of generally accepted accounting principles (GAAP) and generally accepted auditing standards (GAAS). The IG review resulted in the identification of numerous alleged deficiencies relating to the work performed by independent public accountants.

As a follow-up to the IG review, the PWBA completed a review of approximately 270 employee benefit plan audits for the plan year of 1992. The report once again found numerous GAAP and GAAS compliance deficiencies made by independent public accountants. As a result of these reviews, the PWBA has established goals to determine the quality of work performed by independent auditors who perform financial statement audits of employee benefit plans. This ongoing review program seeks to ensure better compliance with ERISA's reporting and disclosure requirements. The goal for the DOL's 1999 budget is that no more than 12% of 1999 plan-year audits will contain deficiencies (down from 19% for 1992 plan-year audits) and that no more than 3% of Form 5500 filings will contain reporting and disclosure deficiencies. During 2001, the PWBA will conduct a nationwide review of Form 5500 filings and related audit workpapers to determine the progress made on reducing errors. Because of these goals, plan sponsors and practitioners should be aware that Form 5500s and plan audits for 1999 may come under particular scrutiny.

AUDIT REQUIREMENTS

Administrators of a plan subject to ERISA must file an annual report for that plan each year. Generally, administrators of plans with 100 or more participants at the beginning of the plan year are required to file Form 5500, with the required audited financial statements, attachments, and schedules. Administrators of plans with fewer than 100 participants are required to file Form 5500 C/R (no audit required) with the required attachments and schedules. Under the "80-120 rule," if a plan has between eighty and 120 participants (inclusive) at the beginning of the plan year, the plan may elect to file the same annual return/report that was filed for the previous year. Plans with 100 or more participants at the beginning of the plan year that file Form 5500 are **required** to have an annual audit of their financial statements. However, plans with fewer that 100 participants at the beginning of the plan year that file Form 5500 C/R are exempt from the audit requirement. Plans with fewer than 100 participants that elect to file Form 5500 are required to have an annual audit of their financial statements. (The most common example is a plan that files a Form 11-K with the SEC but has fewer than 100 participants.) Also, if a plan with fewer than 100 participants elects to file a Form 5500 rather than Form 5500 C/R, that plan is also required to engage an independent qualified public accountant to audit the plan. For a more complete description of Form 5500 filing requirements, refer to Chapter 11, Form 5500.

A participant is defined by ERISA as any employee or former employee who is or may become eligible to receive a benefit of any type from the employee benefit plan. It also covers beneficiaries of such employees. In a defined contribution pension plan, ERISA considers each individual who is **eligible** to participate in the plan to be a participant, even if he chooses not to participate. A participant for a fringe benefit plan is defined as any individual who has had at least one dollar excluded from their income to be used for that fringe benefit plan. For a health and welfare benefit plan, if the individual is eligible to receive benefits, he is counted as a participant. Dependents, however, are not considered to be participants for these plans.

If an audit is required, the plan sponsor must engage an independent qualified public accountant. The independent qualified public accountant (IQPA, as referred to by the DOL) has the responsibility, under generally accepted auditing standards, to express an opinion as to whether the financial statements fairly present the financial position of the employee benefit plan in conformity with generally accepted accounting principles. The IQPA must also determine that the related supplemental schedules are presented fairly, in all material respects, with respect to the financial statements taken as a whole. Note, however, that a GAAS audit is not designed to ensure compliance with all legislative and regulatory requirements. The financial statements, the supplemental schedules, and the Form 5500 remain the responsibility of the plan sponsor or administrator(s).

LIMITED-SCOPE AUDITS

As permitted by 29 CFR 2520.103-8 of the Department of Labor's Rules and Regulations for Reporting and Disclosure under ERISA, the plan administrator is permitted to instruct the auditor not to perform any auditing procedures with respect to information prepared and certified by a bank or similar institution or by an insurance carrier that is regulated, supervised, and subject to periodic examination by a state or federal agency and that acts as trustee or custodian for the plan's assets. The election is available, however, only if the trustee or custodian certifies both as to the **accuracy and completeness** of the information submitted. Certifications that address only accuracy **or** completeness, but not both, do not comply with the DOL's regulations, and therefore are not adequate to allow plan administrators to limit the scope of the audit.

This limited-scope audit provision does not apply to information regarding investments held by a broker/dealer or some investment companies, namely those that are not chartered and regulated by a federal or state agency. The exemption applies only to investment information (including investments, investment income, and related expenses), and does not extend to withdrawals, contributions, individual participant allocations, or other information, whether or not it is certified by the trustee or custodian. Thus, an auditor would perform tests of withdrawals, contributions, and expenses irrespective of whether a limited-scope or full-scope audit is being performed.

Thus, except for the investment-related activity certified by the trustee/custodian, an auditor conducting a limited-scope audit would need to include in the scope of the audit all other functions performed by the plan sponsor or other third-party service organizations.

The limited-scope exemption does not relieve the plan from the requirement to have an audit performed. The limited-scope exemption also does not relieve the plan from making all required disclosures regarding investments. Some of these requirements include disclosures on derivatives, if applicable--individual investments that exceed 5% of the plan balance at the end of the plan year and the net appreciation (depreciation) in fair value of investments by major class of investment.

Plan investments not held by a qualified trustee/custodian should undergo appropriate audit procedures. A plan may have only a portion of its investment assets which are covered by a certification by a qualified trustee/custodian. In such a case, the balance of the investments not eligible for the limited-scope exemption should be subjected to auditing procedures by the plan auditor. In these circumstances, the limited-scope audit report would be required if the plan's assets that are not audited (i.e., those assets covered by the trustee/custodian's certification) are material to the plan's financial statements taken as a whole.

SINGLE-EMPLOYER, MULTIEMPLOYER, AND MULTIPLE-EMPLOYER PLANS

Employee benefit plans are considered to be either single-employer, multiemployer, or multiple-employer. A single-employer plan is one that is generally established and administered by the management of one employer (or a group that is controlled by one employer). The sponsor of a single-employer plan is almost always the employer. Conversely, a multiemployer plan is one that is established subject to a collective bargaining arrangement between a related group of employers (e.g., construction) and the union that represents the employees. The sponsor of a multiemployer plan is comprised of members of the joint employer/union board of trustees as required by the Taft Hartley Act (discussed later). A multiple-employer collectively bargained plan is one that involves more than one employer, is collectively bargained and collectively funded, and, if covered by PBGC termination insurance, had properly elected before September 27, 1981, not to be treated as a multiemployer plan under ERISA. An example of a multiple-employer plan is one sponsored by a trade group or a not-for-profit entity.

The Taft Hartley Labor Act, officially known as the Labor-Management Relations Act (LMRA), was enacted into legislation by Congress in 1947. Sponsored by Robert Alphonso Taft and Fred Allan Hartley, the Act established the first significant regulations concerning union pension and health and welfare funds. Under the LMRA, employers and unions are permitted to create benefit trust funds of which sponsors and participants must have equal representation by the trustees of the fund(s).

FIDUCIARY RESPONSIBILITY AND TRUSTS

The ultimate responsibility for the oversight of the single-employer multiemployer, and multiple-employer plan rests with the fiduciary, the one responsible for the operation and administration of the plan, including the identification of a plan administrator. However, the plan's day-to-day administration (e.g., collecting contributions, paying benefits, managing cash and investments, administering loans, maintaining records, and preparing reports) is often assigned to various entities such as (1) the plan sponsor, (2) a trustee or custodian of plan assets, such as a trust department of a bank or insurance company, (3) an investment advisor, (4) a third-party administrator or recordkeeper, or (5) a person or persons designated as the plan administrator.

ERISA imposes specific restrictions and responsibilities on fiduciaries. These responsibilities include managing and operating the plan in the best interests of the plan participants. The fiduciary is prohibited from permitting the plan to engage in prohibited (nonexempt) party-in-interest transactions. (Party-in-interest transactions will be discussed in Chapter 3, Employee Retirement Income Security Act of 1974 and Chapter 10, Other Accounting and Auditing Considerations).

A plan usually has a trust instrument or document that details the authority and responsibilities of the trustee(s) and any investment advisors or managers. This document should include or be consistent with the plan's investment policy and, therefore, may restrict the investment options permitted by the plan. In addition, the trust agreement should describe the fees to be paid to the trustees, investment advisors, and managers for services provided to the plan. It also may describe who is responsible for payment of these services, for instance, the participants or the plan sponsor.

Three different types of trusts exist: a directed trust, a discretionary trust, and a combination of directed and discretionary. The distinction among the three is where the ultimate responsibility to make investment decisions resides (the authority to purchase and sell investment assets within the framework of the trust instrument). In a directed trust, including a participant-directed trust, the trustee acts only as custodian of a plan's investments and is responsible for collecting investment income and handling trust asset transactions, as directed by the person(s) responsible for making investment decisions. This person(s) may be the plan administrator, the plan's investment committee, the participant, or the plan's investment advisor. A discretionary trust is different from a directed trust in that a trustee is appointed and has authority to make investment decisions within the framework of the trust agreement. A plan may have any combination of directed and discretionary arrangements within the trust. Also, a plan may have one or more trusts as well as one or more custodial or safekeeping accounts.

ACCOUNTING RECORDS

Accounting records should be maintained in a manner so as to permit effective management and operation of the plan. The complexity of the plan will determine the nature of the accounting records and will vary with such factors as the frequency of sponsor contributions, the number of investment options available for participants to select (if applicable), rules regarding the administration of loans, the variety of options available to terminated participants, and the delegation of administrative duties.

The various accounting and plan records are often maintained at several locations. Depending on the nature of the plan, how fiduciary responsibilities are allocated, and who is responsible for various administrative duties, plan records may be maintained by the trustee or custodian of plan assets, insurance companies, service bureaus, the plan administrator, and the plan sponsor, including the payroll and human resources departments.

The records of the plan should typically include the following:

1. Investment asset records. ERISA requires reporting of investment assets in line item 31 of the current Form 5500 (Schedule H or I of the new Form 5500) in addition to the supplemental schedules. The supplemental schedules include
   - Schedule of assets held for investment purposes
   - Schedule of assets held for investment purposes which were both acquired and disposed of within the plan year
   - Schedule of loans or fixed income obligations
   - Schedule of leases in default or classified as uncollectible
   - Schedule of reportable (5%) transactions
   - Schedule of nonexempt transactions.

   These supplemental schedules will be discussed more fully in Chapter 11, Form 5500. These records are generally maintained by the trustee/ custodian and/or plan sponsor.

2. Participants' records. Records should be maintained to determine each employee's eligibility to participate in the plan. Many plans have age and service requirements that the employee must satisfy before s/he is eligible to participate in the plan. Eligibility also can be affected by breaks in service (leaving the employment of the plan sponsor and then returning or taking long-term disability, for example). These records are generally maintained by the human resources and payroll departments at the plan sponsor or the administrative office or a third-party administrator for a multiemployer plan.
3. Contribution records. Separate contribution records should be maintained for employee and sponsor contributions. The plan sponsor generally retains payroll records detailing employee contributions as these contributions are deductions made directly from the participants' paychecks. Sponsor contributions should be accounted for separately to ensure that the contributions are being made in accordance with the plan document. As with participant contributions, the plan sponsor would normally maintain records of sponsor contributions. In the case of multiemployer plans, the contribution records would normally be maintained by each of the participating employers who are sponsoring the plan.
4. Claim records. Claim records for health and welfare benefit plans are generally quite voluminous. They are used for a number of purposes.

- To document the description of the claim paid on behalf of the participant (if the participant has coverage from more than one insurance carrier)
- To document that the appropriate coordination of the payment of benefits has occurred
- To determine when benefit limits, if limits exist, have been reached by individual claimants
- To accumulate various historical data regarding types, amounts, and dates of claims submitted and paid

The claim records may either be maintained by the plan sponsor or by the third-party administrator. For multiemployer plans, the claim records would normally be maintained by the plan's third-party administrator.

5. Distribution records. Records of all distributions to participants (for persons who have left employment at the plan sponsor, retired, or elected to cease contributing to the plan), including loans, should be maintained. These records will detail distribution amounts, payment schedule (lump sum or over a period of several years), payment commencement date, forfeitures, if any, and information to determine the tax consequences of the distribution to the participant. Distribution records may be maintained by the plan sponsor, recordkeeper, trustee/custodian, or other third-party administrator depending upon the arrangements used by the plan to pay benefits to participants. For multiemployer plans, the distribution records would be maintained by the plan's third-party administrator.
6. Individual participant's account information. For each employee who participates in a defined contribution pension plan, a separate participant statement that identifies the participant's share of the total net assets of the plan must be maintained. The plan instrument describes how changes in the value of net assets are to be allocated to the participant's account. The individual participant account records must be reconciled with the plan sponsor's records to determine that the total of all individual participants' accounts equals the total net assets of the plan. According to Revenue Ruling 70-125 of the Internal Revenue Code, the individual participant account records must be reconciled to the plan sponsor's records in order for the plan sponsor to be permitted to deduct on its tax return the amount of the sponsor contribution to the plan (as reported in the plan sponsor's records). For defined contribution pension plans or health and welfare plans, a plan may use a voice response system or internet system that permits a participant to enroll in the plan or make several changes to their investment choices offered by the plan. Some of the changes permitted through the voice response system or

internet system may be changes in their investment options, a change in the percentage of their contribution to the plan, obtaining a loan from their account, or requesting a distribution. In many cases the types of paper records which are available with a voice response or internet recordkeeping system are very limited due to the fact the transactions initiated by the participant are processed via the phone or internet. Typically, the types of hard-copy records that exist include the separate participant statements described above, promissory notes for participant loans, summary totals of net assets for each of the investment funds offered by the plan, and occasionally a reconciliation of total net assets and activity for the plan year between the recordkeeper's system and the trustee/custodian records. In many cases, these records are maintained by the plan recordkeeper and copies of this information are sent to the plan sponsor.

7. Administrative expenses. Invoices, contracts, agreements, or other written evidence will normally be provided to verify these expenses. These expenses may include fees for the recordkeeper, trustee fees, attorney's fees (e.g., to write a plan amendment), independent auditor fees (e.g., performance of the audit), and actuarial fees (for preparation of the actuarial valuation). Records for administrative expenses are maintained by the plan sponsor or the individual participating employers for a multiemployer plan.
8. General accounting records. Plans are required to maintain records of all receipts and disbursements; however, in many cases, these records are prepared and maintained by the trustee/custodian of plan assets.

ERISA requires that workpapers prepared in conjunction with an audit of an employee benefit plan be maintained for a period of six years.

Employee benefit plans provide unique fringe benefits that carry with them many reporting and disclosure requirements. The focus of this guide will be to discuss various topics concerning defined benefit pension plans, defined contribution pension plans, and health and welfare plans, including a description of the types of plans, a discussion of ERISA and Form 5500, and a detailed discussion of the accounting and reporting requirements for the employee benefit plans. *GAAP for Employee Benefits Plans* includes chapters regarding accounting and auditing considerations for employee benefit plans as well as sample financial statements and sample independent auditors' reports.

2 TYPES OF PLANS

INTRODUCTION

As discussed in Chapter 1, companies sponsor various types of benefit plans in an effort to provide retirement, medical, insurance, and other benefits to their employees, owners, directors, outside consultants, and other employees. In order to maintain a competitive advantage in hiring and retaining employees, companies must understand the benefit structures that have become standard in their industry and know the benefits offered by their key competitors. Employers should encourage employees who are making decisions about employment to consider the benefits offered by the employer as part of their compensation package.

The type of employee benefit plan, as well as its tax status, funding, and the inclusion of company stock as an investment option of the plan, generally determine the reporting requirements the plan must meet for the Department of Labor (DOL), Internal Revenue Service (IRS), and the Securities and Exchange Commission (SEC).

Following is a description of the various types of pension and health and welfare plans that may be offered by employers.

DEFINED BENEFIT PENSION PLANS

Defined benefit pension plans provide retirement benefits to retirees based on factors as specified in the plan document, such as final compensation, years of service and age. In a defined benefit pension plan, the sponsor assumes the risk associated with providing the benefit, including the risk of investment loss. Alternatively, a plan sponsor may purchase annuities to provide for the plan's benefits thereby insuring the plan and transferring the risk to the insurance company. Because the future benefit to retirees is defined and is payable over future years, plan sponsors are required to (1) utilize an actuary to calculate the accumulated benefit obligation of the plan and to (2) determine the plan sponsor's annual minimum and maximum contribution to be made to the plan to ensure that the plan will be sufficiently funded to provide the guaranteed benefits to participants and their beneficiaries.

One of the types of specialized defined benefit pension plans is the *cash balance plan*. A *cash balance plan* is typically defined as a defined benefit pension plan that maintains hypothetical "accounts" for participants. The plan sponsor credits a participant's "account" with a certain number of dollars each plan year and promises earnings at a specified rate. Interest on the amount contributed is credited at the stated rate, which may be different from the plan's actual rate of investment return. The interest rate may be modified prospectively, as long as there are no reductions in the participant's benefit accrued thus far. The formula for determining the amount to be credited as a "contribution" to participants' "accounts" may vary from year to year, if the plan sponsor properly amends the plan prior to the beginning of the year and provides notice to participants. The principal advantage of a cash balance plan is the ability of participants to watch their hypothetical "account balances" grow (similar to a defined contribution pension plan) while providing certainty as to the interest to be credited to participants. With the cash balance defined benefit pension plans, participants bear no investment risk. The plan sponsor bears the risk that the plan's actual rate of return may fall below the stated rate of interest to be credited to participants' "accounts." See Chapter 8, Accounting, Auditing, and Reporting for Defined Benefit Pension Plans, for additional information regarding defined benefit pension plans.

DEFINED CONTRIBUTION PENSION PLANS

Defined contribution pension plans provide an individual account for each participant. The future value of the individual account determines the benefits payable to the retiree. The individual account is an accumulation of contributions by the employee, employer, or both, as well as investment gains and losses, allocated forfeitures (if any), minus any plan expenses. In a defined contribution pension plan, the participant assumes the risk of investment loss. A variety of types of defined contribution pension plans exist. Employers may choose the type of plan to be offered depending on whether their desire is to provide benefits only or to also create incentives for employees.

In defined contribution pension plans, if applicable, forfeitures of the nonvested portion of participant balances as a result of termination of employment are designated by the plan document and can provide that the forfeitures be used to reduce future employer contributions, pay the plan's administrative expenses, or be allocated to the remaining participants. Participants become vested in the employer contributions and their related earnings credited to their account according to a vesting schedule laid out in the plan document. By law, participants are immediately vested in the contributions they make to the plan as well as in the related investment gains or losses generated from those contributions.

Pension plans that allow employees to purchase the plan sponsor's stock with their individual contributions generally are required by the SEC to file a Form S-8 to register a defined number of shares for the plan. Alternatively, the plan sponsor may establish in the plan document that the participants may invest in company stock through the plan's purchase of the stock on the open market or from the company's treasury stock. The Form S-8 must be updated annually by filing an Annual Report for the plan on Form 11-K or by including the plan information in the plan sponsor's Annual Report on Form 10-K filed with the SEC. These requirements are applicable to both public and private companies (i.e., even if the stock is not publicly traded the SEC filings may be required); however, exceptions exist for private companies that offer and sell a limited amount of securities under a plan. Because the SEC's rules regarding Form 11-K filing requirements are not clear cut, it is recommended that the plan sponsor's SEC counsel be consulted to assess the requirements, if any, for the plan to file an Annual Report on Form 11-K with the SEC.

The following describes various types of defined contribution pension plans that are commonly offered by plan sponsors to their employees. For additional information regarding defined contribution pension plans, see Chapter 7, Accounting, Auditing, and Reporting for Defined Contribution Pension Plans.

401(k) Plan

A **401(k) defined contribution pension plan** or "cash or deferred arrangement" (CODA) allows participants to elect to defer a portion of their salary by contributing the amount (pretax) to the plan. The participant is therefore not currently taxed on the deferred amount. A 401(k) feature may be added to a profit-sharing, stock bonus plan or Employee Stock Ownership Plan (ESOP). Also, a 401(k) plan may include a thrift plan feature to allow employee contributions which are matched by an employer contribution. The 401(k) plan is subject to various nondiscrimination requirements under the Tax Reform Act of 1986, including the limitation on the annual amount of employee contributions, specific limitations on the amount of contributions by highly compensated employees, as well as other requirements.

Money Purchase Plan

A **money purchase plan** is a defined contribution pension plan in which the employer's contribution is mandatory or nondiscretionary. The required contribution is based on a formula, generally a percentage of the employee's compensation. A money purchase plan may be structured to permit employees to make after-tax contributions to the plan. Although contributions, which are subject to minimum funding requirements, are required by the employer, a money purchase plan is a defined contribution pension plan because a future benefit is not defined and the risk of investment gains and losses remains with the participants.

Stock Bonus Plan

A **stock bonus plan** is a defined contribution pension plan in which benefit payments to participants are most often in the form of shares of stock of the employer. A stock bonus plan is a discretionary plan; in other words, contributions are not required to be made to the plan by the plan sponsor. The plan may make distributions in stock or cash, as the participant elects, or cash may be designated as the only form of distribution if the plan meets certain requirements, particularly for private companies. If the contribution is made in cash, the trust generally purchases stock issued by the sponsor to hold for the retirement benefit of participants. Stock bonus plans do not require employer contributions to be made from company profits or to be a specified amount; however, the method of allocating the contribution to participants must be defined within the plan document.

Employee Stock Ownership Plan (ESOPs)

An **employee stock ownership plan** is a type of stock bonus plan which generally invests primarily in securities of the plan sponsor. ESOPs may be funded through employee or employer contributions (for example, as a type of profit-sharing plan). Public or private companies may sponsor ESOPs in an effort to improve employee retention and foster loyalty to the company, since the participants become owners of the company's stock. Employer securities of a private company are defined as "employer-issued" common stock shares, which provide a combination of voting and dividend rights at least equal to each of the classes of stock with the most voting power and dividend rights. ESOPs may be used as estate planning tools for owners of closely held corporations.

An ESOP may borrow money from the employer or a third-party lender in order to finance the purchase of the plan sponsor's securities. These plans are termed **leveraged ESOPs**. In a leveraged ESOP, the ESOPs loan is collateralized by the stock and is guaranteed by the employer. The ESOP pays off the loan with cash contributions from the employer, and the employer may also utilize dividends earned on the unallocated shares to make payments on the loan. As the loan is repaid, shares are released from collateral and allocated to participants' accounts based upon the formulas specified within the plan document. This allocation of shares to the participant represents the employer contribution to the participants' account. In a leveraged ESOP, contributions by the plan sponsor are required to pay the principal **and** interest on the loan. In an **unleveraged ESOP**, the employer contributes cash to the plan to purchase company stock or contributes stock directly. In this case, contributions by the plan sponsor are discretionary.

ESOPs are an attractive option to many employers due to the tax advantages they provide, such as the deductibility of dividends paid to an ESOP, under certain circumstances, and the deductibility of contributions made to the plan, even if the contributions are to a leveraged ESOP and are used primarily to pay its debt. Also, contributions of stock to an unleveraged ESOP result in a tax deduction for the sponsor for the value of the stock contributed, although no cash outlay is required by the employer. There are risks associated with a leveraged ESOP, which include the impact on the plan of a decrease in the fair market value of the stock. If the fair market value of the stock decreases, additional contributions by the plan sponsor or required loan payments may be accelerated.

Target Benefit Plan

A **target benefit plan** is generally a defined contribution pension plan in which the employer's annual contribution is actuarially determined based on a specified benefit "targeted" for the participant to receive at retirement. The contribution is allocated to individual participant accounts. Because the contribution level is determined for each year without regard to actual experience, the future benefit fluctuates and is not a guaranteed amount. If, however, the employer intends to provide a defined benefit and funds the plan to guarantee the amount, the target plan should be considered a defined benefit pension plan for accounting and financial reporting purposes.

Profit-Sharing Plan

A **profit-sharing defined contribution pension plan** allows a contribution by the employer to be allocated to individual participant accounts. The plan document defines the formula and conditions under which a contribution is required, or whether the contribution is discretionary. Also, the plan document defines the formula for the allocation of the contribution to participants. The contribution may be made from current or accumulated earnings of the company. Features of other defined contribution plans may be added to a profit-sharing plan. A 401(k) feature may be added to allow employee contributions to be deposited into the participant's profit-sharing account, based on the percentage of an employee's salary that is elected to be contributed.

Thrift or Savings Plan

A **thrift or savings plan** is a profit-sharing defined contribution pension plan. To participate, an employee makes after-tax contributions that may be matched by the employer or otherwise used in the determination of the employer's contribution, if provided within the provisions of the plan document. Thrift or savings plans may permit additional contributions to be made by employees which are credited to the participant's account but do not affect the amount or allocation of the contribution made by the employer. In addition, a defined contribution pension plan may be structured such that it includes features of more than one type of defined contribution pension plan. For example, a 401(k) plan may also include a profit-sharing or thrift/savings plan component.

403(b) Plan

A **403(b) defined contribution pension plan** or "tax-deferred annuity plan," is specifically available for nonprofit organizations and public schools. This plan is similar to a 401(k) plan as it allows employees to participate in the plan by deferring a portion of their salary. Also, various types of employer contributions are allowed including matching contributions, contributions of a percentage of each employee's salary, or a fixed amount per participant. Although they are similar to 401(k) plans,

403(b) plans that allow only employee contributions are not considered to be qualified plans as they are not required to have a plan document, nor are IRS determination letters issued for them. As a result, 403(b) plans that accept only employee contributions are generally exempt from the IRS and DOL regulations and requirements that are applicable to qualified plans, for example, discrimination testing and the requirement to have a plan audit. 403(b) plans that accept employer contributions, however, are subject to the nondiscrimination rules that apply to qualified plans. Another difference from 401(k) plans is that 403(b) plans may hold only certain types of investments--annuity contracts, mutual fund custodial accounts, and life insurance contracts--while 401(k) plan investment options are virtually unlimited.

457 Plan

A **457 defined contribution pension plan** is a deferred compensation plan sponsored by a state or local government or private tax-exempt organization. This plan is also similar to a 401(k) plan as it allows employees to participate in the plan by deferring a portion of their salary. The IRC classifies 457 plans as either "eligible" or "ineligible" based on the specific provisions of the plan. The plan sponsor considers the IRC requirements when establishing a 457 plan and determines whether to establish an eligible or ineligible plan. Classified as nonqualified plans, 457 plans do not apply to the IRS for determination letters, although they often request private letter rulings to indicate that the plan meets the requirements of Section 457 of the IRC. Also, the DOL does not require 457 plans to be audited; however, some 457 plans have audit requirements based on their state or local legislation. Unlike 403(b) plans, 457 plans do not have limitations on the types of investments the plan may hold.

HEALTH AND WELFARE BENEFIT PLANS

Health and welfare plans may be designed as defined benefit plans or as defined contribution plans. Defined benefit health and welfare plans provide an established benefit (for example, a promise to pay providers or insurers for specified services). The employer contribution generally is either determined actuarially or estimated based on past actual claims experience for defined benefit health and welfare plans. Defined contribution health and welfare plans allocate amounts to individual participant accounts which accumulate contributions, investment earnings and allocated forfeitures (if applicable), less administrative expenses, to provide benefits to participants. The contributions to be made to the plan, rather than the benefits to be received by the participants, are specified for a defined contribution plan.

Health and welfare benefit plans may provide various benefits including the following:

- Health benefits including medical, dental, prescription drug, visual, hearing, long-term care and psychiatric care

- Insurance benefits such as life insurance and accidental death or dismemberment
- Unemployment, severance, and disability benefits
- Dependent care, day care, apprenticeships, educational assistance, and legal services
- Vacation and holiday
- Postemployment benefits (such as salary continuation, job training and counseling, etc.) extended to former or inactive employees, beneficiaries, and covered dependents

Health and welfare plans may offer benefits while a participant is employed, after the employee retires, or throughout a person's employment and retirement.

Defined Benefit Health and Welfare Plans

A medical plan that would be considered to be a defined benefit health and welfare benefit plan may permit an eligible employee to visit a medical professional, be examined, receive treatment, and the benefit plan would cover all or a portion of those medical expenses, as prescribed in the plan document. Payment for these medical expenses may be made directly to the party providing the medical services, or the employee may pay for the services and then be reimbursed by the defined benefit health and welfare benefit plan.

In many cases, defined benefit health and welfare plans are unfunded, particularly in cases where the employer pays premiums directly to the insurance carrier or other third-party administrator who then pays the claims submitted by plan participants. As such, the use of a trust-funding vehicle is often not necessary.

Employers choose whether to fully insure, self-insure, or partially insure benefits provided through defined benefit health and welfare plans. The insurance arrangement in effect for the plan affects the reporting requirements for the plan as well as the risk assumed by the plan sponsor. In insured arrangements, the plan sponsor shifts a portion or all of the risk of the claims to the insurance company. Insured plans also generally contain provisions limiting the total amount which will be paid for the type of claim submitted (for example, a maximum of $1 million for transplant surgery), and they may also specify a lifetime maximum benefit per participant. For example, a participant may have a lifetime limit of $2 million in claims which may be paid by the plan for claims submitted for that participant.

For an insured plan, the plan, through plan sponsor and participant contributions, pays premiums to the insurance company based on the insurance policy or contract. The plan sponsor establishes how the cost of the plan (i.e., the premiums) is divided between the participant, if any, and the plan sponsor.

In addition to dividing the premium between the plan sponsor and participants, there are other types of cost-sharing arrangements available under insured arrangements. In a coinsurance arrangement, the participant pays a defined portion of the costs for the health care services and the plan sponsor pays the remaining portion.

The percentage of the cost paid by each party generally depends upon the provider of the services and the type of services received. Also, the participant may be required to pay a deductible before the defined percentage of additional costs are covered by the plan sponsor. For example, under a coinsurance arrangement, the plan document may provide that a participant would be required to contribute to the plan an amount representing 50% of the cost of annual medical physicals while the plan sponsor pays the remaining 50% of the cost. The amount that the participant is required to contribute to the plan is dependent upon the nature of medical services received by the participant and the predetermined cost-sharing arrangement for that particular medical service rendered.

Another type of cost-sharing arrangement is the use of copays. In this arrangement, participants are required to pay a copay upon the receipt of health care services. A copay is distinguished from a deductible in that a copay represents a partial payment of the total cost of a medical service which is required to be paid each time a medical service is rendered. A deductible represents a fixed onetime amount that the employee pays (on an annual basis), in addition to any premiums the employee pays, for benefits to be paid under the provisions of the plan. Generally copays are used in arrangements where the insurance premiums are being paid partially by the plan sponsor and partially by the participant.

In uninsured (or self-funded) arrangements, the plan sponsor assumes the risk of the plan and pays for claims submitted by participants. Insurance companies do not pay the claims in uninsured plans, rather the plan sponsor pays claims from its assets.

As in an insured plan, the plan sponsor determines the amount of contribution that it will require from the participant. A plan sponsor may provide for several types of health and welfare benefits under one plan and use insurance to provide for some benefits and cost-sharing arrangements for other benefits.

Defined Contribution Health and Welfare Plans

A medical plan that would be considered to be a defined contribution health and welfare plan may permit an eligible employee to visit a medical professional and receive treatment. However, the amount of the employee's benefit is limited to the amount of money in the employee's account, rather than the amount of benefits prescribed by the plan. In other words, the benefit the participant receives is limited to the amount contributed to the participant's account through his own contributions, contributions by the sponsor, if any, investment gains or losses, administrative expenses assessed against his/her account, and any forfeitures allocated to the participant's account. Any expense over and above the amount in the participant's account must be paid for by the participant and is not covered by the defined contribution health and welfare benefit plan.

An exception to this scenario is medical savings accounts plans whereby the plan sponsor is responsible to make up any shortfall in an employee's account. In other words, the amount of the employee's benefit is that amount prescribed by the plan as opposed to only that which is available in the employee's account. Such shortfalls normally represent timing differences in which a participant has a significant expenditure early in the year before s/he has accumulated sufficient monies in his/her spending account. However, if the participant is terminated prior to accumulating sufficient funds, the plan sponsor will not be reimbursed.

Health and welfare benefits are provided through various types of welfare benefit plans, also referred to as "fringe-benefit plans" in the Internal Revenue Code. Examples of welfare plans are group insurance plans, Section 125 cafeteria plans (including flexible spending plans), Section 129 dependent-care plans, and postretirement medical plans. Often, insurance plans, for example, life and disability insurance and postretirement medical plans, are defined benefit plans while flexible spending plans, such as medical or transportation plans, are defined contribution plans.

401(h) Accounts

In addition, employers may establish 401(h) accounts to fund a portion of their postretirement benefit obligations. The 401(h) account is included as a part of the employer's sponsored defined benefit pension plan. Essentially, use of the 401(h) account permits an employer to fund a portion of their postretirement medical benefit obligations with excess assets from the defined benefit pension plan. The benefits can be paid from the 401(h) account, which is funded with excess defined benefit pension plan assets or certain additional contributions. For additional discussion of the 401(h) accounts, see Chapter 8, Accounting, Auditing, and Reporting for Defined Benefit Pension Plans, and Chapter 9, Accounting, Auditing, and Reporting for Health and Welfare Plans.

Other

Specific types of health and welfare plans include plans established under group insurance arrangements, fringe-benefit plans, multiple-employer welfare associations (MEWAs), and many others. These plans may cover any of the types of benefits (medical, dental, and others) described earlier. Group insurance arrangements are established by insurance companies to provide welfare benefits to two or more unaffiliated employers through separately sponsored plans. Fringe-benefit plans include plans established pursuant to IRC Section 125 (cafeteria plans), IRC Section 120 (group legal services), IRC Section 127 (educational assistance), and IRC Section 129 (dependent care), and others. MEWAs may be established by a group of employers joining together, generally to purchase group health insurance and often using self-funded arrangements. The general distinction between group insurance arrangements and MEWAs pertains to the entity establishing the plans--either the insurance company or the group of employers.

To maximize the deductibility of health care expenses, an IRC Section 501(c)(9) Voluntary Employee Benefit Association (VEBA) trust may be established to fund some or all of the obligations of a welfare benefit plan. A VEBA allows an employer that self-insures part or all of its health programs to obtain an accelerated tax deduction by partially prefunding the plan. Employers may deduct their VEBA contribution, to a maximum amount defined by the IRC Section 419A, in the year the contribution is made rather than in the year in which the benefits are incurred or paid.

Employers may also offer postemployment plans to their employees. Postemployment benefits may be paid to the former employee, their beneficiaries, or their dependents. Postemployment benefits include severance benefits, continuation of medical and life insurance coverages, supplemental unemployment benefits, and others. Depending on the type of benefit offered, the employer chooses whether to insure the benefits or to provide them from its general assets (self-funded), or a combination of each approach.

For additional information regarding health and welfare plans, see Chapter 9, Accounting, Auditing, and Reporting for Health and Welfare Plans.

3 EMPLOYEE RETIREMENT INCOME SECURITY ACT OF 1974

INTRODUCTION

The Employee Retirement Income Security Act of 1974 (ERISA) is the single most significant piece of legislation governing employee benefit plans. ERISA was enacted by Congress to protect the interests of participants in employee benefit plans and their beneficiaries by requiring financial reporting and disclosure to participants, by establishing standards of conduct and responsibilities for fiduciaries of the employee benefit pension plans, and by providing remedies, sanctions, and access to the federal courts. Another objective of ERISA is to improve the overall soundness of employee benefit plans by requiring the vesting of accrued benefits of participants who have significant years of service with their employers; it also seeks to require defined benefit pension plans to meet minimum funding standards and also by requiring defined benefit pension plans to maintain adequate plan termination insurance through the Pension Benefit and Guaranty Corporation (PBGC).

This chapter will provide a general discussion of the provisions of Title I of ERISA. Title I of ERISA generally applies to employee benefit plans--including defined benefit pension plans, defined contribution pension plans, and health and welfare plans--which are established or maintained by an employer or employee organization to provide retirement, medical, surgical, or hospital benefits to the participants and their beneficiaries. The remaining sections of ERISA, Titles II through IV, address certain amended sections of the Internal Revenue Code relating to pension and benefit plans, including jurisdiction, administration and enforcement provisions, and plan termination insurance provisions.

The provisions of ERISA do not pertain to the following plans:

- Government plans (a plan established or maintained by the government of the United States for its employees, by the government of any state or political subdivision of any agency of the United States or of the individual states)
- Church plans (a plan established and maintained by a church or a convention or association of churches which is exempt from tax under Section 501 of the Internal Revenue Code)
- Plans which are designed solely for the purpose of complying with workers' compensation or disability insurance laws
- Plans maintained outside of the United States primarily for the benefit of participants who are mainly nonresident aliens (Note that ERISA does apply to plans which are sponsored in Puerto Rico, the Virgin Islands, American Samoa, Guam, Wake Island and the Canal Zone.)
- Excess benefit plans (plans maintained by an employer to provide benefits to participants in excess of the contributions and benefits limitations as set by Section 415 of the IRC, even if the plan is a funded plan. These excess benefit plans are typically created by employers for the benefit of highly compensated executives to enhance their overall benefit packages.)

DISCLOSURE AND REPORTING REQUIREMENTS

As previously stated, one of the primary objectives of ERISA is to establish uniform reporting and disclosure requirements to the participants of employee benefit plans. According to the provisions of ERISA, employers must provide plan participants with the following information relative to all employee benefit plans sponsored by the employer:

- A summary plan description
- A summary annual report
- Information regarding the participant's individual benefits as requested by the participant
- A summary of material modifications or changes made to the plan document.

Summary Plan Description

For purposes of ERISA, a summary plan description should be provided to all participants and their beneficiaries. The purpose of the summary plan description is to provide the participants with a brief synopsis of the plan document in order to explain to them their rights and obligations under the plan. In general, the summary plan description should include the following type of information:

- Name and address of the plan administrator (or the individual designated by the employer for claims or related matters)
- Name and address of plan trustees

- Description of any applicable collective bargaining agreements
- Description of the plan's provisions regarding eligibility for participation in the plan and benefits
- Description of the nonforfeitable pension benefits of the plan, if applicable

  NOTE: This does not apply to health and welfare plans.
- Description of the conditions which may result in the denial or loss of benefits
- Funding sources for the plan (i.e., employer, employee contributions, or both)
- Date of the end of the plan year
- Procedures to be followed for purposes of presenting claims for benefits under the plan and the remedies available under the plan when claims for benefits are denied
- Any other information that the employer deems appropriate to provide the participants with a description of the various features of the plan

It is required that the summary plan description and a summary of any material modifications made to the most recent version of the plan document be provided to plan participants and beneficiaries within ninety days after s/he becomes a participant in the plan, and in the case of beneficiaries, within ninety days after s/he begins to receive benefits. The plan administrator is also required to provide participants and beneficiaries with an updated summary plan description every five years. The updated summary plan description should incorporate all plan amendments made within the most recent five-year period. The only exception to this requirement is in cases wherein the plan document has not been amended during the five-year period. In such cases, the plan administrator shall provide a summary plan description to participants and beneficiaries every ten years.

Summary Annual Report

The summary annual report is a document which is provided to participants on an annual basis, specifically, no later than 210 days following the end of the plan year. The purpose of the summary annual report is to provide participants with financial information regarding the plan. The report should provide

1. A comparative statement of net assets available for benefits for the plan
2. A statement of changes in net assets available for benefits for the most recently completed plan year
3. Any other disclosures necessary to fairly summarize the plan's latest annual report filed with the Department of Labor (DOL).

It is not required for the information presented in the summary annual report to be presented in financial statement format, but rather it often describes the plan's financial information in a narrative style. Accumulated benefit information for a defined benefit pension plan or health and welfare plan is not required to be presented.

This descriptive format is acceptable to the DOL since they receive the plan's financial information in financial statement format as part of the Form 5500 filing and, at any time, participants and beneficiaries may request copies of the plan's audited financial statements directly from the plan administrator.

Section 2520.104b-10 of the DOL's Rules and Regulations provides an example of a commonly used template that employers may use when preparing the summary annual report for their employee benefit plans.

Information Requests by Participants

If a participant of a single-employer sponsored defined benefit pension or defined contribution pension plan requests information in writing, the employer is required to provide information regarding the participant's total benefits accrued under the provisions of the plan and also the nonforfeitable pension benefits, if any, that have accrued, or the earliest date on which benefits will become nonforfeitable. Such information should be based on the latest available information. In an effort to improve overall communications with employees regarding their benefits and pension benefits, employers are increasingly providing their employees with annual information regarding the benefits which they have earned under the employer's various employee benefit plans, as well as under any employer sponsored defined contribution pension and health and welfare plans.

Summary of Plan Modifications

In the event that material modifications or amendments are made to the plan during the plan year, a summary description of such modifications shall be provided to participants and beneficiaries within 210 days after the end of the plan year during which the amendments were adopted.

Additional Reporting Requirements

In addition to these reporting requirements to participants, employers are required to provide the following information to the appropriate agency, if applicable:

- A plan description, including any significant changes to the information required to be included in the summary plan description (only if requested by the DOL)
- Reports for plans which are terminating are to be filed with the DOL, the IRS, and the PBGC as required by those entities, notifying them of the intent to terminate the plan and requesting approval to do so (PBGC and IRS only)

The plan sponsor of a plan which has significantly failed to meet the ERISA minimum funding standards for the year (discussed in more detail later) is required to notify the participants and beneficiaries of this failure.

In addition to the items previously mentioned, one of the most important reports required to be filed for a plan is the annual report, otherwise known as the Form

5500. The annual report is to be filed with the DOL seven months following the end of the plan year (extensions are available to provide for up to an additional seventy-five days). Developed jointly by the DOL, the IRS, and the PBGC, Form 5500 is designed to provide each of the agencies with relevant information regarding the plan and to minimize the filing burdens for employers. According to the provisions of ERISA, a plan administrator may, in lieu of filing Form 5500, elect to the file under the statute, which will be described briefly below. However, almost all plan administrators elect to file their plans' annual reports via use of the Form 5500 series. Chapter 11, Form 5500, describes in detail the contents of Form 5500, including its supplemental schedules.

In general, the plan administrator is required to file a Form 5500 on an annual basis for each plan sponsored by the employer. For plans with more than 100 participants at the beginning of the plan year, the financial statements of such plans are generally required to be audited by independent public accountants. The definition of who is considered to be a participant varies by the type of employee benefit plan. For defined benefit pension plans and for some types of defined contribution pension plans, ERISA defines a participant as "any employee or former employee of an employer, or any member or former member of an employee organization, who is or may become eligible to receive a benefit of any type from an employee benefit plan that covers employees of such employer or members of such organization, or whose beneficiaries may be eligible to receive any such benefit." For a defined benefit pension plan, participants include active employees, retirees, terminated vested former employees, and beneficiaries who are currently receiving benefit payments. For purposes of defined contribution pension plans, participants are defined as all employees who satisfy the plan's eligibility requirements for participation in the plan, irrespective of whether the employee actually elected to participate in the plan by making contributions to the plan. In general, for a defined benefit pension plan, an employee becomes a participant when s/he has satisfied the plan's age and service requirements for participation in the plan. For a health and welfare plan, an individual becomes a participant when s/he becomes eligible for a benefit.

There are certain exceptions which eliminate the requirement for an audit but still require that a Form 5500 be filed for the plan. These exceptions include the following:

1. If the plan is unfunded, fully insured, or a combination of both. In general, the DOL and tax laws which govern employee benefit plans require that the plan's assets be funded through the establishment of a trust. For unfunded plans, audits are not required. Note that for plans which include an unfunded portion as well as a funded portion, an audit is required of the entire plan. For a health and welfare plan which pays a portion of claims through a trust and a portion of claims directly from the assets of the plan sponsor, the plan's audit would include an audit of all claims paid by the plan for the entire plan year. For example, for a health and welfare plan whose medical

benefits are covered by an HMO (health maintenance organization) and whose dental benefits (and claims) are paid from the assets of the plan sponsor, the audit of the health and welfare plan would include the audit of the medical benefits/claims paid and the dental benefits/claims.

2. A plan whose only asset consists of allocated insurance contracts (these assets are not considered to be plan assets--for more information see Chapter 6, Investments). In general, allocated insurance contracts are contracts whereby the insurance company that issues the contract unconditionally guarantees, upon receipt of the premiums, to provide a retirement benefit of a specified amount, without adjustment for market value conditions, to each participant who has a legal benefit that is enforceable directly against the insurance company. As such, this exception would only apply to defined benefit pension plans.
3. A health and welfare plan (these plans may provide medical, surgical, hospital, accident, disability, severance, vacation, and/or training benefits for employees) that meets the following conditions:
   - The plan pays benefits solely from the general assets of the employer or employee organization maintaining the plan, or
   - The plan provides benefits exclusively through insurance contracts or policies issued by a qualified insurance company or through a qualified HMO, the premiums of which are paid directly out of the general assets of the employer or employee organization, or partly from general assets and partly from employee or member contributions, or
   - The plan provides benefits partly from the general assets of the employer or employee organization and partly through insurance **and** forwards any employee contributions to the insurance company within three months of receipt **and** pays any employee refunds to employees within three months of receipt.

   NOTE: Due to the PWBA's Technical Release 92-1, a nonenforcement release, an audit is not required for cafeteria plans with participant contributions that are used to pay benefits and not held in a trust.

Under ERISA, all participant contributions are considered to be plan assets that then need to be put in trust. As the use of trusts is not being enforced by the DOL under this release, there is no audit required for the plan. Also, for other contributory welfare benefit plans where participant contributions are applied to premium payments and such contributions are not held in a trust, an audit of the plan may not be required. This nonenforcement position reflected in Release 92-1 will continue to apply until final regulations are issued with respect to welfare plans with participant contributions.

One additional situation that requires a Form 5500, which may not initially be accompanied by an auditor's report, is to be filed when a plan's first year is a short-plan year, (i.e., less than seven months). In these cases, the plan administrator may defer the initial audit of the plan until the following plan year and, as such, would not include an accountant's opinion with the plan's initial filing with the DOL. In the following year when an audit of the plan is performed, two separate audits are required: one for the short-plan year and one for the following full-plan year just completed. For example, if a plan's initial year covered a four-month period (year 20X1), one audit needs to be performed for the initial four-month period during year 20X1 and another audit of the plan is needed for the following full year.

An important point to remember with respect to employee benefit plans is the definition of the entity subject to audit. ERISA requires that the actual employee benefit plan itself be audited, not the trust which holds the plan's assets. This point is particularly important in instances wherein one trust may hold the assets of several plans, such as with master trust arrangements and with VEBA trusts; the reporting entity in such situations is each individual employee benefit plan.

FILING UNDER THE STATUTE

As previously mentioned, plan administrators may elect to file the plan's annual report under the statute, that is, Section 103 of ERISA, as opposed to using the plan's Form 5500. A filing in accordance with the statute, however, will not satisfy a plan administrator's obligation to file an annual Form 5500 under the IRC. Therefore, filing under the statute is quite uncommon due to the burden of having to provide information in two different formats.

In general, filing by the statute includes, in addition to the type of financial statement information required by ERISA (statement of net assets and statement of receipts and disbursements, namely, changes in net assets), that the accountant's report disclose the following:

- Any omitted auditing procedures deemed necessary by the accountant, and the reasons for omission
- The statements and schedules covered by the report
- The consistency of the application of accounting standards between the current year and the prior year
- Any matters to which the accountant takes exception, and the impact of such matters upon the plan's financial statements

In addition, under the statute, filing the annual report is required to include the current and prior year statement of net assets available for benefits, the current year statement of changes in net assets available for benefits, and financial statement footnotes, the types of which are discussed in the individual chapters of this book for defined benefit pension, defined contribution pension and health and welfare plans. In essence, while the information required for filing under the statute is very similar to the information already included in the plan's audited financial statements and report issued by the independent public accountant, it carries an additional burden for the plan administrator to prepare a filing under these circumstances, which is different from the Form 5500, which the administrator must also file to satisfy the IRC.

INDEPENDENCE OF THE QUALIFIED PUBLIC ACCOUNTANT

Throughout this chapter, reference has been made to the engagement of an independent qualified public accountant (IQPA) to audit the plan's financial statements. ERISA requires that the accountants performing a plan audit be independent for purposes of auditing the plan's financial statements and for rendering an opinion on such financial statements. The DOL has issued limited guidelines for determining when an auditor is considered to be "independent."

As per Section 29 CFR 2509.75-9 of the DOL's Rules and Regulations, an accountant will not be considered to be independent if the following circumstances exist:

- *During the period of professional engagement to examine the financial statements being reported on or upon, at the date of the opinion, or during the period covered by the financial statements the accountant or his/her firm or a member thereof had or was committed to acquire any direct financial interest or any material of indirect financial interest in the plan or plan sponsor; was connected as a promoter, underwriter, investment advisor, voting trustee, director, officer, or employee of the plan or plan sponsor except that a firm will not be deemed not independent if a former officer or employee of the plan or plan sponsor is employed by the firm and such individual has completely disassociated themselves from the plan or plan sponsor and does not participate in auditing financial statements of the plan covering any period of their employment for the plan or plan sponsor.*
- *An accountant or a member of an accounting firm maintains financial records for the employee benefit plan.*

There are certain situations in which the IQPA is permitted to engage in certain activities that will not impair the independence of the accountant or his/her firm, such as the retention of the accountant to provide professional services to the plan sponsor, auditing the financial statements of the plan sponsor, and also the rendering of services by an actuary who is associated with the accountant or his/her firm is also not deemed to impair objectivity. With respect to services provided by an actuary who is associated with the accountant or his/her firm, the DOL has not taken exception to this activity but the SEC has expressed reservations regarding this situation. There are other circumstances in which an accountant may provide other services to the plan without jeopardizing his/her independence, but they should be considered on an individual basis.

Effective May 31, 1999, the AICPA Professional Ethics Executive Committee revised the interpretations under Rule 101 regarding independence. The AICPA has indicated

> *In the performance of professional services requiring independence, a member should consult the rules of his or her state board of public accountancy, his or her*

state CPA society if applicable, the Independence Standards Board if the client is a registrant of the U.S. Securities and Exchange Commission, the U.S. Department of Labor (DOL) if the client or the client's sponsor is required to report to the DOL, and any other regulatory or private organization that issues or enforces standards of independence. Such bodies may have independence interpretations or rulings that significantly differ from and are more restrictive than those of the AICPA.

In addition, a member in public practice or his or her firm (member) who performs services for a client requiring independence (attest services) for that client may also perform other nonattest services (other services) for that client. Before a member performs other services for an attest client, he or she must evaluate the effect of such services on his or her independence. In particular, care should be taken not to perform management functions or make management decisions for the attest client, the responsibility for which remains with the client's board of directors and management.

The following are some general activities that would be considered to impair a member's independence:

- Authorizing, executing, or consummating a transaction, or otherwise exercising authority on behalf of the plan (for example, negotiating a transaction), or having the authority to do so
- Preparing source documents or originating data, in electronic or other form, evidencing the occurrence of a transaction (for example, broker's advices for purchases/sales of investments)
- Having custody of plan assets
- Supervising plan sponsor employees in the performance of their normal recurring activities
- Determining which recommendations of the member should be implemented
- Reporting to the board of directors on behalf of plan management
- Serving as a plan's stock transfer or escrow agent, registrar, general counsel, or its equivalent

The examples in Exhibit 1 identify the effect that performance of other services for an attest client can have on a member's independence. These examples are not intended to be all-inclusive of the types of other services performed by members.

Exhibit 1

Type of Other Service	*Independence Would Not Be Impaired*	*Independence Would Be Impaired*
Bookkeeping	Record transactions for which plan management has determined or approved account classification, or post coded transactions to a plan's general ledger.	Determine or change journal entries, account codings, or classification for transactions or other accounting records without obtaining plan management approval.
	Prepare financial statements based on information in the trial balance.	Authorize or approve transactions.
	Post client-approved entries to a client's trial balance.	Prepare source documents or originate data.
	Propose standard, adjusting, or correcting journal entries or other changes affecting the financial statements to the plan sponsor.	Make changes to source documents without plan management approval.
Benefit plan administration *NOTE: When auditing plans subject to ERISA, DOL regulations regarding these examples, which may be more restrictive, must be followed.*	Communicate summary plan data to plan trustee.	Make policy decisions on behalf of plan management.
	Advise plan management regarding the application or impact of provisions of the plan document.	When dealing with plan participants, interpret the plan document on behalf of plan management without first obtaining plan management's approval.
	Process transactions (e.g., investment/benefit elections or increase/decrease contributions to the plan; data entry; participant confirmations, and processing of distributions and loans) initiated by plan participants through the member's electronic medium, such as an interactive voice response system or Internet connection or other media.	Make disbursements on behalf of the plan.
	Prepare account valuations for plan participants using data collected through the member's electronic or other media.	
	Prepare and transmit participant statements to plan participants based on data collected through the member's electronic or other media.	
Investment--advisory or management	Recommend the allocation of funds that a plan should invest in various asset classes, depending upon the plan's desired rate of return, risk tolerance, etc.	Make investment decisions on behalf of plan management or otherwise have discretionary authority over plan's investments.

Type of Other Service	*Independence Would Not Be Impaired*	*Independence Would Be Impaired*
	Perform recordkeeping and reporting of plan's portfolio balances including providing a comparative analysis of the plan's investments to third-party benchmarks.	
	Review the manner in which a plan's portfolio is being managed by investment account managers, including determining whether the managers are (1) following the guidelines of the plan's investment policy statement; (2) meeting the plan's investment objectives; and (3) conforming to the plan's stated investment styles.	Execute a transaction to buy or sell a plan's investment.
	Transmit a plan's investment selection to a broker-dealer or equivalent, provided the plan has authorized the broker-dealer or equivalent to execute the transaction.	Have custody of plan assets, such as taking temporary possession of securities purchased by a plan.
Appraisal, valuation or actuarial	Test the reasonableness of the value placed on an asset or liability included in a plan's financial statements by preparing a separate valuation of that asset or liability.	Prepare a valuation of an employer's securities contained in an employee stock ownership plan (ESOP) to support transactions with participants, plan contributions, and allocations within the ESOP, when the plan is not in a position to have an informed judgment on the results of this valuation.
		Prepare an appraisal, valuation, or actuarial report using assumptions determined by the member and not approved by the plan.

MINIMUM PARTICIPATION STANDARDS

In addition to the reporting and disclosure requirements, ERISA also provides for minimum participation standards whereby pension plans are prohibited from requiring as a condition of participation that an employee complete a period of service with the employer which extends beyond the later of (1) the date on which the employee reaches the age of twenty-one or (2) the date on which the employee completes one year of service. However, if a plan provides for the vesting of benefits in a two-year period, then the pension plan may defer participation until the employee has reached age twenty-one and two years of service. For purposes of ERISA, one year of service is defined as a twelve-month period during which the employee has rendered 1,000 hours of service with the employer.

MINIMUM VESTING STANDARDS

ERISA also has established minimum vesting standards for participants in both employee and employer contributions. For purposes of employee contributions, participants' rights to accrued benefits derived from their own contributions are nonforfeitable. In addition, pension plans must provide that the employees' rights to accrued benefits derived from employer contributions must vest in a manner that meets or exceeds one of the two following vesting schedules:

- 100% vesting of accrued benefits after the participants have completed five years of service (often referred to as "cliff vesting")
- The graded vesting of accrued benefits with at least 20% vesting after three years of service, at least 20% for each year thereafter for four years, so that the employee's accrued benefit would be 100% after the completion of seven years of service

The vesting standards as previously stated are the general vesting provisions as provided by ERISA. In the event that plans are terminated or partially terminated, more stringent and aggressive vesting standards apply. In the case of partial plan termination or full plan termination, plan sponsors are generally required to fully vest participants in their accrued benefits.

REQUIREMENTS FOR PAYMENTS OF BENEFITS

ERISA also has provisions regarding the forms of benefit payments to be made under pension plans. For defined benefit pension plans, in the case of vested participants, the accrued benefit payable to such participants shall be provided in the form of a qualified joint-and-survivor annuity unless the participant waives the joint-and-survivor annuity and the participant's spouse consents to such waiver in writing. A qualified joint-and-survivor annuity means that benefits will be paid in the form of an annuity to the surviving spouse for the duration of his or her life. The payments that a participant receives are reduced when an election has been made for the joint-and-survivor annuity option. If a vested participant dies before the retirement benefit annuity commences and the participant has a surviving spouse, a qualified preretirement survivor annuity shall be provided to the surviving spouse. Plan sponsors have the obligation to provide information to participants prior to the commencement of the annuity payments, such as the terms and conditions of the qualified joint-and-survivor annuity, the participant's right to make an election to waive the joint-and-survivor annuity, the right of the participant's spouse and the right of the participant to revoke any elections made relative to the joint-and-survivor annuity options.

According to ERISA, a pension plan shall also provide that unless the participant otherwise elects, the payment of benefits under the plan to the participant shall begin not later than sixty days after the latest of the close of the plan year in which (1) the participant terminates his service with the employer or (2) the date on which the participant attains the earlier of age sixty-five or the normal retirement date as established by the plan document. For example, if a retired participant reached age sixty-five (normal retirement date per the plan document) on November 30, the payment of pension benefits to the participant must commence on or before February 28 of the following year (note that this example assumes that the plan has a year-end of December 31).

MINIMUM FUNDING STANDARDS

The concept of minimum funding standards applies to defined benefit pension plans and also to certain types of defined contribution pension plans, such as money-purchase plans. Specifically, ERISA requires that plans that are subject to the minimum funding standards maintain an account called the funding standard account, which is a memorandum account used to determine compliance with ERISA's minimum funding standards. The concept of minimum funding relates to contributions required to be made to the plans by the employer sponsoring the defined benefit pension plan. In general, for most defined benefit pension plans, the employer's annual contributions to the plan must be sufficient to cover the normal cost for the period (annual cost of pension benefits which will be earned and paid in the future) and the amount needed to amortize the initial unfunded past service liability (the excess of accumulated plan benefits over the present value of the plan's assets) and the increases and decreases in the unfunded past service liability resulting from activities such as plan amendments, actual plan experience, and actuarial gains and losses.

A plan is deemed to meet the ERISA minimum funding standards if at the end of the plan year, the plan does not have an accumulated funding deficiency. An accumulated funding deficiency is the excess of the total charges (required contributions as determined by the actuary) to the funding standard account for all plan years (beginning with the first plan year since 1974) over the total credits (actual contributions and earnings on such contributions) to the funding standard account for those years. In the event that a plan has accumulated funding deficiencies which are not waived by the IRS, the plan sponsor may be required to pay excise taxes as they have failed to meet the minimum funding standards as prescribed by ERISA. In these circumstances, the plan's financial statements may need to reflect a contribution receivable (and to the extent applicable, an allowance for uncollectible contributions receivable) from the plan sponsor for contributions to be made to the plan to satisfy the minimum funding standards. In addition to the extent that a plan becomes 85% or less of being fully funded, the plan administrator is required to notify the participants of the plan's funding status.

Additionally, disclosures may be required in the footnotes to the plan's financial statements to explain the situation resulting in the contribution receivable from the plan sponsor. In certain cases, the IRS may waive a portion or all of the minimum funding requirements for a plan year if meeting the minimum funding standard would result in substantial hardship for the employer, as long as an approved arrangement exists between the plan sponsor and the IRS which provides for the plan sponsor to make all of the required contributions to the plan. In the event that this circumstance exists for the plan, this matter should be disclosed in the footnotes to the plan's financial statements.

ALTERNATIVE MINIMUM FUNDING STANDARD

If a plan uses a funding method which would require that contributions be made to the plan in all years in an amount not less than the entry age normal funding method, the plan may maintain an alternative minimum funding standard account for any plan year. For a given plan year, the alternative minimum funding standard account shall be charged with the sum of

- The lesser of normal cost under the funding method used by the plan or normal cost determined under the unit credit method
- The excess, if any, of the present value of accumulated plan benefits of the plan over the fair market value of the assets
- The amount equal to the excess of credits to the alternative minimum funding standard account for all prior plan years over charges to the account for those years

The alternative minimum funding standard account should be credited with the amount contributed by the employer to the plan for that plan year. Note that the alternative minimum funding standard account is credited with interest in the same manner as the funding standard account previously discussed.

FIDUCIARY RESPONSIBILITIES

One of the key provisions of ERISA was to establish standards for plan investments and transactions and to impose restrictions and responsibilities on plan fiduciaries. A **fiduciary** to a plan is the individual(s) who is(are) responsible for the operation and administration of a plan. Typical examples of such fiduciaries include the plan administrator or an officer or other employee of the plan sponsor who reports to the plan sponsor's management or governing body such as the board of directors. According to ERISA, a fiduciary has the obligation to discharge his duties solely in the interest of the plan participants and their beneficiaries for the purpose of

- Providing benefits to participants and their beneficiaries
- Defraying reasonable expenses of administering the plan

In accomplishing these objectives, a fiduciary is to exercise care, skill, prudence, and diligence in handling the administration of the plan in accordance with the plan document and other documents and agreements which govern the operation of the plan. Furthermore, the fiduciary should diversify the plan's portfolio of investments so as to minimize the risk of large losses (unless under the circumstances it would not be prudent to do so).

According to Section 404(c) of ERISA, in the case of employee benefit plans which provide for individual accounts (such as defined contribution pension plans) and permit the participants to exercise control over the assets in his or her individual account, no person who is a fiduciary shall be liable for any losses which result from the participant's investment elections. When a plan chooses to avail themselves of Section 404(c) safe harbor provisions, there are twenty-five requirements that the plan must satisfy in order to attain this protection. The main requirements are

1. The trustee is responsible to provide notice to the participants that will:
   - Inform participants that the plan intends to be a 404(c) plan
   - Identify a 404(c) fiduciary to the participants
   - Explain that the legal responsibility of the investments transfers from the trustee to the participants
2. The trustee must provide a broad range of investment options to the participants. A broad range is described as at least three diversified core investments. The investments offered must allow the participant the ability to affect his potential return on the investment and the degree of risk associated with those investments.
3. The trustee must have someone available to the participants to explain commonly recognized participant concerns. This person, typically a representative from the bank, investment company, or brokerage firm that is acting as the 404(c) fiduciary, will be available to answer commonly asked questions such as
   - How do I monitor the performance of my investments?
   - How often may I change from one investment option to another?
   - How do I make a change in my investment options?

The fiduciary must be a responsible and qualified individual that can answer the above questions and be available to the participants to explain their investment choices and the administrative feasibility of administering the plan.

Plan fiduciaries should not cause the plan to engage in a prohibited transaction with a party-in-interest. Parties-in-interest to a plan include the following: an employee of the plan, any person who provides services to the plan, the plan sponsor, a person who owns 50% or more of the plan sponsor, or a relative of any of the above.

The prohibited transactions generally fall into the following categories:

- A sale, exchange, or lease of property between the plan and the party-in-interest
- Lending of money or other extension of credit between the plan and a party-in-interest
- Furnishing of goods, services, or facilities between the plan and a party-in-interest

- Transfer to, use by, or for the benefit of a party-in-interest of any assets of the plan
- Acquisition, on behalf of the plan, of any nonqualified employer securities or real property whose value exceeds 10% of the fair value of total assets held by the plan

Furthermore, a fiduciary is prohibited from using the assets of the plan for his/her own interest and also may not act in any transaction involving the plan on behalf of a party whose interests are adverse to the interests of the plan or the plan participants and beneficiaries. Finally, a fiduciary may not receive any special consideration from any party dealing with the plan in connection with a transaction involving the assets of the plan (for example, the fiduciary may not receive commissions related to the investment of plan assets).

ERISA does provide for exceptions related to the rules on prohibited transactions of fiduciaries. Some common examples of such exceptions include

- For 401(k) plans and Employee Stock Ownership Plans, the employer can make matching contributions in the form of employer securities
- The payment of fees to other service providers of the plan from plan assets is also usually acceptable provided that the fees charged are reasonable
- A bank is permitted to serve as the trustee for an employee benefit plan that it sponsors for its employees
- Loans made by the plan to parties-in-interest who are participants or beneficiaries of the plan if such loans (1) are available to all participants and beneficiaries on a reasonably equivalent basis, (2) are not made available to highly compensated employees in an amount greater than the amount made available to other employees, (3) are made in accordance with provisions regarding such loans as set forth in the plan document, (4) bear a reasonable interest rate, and (5) are adequately secured
- A loan to an Employee Stock Ownership plan if (1) such loan is primarily for the benefit of participants and beneficiaries of the plan and (2) such loan is at a reasonable interest rate
- Any transaction between a plan and a common/collective trust fund or pooled investment fund maintained by a party-in-interest which is a bank or trust company supervised by a state or federal agency if (1) the transaction is a sale or purchase of an interest in the fund, (2) the bank or trust company receives only reasonable compensation and (3) the transaction is permitted by the plan document, trust agreement or by a fiduciary who has the authority to manage and control the plan's assets
- A merger of multiemployer plans or the transfer of assets or liabilities between multiemployer plans determined by the PBGC to satisfy the requirements of ERISA Section 4231
- In certain cases plan documents provide for the payment of plan expenses from plan assets which may result in payments being made to the plan spon-

sor. For example, the salary and benefits costs of employees of the plan sponsor who provide services to the plan such as plan accounting and administration might be charged to the plan. These cases are not very prevalent, particularly with single-employer sponsored benefit plans, as the IRS has imposed strict restrictions on the types of "internal" costs which may be paid by the plan to the plan sponsor.

Ultimately, the Secretary of Labor has the authority to grant the administrative exceptions for various transactions, provided that the plan satisfies the statutory exemptions required under ERISA. In general, the Secretary may grant the exceptions only if all of the following conditions are satisfied:

- The exemption is administratively feasible
- The exemption is in the best interests of the plan and its participants and beneficiaries
- The exemption is protective of the rights of participants and their beneficiaries

To the extent that a plan fiduciary breaches any of his/her responsibilities, obligations, or duties imposed to the fiduciary by ERISA, the fiduciary shall be personally liable to make the plan whole for any losses resulting from the fiduciary's actions. The fiduciary may also be subject to other penalties as deemed appropriate by the courts. Similarly, if a plan's Form 5500 filing is rejected and penalties are assessed by the DOL, the penalties are assessed to the plan administrator and are payable by the plan sponsor, not the plan.

In addition, a fiduciary is responsible for the breach of fiduciary responsibility by another fiduciary under the following circumstances:

- If s/he knowingly participates or undertakes to conceal an act or omission of such other fiduciary with the knowledge that such an act or omission is a breach
- If by failing to comply with his/her fiduciary responsibilities, s/he has enabled another fiduciary to commit a breach
- If s/he has knowledge of a breach by another fiduciary, and does not make reasonable efforts to remedy the breach

In cases where assets of a plan are held by more than one trustee, each trustee shall use reasonable care to prevent a cotrustee from committing a breach of fiduciary responsibility. In the event that investment managers are appointed to control and manage the plan's investments, the trustee is not liable for the acts or omissions of such investment managers.

PLAN TERMINATION INSURANCE

The insurance provisions of ERISA apply to qualified defined benefit pension plans and do not generally apply to health and welfare plans and defined contribution pension plans (money purchase plans are the exception). The entity which provides the insurance to defined benefit pension plans is the PBGC. The PBGC's termination insurance program provides retirement benefits to participants and their beneficiaries when underfunded plans are terminated. The insurance program is funded substantially through premium payments which are required to be made to the PBGC.

The plan sponsor or employer is required to make annual premium payments to the PBGC for a single-employer plan. For multiemployer plans, the plan administrator is the designated payor of the premiums. For single-employer plans, the premiums are determined based upon the number of participants in the plan and the amount by which the plan's benefits are underfunded (i.e., the variable-rate portion), with a minimum amount to be charged per plan participant (i.e., the fixed portion). For multiemployer plans, premiums are based solely on the number of participants in the plan. The premium payments are permitted to be paid either by the plan sponsor or by the plan itself if this is in keeping with the provisions of the plan document.

The PBGC premiums consist of a fixed portion and a variable-rate portion. The fixed portion of the PBGC premiums represents an amount which is paid for each participant in the plan. The basic fixed premium paid by all single-employer defined benefit pension plans in 1999 was $19 per participant per year. The variable-rate portion of the PBGC premium is charged only to underfunded defined benefit pension plans. The variable-rate charge for 1999 was $9 per $1,000 of unfunded vested benefits. The premium rate for multiemployer plans was $2.60 per participant, per year.

There are two premium filing due dates each year: the first filing due date and the final filing due date. The first filing due date is the deadline for the fixed portion of the premiums for large plans only (i.e., those required to pay premiums for 500 or more participants for the preceding plan year). The first filing due date is the last day of the second full calendar month in the premium payment year (e.g., the end of February for calendar year plans). The final filing due date is the deadline for large single-employer plans to pay their variable-rate premiums and also the deadline for all premiums for small plans (i.e., those required to pay premiums for fewer than 500 participants for the preceding plan year).

For plan years that begin on the first day of the month, the final filing due date is nine and one-half months from the beginning of the plan year. For example, a plan whose plan year begins on January 1 has an October 15 final filing due date. A plan whose plan year begins on a date other than the first day of the month has an additional two months in which to file premiums. For example, if the plan year begins on January 2, the final filing due date is November 15.

When a reportable event occurs, such as a bankruptcy of the plan sponsor or inability of the plan to make its benefit payments, the plan sponsor or plan administrator must notify the PBGC. For plan terminations, ERISA provides for two different types of terminations: a standard termination and a distressed termination. A plan may be terminated voluntarily in a standard termination only if the plan has the resources to pay all benefit liabilities when due under the plan. In general, a plan sponsor is not permitted to simply terminate an underfunded defined benefit pension plan. A distressed termination may only occur if the distress criteria are satisfied. A distressed plan is one in which the plan sponsor is in liquidation, in bankruptcy or insolvency proceedings, or has filed for Chapter 11 bankruptcy, and the costs of providing pension coverage have become unreasonably burdensome to the plan sponsor. In either type of termination, the plan must submit to the PBGC a certification from an enrolled actuary regarding the value of the plan's assets and accumulated plan benefits.

In general, the PBGC guarantees most vested normal age retirement benefits, early retirement benefits, and certain disability and survivors' benefits. Vested benefits are guaranteed at the level in effect on the date of the plan's termination, subject to a statutory ceiling on the amount of an individual's monthly benefit. Also, to the extent that a plan has been amended within the last five years prior to its termination, such amendments are not usually covered by the PBGC guarantees.

ENFORCEMENT OF ERISA

The responsibility for the enforcement of ERISA rests primarily with the DOL, and the IRS is responsible for enforcing its own rules which were written in relation to ERISA. The IRS and DOL are empowered to pursue violations of ERISA in the federal courts in criminal actions, civil actions, or both. The failure to satisfy ERISA's various requirements may result in the imposition of penalties, including the possible loss by a plan of its tax-exempt status. When ERISA was enacted, it was intended to supercede the individual state laws regarding employee benefit plan matters. As such, most plans are not subject to state regulation if they are subject to the provisions of ERISA.

ERISA provides that in the event of violations of the provisions of ERISA, civil actions may be brought by

- A participant or beneficiary to recover benefits due under the terms of the plan document, to enforce his rights under the terms of the plan, or to clarify his rights to future benefits under the terms of the plan
- The Secretary of the DOL or a participant or beneficiary for appropriate relief related to breaches of fiduciary responsibilities by a plan fiduciary

An employee benefit plan may be sued or may sue as a legal entity under Title I of ERISA. Any judgments rendered against an employee benefit plan are only enforceable against the plan as an entity and are not enforceable against other individuals unless liability is established for that individual, such as against a fiduciary for breach of responsibilities to the plan participants.

ERISA and the IRC also provide for the assessment or imposition of penalties if a plan fails to comply with the reporting and disclosure requirements established for employee benefit plans. The following represents the various penalties which may be assessed as summarized in the AICPA's *Audit of Employee Benefit Plans* for failure or refusal to file reports in accordance with statutory and regulatory requirements:

- Up to $1,000 per day for each day that the plan administrator fails or refuses to file a complete annual report
    - Perfection penalties for deficient filings--Currently, the DOL assesses penalties of (1) $150 per day (up to $50,000) per annual report filing where the required auditor's report is missing; (2) $100 per day (up to $36,500) per annual report filing that contains deficient financial information, such as a missing required supplemental schedule; and (3) $10 per day (up to $3,650) for information required on the Form 5500 Series reports which is not answered.
    - Nonfiler and late-filer penalties--The DOL assesses nonfiler penalties of $300 per day, up to $30,000 per annual report, per year. Late-filer penalties are assessed at $50 per day.
    - Egregious penalties may be assessed in addition to other penalty amounts.
- $25 per day (up to $15,000), for not filing returns for certain types of deferred compensation plans, and certain trusts and annuities by the due dates
- $1 per day (up to $5,000), for each participant for whom a Schedule SSA per the Form 5500 is required but not filed
- $1 per day (up to $1,000), for not filing a notification of change status of a plan
- $1,000 for not filing an actuarial statement (for defined benefit pension plans only)

The above penalties may be waived or reduced if reasonable cause is determined to exist under the circumstances for the plan. When any of the previously mentioned reporting failures is identified by the DOL or IRS, a letter is sent by either the DOL or IRS to the plan sponsor, to the attention of the plan administrator, to notify them that a deficiency was detected. The letter provides the plan sponsor with a forty-five day period to correct the deficiency and to submit the appropriate documentation to either the DOL or IRS without the assessment of a penalty. If the plan sponsor fails to respond to the letter, further action will be taken by the DOL and/or IRS and penalties will be assessed.

Some additional penalties include the following:

- Any individual who willfully violates any provision of Part I of Title I of ERISA shall be fined not more than $5,000 or imprisoned not more than one year or both
- A penalty of up to $10,000, five-year imprisonment, or both, for making any false statement or representation of fact, knowing it to be false, or for knowingly concealing or not disclosing any fact required by ERISA

- Any employer maintaining a plan who fails to meet the notice requirement of Section 101(d) of ERISA with respect to any participant or beneficiary may be liable to such participant or beneficiary in the amount of up to $100 per day from the date of such failure, and a court may order other amounts of relief as deemed appropriate
- Civil penalties may be assessed against parties-in-interest or disqualified persons who engage in prohibited transactions. There is also an excise tax imposed by the IRS of 15% of the amount for prohibited transactions. The excise tax is to be reported on IRS Form 5330, Return of Excise Taxes Related to Employee Benefit Plans. When a prohibited transaction is identified, this form should be completed and the plan sponsor must pay the required excise tax.
- ERISA requires a civil penalty to be assessed by the DOL against a fiduciary who breaches his or her fiduciary duty or commits a violation of Part 4 of Title I of ERISA or any other person who knowingly participates in such a breach or violation. The civil penalty is 20 percent of the amount recovered pursuant to a settlement agreement with the DOL, which is ordered to be paid by a court.

Other penalties are available under the provisions of ERISA and also by the IRC and DOL for various other violations, such as the excise tax imposed by the IRS on prohibited transactions described above. Although the IRS and DOL may impose various penalties for reporting and/or operational noncompliance violations by employee benefit plans, both the DOL and IRS offer various voluntary compliance programs which plans may enter to mitigate such penalties.

As discussed in Chapter 1, Background of Employee Benefit Plans, for example, the PWBA sponsors the Delinquent Filer Voluntary Compliance Program, which was initiated in April 1995, to encourage filer compliance by allowing plan administrators to obtain relief from full late-filer and nonfiler penalties. Under this program, plan administrators must pay minimum penalties which are substantially less than the penalties that could be imposed.

In addition, the IRS sponsors various voluntary compliance programs, such as the Employee Plans Compliance Resolution System (EPCRS), which was created in 1998 and includes five former IRS voluntary compliance programs within its provisions. EPCRS offers plan sponsors the opportunity to correct plan operational failures and reduce potential sanctions that could be imposed by the IRS. For additional information regarding the various IRS compliance programs, see Chapter 10, Other Accounting and Auditing Considerations.

MERGERS AND CONSOLIDATIONS OF PLANS OR TRANSFERS OF PLAN ASSETS

Section 208 of ERISA provides guidance regarding plan mergers and transfers of assets related to such mergers. In recent years, employers have in many cases merged one or more of their defined benefit and/or defined contribution pension plans to facilitate administration of the benefit plans and to generate cost savings. In merging employee benefit plans, ERISA provides that for single-employer sponsored plans, pension plans may not merge with, or transfer assets/liabilities to, any other plan unless each participant in the plan would receive benefits after the merger/transfer of assets; these benefits would need to be equal to or greater than the benefit that the participant would have received under the original pension plan. In other words, a plan merger/transfer of assets is not permitted to occur if it would result in reduced benefits payable to participants.

With respect to the filing requirements, plan administrators are required to file a merging plan's final Form 5500 seven months after the transfer of assets has occurred. The asset transfer date may, in many cases, be different than a plan's effective merger date. However, the DOL views plan mergers as being finalized once the final asset transfer from the merging plan has actually occurred.

ESTABLISHMENT OF TRUST

Section 403 of ERISA provides that plan assets be held in a trust (subject to certain exceptions listed below) by one or more trustees. The trustees must be identified either within the plan document or trust instrument or be appointed by an individual who is a fiduciary to the plan. The trustee of a plan has the authority to manage and control the assets of a plan unless one of the following conditions apply:

- The plan document provides that the trustee is subject to the direction of a named fiduciary who is not a trustee or
- The authority to manage the plan's investment assets is delegated to one or more investment managers, as provided by the plan document.

There are certain exceptions which do not require plan assets to be held in a trust. These exceptions are

- Plan assets which consist of insurance contracts or policies issued by a qualified insurance company
- Assets of a plan which are held by an insurance company
- Plan assets for participants who are self-employed individuals
- Plan assets that consist of individual retirement accounts (IRAs) to the extent such assets are held in qualified custodial accounts
- Assets of contracts established under foundations, religious or educational sponsors

ERISA also provides that plan assets are to be held exclusively for the purpose of providing benefits to plan participants and are not to be used by the plan sponsor for any other purpose. ERISA does permit, however, that plan assets may be used to pay reasonable administrative expenses incurred to administer the plan.

BONDING

Every fiduciary of an employee benefit plan and any person who handles assets of an employee benefit plan is required to be bonded as per Section 412 of ERISA. The only exceptions to the bonding requirement consist of the following:

- If the employee benefit plan is one in which the only assets of the plan used to pay benefits are those from the general assets of the employer or union, in which case the employers of such plan are exempted from the bonding requirements.
- No bond shall be required if the fiduciary is (1) a corporation organized and doing business under the laws of the United States, (2) authorized under laws to conduct an insurance business, (3) is subject to supervision or examination by a federal state agency, and (4) has a combined capital and surplus in excess of $1,000,000.

The amount of the bond shall be fixed at the beginning of each plan year and should not be less than 10% of the funds (assets) handled by the fiduciary. The bond shall not be less than $1,000 nor shall the bond exceed $500,000 except as determined by the DOL. The purpose of the bond is to provide protection to the plan against losses by reason of fraud or dishonesty on the part of the fiduciary.

CONTINUATION OF COVERAGE

Section 600 of ERISA provides that the sponsor of a group health plan (an employee welfare benefit plan providing medical coverage to participants directly or through insurance or reimbursement) shall provide continuation of coverage under the provisions of the plan to qualified beneficiaries who would otherwise lose coverage under the plan as a result of a qualifying event. The only exception to the continuation of coverage provision is for a group health plan whose employers had less than twenty employees during the previous calendar year. A qualifying event consists of any of the following events which would result in the termination of benefits if not for the provisions of ERISA:

- The death of the covered employee
- The termination of the employee's employment
- The divorce or legal separation of the covered employee from the employee's spouse
- The covered employee being entitled to receive Social Security benefits
- A dependent child ceasing to be a dependent child under the provisions of the plan

The type of coverage to be extended to the beneficiary with a qualifying event should be the same coverage provided to all beneficiaries under the provisions of the plan. The coverage begins from the date that the qualifying event occurred and ends either eighteen months or thirty-six months following such date, depending upon the specific qualifying event which occurred. In addition, to the extent that the beneficiary fails to make timely payments of any required premiums, the continuation of coverage may cease. ERISA also provides that employees and spouses of employees be notified in writing of the provisions of benefit continuation, and communications are required by employees and employers regarding the occurrence of a qualifying event.

This chapter has summarized key provisions of Title I of ERISA. Additional information regarding the topics covered herein is available within the full text of the Employment Retirement Income Security Act of 1974.

4 PLANNING

INTRODUCTION

This chapter is the first in a series of chapters that discuss various accounting and auditing concepts associated with employee benefit plans. This chapter focuses on matters that should be considered by an auditor in the planning stages of an employee benefit engagement and also addresses items for the plan administrator to consider during the audits of the plans. The concepts discussed within this chapter apply to audits of defined benefit pension plans, defined contribution pension plans, and health and welfare plans.

As a general reminder, if a plan sponsor files a Form 5500 for a pension plan with the IRS, an audit of the plan's financial statements is generally required. For certain health and welfare plans, audits may not be required if trusts are not utilized; however, a Form 5500 is still required for a plan if there are in excess of 100 participants at the beginning of the plan year. Generally, plan sponsors for defined benefit and defined contribution pension plans with 100 or more participants at the beginning of the plan year must file a Form 5500 which requires an audit. Welfare benefit plans, which satisfy the following criteria, also generally require an audit:

- More than 100 participants at the beginning of the plan year
- The plan utilizes a trust which is used to hold all or a portion of the plan's assets

In other words, a portion of the plan's assets may be held in a trust for employee contributions to the plan, while the plan sponsor pays claims from the general assets of the company. In that case, an audit would be required for the plan. For purposes of a health and welfare plan, dependents are not considered to be plan participants.

AUDIT SCOPE

In determining the nature, timing, and extent of auditing procedures to be performed, the auditor needs to know the extent of services, or scope, requested by the plan administrator. This scope must be clearly defined before beginning the planning of the audit engagement. The auditor must also have a clear understanding of the auditors' reporting responsibilities regarding any supplemental schedules that will accompany the plan's financial statements. Such responsibilities and scope should be defined in an engagement letter.

Full-Scope vs. Limited-Scope Audit

The plan administrator must elect whether a full-scope or limited-scope audit is to be performed. Not all plans will qualify for the limited-scope election. A full-scope audit is one that is performed in accordance with generally accepted auditing standards. The plan's investment assets, investment income generated by those assets, contributions to the plan, benefits paid from the plan, and any other activity in the plan is subject to audit with a full-scope audit. Alternatively, ERISA Section 103(a)(3)(c) permits the plan administrator, in certain circumstances, to elect a limited-scope audit and, in such situations, the auditor would not perform any auditing procedures with respect to investment-related information that is prepared and certified by a bank or insurance carrier or similar qualified institution, such as a trust company. To be qualified, a bank or insurance carrier or similar institution must act as the trustee or custodian of the plan or of its investments. To qualify for the limited-scope audit exemption, the "similar institution" is an entity that must be federally or state chartered and supervised and subject to periodic examinations by state or federal agencies. The limited-scope election does not apply to assets held by a broker/dealer. Additionally, while it is the plan administrator who has the responsibility to engage the independent auditor to perform either a full-scope audit or limited-scope audit, the auditor needs to ascertain the appropriateness for performing a limited-scope engagement on the certifying entity. If the DOL determines that the trustee or custodian does not qualify to certify as to the plan's financial information, it will reject a Form 5500 on the grounds of an inappropriate report.

Additionally, the trustee or custodian must certify to both the accuracy and completeness of the investment information provided. The auditor should be cautious with respect to the certification statement received from the trustee/custodian since in many cases the certifications are not adequate according to the provisions of the DOL's Rules and Regulations. The certifications received from the trustee or custodian are often in flux, which may result in unacceptable certifications. Modifications include adding phrases such as (1) "based upon our review of the statements provided from another entity...," or (2) only addressing the "foregoing summary," or (3) listing with no transactions provided, (4) or "the information provided within the attached report is a summary of your accumulated plan benefits and includes all applicable contributions made to the plan through the end of the plan year (does not address the plan's investments and related investment activity)." Signatures of trust officers are often missing, rubber stamped, or signed by a secretary on behalf of the trust officer. Additionally, many certifications now include a statement that they qualify for the limited-scope audit, when in fact, the entity issuing the certification does not qualify for the limited-scope audit. Finally, some "certifications" often seem to also include many of the plan's other accounts such as contributions, benefit payments, and administrative expenses, rather than just covering investments and investment income.

Another common scenario is when the certification appears to be in proper order, reflecting that the trustee holds investment assets; however, when the report on the trustee is read, it is clear that the certifying entity does not hold the investments of the plan. The assets of the trustee may be held by another entity within the trustee "family," or by an unrelated third party. In some instances, this second entity holding the assets could certify as to the existence and valuation of the investments although there may be instances in which this second entity cannot certify because the assets of a number of plans have been commingled and individual plan information is not readily available. The subject of "certification" is a rapidly changing environment to which auditors should apply due caution.

Engagement Letter

The scope of the audit and the auditor's understanding of the objectives and services to be performed should be documented in an engagement letter. The following are items that should be considered:

- The scope of the audit (full vs. limited)
- The auditor's responsibility regarding supplemental schedules accompanying the basic financial statements
- The auditor's responsibility regarding Form 5500 information
- Consideration of the plan's qualification for tax-exempt status
- The auditor's responsibility for reporting matters that come to his/her attention regarding lack of compliance with ERISA requirements. An engagement letter should clearly state that the objective of the audit is not to determine compliance with such requirements, as this is the responsibility of the plan and the plan's management.

The following exhibit shows an illustrative engagement letter for a full-scope audit of a defined benefit pension plan which appears in the AICPA audit and accounting guide, *Audits of Employee Benefit Plans*. This letter should be modified for the specifics of the engagement as appropriate.

Exhibit 1

Sample Company Employee Benefit Plan and
Sample Company
Address

Attention: Plan Administrator, Sample Company Employee Benefit Plan or President, Sample Company or CFO of Sample Company

This letter will confirm our understanding of our engagement to audit the financial statements and supplemental schedules of Sample Company Defined Benefit Pension

Plan (the plan) as of December 31, 20X1, and for the year then ended, all of which are to be included in the plan's Form 5500 filing with the Internal Revenue Service.

We will audit the plan's financial statements for the year ending December 31, 20X1, for the purpose of expressing an opinion on the fairness with which they present, in all material respects, the financial status of the plan, and changes in financial status of the plan in conformity with generally accepted accounting principles, and whether the supplemental schedules are fairly stated in all material respects in relation to the basic financial statements taken as a whole and in conformity with the Department of Labor's (DOL) Rules and Regulations for Reporting and Disclosure under ERISA.

NOTE: The term "financial status" is used for defined benefit pension or health and welfare plans--defined contribution pension or health and welfare plans use net assets available for benefits and changes in net assets available for benefits. If the plan's financial statements are prepared based on an other comprehensive basis of accounting, this should be mentioned in the management representation letter as well as a statement that all required footnote disclosures have been included as part of the plan's financial statements.

We will conduct our audit in accordance with generally accepted auditing standards. Those standards require that we obtain reasonable, rather than absolute, assurance about whether the financial statements are free of material misstatements, whether caused by error or fraud. Accordingly, a material misstatement may remain undetected. Also, an audit is not designed to detect error or fraud that is immaterial to the financial statements, therefore, the audit will not necessarily detect misstatements that might exist due to error, fraudulent financial reporting, misappropriation of assets, prohibited transactions with parties-in-interest, or other violations of ERISA rules and regulations. The plan administrator is responsible for establishing and maintaining a sound system of internal control, which is the best means of preventing or detecting such matters. Our report will be addressed to the plan administrator and participants.

NOTE: If a limited-scope audit is to be performed for the plan, the second paragraph above should be deleted. In addition, the following paragraph should be substituted for the third paragraph of the sample letter above.

We will conduct the audit in accordance with generally accepted auditing standards except that, as permitted by 29CFR 2520.103-8 of the DOL's Rules and Regulations for Reporting and Disclosure under ERISA and as instructed by you, we will not perform any auditing procedures with respect to information prepared and certified to by [*name of trustee or custodian*], the trustee (or custodian), other than comparing that information with the related information included in the financial statements and supplemental schedules. Because of the significance of the information that we will not audit, we will not express an opinion on the financial statements and supplemental schedules taken as a whole. The form and content of the information included in the financial statements and supplemental schedules, other than that derived from the information certified to by the trustee (or custodian), will be audited by us in accordance with generally accepted auditing standards, and will be subjected to tests of your accounting records and other procedures as we consider necessary to enable us to express an opinion as to whether they are presented in compliance with the DOL's Rules and Regulations for Reporting and Disclosure under ERISA. Our report will be addressed to the plan administrator and participants.

We cannot provide assurance that an unqualified [limited scope opinion as permitted by 29CFR 2520.103-8 of the DOL's Rules and Regulations for Reporting and Disclosure under ERISA] opinion will be rendered. Circumstances may arise in which it is necessary for us to modify our report or withdraw from the engagement. In such circumstances, our findings or reasons for withdrawal will be communicated to [*the trustees of the plan or the members of the plan sponsor's audit committee*].

The financial statements are the responsibility of the plan administrator. Management is also responsible for (1) establishing and maintaining effective internal control over financial reporting, (2) identifying and ensuring that the plan complies with the laws and regulations applicable to its activities, (3) making all financial records and related information available to us, (4) properly recording transactions in the accounting records, (5) making appropriate accounting estimates, (6) safeguarding assets, and (7) providing to us at the conclusion of the engagement a representation letter that, among other things, will confirm management's responsibility for the preparation of the financial statements in conformity with generally accepted accounting principles and the supplemental schedules in conformity with the DOL's Rules and Regulations for Reporting and Disclosure under ERISA, the completeness and availability of financial records and related data, the completeness and availability of all minutes of the Board and committee meetings, and, to the best of their knowledge and belief, the absence of fraud involving management or those employees who have a significant role in the plan's internal control.

The plan administrator has responsibility for the financial statements and all representations contained therein. The plan administrator also has responsibility for the adoption of sound accounting policies and the implementation of recordkeeping and internal control to maintain the reliability of the financial statements and to provide reasonable assurance against the possibility of misstatements that are material to the financial statements.

An audit is planned and performed to obtain reasonable assurance about whether the financial statements are free of material misstatement, whether caused by error or fraud. Absolute assurance is not attainable because of the nature of audit evidence and characteristics of fraud. Therefore, there is a risk that material errors or fraud (including fraud that may be an illegal act) may exist and not be detected by an audit performed in accordance with generally accepted auditing standards.

To the extent that they come to our attention, we will inform management about any material errors, any instances of fraud and, unless clearly inconsequential, any illegal acts. If we become aware of information indicating that an instance of fraud or an illegal act may have occurred which in our judgment would have a material effect on the financial statements of the plan, we will communicate such information to [*the trustees of the plan or the member of the plan sponsor's audit committee*].

While we are not being engaged to report on the plan's internal control, we will furnish to you any recommendations about controls that we note during the audit which appear to be of significance under the circumstances. Additionally, if we become aware of any reportable conditions in the plan's internal control, we will communicate them to you in a separate letter.

The plan and [*Company Name*] (the plan sponsor) agree that all records, documentation, and information we request in connection with our audit will be made available to us, that all material information will be disclosed to us, and that we will have the full cooperation of the plan's and the plan sponsor's personnel.

As a part of our audit, we will perform certain procedures, as required by generally accepted auditing standards, directed at considering the plan's compliance with applicable Internal Revenue Code requirements for tax exempt status, including inspecting the plan's latest tax determination letter from the IRS. As we conduct our audit, we will be aware of the possibility that events affecting the plan's tax status may have occurred. Similarly, we will be aware of the possibility that events affecting the plan's compliance with the requirements of ERISA may have occurred. We will inform you of any instances of tax or ERISA noncompliance that come to our attention during the course of our audit. You should recognize, however, that our audit is not designed to nor is it intended to determine the plan's overall compliance with applicable provisions of the Internal Revenue Code or ERISA.

You have not engaged us to prepare or review the plan's Form 5500 filing with the Internal Revenue Service and Department of Labor. Because the audited financial statements are required to be filed with the Form 5500, professional standards require that we read the Form 5500 prior to its filing. The purpose of this procedure is to consider whether information, or the manner of its presentation in the Form 5500, is materially inconsistent with the information, or the manner of its presentation, appearing in the financial statements. These procedures are not sufficient nor are they intended to ensure that the form is completely and accurately prepared. In the event that our report is issued prior to our having read the Form 5500, you agree not to attach our report to the financial statements included with the Form 5500 filing until we have read the completed Form 5500.

NOTE: This paragraph should be modified or deleted to the extent that the auditor has been engaged to prepare the Form 5500.

The working papers for this engagement are the property of [name of CPA firm] and constitute confidential information. Except as discussed below, any requests for access to our working papers will be discussed with you prior to making them available to requesting parties.

NOTE: If your audit firm participates in a peer review program you may wish to add the following paragraph:

Our firm, as well as other accounting firms, participates in a peer review program, covering our audit and accounting practices. This program requires that once every three years we subject our system of quality control to an examination by another accounting firm. As part of this process, the other firm will review a sample of our work. It is possible that the work we perform for you may be selected for their review. If it is, they are bound by professional standards to keep all information confidential.

We may be requested to make certain working papers available to the Department of Labor (DOL) pursuant to authority given to it by law or regulation. If requested, access to such working papers will be provided under the supervision of [*name of audit firm*] personnel. Furthermore, upon request, we may provide photocopies of selected working papers to the DOL. We will mark all information as confidential and maintain control over the duplication of all such information. However, the DOL may intend, or decide, to distribute the photocopies or information contained therein to others, including other governmental agencies. You will be billed for additional fees as a result of the aforementioned work.

Our fees will be billed as work progresses and are based on the amount of time required at various levels of responsibility, plus actual out-of-pocket expenses. Invoices are payable upon presentation. We will notify you immediately of any circumstances we encounter that could significantly affect our initial estimate of total fees of $XXX.

We shall be pleased to discuss this letter with you at any time. If this letter correctly expresses your understanding, please sign the enclosed copy where indicated and return it to us.

We appreciate the opportunity to serve you.

If the above terms are acceptable to the Sample Company and the plan, and the services outlined are in accordance with your understanding, please sign the copy of this letter in the space provided and return it to us.

Very truly yours,

[*Firm name*]

Accepted and agreed to:

[*Plan Administrator's Signature*]

Sample Company Chief Financial Officer

In addition to the matters included within the sample engagement letter above, the auditor may want to consider adding a discussion of the following matters to the extent applicable under the circumstances of the audit:

- The timing of the audit (dates fieldwork scheduled to begin and end and the expected report issuance date)
- A summary of assistance to be provided by the plan sponsor in connection with the audit and a listing of items to be provided or prepared by the plan sponsor
- A discussion of information which will be communicated by the auditor to the plan sponsor's governing board such as the Board of Directors or Audit Committee, including the communication of any fraud or illegal acts detected during the audit
- An indemnification clause with respect to use of the auditor's report on the plan's financial statements in any other public filing, such as an SEC Form S-8

CONSIDERATION OF FRAUD

SAS 82, *Consideration of Fraud in a Financial Statement Audit,* explains the auditor's responsibility to plan and perform the audit to obtain reasonable assurance that the financial statements are free from material misstatement, whether caused by error or fraud. It also provides guidance in fulfilling those responsibilities, as they relate to fraud, in an audit conducted in accordance with generally accepted auditing standards. Fraud is distinguished from an error based upon whether the underlying event that caused the misstatement was intentional (fraud) or unintentional (error).

SAS 82 distinguishes two types of misstatements which are relevant in an auditor's consideration of fraud: misstatements arising from the misappropriation of assets and misstatements arising from fraudulent financial reporting. The misstatements that arise from the misappropriation of assets involve the theft of the plan's assets which then results in the plan's financial statements not being presented in accordance with generally accepted accounting principles. On the other hand, misstatements that arise from fraudulent financial reporting involve intentional omissions of amounts or disclosures in the plan's financial statements to deceive the users of the plan's financial statements.

Although fraud is usually concealed, there are several risk factors that auditors should consider which may suggest that fraud exists. The following is an excerpt from Appendix K of the AICPA audit and accounting guide, *Audits of Employee Benefit Plans,* which lists examples of fraud risk factors and the suggested responses by auditors. See Appendix K of the AICPA guide for additional examples and information.

Misappropriation of Assets

The misappropriation of assets involves the theft of a plan's assets, and the theft causes the financial statements to not be presented in conformity with generally accepted accounting principles. The theft of assets can occur, for example, by stealing assets, embezzling contributions or by improperly making benefit payments.

SAS 82 lists two broad factors which may alert the auditor to the misappropriation of assets, namely the susceptibility of assets to misappropriation and the lack of controls.

1. ***Susceptibility of Assets to Misappropriation***
   - A company sponsors multiple defined benefit pension plans, some of which are overfunded and some of which are underfunded
   - Lack of a qualified outside service provider to serve as custodian/trustee of plan assets
   - Nonreadily marketable, specialized, or unique investments and management's lack of understanding of such investments. For example, this could include investments such as derivatives, synthetic guaranteed investment contracts, real estate, or limited partnerships
2. ***Absence of Controls.*** The following are examples of control deficiencies which may suggest the misappropriation of assets
   - Lack of appropriate management oversight
   - Lack of review of investment transactions by trustee/custodian, plan sponsor, or the plan's investment committee
   - Lack of segregation of duties related to benefit payments, contributions, investment transactions, claim payments, and participant loans

- Failure to approve transactions with parties-in-interest that could lead to prohibited transactions
- Lack of the independent preparation and review of reconciliations of trust assets to individual participant account records and plan accounting records
- Use of a service provider that does not provide a SAS 70 report
- A SAS 70 report that shows a lack of adequate controls at a service provider
- No independent records are maintained to enable the plan administrator to periodically check the information provided by the trustee/custodian of plan assets

Auditor Responses. The following are examples of auditor responses to the risk factors mentioned above:

- Review reconciliations of the assets held by the trust with participant records throughout the year. Review any reconciling adjustments for propriety.
- Review the account activity for participants who have access to plan assets or assist in administering the plan.
- The auditor may have concluded that a risk of material misstatements exists due to a lack of a qualified outside service provider acting as trustee, custodian, or both for plan assets. In that situation, the auditor could physically inspect assets and examine other evidence relating to ownership. In addition, the fair value of investments could be tested by reference to market conditions.
- The auditor may have concluded that a risk of material misstatements exists with regard to remittance of employee contributions for a defined contribution pension plan because the sponsor is experiencing cash flow problems. In this instance, the auditor may perform a reconciliation of total employee contributions per the payroll register to the recorded amounts for the year, and may select certain months to test for the timely remittance of employee contributions in accordance with DOL regulations.
- The auditor may have concluded that a risk of material misstatement exists because expenses of an underfunded plan are being paid by an overfunded plan. In this instance, the auditor might select expense amounts paid by the overfunded plan and trace them to specific invoices, noting that the expense was recorded by the appropriate plan.
- Review the timeliness of contributions from the plan sponsor throughout the plan year.
- Compare canceled checks to disbursement records. Where benefits are paid by check, compare the signature on the canceled check to participant signatures on other employee documents.

- Confirm benefit payments with participants or beneficiaries.
- Confirm medical bills directly with service providers.

FRAUDULENT FINANCIAL REPORTING

Fraudulent financial reporting may result from several practices: alteration of accounting records or supporting documents which are used to develop the financial statements; misrepresentation or intentional omission of significant information from the financial statements; or the intentional misapplication of accounting principles relating to amounts, classification, manner of presentation or disclosure. SAS 82 lists three broad categories that may alert the auditor to potential instances of fraud. The categories are listed below along with suggested auditor responses to address the items.

1. ***Management Characteristics and Influence Over the Control Environment***

   Consider the following management characteristics and influence over the control environment:

   - A motivation for plan management to engage in fraudulent financial reporting. For example, senior management of the plan sponsor appoints itself trustee of the plan and uses that position to benefit the plan sponsor, such as by using the plan's money to do speculative investing or to support the company through buying employer assets or supporting a supplier.
   - A failure by management to display and communicate an appropriate attitude regarding internal control and the financial reporting process. For example, a failure by management to have adequate valuations performed, including actuarial valuations and calculations for postretirement benefit obligations for a health and welfare plan.
   - Management displaying a significant disregard for regulatory authorities. For example, the plan administrator has been investigated by the DOL or IRS for fiduciary violations in operating the plan.

2. ***Industry Conditions***

   - A declining industry, with increasing business failure and significant declines in customer demands. For example, the plan sponsor is in an industry that is declining in stability. This could lead to difficulties in meeting financial commitments to the plan, including contributions.
   - The plan holds employer securities and the employer is in an industry in which the value of the securities is subject to significant volatility or is not readily determinable.
   - The plan has limited investment options and the plan has invested heavily in employer securities.

3. ***Operating Characteristics and Financial Stability***

   - Significant related-party transactions not in the ordinary course of business or with related entities not audited or audited by another firm.
   - Indications of significant or unusual party-in-interest transactions not in the ordinary course of business.
   - Excessive or unusual transactions with the plan sponsor.

Auditor Responses. The following are examples of audit responses to the risk factors mentioned above:

- Obtain the investment information directly from the plan trustee, and obtain the same information from the party named as having discretion to make investment decisions. Review and reconcile the third party's reports (investment position and activity) with those of the trustee.
- In order to fully understand party-in-interest transactions, confirm transaction amount and terms with the other parties to the transaction.
- Confirm significant information with agents or attorneys to obtain a better understanding of the transaction.
- For single-employer plans, obtain the most recent financial statements of the plan sponsor and review them for indicators of financial difficulties.
- For multiemployer plans, obtain an understanding of the industry sponsoring the plan.
- For plans with investments in insurance contracts, obtain financial information regarding the stability of the insurance company and its rating.

SAS 82 requires that an auditor must document in the workpapers the assessment of the risk of material misstatement due to fraud. The documentation should include the risk factors identified at present; additionally, the response to those current fraud risk factors or other conditions should be identified during the performance of the audit.

RISK ASSESSMENT

As with any other type of audit, an auditor should plan an audit of an employee benefit plan to obtain reasonable assurance that the plan's financial statements are not materially misstated. The nature, timing, and extent of audit procedures to be performed will be determined based upon the size and complexity of the plan's operations and the complexity of the investment portfolio held by the plan. When assessing risks associated with employee benefit plan audits, the auditor should use a methodology similar to that used for other audit engagements. For example, the auditor should be aware that some account balances and transactions have a higher level of risk associated with them than others. Some areas which may represent an audit risk include plans with investments in non-readily-marketable investments or various derivatives, new types of investments such as synthetic guaranteed investment contracts, and voice response or Internet recordkeeping systems (used primarily by defined contribution pension plans). The auditor's assessment of risk should affect the engagement staffing, extent of supervision which will be required during the audit, and the overall strategy for expected conduct and scope of the audit.

During the risk assessment phase, the auditor also determines the level of materiality to be applied to the various plan accounts (i.e., investments, contributions, benefit payments, investment income, and expenses) to determine the scope of audit procedures. For defined benefit and defined contribution pension plans, materiality is often determined by applying a percentage factor to the plan's net assets available for benefits as of the end of the plan year, or the net additions to the plan. For health and welfare plans, materiality is often determined by applying a percentage factor to the contributions, benefit payments, or claims paid by the plan during the plan year. That materiality factor and assessment of overall risk for the engagement determines the extent of testing to be performed on the various accounts.

COORDINATION OF AUDIT

One of the keys to performing a successful audit for an employee benefit plan is the communication and coordination between the auditor, the plan sponsor, and any outside service providers. As there are numerous parties involved in the operation of the plan, communication with and coordination among these parties in planning the audit is essential. Such parties include the plan sponsor, trustee, plan administrator, actuary, recordkeeper, and attorney.

SAS 61, *Communication With Audit Committees,* requires the auditor to communicate certain matters relating to the audit to the appropriate level of management responsible for overseeing the financial reporting process. This level of management is typically the audit committee of the board of directors of the plan sponsor or similar group. When certain conditions exist in an audit, communication of such matters is also required under other standards, including

- SAS 54, *Illegal Acts by Clients*
- SAS 60, *Communication of Internal Control Related Matters Noted in an Audit*
- SAS 71, *Interim Financial Information*
- SAS 82, *Consideration of Fraud in a Financial Statement Audit*
- SAS 90*, Audit Committee Communications* (amends portions of SAS 61 and SAS 71)

The auditor needs to obtain sufficient evidential matter to support the opinion on the financial statements. The auditor should consider performing the procedures outlined below in order to obtain the necessary information to plan the audit.

1. Make inquiries of plan management regarding the following:

- Whether the financial statements will be prepared in conformity with generally accepted accounting principles (GAAP) or an other comprehensive basis of accounting. To the extent that the plan uses a comprehensive basis of accounting other than GAAP, the plan's financial statements need to discuss the differences between the method of accounting used and GAAP. Additionally, if a comprehensive basis of accounting other than GAAP is used, there will generally exist differences between amounts per the plan's financial statements and the Form 5500, and such differences will need to be discussed in a footnote to the plan's financial statements.
- Who performs the maintenance or support of the plan's financial accounting records and prepares the financial statements of the plan and the Form 5500
- Who identifies and monitors party-in-interest transactions. See the discussion in Chapter 3, Employee Retirement Income Security Act, for a description of certain types of transactions which constitute party-in-interest transactions.
- Whether there is any intention by the plan sponsor to terminate the plan
- Whether there have been any legal matters which affected the plan during the year

2. Obtain and review the following items:
   - Minutes of the retirement committee or similar group designated to oversee the plan
   - The summary plan description, plan document, and amendments, if any
   - The prior year Form 5500
   - Agreements or contracts with trustees
   - The IRS determination letter
   - Service auditors' reports prepared for third-party service organizations that have a role in the operation of the plan. See the discussion below regarding service auditor reports (SAS 70 reports).
   - Reports from the actuary, trustee, insurance company, or internal auditors
   - A list of all known party-in-interest transactions which occurred during the plan year
   - Notifications received by the plan sponsor during the year from any of the regulatory authorities, namely the IRS, DOL, or PBGC, if applicable
   - Results of any audits performed by either the IRS or DOL of the plan's operations during the plan year

ANALYTICAL PROCEDURES

SAS 56, *Analytical Procedures,* requires the auditor to perform preliminary and overall analytical procedures in all audits. When planning the audit, preliminary analytical procedures are performed to identify unusual or unexpected fluctuations in amounts usually aggregated at the financial statement level. The absence of expected fluctuations should also be considered. For example, if the plan holds investments in common stock and the stock market experienced an increase of 20% during the year, yet the net investment income earned by the plan remained flat as compared to the prior year, that situation could suggest a specific risk regarding the valuation of investments or recording of investment income. Significant differences should be investigated. These procedures aid the auditor in assessing the overall level of risk as well as planning the audit procedures to be performed.

INTERNAL CONTROLS

SAS 55, *Consideration of Internal Control in a Financial Statement Audit,* as amended by SAS 78, *Consideration of Internal Control in a Financial Statement Audit: An Amendment to SAS 55,* describes and defines internal control and the auditor's role in considering controls during planning and performance of the audit. Chapter 5, Internal Control, discusses internal control in more detail.

TRANSACTIONS PROCESSED BY OUTSIDE SERVICE ORGANIZATIONS

SAS 70, *Reports on the Processing of Transactions by Service Organizations,* as amended by SAS 88, *Service Organizations and Reporting on Consistency,* provides guidance on the factors an auditor should consider when the plan uses an outside service organization for the processing and performance of significant plan operations. Many employers outsource numerous administrative functions, such as recordkeeping and payments of benefits, to such outside service organizations. SAS 70 provides guidance to the auditor who audits plans that use a service provider (e.g., data processing provider, custodian/trustee of plan assets, plan recordkeeper, payroll processor) to process transactions. A SAS 70 report, or service auditor report, provides an understanding of the controls in place at the service provider organization. The use of SAS 70 reports for transactions processed by outside service organizations will be discussed in Chapter 5, Internal Control.

ACCOUNTING ESTIMATES

SAS 57, *Auditing Accounting Estimates,* provides information on obtaining and evaluating sufficient audit evidence necessary to support significant accounting estimates made in the financial statements. Ultimately, plan management is responsible for the fair presentation of the amounts in the financial statements; however, it is the auditor's responsibility to audit and assess the reasonableness of such amounts. The audit procedures should be planned and performed to consider both subjective and objective factors used in determining the accounting estimates.

GOING CONCERN CONSIDERATIONS

SAS 59, *The Auditor's Consideration of an Entity's Ability to Continue as a Going Concern,* as amended by SAS 77, provides guidance regarding the evaluation of whether there is substantial doubt about the entity's ability to continue as a going concern. For financial reporting purposes, continuation of a plan as a "going concern" is assumed in the absence of significant information to the contrary. Information that significantly contradicts the going concern assumption would relate to the plan's inability to meet its obligations as they become due. During the audit, the auditor may become aware of information that raises doubt about the plan sponsor's ability to continue as a going concern. Difficulties encountered by the plan's sponsor may not automatically and necessarily affect employee benefit plans. However, the auditor should determine whether these difficulties pose any imminent danger to the plans and should consider the plan sponsor's ability to deal with them.

SAS 59, as amended, states that the auditor has the responsibility for evaluating whether there is substantial doubt about the plan's ability to continue as a going concern for a reasonable period of time, not to exceed one year from the date of the financial statements. During the planning process, the auditor should assess the entity's ability to continue as a going concern. If substantial doubt exists, a going-concern uncertainty paragraph is required regardless of the auditor's assessment of asset recoverability and amount and classification of liabilities. In general, for defined contribution pension plans which provide for discretionary employer contributions, if there is doubt regarding the plan sponsor's ability to continue as a going concern, that usually does not result in a going concern situation for the plan. This is because a participant's benefit is limited to the balance in his/her individual account, and to the extent that a plan sponsor may not be able to continue as a going concern and not be able to make matching contributions to the plan (for example, for a 401(k) plan), this does not affect the plan's ability to make benefit payments to participants. Participants are fully vested in their own contributions to the plan and are not affected by the viability of the plan sponsor. However, for defined benefit pension plans, the viability of the plan sponsor may significantly affect the ability of the plan to continue, particularly if employer contributions are required to be made to the plan for funding purposes and if such contributions are not made. Finally, for health and welfare plans, the impact upon the plan depends upon whether the plan is fully or partially insured or not insured at all. In the event that a plan is not insured (all claims are paid from the general assets of the plan sponsor), and if the plan sponsor's ability to continue as a going concern is in jeopardy, this will likely significantly affect the ability of the health and welfare plan to continue.

5 INTERNAL CONTROL

INTRODUCTION

This chapter focuses on matters that should be taken into consideration by an auditor when evaluating an employee benefit plan's internal controls. It also contains information that plan administrators should consider with regard to the structure of their plans and the course of action plan auditors will be taking during plan audits. The concepts discussed here apply to audits of defined benefit pension plans, defined contribution pension plans, and health and welfare plans.

Statement on Auditing Standards (SAS) 78, *Consideration of Internal Control in a Financial Statement Audit: An Amendment to Statement on Auditing Standards No. 55,* and SAS 55, *Consideration of Internal Control in a Financial Statement Audit,* provide the auditor with detailed guidance for implementing the second standard of fieldwork included in the generally accepted auditing standards. SAS 78 states that "a sufficient understanding of internal control is to be obtained to plan the audit and to determine the nature, timing, and extent of tests to be performed." In all audits, regardless of scope or size, the auditor should obtain an understanding of internal control sufficient to plan the audit, by performing procedures to understand the design of controls relevant to an audit of financial statements, and whether they have been placed in operation. In other words, the auditor is required to obtain an understanding of the control environment and to document the understanding of those controls, whether it be for a full-scope or limited-scope audit. Note, however, that if a limited-scope audit is performed, the auditor is not required to obtain an understanding of the control environment for investments and investment-related accounts.

As defined by SAS 78, internal control is

> *a process--effected by an entity's board of directors, management, and other personnel--designed to provide reasonable assurance regarding the achievement of objectives in the following categories: (1) reliability of financial reporting, (2) effectiveness and efficiency of operations, and (3) compliance with applicable laws and regulations.*

Such laws and regulations include ERISA, the Internal Revenue Code, and the DOL's Rules and Regulations.

The areas to be focused upon in understanding a plan's internal control are

- Plan administration (including participant enrollments/eligibility)
- Investments and related investment income (for a full-scope audit only)
- Contributions (both employee and employer, rollover contributions, and forfeitures of employer contributions)
- Benefit payments/withdrawals/claim payments
- Participant loans (defined contribution pension plans only)
- Transfers between investment options (defined contribution pension plans only)
- Recordkeeping system (for individual account records)
- Demographic data information system
- Compliance with rules and regulations affecting the plan

THE COMPONENTS OF INTERNAL CONTROL

The internal control structure is made up of five related components, which are defined in SAS 78 as follows:

1. Control environment sets the tone of an organization, influencing the control consciousness of its people. It is the foundation for all other components of internal control, providing discipline and structure.
2. Risk assessment is the entity's identification and analysis of relevant risks to the achievement of its objectives, forming a basis for determining how the risks should be managed.
3. Control activities are the policies and procedures that help ensure those management directives are carried out.
4. Information and communication are the identification, capture, and exchange of information in a form and time frame that enable people to carry out their responsibilities.
5. Monitoring is a process that assesses the quality of internal control performance over time.

According to the provisions of SAS 78, the auditor should consider these five components in obtaining an understanding of the plan's internal control to effectively plan the audit and to determine the extent to which the controls in place are operating as intended. When planning the audit, this understanding would be used to

- Identify types of potential misstatements
- Consider factors that affect the risk of material misstatement
- Design substantive tests

Control Environment

The organization's control environment consists of the attitude, awareness, and actions of the plan administrator, board of directors, or other parties. The auditor should obtain an understanding of this environment and whether the emphasis is on implementing internal controls within the organization. This environment is further influenced by management's philosophy and operating style, the plan's organizational structure, plan management's integrity and ethical values, the participation by the board of directors/trustees in the plan's operations, management's commitment to competence, assignment of authority and responsibility, human resource policies and practices, and other similar types of control environment factors. In many cases, the individuals who are responsible for the plan's operations do not have an understanding of ERISA or the accounting and tax reporting/compliance issues surrounding employee benefit plans. This factor should be considered when an auditor is evaluating a plan's control environment.

Risk Assessment

The risk assessment of the plan is its identification, analysis, and management of risks relevant to the operation of the plan and the preparation of financial statements. The risks relevant to a plan's operation and financial reporting include external and internal events that may occur and adversely affect the plan's ability to operate as intended, per the provisions of the plan document, and to record, process, summarize, and report the financial data. Risks can arise from any series of events including, for example, changes in the trustee/custodian of plan assets or the recordkeeper, change to a new recordkeeping system, such as a voice response or internet system for a defined contribution pension or health and welfare plan, or the merger of a plan into another plan resulting from corporate acquisitions. The auditor should obtain sufficient knowledge of the plan's risk assessment process to understand how management considers risks relevant to the plan's operations and financial reporting issues and how they address such risks.

Control Activities

Control activities are the policies and procedures that help ensure that plan management directives are enacted within the organization. Some examples of control activities that may be relevant to an audit of a plan's financial statements include

- Information processing, such as the processing of benefit payment requests for a defined benefit pension plan or changes to a plan's investment elections with a defined contribution pension plan.
- Physical controls over assets, for example, controls at the trustee/custodian level and segregation of duties of both the plan sponsor (such as the processing of participant enrollment forms), and duties (for example, the recordkeeper who processes transactions at the individual participant account level and the trustee who controls the investments for a defined benefit pension plan). The auditor should obtain an understanding of those control activities relevant to planning and performing the audit.

Information and Communication

The information system consists of the methods and systems established to record, process, summarize, and report plan transactions to maintain accountability for the net assets of the plan. Communication involves defining each individual's roles and responsibilities pertaining to internal control over financial reporting. The auditor should obtain sufficient knowledge of the plan's information system to understand the following as it relates to recording, processing, summarizing, and reporting plan transactions:

- The classes of transactions that are significant to the plan's operations and the financial statements, and how such transactions are initiated. For example, for a health and welfare plan, this would involve the claims processing system, which is one of the most significant components relative to the plan's operations. Obtaining an understanding of the claims processing system would include obtaining an understanding of how claims are submitted for payment, how claims are processed by either the plan sponsor (insured plan) or by a third-party administrator, and the controls in place regarding duplication of payments for a claim.
- The accounting records, supporting information, and specific accounts in the plan's financial statements that are involved in the processing and reporting of transactions. For example, this could include the investment records for a plan--how investment transactions are initiated, approved, and processed by the investment managers, trustee, or custodian of plan assets and ultimately recorded into the trust statements prepared for the plan. In addition, for a multiemployer plan, this could include the payroll and contributions records, including how contributions to the plan are processed by the various employers, how supporting records are maintained by the employers, and how such amounts are ultimately recorded in the plan's financial statements.
- The processing steps that are involved from the initiation of a transaction to its inclusion in the financial statements. For example, this could include the enrollment of a plan participant into a 401(k) plan, beginning with the com-

pletion of an enrollment form for the participant to the establishment of an individual account record. Another example would be the processing of a participant loan request from the completion of the initial request by the participant to the recording of the transaction by the plan recordkeeper to the disbursement of the loan monies to the participant and the subsequent repayment of the loan by the participant.

- The financial reporting process that is used to prepare the plan's financial statements and related footnote disclosures. This would include significant accounting estimates, such as postretirement benefit obligations and incurred but not reported benefit claims for a health and welfare plan, and accumulated plan benefits for a defined benefit pension plan. This could also include the valuation or independent appraisal for nonreadily marketable securities held by a plan.

Monitoring

Monitoring is a process that measures and reviews the quality of internal control performance over time. Plan management should monitor and evaluate controls to assess their effectiveness and whether they are operating as intended. Necessary and timely corrective action is required for controls that are not operating effectively. The auditor should obtain an understanding of the major types of resources the organization utilizes to monitor the effectiveness of internal controls. In some cases, efficiencies may be gained by reviewing the work of the internal auditors if their audits include the employee benefit plans of the plan sponsor (e.g., payroll system activities, health claim audits, or payroll audits for multiemployer plans). SAS 65, *The Auditor's Consideration of the Internal Audit Function in an Audit of Financial Statements,* provides guidance regarding the auditor's responsibility when reviewing and relying upon the work of the internal audit function.

UNDERSTANDING THE CONTROLS

As previously noted, the auditor should obtain an understanding of the components of internal control in sufficient detail in order to properly plan and perform the audit. The nature and extent of procedures to be performed will vary depending upon the size, scope, prior experience with, and complexity of the plan.

The auditor should obtain adequate knowledge and understanding of the design of the relevant controls pertaining to each of the five internal control components and whether they are being exercised within the organization. This knowledge is most often acquired through

- Prior experience with the organization
- Procedures such as inquiries of plan management, supervisory, and staff personnel
- Inspection of plan documents and records
- Observation of plan activities and operations

However, not all of the plan's transactions may be processed within the organization. Many transactions are processed by outside service providers. See discussion of third-party service providers later in this chapter.

Additionally, efficiencies may be achieved by relying on the testing performed during the general audit of the plan sponsor. Such testing may include control work related to the payroll and accounts payable systems as well as to the general ledger. Often, steps necessary to complete the audit of the plan can be incorporated into the control work performed on the systems of the plan sponsor, provided that the controls identified are those which directly impact the operation and administration of the plan sponsor's employee benefit plans. For example, to the extent that the plan utilizes a voice response or internet recordkeeping system, the controls documented and tested regarding the plan sponsor's payroll and human resources department as part of the general audit of the plan sponsor may not be sufficient to address the actual internal controls in place for the defined contribution pension plan.

DOCUMENTATION

Once the auditor has obtained an understanding of the controls in place within the organization, generally accepted auditing standards require this understanding to be documented. The auditor's assessment of control risk and the reasons for such an assessment also need to be documented. The design of tests of controls should support the control risk assessment. The extent to which an auditor decides to perform tests of controls for an employee benefit plan audit will depend upon the decision made by the auditor to either adopt a control reliance strategy or not to adopt such a strategy. The control reliance strategy refers to the extent that an auditor has decided to rely on the internal controls in place for the plan, which s/he would do after testing the controls and performing a reduced amount of substantive testing on the plan's financial statement accounts. In the event that the auditor decides not to adopt a control reliance strategy, tests of a plan's internal controls would not be performed, which then increases the amount of substantive testing performed on the plan's financial statement accounts. Controls may be tested through inquiries of plan management and personnel involved with the administration of the plan, examination of supporting records and documents, review of service auditor reports (SAS 70 reports) prepared for the service organizations of the plan, testing of computer controls in regard to the plan (including plan sponsor computer controls and service provider computer controls), and through the observation of the processing of transactions. The following summary presents various internal control objectives--such as investments, plan administration, or compliance--which may be in place for an employee benefit plan, as well as other related controls. The information was excerpted from the AICPA's *Audits for Employee Benefit Plans*, which presents a comprehensive summary of internal control objectives and controls. The reader should refer to the AICPA audit guide for additional information.

Investments

Control objective: Investment transactions are recorded at the appropriate amounts and in the appropriate periods on a timely basis.

Examples of controls: Reports submitted by the trustees or investment management are reviewed. Detailed subsidiary records are reconciled to the general ledger on a regular basis.

Control objective: Investments (other than insurance contracts with insurance companies) are measured at fair value.

Examples of controls: Quotation sources and appraisal reports are compared with recorded values. Valuation methods are documented in the trust agreement or plan committee minutes. Basis for "good-faith" estimates including independent appraisals, if any, is documented. "Good-faith" estimates are approved by plan committee.

Control objective: Obligations under insurance companies' insurance contracts can be met.

Examples of controls: Financial statements of insurance companies are reviewed. Rating bureau reports are reviewed.

Control objective: Investment criteria and objectives are authorized, and investment strategies are executed in accordance with formal authorizations.

Examples of controls: Investment criteria or objectives are documented in the plan instrument or plan committee minutes. Authority to execute transactions is specified in the plan instrument or plan committee minutes. Investment transactions are reviewed by a plan committee for adherence to investment guidelines.

Investment Income

Control objective: Investment income and expenses are recorded at the appropriate amount and in the appropriate period on a timely basis.

Examples of controls: Commissions and management fees are reviewed for appropriateness and adherence to the contract. Interest, dividends, and other sources of income are reviewed for receipt and for accuracy by reference to reliable sources.

Contributions

Control objective: Amounts of contributions by employers and participants meet authorized or required amounts.

Examples of controls: Contribution requirements or limitations are described in the plan document or collective bargaining agreement. Contributions are determined using approved eligibility lists. Actuary is used to make periodic valuations and reports (defined benefit pension plan and health and welfare plan only).

Control objective: Contributions are recorded at the appropriate amount and in the appropriate period on a timely basis.

Examples of controls: Sponsor or employer payroll records are compared with contribution calculations. In the case of multiemployer plans, some form of periodic payroll audit is performed. Initial controls are established over contribution records for both employer and participant contributions (e.g., salary reduction amounts). Clerical accuracy of contribution forms is checked. Subsidiary contribution records are reconciled to the general ledger. Contribution forms are reconciled to cash receipts ledger and bank deposits. Control totals for contributions withheld from participant records are maintained. Contribution receipts are issued to participants containing notices requesting reviews of discrepancies.

Control objective: Access to cash receipts, cash receipts records, and contribution records is suitably controlled to prevent or detect within a timely period the interception of unrecorded cash receipts or the removal of recorded cash receipts.

Examples of controls: Cash is independently controlled upon receipt. Cash receipts are deposited intact daily. Checks are restrictively endorsed upon receipt. Responsibility for receiving and processing contributions is adequately segregated. Bank accounts are reconciled monthly. Past-due contributions are investigated on a timely basis.

Benefit Payments

Control objective: Benefit payments are determined and authorized in accordance with the plan document.

Examples of controls: Changes in participants' eligibility are approved by the plan committee. Eligibility lists are approved. Signed benefit application forms are used. Benefit applications that provide for review of eligibility, benefit amounts, or plan compliance require approval.

Control objective: Benefit payments are recorded at the appropriate amount and in the appropriate period on a timely basis.

Examples of controls: Benefit calculations supporting payments are checked for clerical accuracy. Benefits payable outstanding for a long period are investigated. Initial controls are established over benefit applications. Benefit amounts are compared with plan or insurance company records. Control totals for monthly pension benefits are maintained. Participants or beneficiaries are notified of their right to have denied claims reviewed.

Participant Data

Control objective: Participant eligibility is determined in accordance with authorization.

Examples of controls: Eligibility is defined in the plan document. Enrollment applications are reviewed by the plan committee or a responsible official.

Control objective: Participant data are properly recorded on a timely basis.

Examples of controls: The number of plan participants is reconciled using enrollment forms. Subsidiary records are maintained for participants who are active, retired, or terminated with vested benefits. Participants' subsidiary records are reconciled with general ledger. Participant data is updated and reconciled to employer's personnel and payroll records before being sent to the actuary.

Control objective: Accumulated benefit amounts and other actuarially determined information are determined periodically and recorded in the plan's records at the appropriate amounts.

Examples of controls: Valuation report prepared by an actuary's valuation report are reconciled with the participants' subsidiary records.

Plan Administration

Control objective: Only participants who satisfy eligibility criteria are able to participate in the plan.

Examples of controls: Review of enrollment forms by plan management to ensure that only eligible participants are able to open individual account records. For voice response recordkeeping systems, information from the employees' personnel file is linked with the recordkeeping system to allow only valid enrollments. Eligibility criteria is clearly defined within the plan document.

Transfers Between Investment Options

Control objective: Participant-initiated transfers are recorded on a timely basis.

Examples of controls: Confirmation statements sent to participants within a two- to three-business-day period to confirm the investment transfer transaction. Immediate updating of the recordkeeping system for participant-initiated transactions.

Participant Loans

Control objective: Participants are permitted to have only one outstanding loan at a time.

Examples of controls: Review and approval of loan request by plan management. For voice-response recordkeeping system, revise controls in place which reject a loan application if one loan is already outstanding for the participant.

Compliance With Rules and Regulations Affecting the Plan

Control objective: Plan satisfies the required antidiscrimination tests.

Examples of controls: Plan management review of antidiscrimination test results. If plan fails tests, corrective action is taken on a timely basis and approved by plan management. Outside service provider is engaged to perform the discrimination tests for the plan.

The documentation of controls may include narratives, flowcharts, and programs and will depend on the nature and complexity of the plan's control environment. Also, if any exceptions are encountered during control testing, they should also be documented along with resolution of such exceptions and any resulting constructive service comments. See further discussion on management letter comments later in this chapter.

MULTIEMPLOYER SPONSORED PLANS

As discussed in previous chapters, a multiemployer sponsored plan is a plan which is generally negotiated and established pursuant to a collective bargaining agreement between an associated group of employers and the union representing the employees.

In the multiemployer sponsored plan environment there are additional matters which must be considered in assessing the plan's internal controls. The control environment of the plan is affected by all the parties involved in the administration of the plan, including the employers sponsoring the plan, the union representing the plan, and the plan sponsor (usually a joint employer/union board of trustees). Essentially, all of the matters previously mentioned with regard to the documentation and testing of controls remain applicable for multiemployer plans; however, the impact due to the involvement of multiple employers and a representative union in the structure of the plan must enter into the consideration of internal controls. For example, for contributions made to a multiemployer sponsored plan, the approval of contributions may need to be tested through examination of individual employer records against minutes from meetings of the board of directors. Additionally, for testing performed on participant eligibility, testing should be performed on participant data for a sample of the various employers. Finally, for multiemployer plans, payroll audits are to be performed for each of the sponsoring companies on a rotational basis. The results of the audits should be reviewed by auditors and considered in the context of procedures to be performed relative to payroll systems and employee and employer contributions.

USE OF THIRD-PARTY SERVICE PROVIDERS

Plan transactions are often executed and maintained by a third-party service provider, such as a bank trustee, insurance company, or contract administrator (herein referred to as a service provider). The auditor must obtain an understanding of the internal control structure in place at the service provider, unless a limited-scope audit is being performed for the plan and the plan's only service provider is a bank. The level of service provided to the plan by the service provider, as well as the degree of discretionary authority for trustees/custodians of plan assets, will determine the extent to which the auditor must consider the control components at the service provider.

If the trustee/custodian executes transactions only as specifically directed by the plan, the trustee/custodian is considered to have **nondiscretionary** authority over plan assets. In this case, the plan should maintain independent records of transactions to be executed by the trustee/custodian. In this case, the auditor may not need to consider the control components in place for the trustee/custodian when obtaining an understanding of the internal control structure required under SAS 78.

If, however, the trustee/custodian has the authority of the plan to execute transactions without being directed by the plan, the trustee/custodian is considered to have **discretionary** authority over plan assets. In this case, the plan will generally not be able to maintain independent records of transactions executed by the trustee/custodian. The auditor would need to consider the control components in place for the trustee/custodian when obtaining an understanding of the internal control structure required under SAS 78.

Factors to Consider When a Service Provider Is Used

SAS 70, *Reports on the Processing of Transactions by Service Organizations,* as amended by SAS 88, *Service Organizations and Reporting on Consistency*, describes the factors that should be considered when auditing the financial statements of a plan that utilizes a service provider to process transactions such as recordkeeping or disbursement transactions. It also provides guidance for independent auditors who issue reports on the processing of transactions by a service organization for use by other auditors. A report prepared in accordance with SAS 70, as amended, should be designed to provide user auditors with a sufficient understanding of controls in place at the service provider to plan the audit in accordance with SAS 78.

The AICPA publication, *Auditing Procedure Study--Implementing SAS No. 70, AICPA Reports on the Processing of Transactions by Service Organizations,* offers additional guidance. SAS 88 provides the following guidance to be considered when planning the audit:

> *Information about the nature of the services provided by a service organization that are part of the user organization's information system and the service organization's controls over those services may be available from a wide variety of sources such as user manuals, system overviews, technical manuals, the contract between the user organization and reports by service auditors, internal auditors or regulatory authorities on the service organization's controls. If the services and the service organization's controls over those services are highly standardized, information obtained through the user auditor's prior experience with the service organization may be helpful in planning the audit.*

For purposes of an audit of an employee benefit plan, information regarding the services provided by the service organization (e.g., recordkeeping services or management of the plan's investments) may be available from many sources such as the SAS 70 report, user manuals, and the contract between the plan and the service provider. Such information, as well as the auditor's prior experience with the service organization, should be considered in planning the audit.

SERVICE AUDITOR REPORTS

As discussed in SAS 70, there are two types of service auditor reports.

1. **Reports on controls placed in operation (Type I report).** Report on a service organization's description of its controls that may be relevant to a user organization's internal control as it relates to an audit of financial statements. This type of report should be useful in providing the user auditor with a sufficient understanding of the controls in place at the service

provider and whether such controls were suitably designed to achieve specified control objectives. These reports are not intended to provide the user auditor with a basis for reducing their assessment of control risk below the maximum. In order to reduce control risk below the maximum, additional testing procedures would be required, including testing of the plan's controls over the activities of the service provider and testing controls at the service provider. The Type I report is usually used to document the auditor's understanding of controls in place at the service provider.

2. **Reports on controls placed in operation and tests of operating effectiveness (Type II report).** Report on a service organization's description of its controls and tests of those controls that may be relevant to a user organization's internal control as it relates to an audit of financial statements. It addresses whether such controls were suitably designed to achieve specified control objectives, whether they had been placed in operation as of a specific date, and whether the controls that were tested operated effectively enough to provide reasonable, but not absolute, assurance that the related control objectives were achieved during the period specified. This report differs from the Type I report in that tests of controls by the service auditor are included. It could also be useful in providing the user auditor with an understanding of the controls sufficient enough to plan the audit as well reduce the assessment of control risk below the maximum for financial statement assertions affected by the controls.

There are a few other items to be aware of when utilizing a service auditor report. The report should cover all services that the service provider is performing for the plan. If the service provider maintains participant accounts, performs the required antidiscrimination tests, prepares Form 1099Rs for distributions, prepares the Form 5500, and reconciles participant data records to trustee/custodian records, all of these services should be described in the service auditor report. With a very large service provider, there may be numerous service auditor reports prepared to cover all of the services provided (e.g., the investment of assets and related activities are often separate from any recordkeeping functions). The auditor should obtain each report necessary to provide coverage of all controls relevant to the plan. Also, the professional reputation of the service auditor should be considered to ensure adequate qualifications.

In addition, a service auditor report should include a section which discusses the general types of controls that should be in place at the user organization (in this case, the employee benefit plan) in order for the controls at the service organization to be effective. The auditor should consider these comments regarding user controls and the existence and effectiveness of such controls in relation to the employee benefit plan subject to the audit.

Finally, auditors should read the service auditor reports for all of the service organizations providing services to the employee benefit plan under audit. An exception is in the case of limited-scope audits in which the auditor is not required to obtain a copy of the SAS 70 report for the trustee/custodian of the plan's investments. However, even with limited-scope audits, the auditor should obtain the SAS 70 reports for other service providers, such as recordkeepers or other third-party administrators. The auditors should also be cognizant of instances of noncompliance which may be identified within a Type II SAS 70 report and may need to be considered by the auditor in his assessment of controls for the plan's internal control structure.

Period Covered by Service Auditor's Report

The service auditor's report should cover a period of at least 6 months of the plan's year in order for the auditor to use it in documenting his or her understanding of the controls in place at the service provider. This is true for both Type I and Type II reports. If the period covered is less than 12 months but more than 6 months, the service auditor reports may be relied upon. However, additional inquiries and procedures should be performed to assess whether significant changes have occurred in the internal controls of the service provider during the period of the plan's year under audit to which the service auditor report does not provide coverage.

For example, if a service auditor report only covers the first six months of the plan's year, the auditor should perform additional procedures to assess whether significant changes have occurred in the internal controls of the service provider during the last six months of the plan's year under audit. Such procedures include making inquiries of plan management and the service provider, performing tests of controls at the service provider, or reviewing work performed by the internal audit function at the service provider.

Exceptions

The service auditor's opinion and report should be reviewed for instances of noncompliance with the service provider's controls and objectives. In the event that deficiencies are identified within the service auditor report, these significant findings will be mentioned within the service auditor's opinion and report, which is generally included in the beginning portion of the service auditor report. The user auditor should consider the effect of the identified instances and assess whether the level of control risk should be modified. If modification is necessary, additional procedures may need to be performed at either the service provider or at the plan level.

Unavailability of a Service Auditor's Report

In certain circumstances, a SAS 70 report may not be available for the service provider of the plan if such service provider did not engage auditors to issue a report on its internal controls. Actuaries, some insurance companies, claims processors, and recordkeepers typically do not have service auditor reports prepared to cover the services rendered to employee benefit plans. A SAS 70 report is not mandatory although many institutions have them prepared. Even if no service auditor report is available, the auditor is still required under SAS 55, as amended, to obtain and document his or her understanding of the internal controls at the service provider. Information necessary to obtain this understanding would be available by contacting the service provider or its auditor. If this understanding cannot be obtained, the auditor would qualify the audit opinion or disclaim an opinion on the plan's financial statements due to a scope limitation.

VOICE RESPONSE OR INTERNET RECORDKEEPING SYSTEMS

Many defined contribution pension plans are using recordkeepers that prepare valuations of individual account record information through voice-activated response systems or internet recordkeeping systems. These systems process participant-initiated transactions such as loans, changes in contribution percentages, or investment allocations. As a result, the plan sponsor does not have a "paper record" of these participant-initiated transactions. Previously, participants were usually required to complete paper forms in order to authorize the transactions. Recently, the IRS has taken the position that signatures on loan requests are no longer required. The participant simply has to call the voice-activated response line or access the internet system.

This has made it increasingly difficult to audit the transactions themselves. In these instances, it will be necessary to either obtain a service auditor's report or perform tests of controls at the service provider. Additional substantive tests may be required as well as alternative means of performing such tests. Often, only confirmations directly with the participants provide enough evidence to satisfy audit requirements. The information needed to prepare such confirmations is derived from transaction reports which need to be generated by the service provider.

REPORTABLE CONDITIONS

SAS 60, *Communication of Internal Control Related Matters Noted in an Audit,* as amended by SAS 78, requires the communication of reportable conditions identified during the course of the audit to the attention of the plan's audit committee, or to the plan administrator or other responsible party with the authority of an audit committee, in the absence of one. For multiemployer plans, such communication should be made to the board of trustees. Reportable conditions are matters that represent significant deficiencies in the design or operation of internal control that could adversely affect the plan's ability to record, process, summarize, and report financial data consistent with the assertions of plan management in the financial statements. Reportable conditions should generally be communicated in writing to the audit committee (or equivalent authority) or to the plan sponsor or the plan sponsor's board of directors or trustees, in the absence of an audit committee.

MANAGEMENT LETTER COMMENTS

A weakness in the plan's design or operation that is not a reportable condition should also be communicated to the plan sponsor orally or through a management letter. Such a letter enables the auditor to document any findings related to weaknesses noted and observed during the course of the audit. Management of the plan generally will address the issue and make improvements to reduce or eliminate the weakness. The internal control environment of an employee benefit plan is an area which in many cases is in need of improvement and offers opportunities for the auditor to offer suggestions for enhancing the effectiveness of a plan's control environment. It also adds value to the audit and enhances the level of service provided to the plan.

6 INVESTMENTS

INTRODUCTION

Investments comprise the largest portion of the assets in almost all employee benefit plans. Plan sponsors have a wide selection of investment options from which to choose when selecting investments for the employee benefit plan. When selecting investments, plan administrators should consider the need for liquidity to pay benefits, return on investment and how to safeguard plan assets. Investment options may include marketable securities--such as money market funds, equity funds, fixed income funds, or investment contracts--to non-readily-marketable investments such as real estate or stock of the plan sponsor. For defined contribution pension plans, sponsors may choose which investment options to make available to plan participants, or they may allow plan participants to select their own individual investments. Some of the most common types of investment options will be discussed in this chapter along with suggested audit procedures. The concepts included within this chapter relate primarily to full-scope audits being performed for an employee benefit plan. However, limited-scope audit procedures are also considered.

VALUATION OF INVESTMENTS

In most cases, investments in an employee benefit plan should be reported in the financial statements at fair market value, which is the amount that would be expected to be received in a current sale between a willing buyer and a willing seller. For most plans, investments are valued by the trustee. For non-readily-marketable securities, plan management needs to have audit procedures in place to determine the fair value of these investments since market quotations are not available. When performing a full-scope audit of an employee benefit plan, it is the auditor's responsibility to assess whether plan management's procedures are reasonable. In order to assist in accomplishing this objective, the auditor should obtain a copy of and read the latest available SAS 70 report (see Chapter 5, Internal Control, for additional information) for the trustee/custodian of plan assets, as discussed below. If the auditor determines that plan management's procedures are not reasonable, the auditor should consider the need to express a qualified opinion or disclaim an opinion because of a scope limitation (if sufficient evidential matter does not exist), or issue a qualified or adverse opinion because of a departure from generally accepted accounting principles (because of inadequate procedures to value investments).

DISCRETIONARY VS. NONDISCRETIONARY TRUSTS

A **discretionary trust** gives the trustee sole discretion as to how the assets of the plan are to be invested. The investment committee normally provides investment guidelines for the trustee to follow but gives total control to the trustee to purchase and sell investment assets within the guidelines established by the investment policy of the plan. Most defined benefit pension plans operate under a discretionary trust arrangement. Conversely, a **nondiscretionary trust** gives no control to the trustee in making decisions as to which investments are to be bought or sold. The trustee acts as custodian for the plan and is responsible for collecting investment income and investing assets as directed by the appropriate party, whether it be the plan administrator, the participant, or the plan investment committee. Most defined contribution pension plans use a nondiscretionary trust. For example, a plan may indicate that monies will be invested in four types of investment funds--an equity, balanced, fixed-income, and a liquid, short-term fund (therefore discretionary)--or it may state four specific funds in which monies may be invested (nondiscretionary).

A discretionary trust generally is associated with a higher level of risk. This results from the trustee having authority to purchase and sell securities without specific instructions from the plan administrator or plan participants (not with respect to participant-directed transactions but with respect to the purchase and sales, for example, within a trustee-directed equity fund). In order to gain sufficient support for transactions executed by the discretionary trust, consider the following:

- If the trustee has engaged an independent auditor to prepare a SAS 70 report, the auditor should obtain and read a copy of the latest available report to determine if the trustee's internal control system is sufficient to ensure that transactions are processed properly by the trustee. This would need to be a Type II SAS 70 report. (See discussion of Type I and Type II SAS 70 reports in Chapter 5, Internal Control.) It is generally not necessary to examine the workpapers of the trust department's auditor if satisfied with the professional reputation and independence of the other auditor. If an auditor is satisfied that the trustee's internal control procedures are reliable, the auditor may be able to reduce but not eliminate the amount of testing performed.
- If a SAS 70 report on the internal control procedures of the trust department cannot be obtained, the auditor should apply alternative procedures with respect to the trust department. See Chapter 5, Internal Control, for additional information when service auditor reports are not available.

When performing full-scope audit procedures for investments, the auditor should review the plan's investment portfolio to determine whether the portfolio is consistent with the plan's investment policy or strategy, as outlined in either the plan document or trust agreement. In addition, as will be described later, auditors should determine that investments are being valued appropriately at the end of the plan year. For those investments which are non-readily-marketable investments, the auditor should make inquiries of the plan's board of trustees, administrative committee, or other group independent from those determining fair market value, to determine that they have reviewed and approved estimates of the fair value of such investments. If they have, the auditor should read the supporting minutes or other documentation.

For a defined contribution pension plan with participant-directed funds, if an independent record of investment transactions is not available, the auditor should confirm investment information directly with the participants. To accomplish this, the auditor should send to the participants, a copy of their annual participant account summary which is sent to them soon after the end of the plan year in order to confirm the proper allocation of participant monies to the proper investment fund. This confirmation may also be used to verify activity during the year, such as transfers, loan balances, contributions, and distributions to satisfy other audit objectives. For additional information regarding auditing accounts of defined contribution pension plans, see Chapter 7, Accounting, Auditing, and Reporting for Defined Contribution Pension Plans.

MUTUAL FUNDS

The term **mutual fund** is the more common name for an open-end investment company. Most mutual funds offer their shares for sale to the public on a continuous basis, though they are not required to do so. A mutual fund that is issued by a registered investment company is valued at quoted market prices, which may fluctuate daily. The quoted market price represents the net asset value of the underlying assets (i.e., stocks and bonds) in which the mutual fund has invested. As such, understanding how daily net asset values (NAV) are maintained, and how adjustments to NAVs are processed, is very important in a defined contribution participant-directed plan. Units of participation or shares indicate the interest each plan and often, each participant has in the underlying assets of the mutual fund. Earnings and appreciation in value for a plan are generally reinvested back into the mutual fund. The purchase or redemption price is determined periodically by the trustee and is based on the current market values of the underlying assets in the mutual fund. The financial statements of mutual funds are examined and reported on by auditors engaged by the registered investment company.

Mutual funds and other investment options are grouped according to the primary investment objective (e.g., high-growth, fixed income, international, balanced, or combinations of these groups). The types of investments in which these funds invest their money reflect their stated objectives. For example, high-growth funds invest almost exclusively in securities associated with high-risk and high-potential appreciation (e.g., high-technology stocks or stocks offered under initial public offerings).

Common or Commingled Trust Fund

A **common or commingled trust** fund is an investment vehicle that is similar to a mutual fund but is maintained by the trust department of a bank or trust company. Similar to the mutual fund, monies are invested in specified investment vehicles often to achieve specific investment objectives. Earnings and appreciation in value are generally reinvested back into the common or commingled trust fund. As with the mutual fund, each plan and often each participant in a defined contribution pension plan acquires units of participation or shares indicating the undivided interest in the underlying assets of the common/commingled trust fund. The purchase or redemption price is determined periodically by the trustee and is based on the current market values of the underlying assets in the common/commingled trust fund. Common collective trust funds are most commonly valued on a monthly basis; however, they may be valued daily, quarterly, or annually. The frequency of the valuation should be detailed in the common collective trust fund agreement. As such, understanding how daily net asset values (NAVs) are maintained and how adjustments to NAVs are processed is very important in defined contribution participant-directed plans. The financial statements of common/commingled trusts are examined and reported on by auditors engaged by the sponsoring bank or trust company.

Note that mutual funds, common/commingled funds, and pooled separate accounts (described below) are similar types of investments. The primary difference is the issuer of the investment. Mutual funds are issued by registered investment companies, common/commingled funds are offered by banks or trust companies, and pooled separate accounts are offered by insurance companies. These latter investments will be discussed in the next part of this chapter.

INVESTMENTS WITH INSURANCE COMPANIES

Insurance companies offer many different types of investment options for employee benefit plans. The nature of the contract will determine the accounting and reporting requirements in the plan's financial statements. Insurance contracts are defined as either unallocated insurance contracts or allocated insurance contracts.

Unallocated contracts are funding arrangements whereby monies are often held in the general account of the insurance company until such time as a benefit payment comes due or it is necessary to purchase annuities for retirees or for participants who terminate employment. Unallocated contracts are assets of the plan, as responsibility for future benefit payments rests with the plan, not with the insurance company. Two popular types of unallocated contracts are the pooled separate accounts (PSA) and guaranteed investment contract (GIC). A GIC may provide a stated (often referred to as guaranteed) or variable rate of return.

In a defined benefit pension plan, allocated contracts are contracts under which contributions paid to the insurance company are currently used to purchase immediate or deferred annuities for individual participants. These monies are then invested by the insurance company, and the sole responsibility for the payment of these benefits lies with the insurance company as long as premiums are paid. Therefore, monies in an allocated contract are **not** assets of an employee benefit plan since the monies, and the related responsibility for paying the benefits, have been transferred over to the insurance company.

For reporting purposes, a defined benefit pension plan should follow SFAS 110, *Reporting by Defined Benefit Pension Plans of Investment Contracts.* In summary, SFAS 110 states that a defined benefit pension plan should report investment contracts, issued by either an insurance company or other entity, at fair value. (Note that SFAS 35, prior to its amendment by SFAS 110, had permitted investments in investment contracts to be recorded at contract value.) An insurance contract's primary purpose, as described by SFAS 110, is to provide economic protection from identified risks occurring or discovered within a specified period. Examples of such risks include death or disability.

Separate Accounts

There are two types of separate accounts, pooled and individual, that can be established with insurance companies.

Pooled separate account. This type of account is established by an insurance company for the purpose of investing assets of one or more employee benefit plans of one or more sponsors. Pooled separate accounts are valued on a daily basis, and an investor may purchase units or sell existing units of the account at any time. Monies invested in a pooled separate account are not commingled with other pooled separate accounts or with the general assets of the insurance company. The account holds particular assets allocated to that account and is credited or charged with income, gains, or losses from these assets separately from income, gains, or losses of the insurance company's corporate or other accounts. In a pooled separate account, like a common collective trust or mutual fund, units of participation or shares are used to allocate each plan's share of assets.

Individual separate account. This type of account is one in which only one plan participates, while a **pooled** separate account allows two or more unrelated plans to take part. As with the pooled separate account, monies held by the insurance company in the individual separate account are maintained separately from the assets of the insurance company.

Deposit Administration Contracts

Insurance companies may offer **deposit administration** (DA) contracts to defined benefit pension plans. DA contracts refer to a type of contract for which contributions are not currently used to purchase single-payment deferred annuities for individual participants. Under the DA contract, payments which are intended to provide future benefits for current employees, are credited to an account. The account is credited with interest at the rate agreed upon in the DA contract. The account decreases whenever annuities are purchased directly from the account for participants who retire or for benefits paid to participants who die, become disabled, or withdraw from the contract.

DA contracts will guarantee a minimum interest rate be paid on the funds and establish the rates at which annuities may be purchased. However, they do not ensure that sufficient funds will exist to meet the cost of all annuities to be purchased.

There is no contractual obligation for a DA contract to pay a dividend. Experience-rated interest credits are determined solely at the discretion of the insurance company and are not guaranteed. The calculation of these credits is based on records kept by the insurance company for each contract and are determined by the actual investment experience of the insurance company. These interest credits may be paid out, added to the balance of the funds, or considered in an overall dividend calculation that takes into account mortality, other actuarial experience, and reserves required by the insurance company. Only defined benefit pension plans may invest in DA contracts. Investments in DA contracts should be presented at fair value on the plan's statement of net assets available for benefits.

Immediate Participation Guarantee Contracts

The **immediate participation guarantee** (IPG) contract is a variation of the DA contract. In an IPG contract, the account is credited with the contributions received during the contract period plus its proportionate share of the insurance company's investment earnings on that contract. Under an IPG contract, the insurance company is required to make benefit payments for the lifetime of the retired employees. IPG contracts may be written under one of two forms. Under the first option, insurance companies purchase annuities as employees retire; an annual adjustment to the account is made to reflect the insurance company's experience under the annuities. Under the other option, when an employee retires, pension payments are made directly from the account without the purchase of an annuity. However, the balance of the account must be maintained at a specified amount, according to a premium schedule in the contract. This is to ensure that sufficient funds remain to provide benefits for all current retirees. The portion of the funds reserved for remaining pension benefits is called the **retired life fund**. If necessary, that account could always be used to buy all annuities in force. Only defined benefit pension plans may invest in IPG contracts. Furthermore, investments in IPG contracts should be presented at fair value on the plan's statement of net assets available for benefits; the statement would include the amount in the retired life fund and the "remaining assets" of the IPG contract.

INVESTMENT CONTRACTS AND AICPA STATEMENT OF POSITION 94-4

As stated earlier, the majority of investments in an employee benefit plan will be valued based on the current fair market value of the investments. However, certain contracts with insurance companies should be presented at contract value. SOP 94-4, *Reporting of Investment Contracts Held by Health and Welfare Benefit Plans and Defined Contribution Plans*, specifies the accounting for investment contracts issued by either an insurance company or another entity.

Defined contribution health, welfare, and defined contribution pension plans should report fully benefit-responsive contracts at contract value (which may or may not be the same as fair value) on the statement of net assets available for benefits. See Chapter 13, Financial Statements and Disclosures, for examples of such financial statements. Contract value is the amount a participant would receive if s/he were to initiate transactions (e.g., make a withdrawal from the contract) under the current terms of the ongoing contract. Contract value is defined as the accumulated contributions plus accrued net investment income less any withdrawals and administrative expenses. Non-benefit-responsive investment contracts should be presented at fair value on the statement of net assets available for benefits.

Benefit responsiveness is defined as the extent to which an investment contract's terms permit and require withdrawals at contract value for benefit payments, loans, or transfers to other investment options offered to the participants of the plan. For a contract to be fully benefit-responsive, the plan must allow plan participants reasonable access to their funds (i.e., withdrawals from the plan at contract value without a penalty assessed), and the freedom to switch investment options from this contract to another investment option offered by the plan.

If a plan limits the number of times per year (e.g., quarterly, semiannually, etc.) that participants may access their funds or make changes in their investment options to control administrative costs, that limitation generally would not affect the benefit responsiveness of the investment contracts held by the plan.

An exception to the requirement that health and welfare and defined contribution pension plans report fully benefit-responsive contracts at contract value may occur if plan management becomes aware of an event which has occurred that may affect the value of the contract. Two possible events are (1) a decline in the credit worthiness of the issuer of the contract or (2) the possibility of a premature termination of the contract by the plan. If management believes the value of the contract may be affected, in accordance with Statement of Financial Accounting Standards 5, *Accounting for Contingencies*, disclosure of the event or reporting the investment at less than contract value, may be appropriate.

If a plan invests in multiple investment contracts, each contract should be evaluated separately to determine benefit responsiveness. If a plan holds pooled funds that have investment contracts as the underlying securities, SOP 94-4 states that each contract in the pooled fund be evaluated individually for benefit responsiveness. Practically, if the pooled fund places any restrictions on withdrawals from the funds, then none of the underlying investment contracts would be considered to be fully benefit-responsive. See Chapter 7, Accounting, Auditing, and Reporting for Defined Contribution Pension Plans and Chapter 9, Accounting, Auditing and Reporting for Health and Welfare Plans, for a summary of the footnote disclosures required by SOP 94-4.

SYNTHETIC GICs

Another form of a guaranteed investment contract is commonly referred to as a synthetic GIC because it mimics the performance attributes of an investment contract, but it does so through the actual purchase of the underlying financial instruments. The primary difference between a traditional GIC and the synthetic GIC is that with the synthetic GIC, the plan actually owns the underlying investments of the investment contracts; with the traditional GIC, the plan holds an interest in the investment contract but does not directly own the underlying securities, which are owned by the insurance company. The synthetic GIC, like other GICs, offers a guaranteed rate of return.

Typically, an insurance company will offer the synthetic GIC, and then will contract with a financially responsible third party to offer "the wrapper." To enable the plan to realize a guaranteed value for the assets if it needs to liquidate them to make benefit payments, a synthetic GIC utilizes a benefit responsive wrapper contract issued by a third party that provides market and cash flow risk protection to the plan. The wrapper enables the plan to liquidate any or all of the securities that underlie the GIC to make benefit payments and still achieve the guaranteed rate of return. In essence, the wrapper absorbs the increases and decreases in the fair market value of the underlying securities by offsetting any losses realized at the time of sale of the securities, or by absorbing the gains.

The underlying securities are valued at fair market value and the wrapper will have either a negative value (if the fair value of the underlying securities was higher than the guaranteed rate of return) or a positive value (if the fair value of the underlying securities was not high enough to satisfy the guaranteed rate of return). The total value of the wrapper plus the underlying fair value of the investments equals contract value. The wrapper, which absorbs the market fluctuations, makes a synthetic GIC "benefit responsive" because it gives participants easy access to their monies without concern of devaluation of their investment. The financial stability of both the issuer and the provider of the wrapper should be determined to insure that no adjustment to contract value is needed.

Reporting Requirements for Synthetic GICs

Another key difference between traditional GICs and synthetic GICs is the presentation of the plan's financial statements. Because plans that invest in synthetic GICs own the underlying assets, it is necessary to include on the Form 5500 supplemental Schedule 27(a), Schedule of Assets Held for Investment Purposes, each asset that comprises the synthetic GIC, including the wrapper. (Note that in this chapter, reference is made to Schedule 27(a) of Form 5500. The Form 5500 will change for plan years beginning in 1999. As such, refer to Chapter 11, Form 5500, for further discussion of this schedule.) Each underlying asset is to be reported at fair market value while the wrapper will have either a positive or negative fair market value. In addition, for a defined benefit pension plan with an investment in a synthetic GIC, disclosure is required (either within the plan's financial statements or footnotes) regarding the general categories of the assets which comprise the synthetic GIC. Furthermore, for either a defined benefit or defined contribution pension plan, disclosure is required (either within the plan's financial statements or footnotes) for any single asset of the synthetic GIC that exceeds 5% of the plan's net assets available for benefits at the end of the plan year.

Conversely, plans that invest in traditional GICs own the investment contract, not the securities which underlie the investment contract. In the event of default, the plan would have recourse against the assets of the issuer of the investment contract not to any securities in which the investment contract invests. A traditional GIC would be included as one line item on the Schedule 27(a) of Form 5500.

EQUITY AND FIXED INCOME SECURITIES

Equity securities refer to common and preferred stocks and debentures that are convertible into common stocks. A convertible security is one that permits the owner to exchange this security for another security of the issuer or a different issuer. This is most common with respect to preferred stocks or convertible bonds that have the right to exchange for stated amounts of common stock.

A fixed-income security is a preferred stock or debt security with a stated dollar income or guaranteed percentage return on investment. The return, or yield, is the amount of dividends or interest, expressed as a percentage of the current market price of the security. Yield, for stocks, is usually calculated by dividing the total dividends paid in the past calendar year by the price of the stock as of the end of the year. Yield on bonds is the total interest earned during the year divided by the price of the bonds as of the end of the year. Calculating yields on stocks and bonds may be useful in estimating the income earned on such investments, as needed when performing a full-scope audit.

SELF-DIRECTED ACCOUNTS

In addition to the investment vehicles previously described, participants also may have a self-directed account in which they may direct purchases of individual stocks and bonds, investments in real estate, limited partnerships, or other investment vehicles. Self-directed accounts are most common with defined contribution pension plans.

A self-directed account is one that allows participants to invest their account balances in almost any investment desired, although some limitations may be specified in the plan document. (For example, a participant may be prohibited from investing in a derivative instrument, which is discussed later in this chapter.) In other words, a participant may authorize a purchase of an investment other than those investments specifically offered by the plan (e.g., common/commingled trust or pooled separate account). The self-directed account is not a pooled investment; rather it is an account made up of all the individual investments owned by the plan that the participants have authorized to be purchased for them. For purposes of presentation within the plan's financial statements, the investment in self-directed accounts may be shown as one line item on the statement of net assets available for benefits. However, each of the individual investments which comprise the self-directed accounts needs to be presented as a separate line item on Form 5500, Item 27a, Schedule of Assets Held for Investment Purposes.

INVESTMENTS IN MASTER TRUSTS AND SIMILAR VEHICLES

When a company or a group of corporations under common control has more than one employee benefit plan, it may invest some or all of the plans' assets into one combined account, called a **master trust**. There is no requirement that the sponsor include all of the company's benefit plans into this master trust, nor do the benefit plans need to be of the same type (i.e., defined contribution, defined benefit, health and welfare). Often the sponsor sets up a master trust to consolidate the recordkeeping function to reduce administrative expenses and to improve the overall rate of return on the plans' investments via the commingling of assets. Each plan within the master trust has an interest in the underlying assets of the master trust, called units of participation or proportionate dollar interest. The trust instrument will state the method of allocating the total master trust investment between the benefit plans that participate in the master trust. A bank serves as trustee for a master trust, acts as custodian, and may or may not have discretionary control over how the monies are invested.

Under ERISA guidelines, a master trust is not required to be audited, although it does have special filing requirements under ERISA as noted in the instructions to Form 5500. Under ERISA, the basic audit requirement is applied to each separate **plan** and not each separate **trust**. As a result, each plan that is part of a master trust must file a separate Form 5500 and satisfy the audit requirement, if applicable. However, in a full-scope audit, certain audit procedures should be performed on the investments held in the master trust if a material amount of the plan's investments is part of a master trust. If both the master trust and one or more of the plans that have monies invested in the master trust are audited, it is often more efficient first to apply appropriate audit procedures to the master trust and then test that the method for allocating units of participation to the participating plans is reasonable. (In Chapter 11, Form 5500, note that master trusts must file Schedule D of the new Form 5500 for plan years beginning in 1999 as they are considered a Direct Filing Entity [DFE].)

When performing full-scope audit procedures, if another independent auditor audits the master trust, the plan auditor should consider

- Reviewing the workpapers of the other auditor, particularly as it relates to the audit of investments held by the master trust
- Performing procedures to independently test the fair value of the underlying investments of the master trust
- Recomputing the allocation of the proportionate dollar interest of participation and the allocation of net investment gain from the master trust to the plan under audit and any other procedures deemed necessary under the circumstances

When performing full-scope audit procedures for the plans, if the master trust is not audited, the auditor should test the underlying investments of the master trust. If sufficient testing is not possible, and the amount of investments held by the master trust is significant, the plan auditor should qualify or disclaim an opinion on the plan's financial statements.

PARTICIPANT LOANS

Many defined contribution pension plans offer participants the ability to borrow against the vested portion of their individual accounts. ERISA and the Internal Revenue Service have established guidelines that must be followed for participant loans. For example, loans cannot be made for longer than five years, unless the proceeds of the loan are used to purchase a primary residence, in which case, the loan period may be for ten years or longer. The interest rate must also be reasonable when compared to the prevailing market for interest rates. Also, the amount of the loan is limited to no more than 50% of the vested portion of the participant's individual account.

An auditor should read the plan document to learn the specific rules for participant loans available through the plan. The plan document will establish the number of loans that a participant may have, the minimum loan amount, what constitutes a loan in default, and other conditions. When the loan is made, the amount is deducted from the participant's account and then repaid back to the participant's account, generally through payroll deductions based on the repayment schedule for the loan.

The portion of the loan repayment that represents principal is added to the participant's account. The portion of the payroll deduction representing interest is reflected as investment income on the loan fund.

The total of all participant loans outstanding is shown as an asset within the investments total on the Statement of Net Assets Available for Benefits and in the supplemental Schedule of Assets Held for Investment Purposes. In addition, within the description of the loans for the Schedule of Assets Held for Investment Purposes, disclosure should be made of the range of interest rates being charged for participant loans and the range of maturities of the participant loans.

NON-READILY-MARKETABLE SECURITIES

Some employee benefit plans may invest in securities that do not have a ready market price (specialized or unique investments such as junk bonds, options, limited partnerships, real estate mortgage investment conduits (REMICs), and derivative products). Some factors that may be considered in estimating the fair value of these investments include, but are not limited to, the length of time the investment has been held, reported prices and extent of trading of similar investments, a forecast of the expected cash flows from the investment, current interest rates, and the financial condition of the investee or issuer. For these securities, the auditor should review and evaluate the plan's methods and procedures for estimating the fair value of such investments, determine whether the plan's methods and procedures for estimating fair value were followed, and assess whether these methods appear to be reasonable and applied consistently. The plan administrator should also determine that such investments have been reasonably valued. In addition, the plan auditor should test the underlying documentation supporting the estimates. The plan may also use a specialist to assist in assigning a value to these nonreadily marketable securities. See the section on the use of specialists later in this chapter.

The footnotes to the plan's financial statements should describe the methods utilized to value the non-readily-marketable investments. Depending on the facts and circumstances, the auditor may also consider adding an explanatory paragraph in the auditor's report to discuss the investment. (See earlier discussion in the section on valuation of investments in this chapter and Chapter 12, Auditors' Reports.) The auditor should also consider obtaining a representation from plan management regarding the valuation of these types of investments.

MONEY MARKET INVESTMENTS

Short-term investments, such as certificates of deposit, commercial paper, short-term government obligations (e.g., US Treasury notes or bills), and bankers acceptances are bought either at face value or at a discount from the face amount. A bankers acceptance is a draft drawn on a bank by a borrower, usually in connection with a commercial transaction. The borrower is liable to pay the draft at its face amount on the due date. Commercial paper is a short-term, unsecured, promissory note issued by a corporation that is usually sold on a discount basis. Short-term investments are valued based on trade, bid, or asked prices or other acceptable evidence. The amortized cost of money market instruments that will mature within a relatively short period usually approximates market value.

OPERATING ASSETS

Operating assets, which may be used in the administration of an employee benefit plan, consist of buildings, equipment, furniture, and fixtures and leasehold improvements. Operating assets are most frequently used in the administration of multiemployer sponsored plans. Operating assets should be presented on the plan's financial statements at cost, less accumulated depreciation or amortization (carrying amount). For purposes of the Form 5500, operating assets are to be presented at their fair value, which usually differs from the carrying amount of the asset. In these cases, the plan's footnotes to the financial statements will need to include a reconciliation of the amount per the Form 5500 and the plan's financial statements. See Chapter 13, Financial Statements and Disclosures, for an example of such a footnote.

SFAS 121, *Accounting for the Impairment of Long-Lived Assets and for Long-Lived Assets to Be Disposed of*, establishes the accounting standards for the impairment of long-lived assets--for assets to be held and used and for those assets which are to be disposed. In summary, SFAS 121 requires that long-lived assets to be held and used by the plan, such as real estate owned by the plan for plan operations, be reviewed for potential impairment whenever circumstances suggest that the carrying amount of the asset may not be recoverable. SFAS 121 also requires long-lived assets that the plan expects to dispose of to be reported at the lower of its carrying amount or fair value less the cost to sell. Assets which will be disposed should not be depreciated while being held for disposal. When auditing employee benefit plans that hold operating assets as investments, auditors may also want to consider the topics discussed in the non-readily-marketable securities and use of specialists sections of this chapter.

MUNICIPAL BONDS AND NOTES

Municipal bonds and notes are also referred to as general obligation bonds and revenue bonds. General obligation bonds represent the issuer's pledge to pay principal and interest when due. Revenue bonds are paid from a specified revenue source (e.g., sales tax on entertainment). Tax-exempt individual development bonds are usually a type of revenue bond.

Municipal notes generally have a maturity date of less than three years. They are usually classified as tax, revenue, or bond anticipation notes because they are redeemed upon the receipt of specific tax-anticipated revenues or on financing received from the proceeds of municipal bonds.

Because there is limited trading activity for municipal bonds and notes, the value of these securities is estimated using a variety of methods. Fair value may be estimated by the sponsor by taking into consideration such factors as coupon interest rate, maturity, credit rating, market indices, and other market data as they relate to the investment being valued. The intent of these procedures is to estimate the amount the owner of the securities could expect to receive from the sale of the securities, even though there may be no intent at this time to sell them.

USE OF SPECIALISTS

Sometimes, because of the complex or subjective nature of the investment, plan management may engage a specialist to assist in the valuation of such investments, particularly with investments in real estate, limited partnerships, or derivative financial instruments. When a specialist is used by a plan, the auditor should perform procedures to evaluate the specialists' qualifications and relationship to the client (e.g., an external investment manager, appraiser, or advisor). In this regard, the auditor should consider obtaining a letter from the specialist regarding their independence from the plan and plan sponsor. Plan administrators may engage investment consultants to provide fair values for investments. In some instances, investment consultants may provide projections of cash flows that are used to determine fair value. Plan management may also have procedures in place to determine their best estimate of the plan value for these investments. Based upon those procedures, the auditor should document in the audit working papers the basis for the conclusions that support the use of the specialist's or plan management's work and its propriety as audit evidence. Also, the auditor should refer to SAS 73, *Using the Work of a Specialist*, for additional guidance.

In accordance with Statement on Auditing Standards (SAS) 85, *Management Representations*, if the work of a specialist has been used by an entity, the auditor should include additional representations from management relating to that use. Note that during late 1999, SAS 89, which amends SAS 85, was issued to require auditors to obtain written representations from plan management regarding their belief that the effects of any uncorrected financial statement misstatements identified by the auditor are immaterial to the plan's financial statements taken as a whole. See Chapter 10, Other Accounting and Auditing Considerations, for an example of such representations. The following provides an example of a representation regarding the use of specialists, which may be included in the management representation letter as provided in SAS 85:

We agree with the findings of specialists in evaluating the [*describe assertion*] and have adequately considered the qualifications of the specialist in determining the amounts and disclosures used in the financial statements and underlying accounting records. We did not give or cause any instructions to be given to specialists with respect to the values or amounts derived in an attempt to bias their work, and we are not otherwise aware of any matters that had an impact on the independence or objectivity of the specialists.

AICPA SOP 99-3, *ACCOUNTING FOR AND REPORTING OF CERTAIN DEFINED CONTRIBUTION PLAN INVESTMENTS AND OTHER DISCLOSURE MATTERS*

During September 1999, the AICPA issued SOP 99-3, *Accounting for and Reporting of Certain Defined Contribution Plan Investments and Other Disclosure Matters*. This SOP simplifies disclosures for certain investments and rescinds the provisions of AICPA Practice Bulletin 12, *Reporting Separate Investment Fund Option Information of Defined Contribution Pension Plans*. SOP 99-3 is effective for plan years ending after December 15, 1999, although earlier application is encouraged.

The following represents a summary of the provisions of SOP 99-3:

- A defined contribution pension plan that provides participant-directed investment programs is no longer required to disclose amounts relating to those individual programs as a separate fund in the financial statements or in the related footnote disclosures.
- If a defined contribution pension plan provides for participant-directed **and** non-participant-directed investment funds, the plan should disclose information in the financial statements or footnotes about the net assets and significant components of the changes in net assets related to the non-participant-directed investment funds.
- Participant-directed investments may be shown in the aggregate, as one line item, in the statement of net assets available for benefits.
- The nonparticipant-directed investments should be presented in either the financial statements or footnotes by general type, such as mutual funds, government securities, or short-term securities. The presentation should indicate whether the fair value of the investments was measured by quoted market prices or was determined otherwise.
- Defined contribution pension plans should specifically identify those non-participant-directed investments that exceed 5% of total non-participant-directed assets at the end of the year as well as those non-participant-directed investments which exceed 5% of the plan's total net assets at the end of the plan year. This disclosure may be included in the plan's financial statements or in the footnotes. This requirement is in addition to the current requirement to identify the plan's investments which exceed 5% of net assets available for benefits.

- Defined contribution pension plans and defined contribution health and welfare plans are no longer required to disclose, by investment fund option, the information on fully benefit investment contracts, as required by SOP 94-4. For a discussion of SOP 94-4, see the section of this chapter on investment contracts and SOP 94-4 reporting and accounting requirements. In addition, see Chapter 7, Accounting, Auditing, and Reporting for Defined Contribution Pension Plans, and Chapter 9, Accounting, Auditing, and Reporting for Health and Welfare Plans, for a summary of the footnote disclosures required by SOP 94-4. The disclosures required by SOP 94-4 are still required for defined contribution pension plans and health and welfare plans in the aggregate.
- Defined contribution pension plans that assign units to participants are not required to disclose the total number of units and the net asset value per unit during the period and at the end of the period.

DERIVATIVE INSTRUMENTS AND HEDGING ACTIVITIES

Many new forms of investments, such as repurchase or reverse repurchase agreements, futures, options, swaps, and hedges are now available. These types of investments are commonly referred to as derivatives or hedges and it is often difficult to determine a fair market value for these investments. For plan years beginning after June 15, 2000, Statement of Financial Accounting Standards 133 (SFAS 133), *Accounting for Derivative Instruments and Hedging Activities,* will be applicable. The application date of SFAS 133 was delayed to plan years beginning after June 15, 2000, through the issuance of SFAS 137, *Accounting for Derivative Instruments and Hedging Activities--Deferral of the Effective Date of FASB Statement 133.* SFAS 133 was issued in June 1998 and it establishes accounting and reporting standards for these derivative instruments and hedging activities. It requires that an entity (including an employee benefit plan) recognize all derivatives as either an asset or a liability. It also requires the derivative to be valued at fair value. While almost all investments are already valued at fair value, there are certain investments such as hedges or convertible securities, that may need to be considered under this standard.

GENERAL AUDIT OBJECTIVES

The audit objectives in auditing plan investments should determine whether

- The investment transactions (purchases and sales) that are recorded are valid
- Investments that are held at year end exist and are owned by the plan
- Investments and related income earned are appropriately valued and are fairly presented in the financial statements in accordance with generally accepted accounting principles and all necessary reporting disclosures are made. For a summary of the required reporting disclosures for investments, see the individual employee benefit plan Chapters 7, 8, and 9.

GENERAL AUDIT PROCEDURES

SAS 81, *Auditing Investments*, provides guidance on auditing investments in debt and equity securities and investments accounted for under Accounting Principles Board (APB) Opinion 18, *The Equity Method of Accounting for Investments in Common Stock*. SAS 81 is effective for audits of financial statements for periods ended on or after December 15, 1997. The following are suggested procedures for auditing investments when performing a full-scope audit of an employee benefit plan. (Procedures for a limited-scope audit are discussed later in this chapter.) The extent of testing to be done will be determined when planning the audit and by reviewing the SAS 70 report, if available. These procedures may be performed for all investments in general. Additional procedures related to specific investments are covered later.

1. Obtain information regarding the trustee's responsibility relative to the plan's investments and financial capability by performing the following procedures:
   - Review the trust or custodial agreement provisions to determine the trustee's responsibilities
   - Determine whether the trustee has adequate insurance covering the plan assets under its control (ERISA mandates that trustees maintain insurance coverage equal to at least 10% of the value of plan assets.)
   - Read the most recent financial statements of the trustee
2. Develop an understanding of the types of investments in the plan by reviewing the trustee report, obtaining the plan's investment strategy, and understanding the impact of that strategy on the plan's investment portfolio (i.e., a more aggressive investment strategy increases the level of risk associated with those investments). Also, determine whether the types of investments held are consistent with the investment policy (e.g., if the investment policy indicates no derivatives are to be held and interest-rate swaps are held, risk may be increased regarding the trustee's understanding of the trust document). This example also represents a potential fiduciary violation.
3. Obtain from the trustee (custodian), via a confirmation request, a report of all investment activity for the plan year. This report would normally include
   - A statement of net assets available for benefits at plan year-end and a statement of changes in net assets available for benefits for the year then ended
   - A listing of all investments held at year-end including a description of the investment, the number of shares of stock/units of each investment, cost, par value, maturity date, and interest rate
   - A listing of investments purchased during the plan year

- A listing of investments sold during the plan year and realized gains or losses from the sale of those securities
- Interest, dividends, and other income earned on the investments during the plan year
- Unrealized appreciation/depreciation of plan investments held at plan year-end
- Investment information for the supplemental schedules required by the DOL for the Form 5500 filing
- Listing of loans or fixed income obligations--listing of leases in default or classified as uncollectible, listing of reportable 5% transactions, listing of nonexempt transactions

4. Reconcile the information certified by the trustee (custodian) to amounts included in the plan's financial statements.
5. Obtain evidence regarding the existence and ownership of investments and information about any liens, pledges, or other security interests by direct confirmation from the trustee or custodian. When the trustee/custodian confirms the investments, they are legally responsible for assets held in its trust department. Therefore, the auditor may accept a confirmation from the bank as evidence of the existence and ownership of the stated investments.

   The trustee may be the person or organization that determines the assets in the trust, the one buying and selling the various investments. The trustee may decide how the money will be invested--following the instructions of the plan, or trust, or participant--in determining which assets to buy or sell. The trustee may also have "possession" of the investments; a custodian is the person or organization who has "possession" of the investments. Typically, custodians do not have authority to direct how the money in the plan will be invested. For most investments, however, a plan administrator or auditor will need to understand at what point, during the purchase or sale of an investment, the trustee or custodian assumes "possession" of the investment.
6. Select investments from the ending market value column of the trustee report. The number of selections should consider the results of the auditor's risk assessment procedures and the review of the SAS 70 report. For the investments selected, determine that the holding of these investments is permitted by the plan's investment policy. For the selected investments, test the ending fair value by reference to stated market quotations at the plan year end date. The *Wall Street Journal* (WSJ), *Moody's Bond Record*, or other independent sources (as listed in step 7 below) may provide reliable fair value quotations for the investments. For investments that do not have a readily ascertainable market value, determine that the valuation methods used by the trustee/plan administrator appear reasonable, as previously discussed.

7. Make selections from the listing of investments purchased and sold during the current plan year. For the investments selected, trace purchase or sales price to an independent source on the trade date. The following list may be useful in providing independent sources for selected types of securities in order to verify a purchase or sales price:
   - **Equity funds**--*Wall Street Journal*, Standard & Poor's 500 Stock Index, Wilshire 5000 Stock Index, the Wilshire Target Large Company Growth Index, the Wilshire Target Large Company Value Index, Dow Jones Industrial Index, and the Dow Jones Interactive website (djinteractive.com)
   - **Bonds**--Various Shearson Lehman Indices (i.e., long-term or municipal)
   - **Mutual funds**--Various Lipper Indices (growth fund or international) and the CDA Wiesenberger
   - **Money market funds**--Donoghue's 12-month yield and others

   Test the valuation of the investment by multiplying the purchase/sales price by the number of shares/units purchased sold on that date.
8. Review the fair values of investments at year-end for unusual conditions (e.g., unexpectedly large difference between cost and fair values or no fair value assigned). This can be performed when reviewing Schedule 27(a), Schedule of Assets Held for Investment Purposes.
9. If investment transactions are recorded on the settlement date rather than the trade date, determine whether the investments purchased or sold near the plan's year end significantly affect the plan's year-end investment balances and whether the fair value of these purchases and sales changed significantly from the trade date to year-end (to evaluate the impact on net appreciation for the year). The trade date is the date on which the transaction actually occurred while the settlement date refers to the date the transaction was settled (i.e., the security was recorded as either a purchase or sale).
10. Confirm with the plan's trustee or custodian the status of any securities that are in transit (i.e., purchases or sales).

AUDIT PROCEDURES INVOLVING MUTUAL FUNDS OR COMMON/COMMINGLED TRUST FUNDS

In addition to the general audit procedures, the following procedures should be performed if assets are invested in a registered investment company (mutual fund) or common/commingled trust fund:

1. Confirm directly with the mutual fund or common/commingled trust fund the number of units of participation held by the plan.

   NOTE: A separate confirmation is not necessary if the funds were included on the confirmation obtained previously when testing investments in general.

2. Confirm contributions, transfers, withdrawals, and/or account balances with individual participants.
3. Obtain a copy of the audited financial statements of the funds and perform the following procedures:
   - Compare the unit information reported in the funds' financial statements to the unit information recorded by the participating plan. Such information would include market value, purchases and sales values, and earned and accrued income. The funds' financial statements do not need to cover the exact period of time included in the plan's audit period; however, they should be recent enough to satisfy the audit objectives.
   - Test the fair value of the investments in the funds by comparing the per-unit market value at year end to market quotations in the fund's financial statements.
   - To the extent that there are frequent adjustments of the fund's net asset values, the auditor should obtain an understanding of how the recordkeeper is tracking the adjustments and assess the impact of the adjustments upon the individual participant accounts.
   - Calculate the average rate of return realized by the plan and compare that to the rate stated in the funds' financial statements.
   - Consider the effect that any report matters (either in the auditor's report or in the notes to the financial statements) may have on the carrying amount of the units of participation held by the plan. An example of a report matter that may have an impact on the carrying value of the investment would include a statement that the mutual fund invests heavily in the gas and oil industry, and it has been reported recently that gas and oil prices are decreasing dramatically and related companies are being hard hit by the decreased revenues.

The extent of testing necessary to obtain sufficient evidential matter is ultimately a judgment call by the auditor. If unable to obtain sufficient evidential matter, it will be necessary to express a qualified opinion (only to the extent that the plan's investment in the mutual fund or common/collective trust represents a small percentage of the plan's net assets) or disclaim an opinion on the plan's financial statements because of a scope limitation.

AUDIT PROCEDURES FOR ASSETS INVESTED WITH INSURANCE COMPANIES

As suggested in the AICPA audit and accounting guide, *Audits of Employee Benefit Plans*, the auditor should consider the following additional audit procedures for defined benefit pension plan assets invested with insurance companies:

1. Read the contract between the contract holder and the insurance company and evaluate whether they are investment or insurance contracts. (Note that insurance contracts involve the concepts of mortality and morbidity.)
2. Confirm the following directly with the insurance company, if applicable:
   - Contributions or premium payments made to the fund or account during the year
   - Interest, dividends, refunds, credits, and changes in value, and whether such amounts have been charged or credited during the year on an estimated or actual basis
   - The value of the funds in the general or separate account at the plan's year-end and the basis for determining such value
   - The amount of insurance company fee and other expenses chargeable during the year
3. Determine that the issuing insurance company is a financially responsible party that should be able to satisfy the terms of the contract. To accomplish this
   - Inquire of plan management how and why the issuing insurance company was selected.
   - Examine financial statements of the insurance company and obtain the insurance company's rating to assess its solvency and financial stability. Consider whether any reported matters might have any effect on the recoverability of the plan's investment.
   - Determine if any market value or penalty adjustments are included in the contract.
4. Decide whether the characteristics of the contract that restrict the use of assets require disclosure in the financial statements of the plan.

AUDIT PROCEDURES FOR DA AND IPG CONTRACTS

For plans that invest in deposit administration (DA) and immediate participation guarantee (IPG) contracts, the following additional audit procedures should be performed, in addition to the general audit procedures previously listed:

- Confirm the value of the contract with the insurance company
- Obtain the audited financial statements of the insurance company, if applicable
- Determine the financial stability of the insurance company by referring to the Moody's and A. M. Best's Guides. (These guides provide information on the financial stability and general background of insurance carriers, along with assigning grades to each company.)

AUDIT PROCEDURES INVOLVING POOLED SEPARATE ACCOUNTS

For investments in pooled separate accounts, the plan auditor is concerned with the plan's units of participation in the pooled separate account, and therefore should examine documents that provide support for those transactions. To perform these procedures, the plan auditor should consider the following:

- If the pooled separate account's (PSA) financial statements have been audited by an independent auditor, obtain and read the PSA's financial statements and the auditor's report. The financial statements need not cover the exact period covered by the plan's financial statements; they should, however, be recent enough to satisfy the audit objectives. Consider the effect that any reported matters may have on the carrying amounts of the units of participation held by the plan, such as restrictions on redemption.
- If the PSA's financial statements have not been audited by an independent auditor, obtain a copy of a service auditor's report (SAS 70) relating to the PSA's activities, if such a report is available. The service auditor's report (if a Type II report) may provide evidence as to the effectiveness of the insurance company's internal control for determining unit values and control-over-share transactions. If the service auditor's report is not available (or is a Type I report), apply appropriate procedures, including obtaining an understanding of internal control and assessing control risk relating to the pooled separate account. In applying these procedures, consider using the work of the insurance company's independent or internal auditor.

If unable to apply the auditing procedures described above, or unable to obtain satisfactory evidential matter, the auditor should express a qualified opinion or disclaim an opinion on the plan's financial statements because of the scope limitation.

AUDIT PROCEDURES FOR PARTICIPANT LOANS

The objectives in auditing participant loans are to provide the auditor with a reasonable basis to conclude that all participant loans exist and that they are properly recorded and valued in conformity with generally accepted accounting principles.

Perform the following audit procedures when testing participant loans:

- Examine supporting loan documentation
- Confirm loans with participants
- Test that interest is being recorded properly
- Test that the loans were made in accordance with plan provisions
- Verify that loans are properly included in investments in the Statement of Net Assets Available for Benefits as well as in the Supplemental Schedule of Assets Held for Investment Purposes.
- Determine if delinquent participant loans should be classified as distributions. The plan document should state the provisions which must be met in

order for the loan to be classified as a distribution, so the plan document should be read carefully in making this determination. If a loan is determined to be in default and not a distribution, it should be listed on the Form 5500 Schedule, Line 27(b)--Schedule of Loans or Fixed Income Obligations (see Chapter 11, Form 5500, for additional information). Note that delinquent loans continue to be classified as investments of the plan. With the new Form 5500, the Schedule of Loans or Fixed Income Obligations will no longer need to report delinquent participant loans provided that the participant loans are secured by the participant's remaining account balance in the plan.

REAL ESTATE

When real estate is held as an investment in an employee benefit plan (e.g., possibly as an investment of a master trust or by a multiemployer plan), the auditor should perform audit procedures to determine that the investment exists, is owned free and clear by the plan or master trust, and is fairly valued.

Audit Objectives for Real Estate, Loans, and Mortgages

The objectives of auditing procedures that apply to real estate, loans, and mortgages are to provide the auditor with a reasonable basis to conclude that all investments are recorded and exist, the investments are owned by the plan and there are no liens or other encumbrances on the investments, and that all transactions are properly valued in conformity with generally accepted accounting principles.

Perform the following audit procedures when testing real estate:

- Examine closing documents and other information supporting the cost of the property
- Examine deeds, titles, encumbrances, and other evidence related to ownership
- Review current year tax bills and compare the property descriptions to those documents evidencing ownership (i.e., deeds or titles)
- Test investment income from real estate, such as rent. Also test payment of related expenses, such as real-estate taxes and maintenance.
- Test the fair value of the real estate. Use the procedures previously outlined for non-readily-marketable securities and the use of specialists as applicable.
- Inquire whether the plan's investments or other transactions violate applicable laws or regulations.

For plans that hold loans and mortgages as investments, perform the following procedures to determine that the investment exists, is owned by the plan, and is fairly valued:

- Examine documents, including notes, mortgages, deeds, and insurance policies supporting selected loans and mortgages

- Confirm selected loans (including loans to participants as described above) and mortgages with borrowers
- Evaluate the reasonableness of the fair value, including the extent of collateral, if any
- Test to see that interest is recorded properly

LIMITED-SCOPE AUDITING PROCEDURES

As discussed in Chapter 1, Background of Employee Benefit Plans, the plan administrator may make an election to limit the scope of the audit as it relates to investments, investment income and investment expenses, if plan assets are held by a qualifying bank, trust company, or insurance company that is state- or federally-chartered and subject to regulation and periodic examination by a state or federal agency. This election permits the auditor not to perform any auditing procedures with respect to investments, investment income/loss, and the supplemental schedules related to investment transactions, provided the trustee certifies as to the completeness **and** accuracy of the plan accounting records. Normally, the trustee's certification is stamped on the face of the trustee report. The trustee should manually affix his signature above the "stamp" that certifies completeness and accuracy. If certification by the trustee is provided for plan investments in a master trust, in order for the plan administrator to elect the limited-scope option, the certification as to completeness and accuracy must be for investments at the plan level, not at the master-trust level.

The limited-scope audit exemption does **not** exempt the plan from the requirement to have an audit, **nor** does the exemption necessarily extend to participant loans (unless the participant loan is not initiated through the sponsor) or non-investment-related areas. The plan auditor is still responsible for auditing sponsor/employee contributions, withdrawals, participant loans (if not certified by the trustee), and administrative expenses. Plan investments not held by a qualified trustee should be tested with appropriate audit procedures as described in this chapter. In deciding the type of report to be issued when only a portion of the assets is certified by a qualifying institution, the auditor should consider the proportion of assets for which the auditor's scope was limited. If those amounts are material to the plan's financial statements, the report on the plan's financial statements should be a limited-scope report.

Even though the trustee has certified to the completeness and accuracy of the information on the trustee report, total investments according to the certified trustee report, by type, must agree with the plan's financial statements. If any of the certified information is obviously not correct or is incomplete, it is the responsibility of the auditor to pursue these matters, and if necessary to further modify the audit report on the financial statements and supplemental schedules.

INVESTMENT EXPENSES

Certain parties involved with an employee benefit plan charge fees for the purchase or sale of securities, fees for investment advice, or commission fees. It is common for these parties to take their fee from the income realized on the transaction. As a result, true investment expenses are often not separately identified within investment income. Therefore, participants electing various investment fund options may not be aware of the differences in such expenses that they are paying. Recent hearings and comments by the Department of Labor may result in additional disclosures in the plan's financial statements about these fees, particularly for defined contribution 401(k) plans.

SOFT DOLLARS

Compensation paid to brokers to execute transactions is normally referred to as commission. In some situations, there may also be "soft-dollar" arrangements, commonly referred to as **research credits**, which are generated by the trading activity of investment managers and are used to purchase investment research services, both in-house and through independent third-party research firms. These research credits assist them in their investment decision-making process. Research credits qualify for the safe harbor provided by Section 28(e) of the Securities Act of 1934. Commissions not used for research-related activities that benefit plan and plan participants may be considered to be breaches of fiduciary responsibilities.

Securities law allows these credits to be treated as an exception to the requirement that all broker/dealers obtain the best price in a securities trade. Soft-dollar credits or payments offset higher money manager commissions. As a result, the monies generally do not go to the investors, or the participants, of the fund. Instead, the monies go to the broker/dealer who is placing the trade.

7 ACCOUNTING, AUDITING, AND REPORTING FOR DEFINED CONTRIBUTION PENSION PLANS

INTRODUCTION

Defined contribution pension plans are employee benefit plans that maintain an individual account for each participant. The future value of the individual account determines the benefits payable to the retiree. The individual account is an accumulation of contributions by the employee, employer, investment gains and losses, and allocated forfeitures less plan expenses, as applicable. During recent years, defined contribution pension plans have become increasingly popular, particularly with respect to 401(k) plans and profit-sharing plans. This chapter will provide a discussion of the accounting and auditing concepts involved with defined contribution pension plans.

COMPARISON OF DEFINED CONTRIBUTION AND DEFINED BENEFIT PENSION PLANS

Defined contribution pension plans are similar to defined benefit pension plans in many ways. Both provide for financial monies to be available for specific groups of employees upon retirement. Both have contributions into the plan (either by the employer, the employee, or both) during the years the participant is employed. In both types of plans, these monies are placed in various investment vehicles, as specified by the plan document, and earn interest, dividends, or other income (e.g., rental), which will appreciate or depreciate over time. However, these plans differ from each other in three important ways.

1. The method of calculating the benefit to be paid
2. The form of recordkeeping associated with the plan
3. Who should bear the risk if the investments should decline in value

Method of Calculation

A defined benefit pension plan provides for a benefit based on a calculation usually determined by age, years of service to the company, the participant's salary, or a contractual benefit. The benefit determined by a defined contribution pension plan is the accumulated total of contributions made to the plan by the employer and/or employee, investment return on the contributed funds, and any forfeitures allocated to the participant's account less any administrative expenses charged to the plan. A participant in a defined benefit pension plan may request a calculation of his or her estimated retirement benefit on an annual basis.

Form of Recordkeeping

The second difference between the two types of benefit plans is that for defined contribution pension plans, an individual account for each participant is maintained. This individual account tracks the benefits accumulated for each participant, as well as the allocation of these dollars among the various investment options offered by the plan. For accounts that are valued on a daily basis, it is easy to determine the benefit accrued for each participant by checking his or her individual account balance. (See the example in the next paragraph.) Conversely, in a defined benefit pension plan, the total benefit for all participants is maintained in one combined account, and the exact benefit for each participant is not formally attributed to any one individual until that participant terminates employment (either by death, retirement, or other termination of employment).

Exhibit 1 is an example of the individual account balance in a defined contribution pension plan for the participant, Emma M. Robinsen.

Exhibit 1

	Total	*Global fund*	*Balanced fund*
Account balance at beginning of the year	$14,900	$ 9,690	$5,210
Employee contribution in the current year	3,120	1,870	1,250
Matching employer contributions this year	1,560	935	625
Interest/dividends/appreciation/depreciation	1,120	730	390
Forfeitures allocated to her account this year	40	25	15
Administrative expenses allocated to her account	(80)	(50)	(30)
Outstanding loan balance	1,280	830	450
Account balance at end of the year	$21,940	$14,030	$7,910

The balance at the end of the year for Emma A. Robinsen would be added to the account balances of each of the other participants at the end of the year to arrive at the total net assets available for benefits of the defined contribution pension plan at year-end, provided there are no unallocated forfeitures, liabilities, or receivables related to the plan.

Conversely, the total net assets available for benefits for a defined benefit pension plan are not specifically identified to correspond to each eligible employee. Rather, the total of all assets in the defined benefit pension plan, which will be used to pay out benefits at some future date for eligible participants in the plan, are maintained in one combined account and not specifically identified to each individual that is an eligible participant. Even in a cash-balance plan where there are hypothetical accounts maintained for an individual, the plan is funded and invested on a total plan basis. (See discussion of cash-balance plans in Chapter 2, Types of Plans, and Chapter 8, Accounting, Auditing, and Reporting for Defined Benefit Pension Plans.)

The Bearer of Risk

The participant bears the risk of low-performing investments (or reaps the rewards for high-performing investments) in a defined contribution pension plan, particularly in cases when the participant is responsible for selecting his or her own investment options. If an investment is performing well in a defined contribution pension plan, the participant's account is credited with the higher income, ultimately resulting in a higher benefit at the time it is paid. In a defined benefit pension plan, since the sponsor is the entity that funds this plan, and the amount of benefits to be paid is stated in a formula in the plan document, if an investment is performing poorly, the likelihood exists that the sponsor would have to contribute more to the plan in order to meet future anticipated benefit payments. Note that in some cases, a plan sponsor offers participants benefits in the form of a defined contribution pension plan to supplement the benefits provided under a defined benefit pension plan, which the plan also sponsors on behalf of the participants. This may happen when the plan sponsor no longer wants to enhance the benefits provided under the defined benefit pension plan.

The contribution, if any, to be made to a defined contribution pension plan by an employer is generally determined by the employer or by a contractual agreement, or both. This contribution rate may be increased or decreased at the discretion of the employer, provided it is not a contractual agreement. Under ERISA, the required contribution for a defined benefit pension plan is determined by an actuary, based on the benefits that are expected to be paid to participants at some future point in time.

When the participant retires or withdraws from the defined contribution pension plan, the amount allocated to that individual represents the participant's accumulated account balance. In the example given above for Emma A. Robinsen, if she were to retire at the end of the year and if she were fully vested, her plan benefit would be $20,660 ($21,940 less $1,280 outstanding loan balance). This amount can normally be paid over time through the purchase of an annuity or in a lump-sum distribution. By comparison, if Emma were part of a defined benefit pension plan, her benefit would be determined by the plan benefit formula, which we will assume is determined by the number of years of service with the company and vesting percentage. For example, if Emma retired at age sixty, after working thirty years for the company, the plan document may say she would receive $35 per year of service ($35 x 30 = $1,050 per year). If she lived for twenty years after retirement, her total benefit would be $21,000 ($1,050 x 20).

REPORTING FOR DEFINED CONTRIBUTION PENSION PLANS

The primary purpose of a defined contribution pension plan's financial statements is to provide information as to the plan's present and future ability to pay benefits to plan participants when they retire, die, or otherwise terminate employment with the sponsoring company. To accomplish this objective, a plan's financial statements should provide information about plan assets, the responsibility of the fiduciary to ensure these assets are sound and secure, any events or transactions that may affect the balance of these assets, and any other factors which are necessary for users to understand the information being provided.

Generally, financial statements of defined contribution pension plans should be prepared in accordance with generally accepted accounting principles (GAAP). However, the DOL accepts financial statements prepared on an other comprehensive basis of accounting, such as the modified cash basis. In modified cash-basis financial statements, investments are recorded at fair value and additions to net assets available for benefits are recognized when cash is received and deductions are recognized when amounts are paid, except for the recognition of unrealized gains and/or losses on investments at the end of the plan year. When plan financial statements are prepared on an other comprehensive basis of accounting, Statement on Auditing Standards (SAS) 62, *Special Reports,* should be followed as well as the Auditing Interpretation of SAS 62, AU 9623.88 which provides guidance in evaluating the adequacy of disclosures in the financial statements. See Chapter 10, Other Accounting and Auditing Considerations, for additional information regarding the use of other comprehensive bases of accounting.

Under ERISA, comparative financial statements for net assets available for benefits are required, while the statement of changes in net assets available for benefits may be presented for only the most current year. The DOL also requires that certain information be included in supplemental schedules, which are not required under GAAP. See Chapter 11, Form 5500, for a discussion of the Form 5500 and the required supplemental schedules. Chapter 13, Financial Statements and Disclosures, includes illustrative financial statements for defined contribution pension plans.

OPERATION AND ADMINISTRATION

A defined contribution pension plan is established by the plan document in which the relevant provisions of the plan are contained. These provisions are established and maintained by the plan sponsor. The plan document normally defines such matters as age and service requirements (e.g., the number of months required to work at the company), which must be satisfied to allow an employee to participate in the plan, as well as whether the plan is contributory. Vesting and loan provisions, if any, would also be defined in the plan document. The plan document also identifies the plan's fiduciary(ies) and fiduciary responsibilities, those relating to maintaining control and management of the plan.

ERISA generally states that a pension plan cannot exclude an employee from participating in a pension plan based on age or service if s/he has completed at least one year of service and is at least age twenty-one or older. However, a plan may deny participation until the participant reaches twenty-one years of age and has at least two years of service, provided that benefits vest 100% thereafter. In addition, ERISA specifies that a plan may not deny an individual the right to participate in a pension plan on the basis of having reached a specified age.

A plan subject to ERISA should state it in writing. The majority of these plan documents are prepared by attorneys or consulting firms. Service organizations--for instance banks, insurance companies, or stockbrokers--may also prepare and update standard plans, called master or prototype plans, which are available to plan sponsors. These prototypes may be used by a plan sponsor to prepare a qualified plan by customizing the prototype to meet the plan sponsor's needs. These standardized plans generally have IRS approval.

The plan administrator is responsible for the general operation and administration of the plan. The plan administrator of a single-employer plan is usually an officer, often the chief financial officer or the human resources director, or other employee of the plan sponsor. For a multiemployer plan, the plan administrator is a board of trustees. The plan administrator reports directly to the plan sponsor's board of directors or other management group. The plan administrator has responsibility to ensure that the plan is operating in accordance with the terms of the plan document, trust instrument, if any, and all applicable government rules and regulations. Generally, the plan administrator makes decisions regarding the interpretation of rights of the participants under the plan, how investments are to be managed, and the performance or the delegation of responsibilities for operating and administering the plan.

PARTICIPANT ELIGIBILITY

In conducting an audit of a defined contribution pension plan, one of the areas to be taken into consideration by the plan auditor is whether the plan participants have met the appropriate criteria for participation in the plan. Auditors should perform testing of participant eligibility to determine whether the active employees of the plan sponsor have met the eligibility criteria established by the plan document, whether they have elected to participate in the plan, and whether an individual account record exists for the participant. Auditors should also determine whether terminated employees have received distributions from the plan, or if they are permitted by the plan document to continue to invest their money in the plan for a certain period of time following termination of employment, as specified in the plan document. Also, distributions to participants must begin when retired participants reach age seventy and one-half.

Auditors should test participant eligibility either while testing internal controls for the plan (discussed earlier in Chapter 5, Internal Control) or while testing participant contributions made to the plan. In either case, the procedures to be performed for testing participant eligibility are identical. If testing eligibility while testing contributions (see procedures below), for the selections made for detail contribution testing purposes, determine whether the selected participants have satisfied the criteria for participation in the plan document. In addition, auditors should make selections for testing from the plan sponsor's personnel files; they should determine whether the participant has elected to participate in the plan and whether an individual account record has been established for that participant. Auditors should also consider making selections for testing purposes from the employer's records of terminated employees to test that distributions for these participants have been made appropriately. By using the same selections for testing participant eligibility as for testing contributions, the audit process can be made more efficient by reducing the total number of selections to be subjected to testing.

Testing for participant eligibility effectively requires that information be obtained from the plan sponsor and recordkeeper. Auditors should review information from the plan sponsor's payroll and personnel files to determine the length of time the participant has been employed by the plan sponsor, whether the participant is an active employee, and whether the participant satisfies any other conditions stipulated by the plan document for participation. In addition, auditors should review the recordkeeping statements in order to determine whether an individual account record has been established for the participant.

Similarly, for a multiemployer-sponsored defined contribution pension plan, the auditor should review information from the plan administrator's files to determine that the participant has satisfied the appropriate conditions for participation in the plan, such as belonging to the appropriate union, serving the employer for a specified length of time, or being of a certain age. The auditor should also review recordkeeping statements to determine whether an individual account record has been established for the participant.

For a plan with a voice response recordkeeping system, testing of participant eligibility should not be affected by a voice response feature. The recordkeeper should be able to provide evidence of individual account records for active, eligible participants as well as evidence of account distributions for terminated participants. In addition, for a plan that permits terminated participants to maintain their account balances in the plan for a period of time, the auditor should determine that the recordkeeper has appropriately classified the participant as terminated.

For multiemployer plans, internal controls should be in place to verify that changes to participant data are being made properly. This is most efficiently done through periodic payroll audits of all employers who participate in the multiemployer plan. Some of the information that should be verified in this test include

- Number of hours worked by the participant
- Rate of pay
- Union dues paid
- A new employee is added to the plan
- A terminated employee is removed from the plan

The multiemployer plan may have an internal audit group perform these tests. It is then the responsibility of the external auditor, who is auditing the defined contribution pension plan, to review the procedures performed to ensure that the testing is reliable. If the testing was not sufficient or payroll audits were not performed, this is usually considered a scope limitation with respect to the audit of the defined contribution pension plan and a disclaimer of opinion must be issued on the plan's financial statements.

Audit Objectives

The objectives of testing participant eligibility are to provide the auditor with a reasonable basis to conclude that (1) all employee personnel that are eligible to participate in the plan are given the opportunity to participate, (2) those eligible personnel who choose to participate are properly included in the plan's individual account records, and (3) participants who have terminated employment with the plan sponsor no longer maintain an individual account with the plan unless otherwise permitted by the plan document.

The elements of participant eligibility that should be tested include

- Basic demographic data, such as name, birth date, and date of hire with the company (or rehire date if there was a leave of absence), which is required to determine eligibility and vesting, as specified in the plan document
- Review of the plan's recordkeeping system to determine existence of individual account records for selections

Audit Procedures

Consider the following audit procedures in testing participant eligibility:

- Review applicable sections of the plan document to determine the criteria established for eligibility to enter the plan
- Review personnel files for eligibility data as well as changes to this data, such as salary information, rate changes, termination notices, hire date, and birth date
- Review recordkeeping system for the existence of an individual account record for the individual selected for testing

STATEMENT OF NET ASSETS AVAILABLE FOR BENEFITS

The statement of net assets available for benefits details the assets and liabilities of the defined contribution pension plan. It is comparable to the balance sheet of most other entities' financial statements in that it presents the net assets available for benefits (assets minus liabilities) at a particular point in time (plan year-end). The net assets provide a basis to determine the plan's future ability to pay benefits when they are due.

Participant-directed defined contribution pension plans provide benefits to participants based on the amounts contributed to their individual accounts by the participants, contributions by the plan sponsor, forfeitures, investment earnings or losses, withdrawals, loans, and administrative expenses. Because the amount of benefit that a participant ultimately receives is directly related to the performance of the investment options selected by the participant, participants have a direct interest in understanding and monitoring the performance of their investments. The participants bear the ultimate risk or reward of how much is available to them at the time of their retirement.

The accounting and auditing of investments has previously been discussed in this guide in Chapter 6, Investments. The presentation of financial statements will be illustrated in Chapter 13, Financial Statements and Disclosures. Investments comprise the majority, if not all, of the assets available for benefits for most defined contribution pension plans. The following sections will discuss the accounting and auditing treatment of the other assets and liabilities that may appear in a defined contribution pension plan's statement of net assets available for benefits.

PARTICIPANT LOANS

Many defined contribution pension plans offer participants the ability to borrow against the vested portion of their individual accounts. ERISA and the IRS have established guidelines for such loans, called participant loans. For example, a loan cannot be made for longer than five years, unless it is used to purchase a primary residence, in which case, the loan period may be for ten years or longer. The interest rate must also be reasonable when compared to the prevailing market for interest rates.

The auditor should read the plan document to understand the specific rules for participant loans available through the plan. Often, the plan document will limit the amount of the loan to no more than 50% of the vested portion of the participant's individual account. It may also establish the number of loans that a participant may have, the minimum loan amount, what constitutes a loan in default, and other conditions of the loan. When the loan is made, the amount is deducted from the participant's investment balances and added to the participant's account as a participant loan. The loan is then repaid, generally through payroll deductions, based on a specified repayment schedule. The loan repayments will then decrease the amount of the outstanding loan balance and increase the amount of the participant's investment balances. The portion of the loan repayment that represents principal is added to the participant's account. The portion of the payroll deduction representing interest is added to investment income on the loan fund.

The total of all participant loans outstanding is shown as an asset within the investment total on the statement of net assets available for benefits and in the supplemental schedule, Schedule of Assets Held for Investment Purposes on the Form 5500. In addition to showing the loan balance at the end of the plan year, the Schedule of Assets Held for Investment Purposes must disclose a range of maturities for the loans and a range of interest rates for the loans. See Chapter 11, Form 5500, for more discussion regarding the requirements of the supplemental schedules.

Audit Objectives

The objectives of performing audit procedures on participant loans are to help the auditor determine (1) whether there is a reasonable basis to conclude that all participant loans exist and (2) whether the participant loans are recorded and are properly valued in conformity with generally accepted accounting principles.

Audit Procedures

The following procedures may be performed to verify the reasonableness of participant loans:

- Examine documentation that supports participant loans and ensure that the loans were made in accordance with the provisions of the plan document. The IRS has recently stated that the participants are not required to sign forms to initiate a participant loan. As such, with many plans it is possible to initiate a loan through a voice-response recordkeeping system. This may require that a confirmation be sent directly to the participant.
- Confirm selected loans with participants. Include in the confirmation the outstanding balance of the loan at the plan year-end date and the interest rate and maturity date of the loan.
- Verify that the interest rate on the loan is properly recorded. Reconcile the total withholding per pay and confirm that the proper split is made between principal and interest in accordance with the repayment schedule.

- Ensure that the financial statement presentation is proper (i.e., reported as plan investments and included in the supplemental schedule, Schedule of Assets Held for Investment Purposes, required by the Form 5500). Note that for defined contribution pension plans with investments in a master trust arrangement, it may be unlikely that the master trust truly holds the participant loans. In this case, the auditor should determine the entity which legally holds the loan for proper presentation of the loan in the plan's financial statements. Often, if the plan does permit loans to be initiated through a voice response system, the loans are classified as investments held by the trustee.
- Determine whether delinquent loans should be reclassified as distributions. The plan document determines when a plan is in default and when it is considered to be a distribution to the participant. Participant loans in default at year-end should be disclosed in the supplemental schedule, Schedule of Loans in Default or Uncollectible, as required by Form 5500. Note that in the new Form 5500, participant loans which are in default will no longer be required to be reported on this schedule, provided that the participant loan is guaranteed by the participants' remaining account balance in the plan. Delinquent loans are considered to be assets held for investment purposes. Determine if any valuation allowance is necessary for the participant loan balance. (Normally, with the limitation on the account balance that can be borrowed and ultimately classified as a withdrawal, no valuation allowance is required.)

CONTRIBUTIONS RECEIVABLE

Contributions receivable represent amounts which are due from the plan sponsor for a single-employer plan, a group of employers for a multiemployer-sponsored plan, plan participants (if the plan is a contributory plan), or other entities (such as federal or state agencies for grants). The amount which should be recorded as a contribution receivable on the plan's financial statement should include amounts that represent formal commitments as well as contributions which are required to be paid to the plan subject to legal or contractual obligations. The basis for determining employer and, if applicable, employee contributions receivable is based on contributions that are attributable to the plan that have not yet been made to the plan by the end of the plan year. For example, if the plan sponsor decides to contribute a profit-sharing match, it is possible that the match level cannot be determined until after the end of the plan year, as they are often based on corporate profits, which may not be available until sometime after the plan year-end. Furthermore, the plan document may provide a match of 25 cents for every dollar contributed by the participant if corporate profits exceed $250,000. If it was not determined until two months after the plan year-end that corporate profits totaled $275,000, but it was known that profits would exceed $250,000, a contribution receivable should be recorded on the plan's financial statements as of the plan year-end. The existence or lack of an accrued liability in the plan sponsor's statement of financial position (i.e., balance sheet) does not provide enough support for recognition of a receivable by the plan.

Employer contributions receivable are generally recorded subject to a formal commitment, and the evidence constituting a "formal commitment" may consist of any or all of the following:

- A resolution by the employer's governing board (such as the board of directors or board of trustees for a multiemployer plan) approving a specified contribution
- A consistent pattern of making payments after the plan's year-end pursuant to an established funding policy that attributes such subsequent payments to the preceding plan year
- A deduction of a contribution for federal tax purposes for periods ending on or before the reporting date
- The employer's recognition as of the reporting date of a contribution payable to the plan

Note that for federal tax purposes, a deduction may be taken on a corporate tax return for contributions made by the due date of the company's tax return (including extensions). For example, for a company with a December 31 year-end who has extended their tax return deadline until September 15 of the following year, the company can take as deductions for the year subject to filing, contributions made through September 15 of the following year.

Audit Objective

The audit objective for contributions receivable is to determine that only amounts that represent valid receivables are recorded by the plan as of the end of the plan year.

Audit Procedures

To test employer contributions receivable, the auditor should review the contribution provisions of the plan document and verify compliance with the plan instrument (i.e., criteria that must be met for an employer and/or employee to make a contribution, the formula to determine upper and lower contribution limits, and the rates for determining the contribution). The auditor should compare the amount of the employer contribution recorded in the plan's trustee report to the amount approved by the board of directors of the plan sponsor (if the contribution requires board approval) or compare it to the amount reflected in the sponsor's accounting records. Alternatively, given the period of time after the plan's year-end in which audit procedures are performed, the auditor may test subsequent payments made by the employer to the plan after the plan's year-end to determine if any amounts contributed represented contributions for the plan year currently under audit.

In addition, the auditor should inquire about the timing of employee contributions made to the plan. As with employer contributions, the auditor may test the subsequent receipts of employee contributions to determine if any contribution amounts represented contributions attributable to the plan year under audit. In many cases, the existence of an employee contribution receivable amount on the plan's financial statements will depend upon the timing of the plan sponsor's payroll close to the plan's year-end.

In addition to the points previously mentioned, the plan auditor should evaluate the collectibility of any amounts reported as contributions receivable at the end of the plan year. If a portion of the receivables are deemed to be uncollectible, an allowance for doubtful accounts should also be recorded on the plan's financial statements. This situation most commonly occurs with multiemployer sponsored plans.

If the auditor also performs an audit of the plan sponsor, it is often efficient while performing audit procedures on the payroll system to test the total amount of contributions made to the plan and to reconcile such amounts to the plan's trustee records.

OTHER ASSETS

Other assets of a defined contribution pension plan may include investment income receivable or a receivable from a broker for sales of investments not settled by the end of the plan year. Also, in the case of multiemployer plans, the plan may hold operating assets such as buildings, equipment, and furniture. See Chapter 6, Investments, for a discussion of operating assets.

Audit Objective

The audit objective for other assets is to determine that only amounts that are valid plan assets are recorded by the plan as of the end of the plan year.

Audit Procedures

Consider the following audit procedures when testing other assets:

- Obtain a listing of all accrued investment income amounts held as of the plan's year-end and make a selection of accrued investment income amounts (e.g., accrued dividends, interest) for testing. The auditor may test the selections by examining subsequent receipts or other records supporting the amounts, the timing of the selected accruals, and whether such amounts represent valid accruals at the plan's year-end.
- Consider the existence of sales of investments that are "pending receipt" due to selling near the plan's year-end (i.e., the transaction did not settle until after year-end). The auditor should review trust statements for the first few months of the following plan year to determine if there were amounts received for sales of investments with trade dates before year-end.

- Determine that operating assets reported, if any, exist and are in use by the plan. Test additions made during the year for validity and recording. Also, test dispositions, including any gains or losses realized on the transactions, and depreciation recorded for the period.

ACCRUED LIABILITIES

A plan may have liabilities for securities purchased by the plan but not yet settled, or expenses for administrative fees (e.g., trustee fees) which may still be payable at plan year-end. These liabilities should be deducted to arrive at net assets available for benefits.

NOTE: The plan should not reflect, as benefits payable, amounts allocated to accounts of persons who have elected to withdraw from the plan but have not yet been paid. These amounts should be disclosed only in the notes to the financial statements.

On the benefit claims payable line on Form 5500, the plan should only include the amount of benefit claims for which the checks have been written and signed but which have not yet been distributed or mailed to participants. In many instances, there will be no benefits payable.

In addition, in certain cases, a plan may record liabilities for excess contributions that need to be refunded to plan participants because of the plan's failure under the required antidiscrimination tests. A defined contribution pension plan is required to perform several antidiscrimination tests to determine that the elective deferrals (participant contributions) by highly compensated employees do not favor such employees as compared to the elective deferrals made by other plan participants. Two different antidiscrimination tests are required. The first, the actual deferral percentage (ADP) test compares the actual percentages of compensation deferred or contributed to the plan by highly compensated employees vs. the percentages deferred by the remaining plan participants. The actual contribution percentage (ACP) test measures the average amount of contributions made to the plan by highly compensated employees to those of the remaining plan participants. See Chapter 10, Other Accounting and Auditing Considerations, for additional information regarding the antidiscrimination tests.

One of the errors commonly made in performing these tests is that incorrect amounts of compensation are utilized as the basis for the calculations. For purposes of the antidiscrimination tests, compensation is defined in the IRC, and the definition of compensation for highly compensated employees includes amounts paid to the employee during the plan year, increased by contributions made by the employee to the 401(k) plan during the year and by salary reduction contributions made during the year under a cafeteria plan arrangement. For all other employees, compensation generally includes only the gross income of the participant for income tax purposes. (In other words, it does not include contributions made by the participant to the 401(k) plan.) Plan auditors and plan administrators should refer to the plan document for the definition of compensation applicable to the participants, which varies for the particular plan being audited, the type of employee, and the test being performed.

The auditor should review the antidiscrimination test results to determine that the correct amounts were utilized in arriving at compensation for both the highly compensated employees and the non-highly-compensated participants, according to the IRC's definitions of compensation and the plan document's definition of compensation. The auditor does not need to recalculate the test results (unless separately engaged by the plan administrator to do so) but should become familiar with the general concepts of the tests. For additional specifics regarding the tests, refer to the IRC provisions dealing with the antidiscrimination tests.

In certain cases, a plan may not pass the required antidiscrimination tests for a given plan year. Normally, a plan fails these tests as a result of excess contributions made to the plan by highly compensated employees who participate in the plan. Once the plan administrators have been made aware of the failure of the test, they usually take corrective action by refunding the required amount of money (i.e., contributions) to those highly compensated employees. In many cases, such refunds to participants occur after the end of the plan year currently under audit. In these instances, the plan's financial statements should reflect a liability on the statement of net assets available for benefits for the amounts to be refunded. An alternative way to pass the discrimination test is for the employer to make a contribution to non-highly-compensated employees called a qualified nonelective contribution. The amount may be described within the liabilities section of the plan's financial statements as excess contributions refundable to participants and should be explained in a footnote to the plan's financial statements.

If the plan administrator does not take the required corrective action to enable the plan to pass the required antidiscrimination tests, the plan's tax-exempt status may be jeopardized. This fact will need to be considered when analyzing the plan's financial position, tax status, the related footnote disclosures, and the opinion to be rendered on the plan's financial statements.

In addition, during the planning phase of the engagement, when the understanding of the plan's internal control is being documented, the auditor should consider asking plan management how often the discrimination tests are performed for the plan. With larger 401(k) plans, these tests are often performed quarterly or semiannually so as to monitor more closely the plan's compliance with the required tests. To the extent that the plan continually fails the discrimination tests, the auditor should recommend to plan management that the tests be performed more often during the plan year so that management can monitor the test results more frequently. This may facilitate corrective action to be taken by plan management during the plan year.

Also, in cases of a plan termination or merger, the plan may record amounts payable as distributions to participants or as a transfer payable to another plan, depending on the treatment requested by the participant. If the participant will be paid monies from the plan that will not be reinvested in another qualified pension plan, the monies should be reflected as distributions payable to participants. If the participant will reinvest the monies in another qualified pension plan, the monies should be shown as a transfer payable to another plan.

Audit Objective

The audit objective relative to accrued liabilities is to determine that all liabilities of the plan at the end of the plan year have been recorded in the plan's statement of net assets available for benefits.

Audit Procedures

In order to audit the plan's accrued liabilities at the end of the plan year, the plan auditor should perform the following:

- Review trust statements for the first and/or second months of the following plan year to determine if there were any investment purchases which settled at the beginning of the following plan year which represented liabilities at the end of the plan year currently under audit.
- Review the plan's antidiscrimination test results to determine if any liabilities are to be recorded on the plan's financial statements for amounts to be refunded to participants if the plan has failed the tests.
- Review the supporting documentation for administrative expenses paid during the early part of the following plan year (generally during the first two months of the following plan year) to determine if any amounts paid actually represented administrative expenses which were incurred by the plan during the plan year currently under audit. If so, they should be recorded as liabilities at the end of the plan year.
- Perform any other subsequent disbursements testing procedures deemed necessary.

STATEMENT OF CHANGES IN NET ASSETS AVAILABLE FOR BENEFITS

The statement of changes in net assets available for benefits shows the activity (i.e., additions and deductions) that has occurred in the defined contribution pension plan during the plan year. Additions include net realized gains (for instance, interest, dividends, and gains/losses on sales of investments) earned on the investments of the plan as well as unrealized gains or losses (i.e., the change in market value of the investments). Contributions from the plan sponsor and from participants are additions to the plan. Deductions are usually payments to participants who have retired or terminated employment; administrative expenses also fall under deductions. Transfers are monies that go into one plan from another qualified pension plan or from one investment fund to another. Transfers will appear as either "transfers in" or "transfers out," depending on if the monies are going to or out of this plan or fund. Rollovers are contributions that go from one qualified pension plan to another, generally as the result of a change in participant's employment either to or from the current plan sponsor.

INVESTMENT INCOME

Investment income includes interest, dividends, rental income, and other earnings paid on investments that are or were held by the plan during the plan year. It also includes realized and unrealized gains and losses on those investments. Realized gains and losses result when an investment is bought at one price and later sold at a different price. If the selling price is higher than the purchase price, the plan realizes a gain. If the selling price is lower, the plan realizes a loss. In addition, at the end of the plan year, most investments held at year-end will be priced at fair market value (certain investment contracts may be presented at contract value as discussed in Chapter 6, Investments). If the ending market value of an investment held at the plan's year-end is higher than the fair market value at the beginning of the year (or when purchased, if bought during the current plan year), then an unrealized gain results--unrealized because the investment is still held by the plan at year-end and has not been sold. If the ending market value is lower than the fair market value at the beginning of the year, then an unrealized loss results.

Audit Objectives

The audit objectives for a full-scope audit of investment income are to provide assurance that earnings from the investment vehicles of the plan have been properly recorded in all material respects and appropriately allocated to the individual participant records. Generally accepted accounting principles require that the statement of changes in net assets available for benefits be presented in enough detail to identify the significant changes during the year. These generally should include

- Unrealized appreciation/depreciation or unrealized gains and losses on investments during the year. The amount of unrealized gains and losses on investments represents the increase or decrease in the fair value of investments from the beginning of the plan year to the end of the plan year.
- Realized gains and losses generated from the sale of investments during the year. The amount of realized gains and losses is calculated as the difference between the proceeds from the sales of investments and the original (or historical) cost of such investments. (Note that in some cases, the unrealized gains and losses and the realized gains and losses are combined for financial statement purposes and grouped in a category entitled the net appreciation/depreciation in fair value of investments. Form 5500 requires that the unrealized and realized gains and losses be reported separately.)
- Investment income which includes interest, dividends, rental income, and other types of income (exclusive of unrealized appreciation/depreciation and realized gains and losses). For certain pooled-type investments, investment income should be presented as net investment gain/loss. This net investment gain/loss includes the net appreciation/depreciation on the

pooled-type investments. (Note that this is consistent with the presentation required in Form 5500.)

- For a company that places assets relating to some or all of their plans in a master trust, the method used to allocate investment income to each plan is usually stated in the trust agreement. Each plan has an undivided interest in the assets of the trust, and ownership is represented by a record of proportionate dollar interest or by units of participation. The auditor should examine how ownership is attributed to the individual plans to ensure that the allocation method is reasonable and that it agrees with the provisions of the plan document.

Audit Procedures

When testing investment income in a full-scope audit, it may be efficient to perform substantive analytical procedures or tests in total as compared to performing detailed testing procedures of individual investment purchases and sales transactions. The auditor may calculate the amount of income for a class of securities based upon published indices and compare this amount to the actual amount of investment income recorded. For some investments, it may be more appropriate to perform detail testing procedures. Some suggested analytical and detail audit procedures that may be used to audit investment income are as follows:

NOTE: The average rate of return that the auditor calculates may differ from the independent source if investment fees are netted against investment income. See the discussion of investment fees below.

1. Obtain from the trustee a schedule of investments showing beginning and ending balances, investment income, net unrealized gains or losses, and realized gains or losses. This information should have been obtained in connection with the audit of the statement of net assets available for benefits.
2. To perform analytical review procedures instead of, or in addition to, detail tests, consider performing the following procedures to test investment income:
   - Segregate investments by significant type--government securities, equities, fixed income securities, mutual funds by type (i.e., growth fund vs. money market fund) or temporary investments. It may be necessary to aggregate the investments by other than investment type in order to arrive at a reasonable expectation. Some other aggregations which may be considered include (1) by period (quarterly or monthly), or (2) by trust account or group of trust accounts.
   - Determine the average investment balance for each significant type by adding the beginning and ending investment balances together and dividing by two. This simple average may need to be refined (to adjust for the effects of contributions/distributions) to quarterly or monthly amounts if the activity during the year is not reasonably uniform.

- Divide the investment income earned on each type of investment by its average investment balance, which will result in an average rate of return on that investment.
- Develop separate expectations of investment income for the particular investment based on independent published sources. Note that for most of the indices listed below, quoted returns are often for the total return of the investment (in other words, investment income plus unrealized appreciation/depreciation **plus** realized gains and losses **less** investment expenses incurred). Information regarding the indices and the investment components included should be available when accessing the sources below. Some examples of independent published sources--where to look for investment income data for selected types of investments--follow:

    Equity investments
    Wall Street Journal
    Standard & Poor's 500 Stock Index
    Wilshire 5000 Stock Index
    Dow Jones Industrial Average
    Wilshire Target Large Company Growth
    Wilshire Target Large Company Value
    Wilshire Internet

    Fixed income investments
    Moody's Bond Record
    Various Shearson Lehman or Merrill Lynch Indices
    Interest rates stated on the securities

    Mutual fund investments
    Wall Street Journal
    Various Lipper Indices

    Temporary investments
    Donoghue's 12-month Yield Index

- Compare the average amount calculated for the investment type to the expected amount. Obtain and corroborate an explanation from the plan administrator or trustee for any significant fluctuations.

3. To perform tests of details, obtain from the trustee a listing of all investment purchases and sales (i.e., proceeds and realized gains/losses) during the year. Consider the following procedures:

    - Perform tests of details to test both net realized gains or losses and investment income (e.g., interest and dividends) by making a selection of investment purchases/sales during the year. Reconcile the beginning of the year investment balance (at fair value) to the prior year working papers. Compare purchase/selling prices to published market price ranges on the applicable trade dates (the date an agreement is made to buy or sell the investment). Depending on the nature of the investment, obtain an independent source to compare the purchase/selling price. Compare interest, dividends, and net investment gain/loss received (e.g., for mutual funds) to an independent source (see list above). A business library will typically carry reference books that detail dividends declared and paid. This information may also be obtained from the Internet. The interest rate is generally stated on the investment instrument.

- Examine brokers' advices, cash records, or other supporting documentation for the quantity, description, and date of acquisition/ disposition of the investment. Note that often a trustee may be making large block purchases or sales for a number of plans. Information should exist that identifies investment amounts by plan.
- In the event that brokers' advices or independent cash records are not available, confirm the purchase/sale with the broker.

NOTE: For many pooled investment vehicles (mutual funds, common collective trusts, or pooled separate accounts), quoted returns are often for total return (i.e., investment income plus unrealized appreciation/depreciation plus realized gains and losses less investment expenses incurred). In those cases, testing net investment gain/loss in total may be more efficient.

4. Test the calculation of the realized gain or loss on the transaction and agree the realized gain or loss to the listing of investment sales made during the year. Determine whether the method used for calculating the realized gain or loss on the transaction is in accordance with the DOL's rules and regulations (e.g., realized gains and losses should be based on beginning of year market values rather than historical cost).
5. Recalculate the unrealized gain/loss portion of the net appreciation or depreciation in fair value of investments. Obtain the beginning of the year market value of the selected investment. Add any purchases of that security and subtract any sales. (For the sales number, use the market value for that security from the beginning of the year, not the actual proceeds received.) This will result in the ending fair value of the investment. Compare this balance to the ending fair value recorded for that security on the trustee report. If the recorded fair value is higher, the investment has an unrealized gain. If the recorded value is lower, the investment has an unrealized loss. Compare the total appreciation/depreciation with the amount recorded by the trustee and evaluate any differences.
6. For investments in non-readily-marketable securities, recalculate the unrealized gains/losses during the year by referring to the fair value of the securities at the end of the prior plan year and the end of the current plan year. Any realized gains/losses generated from the sale of the securities should be tested by recomputing such gains/losses as proceeds from the sale less the original cost. In addition, actual income generated from such investments,

such as dividend income from limited partnerships or capital distributions should be audited through referring to independent sources, such as the tax filing for the limited partnership or audited financial statements, if available.

INVESTMENT FEES

The following discussion of investment fees relates to full-scope audits only.

Fees that are assessed by parties involved in the plan for the purchase or sale of securities--brokerage fees for investment advice or commission fees--are considered to be investment expenses. Investment expenses can be (1) assessed as a percentage of the purchase or selling price of the investment being traded, (2) a flat fee charged per transaction, or (3) a flat fee for asset management or percentage of managed assets charged on a per-month basis. Some trustees/brokers show the investment fee on a separate invoice or as a separate total on the brokers' advice. However, it is common practice to either net the brokerage fee with proceeds of the sale or deduct the fee automatically on a periodic basis (e.g., monthly) from the plan account. In each of these two examples, the investment fee is not readily available.

A mutual fund may charge certain distribution costs, such as advertising, promotion, and sales incentives to shareholders. These fees are called 12b-1 fees. The name comes from the Securities and Exchange Commission Rule 12b-1, established in 1980 and updated in 1993. The 12b-1 fee typically ranges from .25% to 8.5% of the invested fund balance. The 12b-1 fees are charged primarily in cases where the funds are sold through brokers, insurance agents, and financial planners. A no-load fund is a mutual fund that charges no sales fees to its shareholders. Individuals wishing to invest their money in a no-load mutual fund buy shares directly from the company who offers the fund, rather than through a broker.

The plan document may address investment fees. The auditor should determine the method used by the trustee/broker to assess fees by discussing this with the plan administrator. Inquiries should also be made of the plan administrator as to how investment fees are monitored. If fees are netted (normally done for mutual funds and common/commingled trust funds), it will be difficult to test this amount as the fees will be shown on the trustee statement netted together with the investment income amount. However, if the investment return is substantially below other comparable indices, it may be worth pursuing with the plan administrator and the trustee. If amounts are not netted, test as necessary the investment expenses for a sample selection to determine that the amounts are properly assessed.

When assets are invested in securities/funds in which investment fees are netted against investment income on the statement of changes in net assets available for benefits, the investment income line should be shown as

Investment income (net of investment expenses)	$ x,xxx

If assets include investments with insurance companies (or other accounts where investment fees are not netted), determine that the investment fees assessed on these investments agrees with the investment fee stated in the investment contract. To do so, the auditor should examine the statement received from the insurance company, which details the plan's investments in the insurance contracts during the year and also summarizes the investment fees charged to the plan during the year. The actual fees and the investment fee rate stated in the investment contract should be compared and significant discrepancies should be investigated with the plan administrator.

LIMITED-SCOPE AUDITS

When the plan administrator has elected to have a limited-scope audit performed, agree the investment income amounts certified on the trustee report(s) with the financial information reported on the plan's financial statements. In the event that the trustee/custodian has failed to report accrued investment income in the plan's trust reports, when such accrued investment income should be reported on the plan's financial statements, the auditor should perform appropriate audit procedures to determine the amount of the accrued investment income. In addition, such amounts would be excluded from the amounts certified by the trustee/custodian in the standard footnote disclosure used for limited-scope audits. See Chapter 13, Financial Statements and Disclosures, for an example of a plan's footnote disclosures for limited-scope audits.

CONTRIBUTIONS FROM EMPLOYERS

Typically, there are two types of employer contributions: an employer match (of all or part of an employee contribution) and a profit-sharing contribution. Some plans provide for no employer contributions, some provide only one type, while still other plans offer both. The plan instrument and related documents provide the information to determine the amount that has been or will be contributed to the plan. For profit-sharing or discretionary plans, the auditor should review board minutes to determine whether and how much the employer will contribute. The auditor should read these documents to determine the basis for calculating the employer contributions and then recalculate the contribution (if a contribution was made) to ensure that it was done in accordance with the provisions of the plan document.

An employer matching contribution may be calculated based on a stated percentage of the employee contribution. For example, the plan document may read "the plan sponsor will match 50 cents for every dollar contributed by the participant up to 3% of his or her regular pay." For an employee who elects to contribute 5% of his pay to the plan, the plan sponsor will contribute 1.5% of his pay (50 cents per $1 x 3%) to the plan.

A profit-sharing contribution may be made when a stated level of profitability is realized by the plan sponsor. An example of this type of contribution may read

If net income after tax is	*Employer match is*
$500,000 to $999,999	25% of employee's annual contribution
$1,000,000 to $4,999,999	35% of employee's annual contribution
$5,000,000 and higher	45% of employee's annual contribution

If net income after tax for the current plan year is $872,000 and a participant has contributed $2,750 to the plan, his employer profit-sharing match contribution would be $687.50 ($2,750 x 25%).

For discretionary plans, the auditor should agree the employer match to the amount approved in the board minutes to determine the propriety and timing of the employer contributions.

Audit Objectives

The audit objectives for contributions received from plan sponsors are to provide assurance that amounts received have been determined and recorded in accordance with the plan documents or minutes of the board. Also, the auditor should ensure that employer contributions are properly recorded in the financial statements in conformity with generally accepted accounting principles. (Note that contributions receivable were covered and tested previously in this chapter.)

Audit Procedures

The following audit procedures apply to single-employer, multiple-employer, and multiemployer plans.

Single-employer plans and multiple-employer plans. To ensure that auditing objectives are met, the auditor should obtain directly from the plan sponsor a schedule of all employer contributions made to the plan. If possible, the auditor should test the plan sponsor contribution in total, then test the allocation to the various participants. If a test of the total plan sponsor contribution is not possible, select a sample of participants from the list and perform the following:

- Recalculate the contribution to ensure that the contribution rate or amount stated in the appropriate documents was applied properly
- Test posting from the employer contribution listing to the participant records on a sample basis, and from these records to the employer contribution listing

The preceding tests should be performed for the various type of employer contributions (i.e., matching, profit-sharing, other discretionary).

For multiple-employer sponsored plans, the steps listed above should be performed for the employer contributions of each sponsoring employer.

Multiemployer plans. For multiemployer plans, obtain a list of participating employers and determine that it is all-inclusive by examining appropriate plan documents (e.g., a collective bargaining agreement) and perform the following:

- Obtain a schedule of contributions received or receivable (usually provided by the administrator or trustee) and note that contributions are made by the employers from the list of participating employers
- Test the schedule of contributions to ensure that it is mathematically correct and that the contribution rate stated in the appropriate document(s) was used
- Test postings on a sample basis from the employer contribution listing (employer contribution reports) to the participant records and from the participant records to the employer contribution reports and recompute amounts allocated to individual participant accounts

These tests should be performed for the various types of employer contribution(s) within that plan (i.e., straight match, profit-share or other). In addition, consider confirming directly with the contributors the amounts contributed to the plan, both already received and those that are receivable at year-end.

NOTE: Efficiencies in testing may be realized if the above procedures are performed for the same participants as those selected when testing employee contributions and participant's eligibility. Consider the coordination of procedures with any payroll audits performed during the plan year as previously discussed. With respect to the importance of payroll audits for multiemployer plans, see the discussion on contributions from participants/individual participant accounts later this chapter.

FORFEITURES

When participants terminate employment with the plan sponsor, it is possible that employer contributions allocated to their accounts are not fully vested. The plan document will indicate whether monies not fully vested are forfeited back to the plan and used to offset future employer contributions, to pay plan administrative expenses or to reinstate the employer portion of account balances for participants who previously left the plan within the past five years and have since returned and reinstated their portion of their accounts. Forfeited monies may also be reallocated to the remaining plan participants, based on each participant's account balance as a percentage of the total. For example, if a participant's account balance was $5,000 out of the total $500,000 in this plan, one percent of the forfeitures would be allocated to the participant's account. Again, it is important to read the plan document to identify the proper treatment of forfeitures.

A participant is always fully vested in his/her own employee contributions and investment earnings thereon. However, many plan sponsors impose incremental vesting percentages which participants have to satisfy to be eligible to receive all the monies the employer has contributed to the participant's account. Plan documents may either provide for 100% vesting after five years of service or 100% vesting after seven years of service as illustrated in Exhibit 2.

Exhibit 2

Number of years of employment		*Vesting percentage*
More than	*But less than*	
0	3	0%
3	4	20%
4	5	40%
5	6	60%
6	7	80%
7		100%

Under the above vesting chart, if Mr. Baker terminated employment after working just over four years, he would be entitled to receive 40% of the employer contributions which had been allocated to his account during those two years. The remaining 60% of the employer contribution would be forfeited and would either be used to offset future employer contributions, to pay administrative expenses, or to reinstate the employer portion of participants' accounts who had previously left and were reinstated within five years. Alternatively, it would be reallocated among the remaining participants, depending on the treatment of forfeitures as stated in the plan document. Remember that Mr. Baker is always fully vested in his own contributions since this was his money that was contributed to the plan; however, depending on the performance of his investment funds, the value of his contributions may have appreciated or depreciated.

If the plan document states that forfeited monies are to be used to offset future employer contributions, the auditor should determine whether forfeited monies were properly used for this purpose. The auditor should also determine whether the amount of such forfeitures has been appropriately disclosed in the plan's financial statements. If forfeited, nonvested amounts exist at year-end that will be used to reduce employer contributions in the subsequent plan year, this information should be disclosed in the footnotes to the plan's financial statements. In addition, the footnotes to the plan's financial statements should disclose the amount of forfeited contributions during the plan year and what such forfeitures were used for during the plan year. The auditor should also consider the appropriateness of how such forfeitures are presented in the statement of net assets available for benefits. Those amounts are essentially unallocated assets that often are identified as prepaid employer contributions. If forfeitures were reallocated to the remaining participants, the auditor should test the reallocation on a sample basis.

If a participant terminates employment with the plan sponsor and then returns to work for that same plan sponsor within a five-year period (i.e., a break in service), any employer contribution monies that were previously forfeited must be reinstated to that participant's account. If the plan document states that forfeitures are to be used to offset future employer contributions, the plan sponsor must contribute additional monies to reinstate the participant's account to the totals that existed before the participant left the company. This contribution offsets the reduction in sponsor contributions that were realized at the time of the participant's separation from the company. Even though the plan sponsor did not receive the benefit of these forfeitures (i.e., a reduction of their sponsor contributions) the sponsor is required to contribute additional monies to make the account of this reinstated employee whole again.

If forfeitures are to be allocated to the remaining plan participants, the monies should be allocated as soon as possible. The forfeited monies should not be placed in a suspense account since monies are not permitted to remain as unallocated assets in a defined contribution pension plan.

CONTRIBUTIONS FROM PARTICIPANTS/ INDIVIDUAL PARTICIPANT ACCOUNTS

The plan document provides the information to determine the formula for upper and lower contribution limits and the rates used to calculate the employee contributions made to the plan. The auditor should read the plan document to determine the basis for calculating the employee contribution, review the employee election form if it exists, and then recalculate the contribution to ensure that it was made in accordance with the plan document and employee election.

Audit Objectives

The objective of auditing procedures for testing individual participant accounts is to provide a reasonable basis for concluding whether net assets have been allocated to the individual participant accounts in accordance with the plan instrument and whether the sum of the participant accounts reconciles with the total net assets available for plan benefits. This test should be made regardless if a full or limited-scope audit is being performed.

The audit objectives for contributions received from participants are to provide assurance that amounts received have been determined and recorded in accordance with the plan document. Also, the auditor must ensure that employee contributions are properly recorded in the financial statements in conformity with generally accepted accounting principles and that the contributions are being allocated to the investment vehicles in accordance with the participant's designation.

The Department of Labor has established regulations related to the timing of the deposit of employee contributions into the trust of a funded plan. As described in DOL Reg 2510.3-102, an employer must "segregate employee contributions from its general assets as soon as practicable for deposit into the trust of a funded plan, but in no event more than (1) ninety days after the contributions are paid by employees or withheld from their wages for a welfare benefit plan or (2) the fifteenth business day following the end of the month in which amounts are contributed by employees or withheld from their wages for a pension benefit plan." The auditor should determine that employee contributions are being deposited with the trustee/ custodian of plan assets on a timely basis and in accordance with the plan's policies and procedures and with the DOL's regulations.

An example of employee contributions follows:

Ms. Cramer elects to have 6% of her salary withheld from her regular pay. She determines that she wants 40% of her contribution invested in the balanced fund, 35% in the growth fund, and 25% in the fixed income fund and did not change her allocations during the entire plan year. Ms. Cramer's gross monthly pay totals $2,000. Her monthly employee contribution totals $120 ($2,000 x 6%) with $48 going to the balanced fund ($120 x 40%), $42 to the growth fund ($120 x 35%), and $30 to the fixed income fund ($120 x 25%).

If Ms. Cramer changes her allocations during the plan year, either through a voice response system or on a paper document, those changes will have to be taken into consideration when testing the allocations of her monies to the various investment funds.

Audit Procedures

Consider the following steps when performing audit procedures on individual participant accounts:

1. Obtain from the recordkeeper the individual account records showing beginning and ending balances and current period additions and deductions by individual account and in total. Test the mathematical accuracy of the report. IRS Revenue Ruling 70-125 states that the total of the individual participant accounts must equal the total amount of investments in the trustee report at the end of the plan year. That is, this ruling does not permit unallocated monies to sit in a suspense account. The monies must be allocated back to the participants or shown as an asset if the forfeitures will be used to offset future employer contributions. Note that contributions receivable, accrued liabilities, and accrued investment income amounts are not usually allocated at plan year-end to the individual participants; therefore, at the individual participant level the totals may not agree. However, once the contributions receivable, accrued liabilities, and accrued investment income amounts are added in on an overall basis, the totals should agree.
2. Agree or reconcile year-end totals shown in the individual account records (in the aggregate) to the year-end balances in the plan's final accounting records and to the trustee report for the following:
   - Beginning balances
   - Employer contributions
   - Employee contributions
   - Net investment income
   - Administrative expenses
   - Withdrawals
   - Forfeitures, if applicable
   - Participant loans, if applicable
   - Fund transfers (e.g., rollovers, merged plans)
   - Ending balances
3. To test employee contributions, allocations, loans, withdrawals, transfers, and individual account balances efficiently, confirm the information with

the participant. The use of confirmations is especially effective when auditing defined contribution pension plans that use voice response or Internet recordkeeping systems. (The participants selected for testing of employer contributions may be used.) The confirmation request should include a copy of the participant's account summary as of the end of the plan year, which details the balance in each of the investment accounts. It also should include a summary of the participant's elections. Try to coordinate sending confirmations soon after the participant's year-end account summaries are originally sent to employees, which may result in a higher response rate from the participants than if the confirmations are sent out four to eight months after the plan year-end.

4. Review the participant election forms (if available) or the plan document to understand how allocations are to be made to individual participant accounts. Evaluate the procedures employed by the plan sponsor or recordkeeper to ensure that allocations made to individual participant accounts are appropriate and applied consistently. Review the SAS 70 report for the recordkeeper, if applicable.
5. Reconcile the total employee withholdings recorded in the plan sponsor's payroll records to the total amount of employee contributions recorded in the plan's financial statements.
6. Determine the plan's policy regarding the timing of deposits to the trustee for employee contributions. DOL regulations require them to be made as soon as those contributions can be segregated by the plan sponsor, but no later than 15 days following the month in which employee contributions are withheld or received by the employer, as previously discussed.
7. Determine whether any withholdings (for employee contributions to the plan) that were authorized by the participant were withheld and included as an addition to the participant's account. Confirm that monies withheld were deposited into the participant's account as soon as practicable. (To the extent monies are held by the sponsor and not deposited in a timely manner to the participant's account, this represents a prohibited transaction which should be reported on Schedule 27(e) of the old Form 5500 and Schedule G of the new Form 5500. This situation is considered to be a prohibited transaction, because it is determined to be either a use of plan assets for the benefit of the employer or a prohibited extension of credit--a loan--to the employer. In extreme circumstances, it may constitute an embezzlement of plan assets.)
8. If the plan allows the participant to determine which investment vehicle his/her monies are contributed to (i.e., participant-directed fund), verify that the participant contribution was allocated in accordance with instructions made by the participant. Consider the frequency with which participants can change their investment option elections and whether there are any records of these changes.

Many defined contribution pension plans are utilizing recordkeepers that prepare daily valuations of individual account records by means of voice-activated response systems or the Internet to process participant-initiated transactions. In these cases, neither the plan sponsor nor the recordkeeper retain paper copies of these transactions. For example, in many cases, the plan sponsors no longer have records of transactions initiated by participants to transfer funds from one investment option to another, whereas in the past, the participants would have been required to complete paper forms to serve as supporting documentation. In addition, recently the IRS has stated that signatures on loan requests are no longer required from participants. Instead, participants may be able to call the recordkeeper to initiate a loan just as they can call to initiate transfers of funds between the various investment options.

In these cases, it may be difficult to obtain a sufficient understanding of the control environment at the service organization without either obtaining a service auditor report or visiting the service organization to perform tests of controls and/or substantive testing procedures. Moreover, the absence of a "paper trail" for the participant-initiated transactions will require alternative procedures for testing transactions, such as confirming specific distributions, loans, or enrollment information directly with the participant. The auditor should consider requiring copies of the tapes that record the participant-directed transactions. However, this may often require giving advance notice to the service provider, since the tapes are normally maintained only for a short period of time. If it is not possible to obtain these tapes, it is important to understand the components of internal control maintained by the service organization. To do so efficiently, obtain and review a copy of the SAS 70 report for the service organization.

The auditor should read the entire SAS 70 report to determine what areas of the service organization were reviewed and tested, the time period for the tests, and the results of the tests. If the SAS 70 report indicates that there are instances of noncompliance with the service organization's controls, consider the effect of the findings on the level of risk that has been assigned to this engagement and the effect these findings will have on the plan's financial statements. Consequently, additional tests may need to be performed at the service organization or at the plan level.

9. Some self-directed funds permit a participant to purchase stocks, securities, shares in mutual funds, and the like--in essence, any security or other investment that is available through the stock market and brokers/dealers--in addition to, or in lieu of, offering a selected number of investment options to the participants. If this investment option exists for the plan being audited, the auditor should test that monies withheld from each participant selected above were appropriately used to purchase the securities chosen by the participant.

10. If the election is made not to verify employee contributions, allocations, and account balance information through the use of confirmations, or if a confirmation is not received back from the participant, select activity in individual participant accounts for testing by sampling individuals from the current period additions column of the current year individual account records. For those selections, perform the following to test current period additions for employee contribution amounts:

    - Agree such amounts recorded in the individual's account to payroll records of amounts withheld
    - Determine whether the amount of withholdings were authorized by the individual

    Investment income allocated to the individual accounts was tested earlier in this chapter.
11. If the election is made not to verify information through the use of confirmations, make a selection of employees from the initial payroll disbursement records and perform the following. Note that for plans which use voice response recordkeeping systems, these procedures are not suggested due to the absence of a paper trail for transactions.

    - Determine that any withholdings (for employee contributions to the plan) that were authorized by the participant on his/her plan enrollment form were withheld and included as an addition to the participant's account. Determine that monies withheld were deposited into the participant's account as soon as practicable.
    - If the plan allows the participant to determine to which investment vehicle his/her monies are contributed (i.e., participant-directed fund), verify that the participant contribution was allocated to the various investment vehicle(s) in accordance with the instructions made by the participant on his/her plan enrollment form.
    - Some self-directed funds permit a participant to purchase stocks, securities, or shares in mutual funds, in essence, any security or other investment that is available through the stock market and brokers/dealers, rather than, or in addition to, offering a selected number of investment options to the participants. If this is true of the plan being audited, test that monies withheld from each participant selected above were appropriately used to purchase the securities selected by the participant.
    - For plan transfer amounts, determine whether amounts from the individual participant account records were (1) properly authorized by the individual, (2) recorded in the proper amount on a timely basis, and (3) properly recorded in the individual's account in the other plan (or fund) in the same period by examining transfer request forms.

12. For multiemployer sponsored plans, including 401(k) plans, in addition to the above procedures, to evaluate whether the participants have been properly included in or excluded from the trustee reports, consider comparing the employer's contribution reports with the information shown in participants' earnings records and comparing hours worked and earnings records with the employer's contributions reports.

    For multiemployer plans, internal controls should be in place to verify that changes to participant data are being made properly. This is most efficiently done through periodic payroll audits of all employers who participate in the multiemployer plan. Some of the information that should be verified in this test include the number of hours worked by the participant, the rate of pay, union dues paid, that a new employee is added to the plan, or that a terminated employee is removed from the plan.

    Often, the multiemployer plan will have an internal audit group perform these tests. It is the responsibility of the external auditor (who is auditing the defined contribution pension plan) to review the procedures performed to ensure that reliance can be placed on the testing. If the testing was not sufficient or payroll audits were not performed, this is usually considered a scope limitation with respect to the audit of the defined contribution pension plan and a disclaimer of opinion must be issued.

BENEFIT PAYMENTS/WITHDRAWALS

For defined contribution pension plans, the vested balance in a participant's individual account (less any outstanding loan balances) represents the amount of benefit due to that individual upon retirement or termination from the company. The method of payment (lump sum or annuity) and the determination of beneficiaries is determined by the plan document and by an election made by the participant.

Audit Objectives

The audit objectives for procedures applied to benefit payments for a defined contribution pension plan are to provide the auditor with a reasonable basis to determine

- That all payments are made in accordance with applicable plan provisions
- That the payments are made to, or on behalf of, only those persons who are entitled to receive those benefits. Persons entitled to receive benefits include participants who have terminated or retired from the company, or their designated beneficiary(ies) if the participant is deceased.
- That benefit payments are recorded in the proper account, amount, and period

Audit Procedures

Consider the following for audit procedures for testing benefit payments:

1. Select a number of participants who are currently receiving benefit payments or received a lump-sum payment in the current plan year. The participants selected should include those who received benefits for the first time in this fiscal year, as well as participants who have received benefits in prior years (those receiving installment payments). The same participants selected for the testing of employer contributions and contributions from participants may be used to test benefit payments, provided that adequate coverage of disbursements is obtained. For each participant selected
   - Read the plan document to obtain an understanding of the benefit that the person is entitled to receive, taking into account vesting and forfeitures
   - Examine the benefit election form to determine the method of payout selected by the participant for the benefit: lump sum, installment payments, or a rollover to another qualified plan
   - Recompute any forfeited balances and outstanding loans, in accordance with the plan document
   - Compare the benefit payment amount to cash disbursement records or to the trustee report. Verify that the benefit paid out equaled the value of the individual account record at the time employment was terminated.
2. The auditor should also determine that procedures exist to determine the appropriateness of continued payments to retired, terminated personnel. If an installment method of paying out benefits is selected, there should be a procedure in place to cease benefit payments once all installments are made.

ADMINISTRATIVE EXPENSES

This line item includes the amount of administrative expenses paid by the plan during the year including any amounts accrued on the statement of net assets available for benefits at the end of the plan year and the corresponding reversal of any accruals for administrative expenses which were recorded at the end of the prior year. For further information regarding the types of administrative expenses which may be paid by a plan, see the discussion above in the section on accrued liabilities.

Audit Objectives

The audit objectives for procedures applied to administrative expenses are to provide the auditor with a reasonable basis to determine

- That all administrative expenses paid by the plan are made in accordance with applicable plan provisions
- That transactions are recorded in the proper account, amount, and period

Audit Procedures

When auditing administrative expenses paid by the plan, although substantive analytical review procedures may be performed, often the most effective type of testing is detail testing whereby the auditor makes a sample selection of administrative expenses paid by the plan and examines supporting documentation, such as copies of invoices and canceled checks, to determine that the expense paid was a valid plan expense. As mentioned previously, the types of administrative expenses incurred by a defined contribution pension plan may include audit fees, trustee fees, and recordkeeping fees. As a matter of practicality, the amount of administrative expenses incurred by a plan during the plan year is not generally a significant amount in comparison to the plan's net assets available for benefits. As such, when planning audit procedures with respect to administrative expenses, the auditor should consider the materiality of the administrative expenses line item to determine the most efficient approach for testing purposes.

TRANSFERS IN/TRANSFERS OUT

The transfer of assets into or from a defined contribution pension plan may result from a plan merger, plan termination (when the terminated plan is replaced by another plan) or, for plan sponsors who sponsor multiple plans for multiple locations, from the transfer of participants from one location to another. In these cases, the plan assets attributable to the transferring participants are transferred from one plan to another plan.

Audit Objective

The audit objective for procedures applied to transfers is to provide the auditor with a reasonable basis to determine that the transfer of plan assets is recorded at the fair market value of the assets at the transfer date.

Audit Procedures

When auditing transfers to and from the plan, the plan auditor should make selections for testing purposes to determine that the plan assets were transferred at the fair market value of the assets as of the transfer date.

OTHER FINANCIAL STATEMENT DISCLOSURES

The financial statements of a defined contribution pension plan should describe the methods used to determine the fair value of investments held by the plan. This would include all investments held by the plan, including insurance contracts, and those for which an active market exists for the investment as well as those which are not readily marketable. In addition to the above, the financial statements of a defined contribution pension plan should also include the following, if they are applicable:

1. A brief general discussion of the provisions of the plan document including, but not limited to, a description of: the employees covered by the plan; vesting schedule for employer contributions; how forfeitures will be utilized (specifically if forfeitures will be used to reduce future employer contributions); the method of allocating earnings to the participant accounts; description of employee contributions, if applicable; and the name of the plan trustee or custodian. Alternatively, the footnotes may include a note which refers readers to the plan document for a summary of the plan's provisions as opposed to discussing the provisions within the footnotes.
2. The plan should disclose significant accounting policies, such as its use of estimates in determining amounts included within the financial statements, any concentrations of risks of investments, and significant costs of administering the plan paid by the plan sponsor.
3. A discussion of the methods used to determine the fair value of investments held by the plan. This would include all investments held by the plan, including insurance contracts as well as those for which an active market exists for the investment and those which are not readily marketable.
4. The plan should disclose the method for determining employer contributions. For plans which are contributory (contributions made by employees), the plan should disclose the method for determining employee contributions. Plans that must follow minimum funding requirements established by ERISA (e.g., a money purchase plan) should disclose whether the requirements have been met. If the requirement was not met but the plan has been granted a waiver by the IRS, or if a request for a waiver has been filed but a response has not been received from the IRS, that fact should be disclosed.
5. For persons who have elected to withdraw from the plan but have not yet received payment, these amounts should be disclosed in a footnote to the financial statements; however, these amounts should not be shown as a liability on the statement of net assets available for benefits. A reconciliation may be required in the footnotes to show the difference between the financial statements and the amounts reported in the Form 5500.
6. The plan's financial statements should separately disclose any single investment which exceeds 5% of net assets available for benefits as of the end of the plan year. To the extent that the investment is already listed separately in the statement of net assets available for benefits, the investment is not required to be disclosed again in the footnotes.
7. The plan's financial statements should disclose the net appreciation (depreciation) in fair value of investments (by major class of investment). In addition, the plan should segregate the net appreciation (depreciation) as generated by investments whose fair value is determined by quoted market prices from the amount generated by investments whose fair value is estimated.

8. If the plan invests in a master trust along with other employee benefit plans of the plan sponsor, the financial statements should include the relevant master trust disclosures including: a general description of the types of investments held by the master trust (equity, debt); the components of investment income earned by the master trust during the year (interest, dividends, net appreciation/depreciation); the plan's percentage of the total master trust's investments at the end of the year; and a discussion of the method used by the master trust to allocate investments and investment income to the participating plans.
9. A description of significant plan amendments which have been adopted during the year and disclosure of the expected impact of such amendments upon the plan's net assets--if significant either individually or in the aggregate--should be included.
10. The federal tax status of the plan should be discussed, which should indicate if the plan has or has not received a favorable determination letter from the IRS. To the extent that the plan has been amended since receiving the latest determination letter from the IRS, that fact should be disclosed as well as plan management's belief as to whether they believe that the plan's tax-qualified status has been maintained. If plan management has not yet requested a determination letter from the IRS, or has requested a letter but not yet received a response from the IRS, that should likewise be disclosed. Information regarding whether a plan has or has not received a favorable determination letter is not required to be disclosed under generally accepted accounting principles, but is required by ERISA.
11. From a tax perspective, to the extent that a plan has entered into a Voluntary Compliance Program sponsored by either the DOL or the IRS, consideration should be given to the disclosure of such a fact as well as plan management's assessment as to the potential impact upon the plan.
12. A description of general policies required to be followed if the plan is terminated should be disclosed. Upon full or partial termination of a plan, affected participants become fully vested in all employer contributions that have been credited to their account.
13. A discussion of any unusual events or transactions occurring after the latest plan year-end but before the issuance of the plan's financial statements that might affect the usefulness of the financial statements should also be disclosed. Such types of events may include plan mergers, plan terminations, or significant plan amendments.
14. In the event that the plan has entered into any nonexempt transactions during the year (i.e., prohibited transactions), disclosure should be made of a description of such transactions and the corrective action being taken by the plan sponsor in relation to the transactions. This information is also required to be reported in the supplemental schedules, which are part of the plan's Form 5500 filing.

15. If the plan engaged in significant transactions during the year with a related party (other than the arm's-length transactions with the plan's trustee/custodian of plan assets), a description of the nature and amount of the transactions should be included in the footnotes to the plan's financial statements.

ADDITIONAL DISCLOSURES FOR FULLY BENEFIT-RESPONSIVE INVESTMENT CONTRACTS

For fully benefit-responsive investment contracts that are described in SOP 94-4, *Reporting of Investment Contracts Held by Health and Welfare Benefit Plans and Defined Contribution Pension Plans,* the following disclosures must also be made (in the aggregate):

- The average yield for each period for which a statement of net assets available for benefits is presented. This information is available from the investment company.
- The crediting interest rate as of the date of each statement of net assets available for benefits presented. Again, this rate is available from the investment company.
- The amount of valuation reserves recorded to adjust contract amounts (for example, due to problems with the creditworthiness of the contract issuer or the third-party guarantor).
- The fair values of fully benefit-responsive investment contracts reported at contract value on the statement of net assets available for benefits. Note, however, that SFAS 126, *Exemption from Certain Required Disclosures about Financial Instruments for Certain Nonpublic Entities*, provides that plans which satisfy all of the following criteria are not required to disclose the fair value of fully benefit-responsive investment contracts: (1) the plan is a nonpublic entity (in other words, a Form 11-K filing is not required for the plan); (2) the plan's total assets are less than $100 million on the date of the plan's financial statements; and (3) the plan has no instrument that, in whole or in part, is accounted for as a derivative instrument under SFAS 133, *Accounting for Derivative Instruments and Hedging Activities*, during the reporting period.

SFAS 105, 107, AND 119

Any additional disclosure requirements pursuant to SFAS 107, *Disclosures about Fair Value of Financial Instruments*, should be included within the plan's financial statements. SFAS 107 requires the disclosure of the fair value of financial instruments for which it is practicable to estimate that value. In addition, any significant assumptions that were utilized to establish the fair value must be disclosed. SFAS 107 states

If it is not practicable for an entity to estimate the fair value of a financial instrument or a class of financial instruments, the following should be disclosed:

- *Information pertinent to estimating the fair value of that financial instrument or class of financial instruments, such as the carrying amount, effective interest rate and maturity, and*
- *The reasons why it is not practicable to estimate fair value*

See description above regarding the effect of the issuance of SFAS 126 on the required disclosures under SFAS 107. Also, the fair value disclosures are not required for plan obligations, including postretirement obligations.

SFAS 105, *Disclosure of Information about Financial Instruments With Off-Balance-Sheet Risk and Financial Instruments With Concentrations of Credit Risk,* established requirements for all entities to disclose information principally about financial instruments with off-balance-sheet risk of accounting loss. SFAS 119, *Disclosure About Derivative Financial Instruments and Fair Value of Financial Instruments*, was issued in October 1994 and superseded SFAS 105. SFAS 119 expanded on the applicability of the disclosure requirements mandated by SFAS 105. The disclosure requirements established by SFAS 105 were as follows:

- The face, contract, or notional principal amount
- The nature and terms of the instruments and a discussion of their credit and market risk, cash requirements, and related accounting policies
- The accounting loss the entity would incur if any party to the financial instrument failed completely to perform according to the terms of the contract and the collateral or other security, if any, for the amount due proved to be of no value to the entity
- The entity's policy for requiring collateral or other security on financial instruments it accepts and a description of collateral on instruments presently held

SFAS 105 also added disclosure requirements related to information about significant concentrations of credit risk from an individual counterparty or groups of counterparties for all financial instruments. The following represent the disclosure requirements related to concentrations:

- Information about the activity, region, or economic characteristic that identifies the concentration
- The amount of the accounting loss due to credit risk the entity would incur if parties to the financial instruments that make up the concentration failed completely to perform according to the terms of the contracts and the collateral or other security, if any, for the amount due proved to be of no value to the entity
- The entity's policy of requiring collateral or other security to support financial instruments subject to credit risk, information about the entity's access

to that collateral or other security, and the nature and a brief description of the collateral or other security supporting those financial instruments

SFAS 105 provided an exemption of the previously described disclosure requirements for the following:

- Insurance contracts, other than financial guarantees and investment contracts
- Unconditional purchase obligations
- Employers' and plans' obligations for pension benefits, postretirement health care and life insurance benefits, employee stock option and stock purchase plans, and other forms of deferred compensation arrangements
- Financial instruments of a pension plan, including plan assets, when subject to the accounting and reporting requirements of SFAS 87, *Employers' Accounting for Pensions*
- Substantively extinguished debt subject to the disclosure requirements of SFAS 76, *Extinguishment of Debt,* and any assets held in trust in connection with an in-substance defeasance of that debt

SFAS 119 requires disclosures about derivative financial instruments--futures; forward, swap, and option contracts; and other financial instruments with similar characteristics, such as interest-rate caps or floors and fixed-rate loan commitments. SFAS 119 established additional disclosure requirements about amounts, nature, and terms of derivative financial instruments that were not subject to the disclosure requirements under SFAS 105 because they did not result in off-balance-sheet risk of accounting loss. This statement also requires that a distinction be made between financial instruments held or issued for trading purposes and financial instruments held or issued for purposes other than trading. For options held and other derivative financial instruments not included in the scope of SFAS 105, an entity is required to disclose either in the body of the financial statements or in the accompanying notes the following information by category of financial instrument:

- The face or contract amount (or notional principal amount if there is no face or contract amount)
- The nature and terms, including, at a minimum, a discussion of (1) the credit and market risk of those instruments, (2) the cash requirements of those instruments, and (3) the related accounting policy pursuant to the requirements of APB Opinion 22, *Disclosure of Accounting Policies*

Additional disclosure requirements based on the classification of the financial instrument (i.e., held or issued for trading purposes or held and issued for purposes other than trading) were also established with SFAS 119.

ADDITIONAL DISCLOSURES FOR DERIVATIVES

SFAS 133 was issued in June 1998 and it establishes accounting and reporting standards for these derivative instruments and hedging activities. The effective date of SFAS 133 was delayed to plan years beginning after June 15, 2000, through the issuance of SFAS 137, *Accounting for Derivative Instruments and Hedging Activities--Deferral of the Effective Date of FASB Statement 133.* In accordance with SFAS 133, the following additional disclosures should be made when a plan invests in the purchase or sale of derivative instruments.

Fair Value Hedges

Fair value hedges are instruments that hedge the exposure to changes in fair value of an asset or liability. For derivative instruments as well as nonderivative instruments that may give rise to foreign currency transaction gains or losses and which have been designated and have qualified as fair value hedging instruments **and** for the related hedged items, the following applies:

- The net gain or loss recognized in earnings during the reporting period representing (1) the amount of the hedges' ineffectiveness and (2) the component of the derivative instruments' gain or loss, if any, excluded from the assessment of hedge effectiveness, and a description of where the net gain or loss is reported in the statement of income or other statement of financial performance
- The amount of net gain or loss recognized in earnings when a hedged firm commitment no longer qualifies as a fair value hedge

Cash Flow Hedges

For derivative instruments that have been designated and have qualified as cash flow hedging instruments and for the related hedged transactions, the following applies:

- The net gain or loss recognized in earnings during the reporting period representing (1) the amount of the hedges' ineffectiveness and (2) the component of the derivative instruments' gain or loss, if any, excluded from the assessment of hedge effectiveness, and a description of where the net gain or loss is reported in the statement of changes in net assets available for benefits
- A description of the transactions or other events that will result in the reclassification into earnings of gains and losses, and the estimated net amount of the existing gains or losses at the reporting date that is expected to be reclassified into earnings within the next 12 months
- The maximum length of time over which the entity is hedging its exposure to the variability in future cash flows for forecasted transactions, excluding those forecasted transactions related to the payment of variable interest on existing financial instruments
- The amount of gains and losses reclassified into earnings as a result of the discontinuance of cash flow hedges because it is probable that the original forecasted transactions will not occur

COMPARATIVE FINANCIAL STATEMENTS

As a plan's financial statements are generally presented in a comparative format to comply with the provisions of ERISA, the disclosures required above for items covered by the statement of net assets available for benefits would need to cover both the current plan year and the prior plan year, while disclosures required for items covering the statement of changes in net assets available for benefits would need to cover only the current year (unless comparative statements of changes in net assets available for benefits are presented).

8 ACCOUNTING, AUDITING, AND REPORTING FOR DEFINED BENEFIT PENSION PLANS

INTRODUCTION

Defined benefit pension plans are employee benefit plans that promise to pay to the plan participants, upon retirement, a specific benefit determined upon a formula included within the plan document. The formula may include such factors as the participant's age, years of service, and compensation earned while an active employee of the plan sponsor. Recently, the rate of introducing new defined benefit pension plans has decreased in comparison to other types of employee benefit plans, such as 401(k) plans and profit-sharing plans, which have become popular alternatives. However, millions of Americans continue to rely upon a substantial portion of their retirement income from defined benefit pension plans, which have continued to evolve into new forms, such as cash-balance plans (see discussion of these plans later in this chapter), to meet the needs of plan sponsors and participants. This chapter will provide a discussion of the accounting and auditing concepts involved with defined benefit pension plans.

COMPARISON OF DEFINED BENEFIT AND DEFINED CONTRIBUTION PENSION PLANS

As mentioned above, defined benefit pension plans provide a promise to pay to participants retirement benefits that are determinable based upon specific formulas in a plan document. The formula to calculate pension benefits payable to a retiree is usually a variation of one of the following:

- Years of service with the plan sponsor multiplied by an amount per year of service (otherwise known as the benefit unit multiplier)
- Average compensation (compensation for the participant's last five years of employment with the plan sponsor or the highest compensation for five out of the last ten years of employment with the plan sponsor) earned while an employee of the plan sponsor multiplied by a percentage or other factor defined in the plan document

In order to fund benefits to be paid to all plan participants, investments are put in a trust. The specific benefit that is payable to a participant is not determined until the participant terminates employment with the plan sponsor through either termination, retirement, or death. This arrangement differs from a defined contribution pension plan which provides an individual account for each plan participant that clearly defines, as of a point in time, the specific benefits payable to each participant of the plan.

Another key difference between a defined benefit pension plan and a defined contribution pension plan is the manner in which the amount of retirement benefits payable under the plan are determined. For purposes of a defined contribution pension plan, the plan's total obligation for benefits is determined based upon the sum total of all of the individual participant accounts. For a defined benefit pension plan, a plan's accumulated plan benefit obligation is estimated by an actuary, who bases the estimate of benefits to be paid to participants on the plan's demographics, participant turnover, mortality statistics, expected returns on investments, the benefit formula, and retirement age as provided by the plan document.

REPORTING FOR DEFINED BENEFIT PENSION PLANS

The purpose of the financial statements of a defined benefit pension plan is to provide financial information that is useful in assessing the plan's present and future ability to pay benefits when they come due.

The primary source of accounting literature for defined benefit pension plans is SFAS 35, *Accounting and Reporting by Defined Benefit Pension Plans.* SFAS 35 applies to ongoing defined benefit pension plans (as opposed to plans that have been terminated or liquidated), and it also applies to plans which are subject to ERISA (note that ERISA does apply to terminated plans). The financial statements of a defined benefit pension plan should include the following:

- Statements of net assets available for benefits as of the end of the current plan year and the prior plan year-end
- A statement of changes in net assets available for benefits for the plan year (see the next item for a discussion of situations that require the presentation of a comparative statement of changes in net assets available for benefits.)
- Information regarding the actuarial present value of accumulated plan benefits for the plan, which may be provided as of the beginning or end of the plan year. Presentation of information on the accumulated plan benefits as of the end of the plan year is the preferred method. This information may be included as a separate financial statement or it may be included within the notes to the plan's financial statements. If the information is presented as of the beginning of the plan year, then the plan is also required to present a comparative statement of changes in net assets available for benefits. In this case, a comparative statement of changes in net assets available for benefits is required in order to match the plan's assets with its related obligations.
- Information regarding the change in the actuarial present value of accumulated plan benefits from the prior year to the current year. This information is required only for significant components of the change in the actuarial present value of accumulated plan benefits. Similarly, this information may be presented in either a separate financial statement or included within the notes to the plan's financial statements.

Generally, financial statements of defined benefit pension plans should be prepared in accordance with generally accepted accounting principles (GAAP). However, the Department of Labor (DOL) accepts financial statements prepared on an other comprehensive basis of accounting, such as the modified cash-basis method. In modified cash-basis financial statements, investments are recorded at fair value, additions to net assets available for benefits are recognized when cash is received, and deductions are recognized when amounts are paid, except for the recognition of unrealized gains and/or losses on investments at the end of the plan year. When plan financial statements are prepared using another comprehensive basis of accounting, Statement on Auditing Standards (SAS) 62, *Special Reports,* should be followed as well as the Auditing Interpretation of SAS 62, AU 9623.88, which provides guidance in evaluating the adequacy of disclosures in the financial statements. See Chapter 10, Other Accounting and Auditing Considerations, for additional information regarding the use of other comprehensive bases of accounting.

ERISA requires comparative financial statements for the statement of net assets available for benefits, while the statement of changes in net assets available for benefits may be presented for only the most current year. However, if the accumulated plan benefit information is presented as of the beginning of the plan year, comparative statements of changes in net assets available for benefits are then required. The DOL also requires that certain information be included in supplemental schedules, which are not required under GAAP. See Chapter 11, Form 5500, for a discussion of the Form 5500 and the required supplemental schedules. Chapter 13, Financial Statements and Disclosures, includes illustrative financial statements for defined contribution pension plans.

OPERATION AND ADMINISTRATION

Defined benefit pension plans may be sponsored by a single employer (single-employer plan) or by a group of employers (multiemployer plan). Single-employer plans are usually sponsored by the management of one employer or a controlled group of companies. With a single-employer plan, the plan sponsor is the employer. With multiple-employer plans, the plan sponsor is a group of employers. Multiemployer plans are established pursuant to collective bargaining agreements between an associated group of employers and the labor unions representing the employees of such companies. For a multiemployer plan, the plan sponsor is a joint employer/union board of trustees.

Plan Document

Defined benefit pension plans are typically established pursuant to a legal document entitled the plan instrument or plan document. The plan document provides information regarding the various provisions of the plan, such as employees covered, eligibility requirements, manner in which contributions are made to the plan, definition of the benefit formula, payment of benefits, and definition of retirement dates. The plan document also identifies the individual(s) who is(are) responsible for the operation and administration of the plan (otherwise known as the plan fiduciary). The plan fiduciary is usually an officer or employee of the plan sponsor, such as the vice president of human resources or the chief financial officer, who generally reports to the board of directors or senior management. The fiduciary's primary responsibilities include operating the plan in accordance with the provisions of the plan document and applicable laws such as ERISA and the IRC, and making policy decisions as they relate to the management of the plan's assets, payment of benefits, and other plan provisions. Plan documents are required by ERISA to be in writing and may take the format of a prototype plan, which is an industry-standard plan document customized by many plan sponsors to address the specifics of the particular plan. Alternatively, the plan document may be one written specifically for the plan by plan management.

Trust Agreement

Defined benefit pension plans are required to establish a trust for purposes of holding the plan's investment assets. There is usually a trust agreement or instrument created to define the terms of the trust arrangement between the trustee or custodian of plan assets and the plan. There may also exist separate arrangements between the trustee and the investment managers to define the responsibilities of the investment managers and to outline the parameters for investment of plan assets. The agreement also should describe the plan's investment policy, the use of investment managers to control and manage the plan's investments, and the reporting of the plan's investments. The provisions of the trust instrument should be consistent with the plan document which, for example, may disallow the investment of plan assets in certain investment vehicles such as derivatives. The trust agreement also typically discusses the payment of fees to the trustee or custodian, investment managers, and advisors for the services provided to the plan. Increasingly, for certain types of defined benefit pension plans, such fees are being paid from plan assets, which would be disclosed within a trust agreement.

STATEMENT OF NET ASSETS AVAILABLE FOR BENEFITS

The statement of net assets available for benefits details the assets and liabilities of the defined benefit pension plan. It is comparable to the balance sheet of most other entities' financial statements in that it presents the net assets available for benefits (assets minus liabilities) at a particular point in time (plan year-end). Defined benefit pension plan liabilities differ from accumulated plan benefit obligations--plan liabilities are generally current amounts owed as a result of the operation of the plan for items other than benefits. Accumulated plan benefit obligations are amounts, often estimated, that a plan is required to pay in the future for benefits, based on the provisions of the plan document. These obligations are to plan participants or on behalf of plan participants for the benefits offered under the plan. The net assets provide a basis to determine the plan's future ability to pay benefits when they are due. Financial statement presentation will be illustrated in Chapter 13, Financial Statements and Disclosures.

The accounting and auditing of investments has previously been discussed in Chapter 6, Investments. Investments comprise the majority, if not all, of the assets available for benefits for most defined benefit pension plans. The following will discuss the accounting and auditing treatment of the other assets and liabilities that may appear in a defined benefit pension plan's statement of net assets available for benefits.

CONTRIBUTIONS RECEIVABLE

Contributions receivable represent amounts that are due from the plan sponsor for a single-employer plan--or a group of employers for a multiemployer-sponsored plan--plan participants (if the plan is a contributory plan) or other entities, such as federal or state agencies for grants. Contribution receivables should be recorded as amounts which represent formal commitments as well as contributions that are required to be paid to the plan subject to legal or contractual obligations. The basis for determining employer and, if applicable, employee contributions receivable is based on contributions that are attributable to the plan that have not yet been made to the plan by the end of the plan year. The existence or lack of an accrued liability in the plan sponsor's statement of financial position (i.e., balance sheet) does not provide enough support for recognition of a receivable by the plan.

According to the provisions of SFAS 35, employer contributions receivable are generally recorded subject to a formal commitment, and the evidence constituting a "formal commitment" may consist of any or all of the following: (1) a resolution by the employer's governing board (such as the board of directors or board of trustees for a multiemployer plan) approving a specified contribution, (2) a consistent pattern of making payments after the plan's year-end pursuant to an established funding policy that attributes such subsequent payments to the preceding plan year, (3) a deduction of a contribution for federal tax purposes for periods ending on or before the reporting date, or (4) the employer's recognition as of the reporting date of a contribution payable to the plan. (Note that the existence of accrued pension costs on the financial statements of the plan sponsor often does not result in a contribution receivable on the plan's financial statements). For federal tax purposes, a deduction may be taken on a corporate tax return for contributions made by the due date of the company's tax return (including extensions). For example, a company with a December 31 year-end that has extended their tax return deadline until September 15 of the following year can take as deductions for the year subject to filing contributions made through September 15 of the following year.

The existence of any or all of the situations previously described would warrant the recording of an employer contribution receivable on the plan's financial statements. One other account that should be considered in relation to contributions receivable is the applicability of an allowance for uncollectible receivables. For example, to the extent that there has been a pattern of contributions that have proven to be uncollectible by a participating plan sponsor in the past, this may necessitate a reserve to be recorded on the plan's financial statements. This situation is likely to be more prevalent with multiemployer-sponsored plans or in cases where the financial stability of the plan sponsor is questionable.

For employee contributions receivable, the amounts may represent amounts that were withheld from the wages of employees for contributions to the plan prior to the plan's year-end but that were not deposited into the plan's trust until the following plan year.

Audit Objective

The audit objective for contributions receivable is to determine that only amounts which represent valid receivables are recorded by the plan as of the end of the plan year.

Audit Procedures

To test employer contributions receivable, the auditor should review the contribution provisions of the plan document and verify compliance with the plan instrument. In other words, the auditor should determine if proper criteria have been met for an employer and/or employee to make a contribution. The auditor should compare the amount of the employer contribution recorded in the plan's trustee report to the amount approved by the board of directors (or board of trustees for a multiemployer plan) of the plan sponsor, if the contribution requires board approval. Such approval should be documented in the board minutes. The auditor should also review the actuarial valuation, specifically the section that details the "recommended contributions" per the actuary to determine that minimum funding standards have been satisfied. In addition, given the period of time after the plan's year-end in which audit procedures are performed, the auditor may test subsequent payments by the employer to the plan.

In addition, the auditor should inquire about the timing of employee contributions made to the plan, if the plan is a contributory defined benefit pension plan. As with employer contributions, the auditor may test the subsequent receipts of employee contributions to determine if any of these receipts reflect contributions attributable to the plan year under audit. In many cases, the existence of an employee contribution receivable amount on the plan's financial statements will depend upon the timing of the plan sponsor's payroll close to the plan's year-end.

The plan auditor should also evaluate the collectibility of any amounts reported as contributions receivable at the end of the plan year. If a portion of the receivables are deemed to be uncollectible, an allowance for doubtful accounts should be recorded on the plan's financial statements. This situation most commonly occurs with multiemployer-sponsored plans.

If the auditor also performs an audit of the plan sponsor, it is often efficient while performing audit procedures on the payroll system to test the total amount of contributions made to the plan and to reconcile such amounts to the plan's trustee records.

OTHER ASSETS

Other assets of a defined benefit pension plan may include investment income receivable or a receivable from broker for sales of investments not settled by the end of the plan year. Also, in the case of multiemployer plans, the plan may hold operating assets such as buildings, equipment, and furniture. See Chapter 6, Investments, for a discussion of operating assets.

Audit Objective

The audit objective for other assets is to determine that only amounts that are valid plan assets are recorded by the plan as of the end of the plan year.

Audit Procedures

Consider the following audit procedures in testing other assets:

- Obtain a listing of all accrued investment income amounts held as of the plan's year-end and make a selection of accrued investment income amounts (e.g., accrued dividends, interest) for testing. The auditor may test the selections by examining subsequent receipts or other records supporting the amounts, the timing of the selected accruals, and whether such amounts represent valid accruals at the plan's year-end.
- Consider the existence of sales of investments that are pending receipt for investments (i.e., investments that were sold near the plan's year-end but did not have a settled transaction until after year-end). The auditor should review trust statements for the first few months of the following plan year to determine if there were amounts received for sales of investments with trade dates before year-end.
- Determine that operating assets reported, if any, exist and are in use by the plan. Test additions made during the year for validity and recording. Also, test dispositions, including any gains or losses realized on the transactions, and depreciation recorded for the period.

ACCRUED LIABILITIES

Two of the most common type of liabilities that may be recorded on a defined benefit pension plan's financial statements consist of (1) liabilities for securities purchased by the plan which had not yet settled by the plan's year-end and (2) administrative expenses payable. In recent years there has been a move to have more and more employee benefit plans share in all or a portion of the payment of administrative expenses incurred in connection with the administration and operation of the plan, particularly with plans that are in an overfunded position (i.e., the fair value of the plan's assets exceeds the actuarial present value of the plan's accumulated plan benefits). In many cases, plan documents are amended or new plans are written with a provision that allows for the payment of some or all administrative expenses by the plan. These types of administrative expenses may include Pension Benefit Guaranty Corporation (PBGC) premiums, actuarial and accounting fees, and internal costs. One of the most common types of administrative expenses paid by defined benefit pension plans are the PBGC premiums. ERISA requires defined benefit pension plans to pay premiums to the PBGC for plan termination insurance. This insurance is required by ERISA to help ensure that for all defined benefit pension plans there will be adequate resources to pay basic pension benefits to qualified participants. For additional information regarding PBGC premiums, see Chapter 1, Background of Employee Benefit Plans, and Chapter 3, Employee Retirement Income Security Act of 1974.

The internal costs may consist of salaries and benefits of those individuals who are employed by the plan sponsor and devote a substantive portion of their employment to operating the plan and dealing with administrative issues associated with the plan. The IRS has very stringent regulations in place regarding the types of internally generated expenses which may be charged back to an employee benefit plan. Based upon the types of administrative expenses incurred by the plan, it may be necessary to record an accrual as of the date of the plan's financial statements, which would represent expenses incurred by the plan prior to the end of the plan year but not paid until the following year.

In general, the only types of benefits payable recorded by a defined benefit pension plan would generally result from either a plan termination or plan merger. (For more discussion regarding plan mergers and plan terminations, see Chapter 10, Other Accounting and Auditing Considerations.) Liabilities for benefits payable in a defined benefit pension plan are not recorded on the plan's financial statements, because all of the plan's benefits payable are reported within the plan's presentation of the accumulated plan benefits information. Actuaries normally use the cash-basis method with respect to recording benefit payments, and therefore, if a liability is recorded on the plan's statement of net assets available for benefits, the liability would be counted twice as it is incorporated within the accumulated plan benefits information. Whether disclosed in the footnotes to the plan's financial statements or in a separate financial statement, information is available within the plan's financial statements that provide the plan's accumulated benefit obligations.

Audit Objective

The audit objective relative to accrued liabilities is to determine that all liabilities of the plan at the end of the plan year have been recorded in the plan's statement of net assets available for benefits.

Audit Procedures

In order to audit the plan's accrued liabilities at the end of the plan year, the plan auditor should perform the following:

- Review trust statements for the first and/or second months of the following plan year to determine if there were any investment purchases that settled at the beginning of the following plan year which represented liabilities at the end of the plan year currently under audit.
- Review the supporting documentation for administrative expenses (generally during the first two months of the following plan year) to determine if any amounts paid represented administrative expenses which were incurred by the plan during the plan year currently under audit that should be recorded as liabilities at the end of the plan year.
- Perform any other subsequent disbursements testing procedures deemed necessary.

STATEMENT OF CHANGES IN NET ASSETS AVAILABLE FOR BENEFITS

The statement of changes in net assets available for benefits shows the activity that has occurred (additions and deductions) in the defined benefit pension plan during the plan year. Additions include net realized gains (interest, dividends, gains/losses on sales of investments) earned on the investments of the plan as well as unrealized gains or losses (the change in market value of the investments). Contributions from the plan sponsor and participants also are additions to the plan. Deductions are usually payments to participants who have retired or terminated employment. Administrative expenses are another type of deduction to the plan. Transfers are monies that go into one plan from another qualified pension plan or from one investment fund to another. Transfers will appear as either transfers in or transfers out, depending on if the monies are going to or out of this plan or fund. Rollovers are contributions that go from one qualified pension plan to another generally as the result of a change in participant's employment either to or from the current plan sponsor.

INVESTMENT INCOME

Investment income includes interest, dividends, rental income, and other earnings paid on investments that are or were held by the plan during the plan year. It also includes realized and unrealized gains and losses on those investments. Realized gains and losses result when an investment is bought at one price and later sold at a different price. If the selling price is higher than the purchase price, the plan realizes a gain; if the selling price is lower, the plan realizes a loss. In addition, at the end of the plan year, most investments held at year-end will be priced at fair market value (certain investment contracts may be presented at contract value as discussed in Chapter 6, Investments). If the ending market value of an investment held at the plan's year-end is higher than the fair market value at the beginning of the year (or when purchased, if bought during the current plan year), then an unrealized gain results--unrealized, because the investment is still held by the plan at year-end and has not been sold. If the ending market value is lower than the fair market value at the beginning of the year, then an unrealized loss results.

Audit Objectives

The audit objectives for a full-scope audit of investment income are to provide assurance that earnings from the investment vehicles of the plan have been properly recorded in all material respects and appropriately allocated to the individual participant records. GAAP requires that the statement of changes in net assets available for benefits be presented in enough detail to identify the significant changes during the year. These generally should include

- Unrealized appreciation/depreciation, or unrealized gains and losses, on investments during the year. The amount of unrealized gains and losses on investments represents the increase or decrease in the fair value of investments from the beginning of the plan year to the end of the plan year.

- Realized gains and losses generated from the sale of investments during the year. The amount of realized gains and losses is calculated as the difference between the proceeds from the sales of investments and the original (or historical) cost of such investments.

  NOTE: In some cases the unrealized gains and losses and the realized gains and losses are combined for financial statement purposes and grouped in a category entitled the net appreciation/depreciation in fair value of investments. Form 5500 requires that the unrealized and realized gains and losses be reported separately.

- Investment income, which includes interest income, dividends, rental income, and other types of income (exclusive of unrealized appreciation/depreciation and realized gains and losses). For certain pooled-type investments, investment income should be presented as net investment gain/loss. This net investment gain/loss includes the net appreciation/depreciation on the pooled-type investments. (Note that this is consistent with the presentation required in Form 5500.)
- For a company that places assets relating to some or all of their plans in a master trust, the method used to allocate investment income to each plan is usually stated in the trust agreement. Each plan has an undivided interest in the assets of the trust, and ownership is represented by a record of proportionate dollar interest or by units of participation. The auditor should examine how ownership is attributed to the individual plans to ensure that the allocation method is reasonable and that it agrees with the provisions of the plan document.

Audit Procedures

In testing investment income in a full-scope audit, efficiencies may be realized by performing substantive analytical procedures or tests in total, as compared to performing detailed testing procedures of individual investment purchases and sales transactions. The auditor may calculate the amount of income for a class of securities based upon published indices and compare the calculated amount of investment income to the actual amount of investment income recorded. For some investments, it may be more appropriate to perform detail testing procedures. The following represents suggested analytical and detail audit procedures that may be used to audit investment income.

NOTE: The average rate of return that the auditor calculates may differ from the independent source if investment fees are netted against investment income. See the discussion of investment fees below.

1. Obtain from the trustee a schedule of investments showing beginning and ending balances, investment income, net unrealized gains or losses, and re-

alized gains or losses. This information should be obtained in connection with the audit of the statement of net assets available for benefits.

2. To perform analytical review procedures instead of, or in addition to, detail tests, consider performing the following procedures to test investment income:

   - Segregate investments by significant type--government securities, equities, fixed income securities, mutual funds (by type, i.e., growth fund vs. money market fund) or temporary investments. It may be necessary to aggregate the investments by other than investment type in order to arrive at a reasonable expectation. Some other aggregations which may be considered include (1) by period (quarterly or monthly), or (2) by trust account or group of trust accounts.
   - Determine the average investment balance for each significant type by adding the beginning and ending investment balances together and dividing by two. This simple average may need to be refined (to adjust for the effects of contributions/distributions) to quarterly or monthly amounts if the activity during the year is not reasonably uniform.
   - Divide the investment income earned on each type of investment by its average investment balance, which will result in an average rate of return on that investment.
   - Develop separate expectations of investment income for the particular investment based on independent published sources. Note that for most of the indices listed below, quoted returns are often for the total return of the investment (i.e., investment income plus unrealized appreciation/depreciation **plus** realized gains and losses **less** investment expenses incurred). Information regarding the indices should be available from the sources below to indicate the components of the return listed. Some examples of independent published sources follow:

     Equity Investments
     Wall Street Journal
     Standard & Poor's 500 Stock Index
     Wilshire 5000 Stock Index
     Dow Jones Industrial Average
     Wilshire Target Large Company Growth
     Wilshire Target Large Company Value
     Wilshire Internet

     Fixed Income Investments
     Moody's Bond Record
     Various Shearson Lehman or Merrill Lynch Indices
     Interest rates stated on the securities

Mutual Fund Investments
Wall Street Journal
Various Lipper Indices

Temporary Investments
Donoghue's 12-month Yield Index

- Compare the average calculated for the investment type to the expectation.
- Obtain and corroborate an explanation from the plan administrator or trustee for any significant discrepancies.

3. To perform tests of details, obtain from the trustee a listing of all investment purchases and sales (i.e., proceeds and realized gains/losses) during the year. Consider the following procedures:

   - Perform tests of details to test both net realized gains or losses and investment income (e.g., interest and dividends) by making a selection of investment purchases/sales during the year. Agree the beginning of the year investment balance (at fair value) to the prior year working papers. Compare purchase/selling prices to published market price ranges on the applicable trade dates (the date an agreement is made to buy or sell the investment). Depending on the nature of the investment, obtain an independent source to compare the purchase/selling price. Compare interest, dividends, and net investment gain/loss received (e.g., for mutual funds) to an independent source (see previous list). A business library will typically carry reference books that detail dividends declared and paid. This information may also be obtained from the Internet. The interest rate is generally stated on the investment instrument.
   - Examine brokers' advices, cash records, or other supporting documentation for the quantity, description, and date of acquisition/disposition of the investment. Note that often a trustee may be making large block purchases or sales for a number of plans. Information identifying amounts by plan should exist.
   - In the event that brokers' advices or independent cash records are not available, confirm the purchase or sale with the broker.

   NOTE: For many pooled investment vehicles (mutual funds, common collective trusts, or pooled separate accounts), quoted returns are often for total return (i.e., investment income plus unrealized appreciation/depreciation plus realized gains and losses less investment expenses incurred). In those cases, testing net investment gain/loss in total may be more efficient.

4. Test the calculation of the realized gain or loss on the transaction and agree the realized gain or loss to the listing of investment sales made during the year. Determine whether the method used for calculating the realized gain or loss on the transaction is in accordance with the DOL's rules and regula-

tions (e.g., realized gains and losses should be based on beginning of year market values rather than historical cost).

5. Recalculate the unrealized gain/loss portion of the net appreciation or depreciation in fair value of investments. Obtain the beginning of the year market value of the selected investment. Add any purchases of that security and subtract any sales. (For the sales number, use the market value for that security from the beginning of the year, not the actual proceeds received.) This will result in the ending fair value of the investment. Compare this balance to the ending fair value recorded for that security on the trustee report. If the recorded fair value is higher, the investment has an unrealized gain. If the recorded value is lower, the investment has an unrealized loss. Compare the total appreciation/depreciation with the amount recorded by the trustee and evaluate any differences.
6. For investments in nonreadily marketable securities, recompute the unrealized gains/losses during the year by referring to the fair value of the securities at the end of the prior plan year and the end of the current plan year. In addition, any realized gains/losses generated from the sale of the securities should be tested by recomputing such gains/losses as proceeds from the sale less the original cost. In addition, actual income generated from such investments, such as dividend income from limited partnerships or capital distributions, should be audited through reference to independent sources such as the tax filing for the limited partnership or audited financial statements, if available.

INVESTMENT FEES

Fees that are assessed by parties involved in the plan for the purchase or sale of securities (i.e., a brokerage fee), for investment advice, or commission fees are considered investment expenses. Investment expenses can be (1) assessed as a percentage of the purchase or selling price of the investment being traded, (2) a flat fee charged per transaction, or (3) a flat fee or percentage of managed assets charged on a per-month basis. Some trustees/brokers show the investment fee on a separate invoice or as a separate total on the brokers' advice. However, it is common practice to either net the brokerage fee with proceeds of the sale or deduct the fee automatically on a periodic basis (e.g., monthly) from the plan account. In each of these two examples, the investment fee is not readily available.

A mutual fund may charge certain distribution costs, such as advertising, promotion, and sales incentives to shareholders. These fees are called 12b-1 fees. The name comes from the Securities and Exchange Commission Rule 12b-1, established in 1980 and updated in 1993. The 12b-1 fee typically ranges from .25% to 8.5% of the invested fund balance. The 12b-1 fees are charged primarily in cases where the funds are sold through brokers, insurance agents, and financial planners. A no-load fund is a mutual fund that charges no sales fees to its shareholders. Individuals wishing to invest their money in a no-load mutual fund buy shares directly from the company who offers the fund, rather than through a broker.

The plan document may address investment fees. The auditor should determine the method used by the trustee/broker to assess fees by discussing this with the plan administrator. Inquiries should also be made of the plan administrator as to the procedures for monitoring investment fees. If fees are netted (normally done for mutual funds and common/commingled trust funds), it will be difficult to test this amount as the fees will be shown on the trustee statement netted together with the investment income amount. However, if the investment return is substantially below other comparable indices, it may be worth pursuing with the plan administrator and the trustee. If amounts are not netted, test as necessary the investment expenses for a sample selection to determine that the amounts are properly assessed.

When assets are invested in securities/funds in which investment fees are netted against investment income on the statement of changes in net assets available for benefits, the investment income line should be shown as

Investment income (net of investment expenses)	$ x,xxx

If assets include investments with insurance companies (or other accounts where investment fees are not netted), determine that the investment fees assessed on these investments agree to the investment fee rate stated in the investment contract/agreement. This may be performed by examining the statement received from the insurance company detailing the plan's investments in the insurance contracts during the year which will also summarize the investment fees charged to the plan during the year. These actual fees and the investment fee rate stated in the investment contract should be compared and significant discrepancies should be investigated with the plan administrator.

LIMITED-SCOPE AUDITS

When the plan administrator has elected to have a limited-scope audit performed, agree the investment income amounts certified on the trustee report(s) to the financial information reported on the plan's financial statements. In the event that the trustee/custodian has failed to report accrued investment income in the plan's trust reports, when such accrued investment income should be reported on the plan's financial statements, the auditor should perform appropriate audit procedures to determine the amount of the accrued investment income. In addition, such amounts would be excluded from the amounts certified by the trustee/custodian in the standard footnote disclosure used for limited-scope audits. See Chapter 13, Financial Statements and Disclosures, for an example of a plan's footnote disclosures for limited-scope audits.

CONTRIBUTIONS

Contributions received during the plan year may be segregated between employer contributions, employee contributions (to the extent that the plan is a contributory plan which is very rare), and other contributions. The contributions recorded (as segregated by employer, employee, and other contributions) would also include the impact of accruals recorded for contributions not yet received by the end of the plan year and the reversal of any accrued contributions recorded as of the end of the prior plan year. To the extent that a defined benefit pension plan is less than 85% funded based on IRS funding rules, the plan sponsor is required to make contributions to the plan on a quarterly basis and to notify the plan participants of the plan's funding status (i.e., that the plan is not fully funded). If a plan exceeds the 85% funding criteria, there are no restrictions on the timing of plan sponsor contributions other than those already discussed regarding the IRS rules for deducting contribution amounts for tax purposes.

Audit Objectives

The audit objectives for contributions received from plan sponsors are to provide assurance that amounts received have been determined and recorded in accordance with the plan documents or minutes of the board. Also, the auditor should ensure that plan sponsor contributions are properly recorded in the financial statements in conformity with generally accepted accounting principles. (Note that contributions receivable were covered and tested previously in this chapter.)

Alternatively, the audit objectives for contributions received from participants are to provide assurance that amounts received have been determined and recorded in accordance with the plan document. Also, the auditor must ensure that employee contributions are properly recorded in the financial statements in conformity with generally accepted accounting principles.

Audit Procedures

The following audit procedures apply to employee contributions for single-employer, multiple-employer, and multiemployer plans.

Employer contributions--single-employer plans and multiple-employer plans. To ensure the auditing objectives are met, the auditor should obtain directly from the plan sponsor a schedule of all employer contributions made to the plan. Select a sample from the list and perform the following:

- Compare the amount of the contributions to the actuarial valuation to determine that the plan sponsor satisfied the ERISA minimum funding requirements. The ERISA minimum funding requirements are discussed later in this chapter in the section on actuarial present value of accumulated plan benefits. If the contributions made by the plan sponsor fail to meet the ERISA minimum funding requirements, the auditor should discuss this situation with the plan administrator to determine what action will be taken to satisfy the ERISA requirements. In some cases, the plan sponsor will make or will have already made a contribution in the following plan year to satisfy the minimum contributions, and in such cases, a contribution receivable should be recorded on the plan's statement of net assets available for benefits. In other cases, particularly if the plan sponsor is experiencing financial hardships, the plan sponsor may request from the IRS a waiver which would either postpone, or in extreme cases, eliminate any additional contributions needed to satisfy the ERISA minimum funding requirements for that plan year. In either of these cases, the appropriate disclosure should be made in the footnotes to the plan's financial statements to describe the plan's failure to meet the ERISA minimum funding requirements and the action which has been taken by the plan sponsor with respect to this situation. See Chapter 13 for an example of a plan's footnote disclosure which deals with this matter. In cases where the plan sponsor has made contributions to the plan which exceed the maximum tax-deductible amounts, this situation should be discussed with the plan administrator as to the reasons for the excess contributions. This situation may also result in an opportunity for a management letter comment to be rendered to plan management.

- Consider confirming directly with the plan sponsor the amounts contributed to the plan, both already received and those that are receivable at year-end.

For multiple-employer sponsored plans, the steps previously listed should be performed for the employer contributions of each sponsoring employer.

Employer contributions--multiemployer plans. For multiemployer plans, the auditor should obtain a list of participating employers and determine that it is all-inclusive by examining appropriate plan documents (e.g., a collective bargaining agreement). The auditor should then perform the following:

- Obtain a schedule of contributions received or receivable (usually provided by the administrator or trustee) and note that contributions are made by employer(s) from the list of participating employers.
- Test the schedule of contributions to ensure that it is mathematically correct and that the contribution rate stated in the appropriate document(s) was used.
- Compare the amount of the contribution to the actuarial valuation to determine that the plan sponsor satisfied the ERISA minimum funding requirements.
- Consider confirming directly with the contributors the amounts contributed to the plan, both already received and those that are receivable at year-end.

Employee contributions. The following procedures may be performed for auditing employee contributions for single-employer, multiple-employer, and multiemployer plans.

- Obtain a schedule of contributions received or receivable from participants and reconcile the totals to the plan's financial accounting records.
- Either perform detail tests for selected transactions or perform substantive analytical review procedures to test the amount of employee contributions.

- To perform detail test transactions, select contributions from the schedule received and trace the amounts contributed to the payroll records and the participant's personnel file to determine whether the amount of the withholding was authorized by the participant and appropriately withheld.
- To test amounts by performing substantive analytic review procedures, develop an expectation of the amount of employee contributions by using prior year activity, specified levels of participants' contributions per payroll information, number of plan participants, and payroll cycle. Compare the expectation to the actual amount of contributions received and recorded and obtain and corroborate explanations for any significant differences through examination of supporting documents.

BENEFIT PAYMENTS

As the caption suggests, this line item would record the amount of benefits paid to retirees and their beneficiaries during the course of the plan year, including amounts which were paid to retirees directly by insurance companies pursuant to the provisions of unallocated contracts held by the plan.

Audit Objectives

The audit objectives for procedures applied to benefit payments are to provide the auditor with a reasonable basis to determine:

- That all payments are made in accordance with applicable plan provisions
- That the payments are made to, or on behalf of, only those persons who are entitled to receive those benefits. Persons entitled to receive benefits include participants who have terminated or retired from the company, or their designated beneficiary(ies) if the participant is deceased and the joint survivor benefit was selected.
- That transactions are recorded in the proper account, amount, and period

Audit Procedures

In auditing benefit payments, the auditor may perform either detail testing or substantive analytical review procedures or a combination of both. Listed below are some suggested approaches for auditing benefit payments.

1. In performing detail testing procedures for benefit payments, the auditor should make a selection of retirees for testing purposes. In the sample of retirees made for testing purposes, the auditor may also consider adding a focus upon (1) new retirees (i.e., participants who have retired during the current year) since this is the first year that they are receiving benefit payments, and/or (2) older retirees (perhaps a population of retirees older than eighty-five years old) to ensure that the older retirees are still alive and that the plan is not making benefit payments to individuals who are deceased.

2. To the extent that the plan sponsor demonstrates an interest in auditing the benefit payments being paid to the older population of retirees, it is possible to access information from the United States Department of Social Security to compare the listing of plan participants against to determine if the plan's older population has not been reported as deceased to the Department of Social Security.
3. For the retirees selected for testing purposes, the auditor should recompute the amount of the monthly and annual benefit payments paid to the retiree based upon the benefit calculations provided within the plan document. In the event that the participant has elected to receive a lump-sum benefit payment, the calculation of the retirement benefit is increasingly complex.
4. The auditor should also confirm the amount of benefits with the retirees, especially for new retirees and the older population of retirees. For confirmations that are not returned from the retirees, the auditor should perform alternative procedures which would consist of obtaining a copy of the canceled check for the retiree's monthly benefit payment and agreeing the amount of the benefit payment to the appropriate documentation maintained within the retiree's personnel file, such as the benefit payment calculation and approval form. In addition, the auditor should compare the retiree's signature on the canceled check to his/her signature maintained within the retiree's personnel file.
5. In the event that the auditor elects to perform substantive analytic review procedures, the auditor should develop an independent expectation of the benefit payments paid by the plan during the year and compare such expectation to the actual amount of benefits paid. The expectation may be determined by the following formula:

   Prior year actual benefit payments = $50,000
   Actual number of retirees during the prior year = 100
   Average benefit payment per retiree = $5,000 ($50,000/100)
   Average number of retirees during the current year = 110
   Auditor's expectation of current year benefit payments = $55,000 ($5,000 per retiree multiplied by 110 average number of retirees during the current year)

   The auditor should also adjust the expectation for benefit payments for the impact of any plan amendments, which have been adopted during the year but would not have been taken into consideration in the prior year actual benefit payments, and also for lump-sum benefit payments made to retirees/beneficiaries during the year. This expectation should be compared to actual benefit payments and any significant differences should be investigated.

6. The auditor should also compare the total benefit payments as reported within the trustee statements to the benefit payments as listed within the benefit payment register to determine that the amounts are consistent.

ADMINISTRATIVE EXPENSES

This line item includes the amount of administrative expenses paid by the plan during the year, including any amounts accrued on the statement of net assets available for benefits at the end of the plan year and the corresponding reversal of any accruals for administrative expenses which were recorded at the end of the prior year. For further information regarding the types of administrative expenses that may be paid by a plan, see the previous discussion in the section on accrued liabilities.

Audit Objectives

The audit objectives for procedures applied to administrative expenses are to provide the auditor with a reasonable basis to determine

- That all administrative expenses paid by the plan are made in accordance with applicable plan provisions
- That transactions are recorded in the proper account, amount, and period.

Audit Procedures

When auditing administrative expenses paid by the plan, although substantive analytical review procedures may be performed, perhaps the most effective type of testing is detail testing, whereby the auditor makes a sample selection of administrative expenses paid by the plan and examines supporting documentation, such as copies of invoices and canceled checks, to determine that the expenses are valid. As previously mentioned, the types of administrative expenses incurred by a defined benefit pension plan may include PBGC premiums, actuarial fees, audit fees, or internal costs. As a matter of practicality, the amount of administrative expenses incurred by a plan during the plan year is not generally a significant amount in comparison to the plan's net assets available for benefits. As such, when planning audit procedures with respect to administrative expenses, the auditor should consider the materiality of the administrative expenses line item to determine the most efficient approach for testing purposes.

TRANSFERS IN/TRANSFERS OUT

The transfer of assets into or from a defined benefit pension plan may result from a plan merger, plan termination (when the terminated plan is replaced by another plan), or from the transfer of participants from one location to another for plan sponsors who sponsor multiple plans for multiple locations. In these cases, the plan assets and the related accumulated plan benefit obligation related to the transferring participants are transferred from one plan to another plan.

Audit Objectives

The audit objectives for procedures applied to transfers are to provide the auditor with a reasonable basis to determine that the transfer of plan assets is recorded at the fair market value of the assets at the transfer date and that the accumulated plan benefit obligation related to such participants also transferred as appropriate.

Audit Procedures

When auditing transfers to and from the plan, the plan auditor should make selections for testing purposes to determine that the plan assets were transferred at the fair market value of the assets as of the transfer date. In addition, the auditor should review the actuarial valuation to determine that the accumulated plan benefit obligations related to the transfer were appropriately reflected in the plan's statement of accumulated plan benefit obligations.

Actuarial Present Value of Accumulated Plan Benefits

Calculation of accumulated plan benefits obligation. The accumulated plan benefit information is provided by an actuary in their actuarial valuation report. The accumulated plan benefits information should include benefits for the following categories of plan participants:

- Retired or terminated employees or their beneficiaries, if applicable
- Beneficiaries of deceased employees
- Current (or "active") employees

In general, the determination of the amount of accumulated plan benefits should be dependent upon the provisions of the plan document, which discuss benefits payable under the plan. Typically, plan documents specify that a certain benefit payment is "earned" by participants for each year of credited service. However, in certain cases, the plan document may not clearly specify the amount of the benefit for each year of service. In these cases, paragraph 17 of SFAS 35 provides some guidelines which include the following:

> *"If the benefit is not clearly determinable...the benefit shall be considered to accumulate in proportion to (a) the ratio of the number of years of service completed to the benefit information date to the number that will have been completed when the benefit will first be fully vested, if the type of benefit is included in vested benefits,...or (b) the ratio of completed years of service to projected years of service upon anticipated separation from covered employment, if the type of benefit is not includable in vested benefits..."*

In measuring accumulated plan benefits, the following five points may need to be taken into consideration:

1. The employee's pay history and years of credited service as of the benefit information date

2. Future service when evaluating an employee's eligibility for certain other benefits provided by the plan, such as early retirement benefits and death and disability benefits
3. Future increases in salaries and benefits only to the extent that they have been specified before the benefit information date, such as cost of living adjustments
4. Plan amendments which have been adopted **after** the benefit information date should generally **not** be recognized. However, if the actuarial valuations are prepared consistently from one year to the next year, specifically with respect to the treatment of plan amendments, then it may be acceptable to recognize plan amendments at their adoption date instead of their effective date. The plan amendments which have been adopted after the benefit information date should be disclosed in the footnotes to the plan's financial statements as well as the anticipated impact of such amendments upon the plan's accumulated plan benefits.
5. Benefits which are guaranteed by an allocated contract should be excluded as the value of the allocated contracts are similarly excluded from plan assets in the statement of net assets available for benefits. However, such benefits which are guaranteed by the allocated contracts should be disclosed in the footnotes to the plan's financial statements.

The actuarial present value of accumulated plan benefits is calculated by an actuary by applying certain actuarial assumptions and by using an actuarial cost method and incorporating the participant information described in items 1 through 5 above. Actuarial assumptions assume that the plan is an ongoing plan and include, but are not limited to the following:

- The interest rate, which is used for discounting the expected future payments, and which should reflect the expected long-term rate of return on the plan's investments, taking into consideration the plan's investment policy and the returns that are reasonable for the types of investments held by the plan. (Note that as provided by SFAS 35, the interest rate used does not normally change very frequently.)
- An allowance for the consideration of employee turnover (which should be based upon historical trends of the employer) and mortality rates (based upon published mortality tables such as the UP 1984 Mortality Table)
- The average retirement age for the plan and consideration of the historical experience for the plan

It is important to note that the actuarial assumptions which are used for purposes of preparing the actuarial valuation (which may sometimes be referred to as the SFAS 35 valuation) are often different from the assumptions used by the actuary for determining the plan's funding and the plan sponsor's pension costs. These are used for purposes of accounting for the pension costs by the plan sponsor (and used in preparation of the SFAS 87 valuation). The actuary uses actuarial cost methods, such as the entry-age-normal cost method or the projected unit credit cost method, in order to determine the plan's funding requirements, the amount and timing of employer contributions to be made to the plan, the annual pension costs to the plan sponsor, the tax deductibility of amounts contributed, and the pension expenses to be recorded by the plan sponsor. Appendix A, Actuarial Concepts, Methods, and Assumptions, provides a discussion of the various actuarial cost methods and assumptions used to prepare the actuarial valuations for defined benefit pension plans. Also, see Chapter 3, Employee Retirement Income Security Act of 1974, for a discussion of the ERISA funding requirements for defined benefit pensions plans.

Presentation of accumulated plan benefits information. Accumulated plan benefits represent the present value of the benefit payments which are to be paid to the participants of the plan upon their retirement. Essentially, the accumulated plan benefit information is intended to present the expected benefits to be paid by the plan for service rendered to date, measured as of a specific point in time. SFAS 35 permits the information regarding accumulated plan benefits to be presented as of either the beginning or end of the plan year, although presentation of the information as of the end of the plan year is preferable. If the accumulated plan benefit information is presented as of the beginning of the plan year, then only one year of accumulated plan benefit information is required to be presented. If the accumulated plan benefit information is presented as of the end of the plan year, then comparative accumulated plan benefit information should be presented. In order for the plan's financial statements to satisfy the objective as set forth by the Financial Accounting Standards Board of providing information that is useful in assessing the plan's ability to make benefit payments when due, the plan's statements of net assets available for benefits and the changes therein and the information regarding accumulated plan benefits and the changes therein need to be presented for the same period. For example, ERISA permits that a plan's financial statements include a comparative statement of net assets available for benefits and only the current year's statement of changes in net assets available for benefits. However, if a plan elects to present the accumulated plan benefit information as of the beginning of the current plan year, then the plan's financial statements should also include a comparative statement of changes in net assets available for benefits. This is required in order to match the plan's assets with its obligations.

Another factor to consider regarding the presentation of accumulated plan benefit information is the dating of the actuarial valuation reports prepared by actuaries. In many cases, the actuarial valuations for accumulated plan benefit information presented as of the end of the plan year (assuming a calendar year-end) are actually dated January 1 as opposed to December 31 of the prior year. In these cases, it is important to note that the plan's assets and obligations need to be presented as of the same date, and to the extent that the plan may have had plan amendments which became effective on January 1, such amendments may be reflected in the accumulated plan benefit information presented in the actuarial valuation. In these cases, because an end of the year presentation for accumulated plan benefits is being used, such amendments should not have been taken into consideration in the actuarial valuation report. In these cases, the plan administrator will need to request that the actuary provide revised calculations of the plan's accumulated plan benefit obligations as of the end of the plan year (December 31).

Also, as mentioned previously, the information regarding accumulated plan benefits and the changes therein may be presented either as a separate financial statement or included within the footnotes to the plan's financial statements. The same location should be selected for presenting the accumulated plan benefits information and the changes in accumulated plan benefits for a given year (i.e., present both series of information either in the footnotes or within the financial statements). Note that information regarding the changes in accumulated plan benefits is only required to the extent that the factors which affected the change in accumulated plan benefits from the preceding year to the current year are significant.

ACCUMULATED PLAN BENEFITS OBLIGATION

The accumulated plan benefit information, which is either disclosed in the footnotes to the plan's financial statements or as a separate financial statement, should stipulate the amounts of accumulated plan benefits attributable to the following categories:

- Vested benefits of participants currently receiving benefits (i.e., current retirees)
- Other vested benefits (for example, this includes benefits for active employees who have sufficient years of credited service to be fully vested in the pension benefits and for employees who have terminated employment with the plan sponsor but had fully vested in the pension benefits prior to the severance of their employment with the plan sponsor, therefore referred to as terminated vested participants)
- Nonvested benefits (i.e., for active employees who have not yet reached the years of credited service to be fully vested in the plan)

Although the majority of defined benefit pension plans are noncontributory (in other words, contributions are not required or even permitted to be made by employees), certain defined benefit pension plans, and multiemployer plans particularly those initiated prior to the enactment of ERISA, do allow contributions to be made by their employees. In addition, within the plan's discussion of accumulated plan benefits for such contributory plans, the accumulated contributions of active employees should be disclosed as well as the interest credited on those contributions (as well as the crediting interest rate).

Changes in Accumulated Plan Benefit Obligations

The information that is to be presented regarding the change in accumulated plan benefits (i.e., difference between prior benefit information and the current benefit information) may be disclosed in the footnotes to the plan's financial statements or within a separate financial statement and should include the following information to the extent applicable for the plan's circumstances: (Note that presentation of information regarding changes in accumulated plan benefits from the preceding benefit information date to the current benefit information date is not required unless the components resulting in the change in accumulated plan benefits are significant.)

1. The impact of plan amendments (For example, a plan could be amended to increase the benefit unit multiplier, which is one of the primary components in determining a participant's future pension benefit. The impact of such a change in a participant's benefit needs to be quantified by the actuary to determine the increase in the plan's accumulated plan benefit obligation. Note that a plan amendment could be approved by plan management in the current year that actually may have benefit unit multiplier rate increases for each of the next three years. The portion of the plan amendment which affects the current year would be included in the plan amendments disclosure.)
2. Changes in actuarial assumptions (for example, to the extent that a change is made to the average retirement age from sixty-five to sixty-two, that change would decrease the plan's accumulated plan benefits). Changing the actuarial assumptions does not result in reducing benefits payable to participants of a defined benefit pension plan; it may only alter the funding of contributions to the plan in terms of the amount and frequency of contributions. When there are changes in actuarial assumptions, such changes are considered changes in accounting estimates and previously reported amounts should not be restated. The actuarial assumptions used for purposes of the SFAS 35 valuation are not expected to be changed annually or even very frequently, (unlike the assumptions used for purposes of SFAS 87 valuations which may change annually, particularly the discount rate). The assumptions used by the actuary should be reviewed annually to determine that they continue to remain applicable particularly in situations when there has been a significant change in the mix or portfolio of the plan's investments or after plan mergers or divestitures of a portion of the plan sponsor company which can have a significant effect on the plan's expected long-term rate of return.
3. Benefits paid by the plan during the year to retirees must be deducted to reflect the reduction in the plan's total accumulated plan benefits. The benefits paid as reported here should agree to the amount of benefits paid as reported on the plan's statement of changes in net assets available for benefits for the period covered.
4. Changes in the plan's composition or coverage due to a termination of the plan, spinoff, merger, or transfer of participants to another participating plan of the sponsor. Any of the items listed could affect the plan's accumu-

lated plan benefits due to the change in the composition of the plan's population. For example, in the event of a plan merger, the accumulated plan benefits of the merging plan may be transferred to another plan and should be reflected as a transfer of the accumulated plan benefit obligation for the plan.

5. Benefits accumulated during the year by active employees. This line item will include the impact of another year of benefits earned by active employees of the plan sponsor, and also the impact of actuarial gains and losses resulting from experiences of participants such as mortality or turnover, which will affect the initial expectations of the actuary. In essence, this line item performs a "true-up" of actuarial estimates to **actual** plan experience.
6. Increase for interest due to decrease in the discount period. This line item reflects the increase in the accumulated plan benefit liability due to the passage of one additional year in the plan's operation and payment of benefits.

As mentioned earlier, the plan may present accumulated plan benefit information as of either the beginning or end of the plan year.

Audit Objectives

The audit objectives relating to the accumulated plan benefit information are to determine that the plan's accumulated plan benefit obligations have been presented and calculated in accordance with the provisions of SFAS 35, and that the actuary has taken into consideration the appropriate plan population and applicable provisions of the plan document and amendments in the preparation of the actuarial valuation.

Audit Procedures

The primary focus for an auditor, when auditing the accumulated plan benefit information presented by the plan within its financial statements or footnotes to the financial statements, is the report prepared by the actuary--the actuarial valuation. As mentioned earlier, for purposes of developing the accumulated plan benefit information, an actuary should be engaged by the plan. As part of the audit process, the auditor should independently receive a copy of the actuarial valuation. The remaining procedures discussed below are applicable for actuarial valuations prepared as of either the beginning or end of the plan year. The procedures listed below are applicable for either full-scope audits or limited-scope audits.

Engaging a specialist. One of the first considerations to be made by the auditor are the requirements with respect to the use of specialists in an audit engagement. Actuaries are considered to be specialists as defined by SAS 73, *Using the Work of a Specialist*. According to the provisions of SAS 73, when a specialist is used by a plan, the auditor should perform procedures to evaluate the specialist's qualifications, reputation, and relationship to the client. In this regard, the auditor should consider obtaining a letter from the actuary regarding their independence from the plan and the plan sponsor. The auditor should document in the audit working papers the basis for conclusions that support reliance on the use of the actuary's work and its propriety as audit evidence. In addition, in accordance with the provisions of SAS 85 (as amended by SAS 89), since the work of a specialist (actuary) has been used by the plan, the auditor should include additional representations from plan management relating to the findings of the actuary. The following represents an example of the item to be included in the management representation letter:

> We agree with the findings of the actuary in evaluating the plan's accumulated plan benefit obligations and have adequately considered the qualifications of the actuary in determining the amounts and disclosures used in the financial statements and underlying accounting records. We did not give or cause any instructions to be given to specialists with respect to the values on amounts derived in an attempt to bias their work, and we are not otherwise aware of any matters that had an impact on the independence or objectivity of the actuary.

The actuarial valuations. A typical actuarial valuation includes a variety of information to be used by the auditor. For instance, the actuary will determine the accumulated plan benefit obligations for the plan. The auditor should agree this information to the plan's financial statements and to the Schedule B of the Form 5500 for the plan to determine that the plan has correctly reported the accumulated plan benefit information within the plan's financial statements, and also to determine that the actuary has the correct information regarding the plan's net assets available for benefits.

Another purpose of the actuarial valuation is to calculate the amount of plan sponsor contributions which are required to be made to the plan during the year to satisfy the ERISA minimum funding requirements, and also the maximum deductible contributions that may be made by the plan sponsor for IRS purposes. The auditor should determine that the contributions made by the plan sponsor, as reported on the plan's statement of changes in net assets available for benefits during the year, are within the range of contributions reported in the actuarial valuation, are at least equal to the ERISA minimum funding requirements, and do not exceed the maximum tax deductible amount.

In order for the auditor to determine that the actuary has all of the relevant information regarding the plan and demonstrates an adequate understanding of it to enable the actuary to prepare the accumulated plan benefit information, the auditor will want to review the section of the actuarial valuation which contains the summary of plan provisions. Within this section, the actuary will highlight key provisions of the plan that are critical to its operation, such as the benefit formula, date of last plan amendment, participants covered by the plan, and date of plan's inception. In order to ensure that the summary of plan provisions as reported by the actuary is accurate, the auditor should compare this information to the plan document and any relevant plan amendments for consistency. In addition, to the extent that the auditor has been made aware of amendments that have been executed by plan management, the auditor should determine that the actuary has received information regarding the amendment. This can be accomplished by reviewing the summary of plan provisions, and specifically, the date listed as the date of the latest plan amendment. The auditor may also review the sections within the plan document which have changed to ensure that the actuary has appropriately reflected the impact of such amendments in the summary of plan provisions.

The actuarial valuation will also include census information regarding the plan, which provides a summary of the total number of active, terminated vested, and retired participants as of the benefit information date. In addition, although not generally provided with the actuarial valuation, the auditor may request from the actuary the detailed demographic information for the plan which will list detailed information for each group of plan participants (actives, retirees, terminated vested participants), such as their hire date, termination date, date of birth, date of retirement, and average salary. In order to determine that the actuary has taken into consideration the complete population for the plan, the auditor may perform either procedure 1 or procedure 2 listed below relative to the census data and demographic data, depending upon the auditor's assessment of the effectiveness of the communication between the plan sponsor and the actuary regarding changes in census data. (Note that procedures 3 and 4 listed below should be performed by auditors in any case.)

1. For each of the significant components (actives, retirees, and terminated vested participants, including beneficiaries), the auditor should independently obtain information from the plan sponsor (such as from the payroll system or benefit payment register) to determine the number of actives, retirees, and terminated vested participants as of the benefit information date. The auditor should then compare the information to that reported by the actuary to determine consistency in the census data.
2. The auditor may also perform detailed testing procedures relative to the demographic data by making a selection of participants from the plan sponsor's personnel files and agreeing relevant information such as birth date, hire date, and salary to the detailed demographic information received from the actuary. The auditor should then perform the same procedures but by making the selections from the actuary's detailed demographic data and agreeing back to the information from the plan sponsor's personnel files to uncover any discrepancies.
3. The auditor should also periodically review the actuarial assumptions to determine that they are still appropriate, particularly if there have been significant changes in the mix of the plan's portfolio of investment assets or if there have been any other such changes which may warrant a revision of the actuarial assumptions.
4. Any exceptions identified in the procedures performed above should be quantified and brought to the attention of the plan sponsor and to the actuary for clarification and resolution. In addition, the auditor should evaluate

the exceptions and determine the effect of such exceptions upon accumulated plan benefits.

With respect to the information included within the changes in accumulated plan benefits from the prior benefit information date to the current benefit information date, the auditor should perform the following procedures.

NOTE: With respect to the line items presented below, while the actuary is a specialist used to determine the accumulated plan benefit obligations, ultimately, the auditors are required to take responsibility for amounts included in the plan's financial statements and should be comfortable with all amounts presented in the financial statements which relate to the plan's accumulated plan benefits.

1. For amounts listed as benefit payments, the auditor should agree such amount to the amount of benefit payments reported in the plan's statement of changes in net assets available for benefits.
2. For the changes in actuarial assumptions line item, while the auditor may not be able to quantify or recompute the amount as a result of a change in an actuarial assumption, the auditor should review the summary of actuarial assumptions which appears as part of the actuarial valuation and compare it to the summary included in the prior year's actuarial valuation. To the extent that the auditor identifies changes in the actuarial assumptions, the auditor should expect to see an amount listed in the accumulated plan benefits summary table as a change in actuarial assumptions. The auditor should also determine that the change in the actuarial assumption appears reasonable, given circumstances for the plan. An absence of a change in assumptions likewise suggests the absence of an amount appearing as a change in actuarial assumptions.
3. For the plan amendment line item, similar to the discussion above, the auditor may not be able to recompute the amount listed as a plan amendment; however, based upon the knowledge obtained about the plan during the course of the audit, the auditor should determine whether any plan amendments have been effective or adopted which would affect the accumulated plan benefits obligation for the plan. In certain cases, depending upon the nature of the plan amendment, the auditor may be able to estimate the impact that an amendment will have upon accumulated plan benefits. This is particularly applicable in the case of plan amendments which increase the amount of benefits payable to participants on a monthly or annual basis.
4. The increase for interest due to decrease in the discount period line item may be readily recomputed by the auditor by multiplying the accumulated plan benefits as of the prior benefit information date by the assumed rate of return on plan assets used by the actuary and disclosed in the summary of actuarial assumptions. In certain cases, the increase for interest may be re-

computed as the average accumulated plan benefit balance multiplied by the assumed rate of return on plan assets.

5. For amounts appearing as benefits accumulated--net, the auditor should determine the reasonability of the amount based upon general knowledge of the plan and review of additional information included within the actuarial valuation, which may discuss the actual plan experience during the year covered by the actuarial valuation. The actual experience of the plan, as determined for the year and compared to the estimate for the year, flows through the benefits accumulated line item generally in the form of actuarial gains and losses. For example, to the extent that a plan realizes an actual return on plan investments which exceeds the estimated return by the actuary, this would result in an actuarial gain for the plan and would lower the plan's accumulated plan benefit obligations.
6. For other amounts which may appear in the reconciliation of accumulated plan benefits, such as transfers due to plan mergers, the auditor should assess the reasonability of the amounts listed based upon activities of the plan during the year.

Any discrepancies identified during the performance of the procedures previously listed should be discussed with the appropriate levels of plan management to be resolved to the satisfaction of the auditor.

These procedures represent suggested approaches for auditing the accounts of a defined benefit pension plan. Consideration should also be given to the concepts discussed in the chapters on planning, internal control, investments, other accounting and auditing considerations, auditors' reports and financial statements and disclosures. The material presented within those chapters is important and applicable to defined benefit pension plans. Chapter 12, Auditors' Reports, includes helpful examples of auditors' reports and Chapter 13, Financial Statements and Disclosures, includes illustrative financial statements and sample footnote disclosures, which are relevant to defined benefit pension plans.

OTHER FINANCIAL STATEMENT DISCLOSURES

In addition to the information regarding accumulated plan benefits and net assets of the plan, the plan's financial statements should include a discussion of additional matters in accordance with the provisions of SFAS 35. These additional disclosures would include the following:

1. A brief discussion of the provisions of the plan document including, but not limited to, a description of: the employees covered by the plan; benefits provided under the plan; forms of benefit payments to be made to retirees (joint and survivor annuities or lump-sum payments); vesting schedule for employer contributions; description of employee contributions, if applicable; and name of plan trustee and/or custodian. Alternatively, the footnotes may include a note which refers readers to the plan document for a sum-

mary of the plan's provisions as opposed to discussing the provisions within the footnotes. It is unusual, however, not to include some basic information regarding the plan within the plan's footnote disclosures.

2. The plan should disclose significant accounting policies such as its use of estimates in determining amounts included within the financial statements, any concentrations of risks of investments, and if significant costs of administering the plan are paid by the plan sponsor.
3. For plans which are contributory (contributions made by employees), the plan should disclose the method for determining employee contributions and the interest rate credited to such contributions.
4. A discussion of the methods used to determine the fair value of investments held by the plan. This would include all investments held by the plan including insurance contracts and those for which an active market exists for the investment and those which are not readily marketable.
5. To the extent that the plan invests in allocated contracts for participants (not considered to be plan assets), disclosure should be made of the amount of such assets held by the plan as well as the plan's policy regarding the purchase of these types of contracts from insurance companies. Any dividend income related to these allocated contracts should be disclosed, although it is permissible to net the amount of administrative expenses paid to the insurance companies for administering the contracts against the amount of dividend income earned.
6. The plan's financial statements should separately disclose any single investment which exceeds 5% of net assets available for benefits as of the end of the plan year. To the extent that the investment is already listed separately in the statement of net assets available for benefits, the investment is not required to be disclosed again in the footnotes.
7. The plan's financial statements should disclose the net appreciation (depreciation) in fair value of investments by major class of investment, such as equities or fixed income securities, as well as segregating the net appreciation (depreciation) as generated by investments whose fair value is determined by quoted market prices (such as an investment in a mutual fund) from the amount generated by investments whose fair value is estimated (such as a limited partnership or real estate).
8. If the plan invests in a master trust along with other employee benefit plans of the plan sponsor, the financial statements should include the following disclosures: a general description of the types of investments held by the master trust (equity, debt, fixed income) and the amounts of such assets at the end of the year; the components of investment income earned by the master trust during the year (interest, dividends, net appreciation/depreciation); the plan's percentage of the total master trust's investments at the end of the year; and a discussion of the method used by the master trust to allocate investments and investment income to the participating plans.

9. A discussion of the significant actuarial assumptions used by the actuary in determining the plan's accumulated plan benefits. This would include disclosure of the average retirement age, mortality tables used, assumed long-term rate of return on plan investments (discount rate), and any other significant assumptions applicable under the circumstances.
10. To the extent that a change has been made in the assumptions used by the actuary during the current year as compared to those used in the prior year, such changes should also be disclosed. For example, the actuary may change the assumed long-term rate of return on plan investments due to a change in the actual performance of plan assets over time, and the prior and current assumed long-term rates of return should be disclosed in the plan's financial statements. As a general note, the actuary's assumptions should not usually change dramatically from one plan year to another in a relatively stable market scenario.
11. Additional changes in circumstances which may significantly affect a plan's accumulated plan benefits would be significant plan amendments or the partial or full termination of a plan. A partial termination of a defined benefit pension plan results in the full vesting of accrued benefits of those participants. If a plan is fully terminated, this would then require the plan's financial statements, including accumulated plan benefit information, to be recorded on the liquidation basis of accounting. Presentation of the accumulated plan benefit information, using the liquidation basis as opposed to the ongoing basis of accounting, normally represents a significant change in actuarial assumptions which would require disclosure. With the liquidation basis of accounting, all participants' (and beneficiaries') benefits become fully vested, which is one of the most significant changes from adopting the liquidation basis of accounting. In addition, the various disclosures which are typically included in the footnotes to a plan's financial statements regarding the vesting of benefits will change with the liquidation basis of accounting.
12. A discussion of the plan's funding policy including the actuarial method used by the actuary for determining required contributions to the plan and a discussion as to whether the plan has satisfied ERISA's minimum funding requirements during the year. If the plan has failed to meet ERISA's minimum funding standards during the year, that fact should be disclosed as well as the remedial action to be taken by the plan sponsor including obtaining the appropriate waivers from the IRS.
13. The federal tax status of the plan, which should indicate if the plan has or has not received a favorable determination letter from the IRS. To the extent that the plan has been amended since receiving the latest determination letter from the IRS, that fact should be disclosed as well as plan management's belief as to if they believe that the plan's tax-qualified status has been maintained. If plan management has not yet requested a determination

letter from the IRS, or has requested a letter but not yet received a response from the IRS, that should likewise be disclosed. Information regarding whether a plan has or has not received a favorable determination letter is not required to be disclosed under generally accepted accounting principles but is required by ERISA.

14. From a tax perspective, to the extent that a plan has entered into a voluntary compliance program sponsored by either the DOL or the IRS, consideration should be given to the disclosure of such a fact as well as plan management's assessment as to the potential impact upon the plan. In addition, consideration should be given to potential modifications that may need to be made to the independent auditors' report relative to the plan's tax-qualified status.
15. A description of significant plan amendments which have been adopted during the year and disclosure of the expected impact of such amendments upon the plan's accumulated plan benefits. The expected impact of such amendments should be available as it would be a rare plan sponsor who would accept an amendment to a plan without knowing the cost of the plan amendment.
16. A description of the general priorities upon termination of the plan including: the priority order of participants' claims to the assets of the plan upon plan termination and benefits guaranteed by the PBGC, including a discussion of the application of the PBGC guaranty to any recent plan amendments. If the above information is included within the plan document, reference can be made to the plan document for a discussion of the priorities in the event of a plan termination, as opposed to discussing the details in the footnotes to the plan's financial statements. The PBGC will not approve a plan termination unless the plan is fully funded or distressed. In other words, a fully funded plan is one in which the plan's net assets available for benefits exceeds the plan's accumulated plan benefit obligations as calculated using the liquidation basis of accounting. A distressed plan is one in which the plan sponsor is in liquidation, in bankruptcy, in insolvency proceedings, or has filed for Chapter 11 bankruptcy, and the costs of providing pension coverage have become unreasonably burdensome to the plan sponsor.
17. A discussion of any unusual events or transactions occurring after the latest benefit information date but before the issuance of the plan's financial statements that might affect the usefulness of the financial statements in determining the ability of the plan to pay its benefits in the future. Such types of events may include plan mergers, plan terminations, or significant plan amendments that increase the amount of benefits payable under the plan. Disclosure should be made of the expected impact of such events upon the plan's financial statements, and if not yet determinable, such a fact

should be explained including the reason why an impact cannot yet be determined.

18. In the event that the plan has entered into any nonexempt transactions during the year (i.e., prohibited transactions), to the extent that such transactions are material to the plan's financial statements, disclosure should be made of a description of such transactions and the corrective action being taken by the plan sponsor in relation to the transactions. This information is also required to be reported in the supplemental schedules which are part of the plan's Form 5500 filing.
19. If the plan engaged in significant transactions during the year with a related party (other than the arm's-length transactions with the plan's trustee/ custodian of plan assets), a description of the nature and amount of the transactions should be included in the footnotes to the plan's financial statements. In addition, any employer securities held by the plan should be disclosed in the footnotes to the plan's financial statements.

SFAS 105, 107, AND 119

Any additional disclosure requirements pursuant to SFAS 107, *Disclosures about Fair Value of Financial Instruments*, should be included within the plan's financial statements. SFAS 107 requires the disclosure of the fair value of financial instruments for which it is practicable to estimate that value. In addition, any significant assumptions that were utilized to establish the fair value must be disclosed. SFAS 107 states

> *If it is not practicable for an entity to estimate the fair value of a financial instrument or a class of financial instruments, the following should be disclosed:*
>
> - *Information pertinent to estimating the fair value of that financial instrument or class of financial instruments, such as the carrying amount, effective interest rate and maturity, and*
> - *The reasons why it is not practicable to estimate fair value.*

Note, however, that SFAS 126, *Exemption from Certain Required Disclosures about Financial Instruments for Certain Nonpublic Entities*, provides that plans which satisfy all of the following criteria are not required to disclose the fair value of financial instruments: (1) the plan is a nonpublic entity (in other words, a Form 11-K filing is not required for the plan); (2) the plan's total assets are less than $100 million on the date of the plan's financial statements, and (3) the plan has no instrument that, in whole or in part, is accounted for as a derivative instrument under SFAS 133, *Accounting for Derivative Instruments and Hedging Activities*, during the reporting period.

SFAS 105, *Disclosure of Information about Financial Instruments with Off-Balance-Sheet Risk and Financial Instruments With Concentrations of Credit Risk,* established requirements for all entities to disclose information principally about financial instruments with off-balance-sheet risk of accounting loss. SFAS 119,

Disclosure about Derivative Financial Instruments and Fair Value of Financial Instruments, was issued in October 1994 and superseded SFAS 105. SFAS 119 expanded on the applicability of the disclosure requirements mandated by SFAS 105. The disclosure requirements established by SFAS 105 were as follows:

- The face, contract, or notional principal amount
- The nature and terms of the instruments and a discussion of their credit and market risk, cash requirements, and related accounting policies
- The accounting loss the entity would incur if any party to the financial instrument failed completely to perform according to the terms of the contract and the collateral or other security, if any, for the amount due proved to be of no value to the entity
- The entity's policy for requiring collateral or other security on financial instruments it accepts and a description of collateral on instruments presently held

SFAS 105 also added disclosure requirements related to information about significant concentrations of credit risk from an individual counterparty or groups of counterparties for all financial instruments. The following represent the disclosure requirements related to concentrations:

- Information about the activity, region, or economic characteristic that identifies the concentration
- The amount of the accounting loss due to credit risk the entity would incur if parties to the financial instruments that make up the concentration failed completely to perform according to the terms of the contracts and the collateral or other security, if any, for the amount due proved to be of no value to the entity
- The entity's policy of requiring collateral or other security to support financial instruments subject to credit risk, information about the entity's access to that collateral or other security, and the nature and a brief description of the collateral or other security supporting those financial instruments

SFAS 105 provided an exemption of the previously described disclosure requirements for the following:

- Insurance contracts, other than financial guarantees and investment contracts
- Unconditional purchase obligations
- Employers' and plans' obligations for pension benefits, postretirement health care and life insurance benefits, employee stock option and stock purchase plans, and other forms of deferred compensation arrangements
- Financial instruments of a pension plan, including plan assets, when subject to the accounting and reporting requirements of SFAS 87, *Employers' Accounting for Pensions*

- Substantively extinguished debt subject to the disclosure requirements of SFAS 76, *Extinguishment of Debt,* and any assets held in trust in connection with an in-substance defeasance of that debt

SFAS 119 requires disclosures about derivative financial instruments--futures; forward, swap, and option contracts; and other financial instruments with similar characteristics, such as interest-rate caps or floors and fixed-rate loan commitments. SFAS 119 established additional disclosure requirements about amounts, nature, and terms of derivative financial instruments that were not subject to the disclosure requirements under SFAS 105 because they did not result in off-balance-sheet risk of accounting loss. This statement also requires that a distinction be made between financial instruments held or issued for trading purposes and financial instruments held or issued for purposes other than trading. For options held and other derivative financial instruments not included in the scope of SFAS 105, an entity is required to disclose either in the body of the financial statements or in the accompanying notes the following information by category of financial instrument:

- The face or contract amount (or notional principal amount if there is no face or contract amount)
- The nature and terms, including, at a minimum, a discussion of the (1) the credit and market risk of those instruments, (2) the cash requirements of those instruments, and (3) the related accounting policy pursuant to the requirements of APB Opinion 22, *Disclosure of Accounting Policies*

Additional disclosure requirements based on the classification of the financial instrument (i.e., held or issued for trading purposes or held and issued for purposes other than trading) were also established with SFAS 119.

ADDITIONAL DISCLOSURES FOR DERIVATIVES

SFAS 133 was issued in June 1998 and it establishes accounting and reporting standards for these derivative instruments and hedging activities. The application date of SFAS 133 was delayed to plan years beginning after June 15, 2000, through the issuance of SFAS 137, *Accounting for Derivative Instruments and Hedging Activities--Deferral of the Effective Date of FASB Statement 133.* In accordance with SFAS 133, the following additional disclosures should be made when a plan invests in the purchase or sale of derivative instruments.

Fair Value Hedges

Fair value hedges are instruments that hedge the exposure to changes in fair value of an asset or liability. For derivative instruments as well as nonderivative instruments that may give rise to foreign currency transaction gains or losses that have been designated and have qualified as fair value hedging instruments and for the related hedged items the following applies:

- The net gain or loss recognized in earnings during the reporting period representing (1) the amount of the hedges' ineffectiveness and (2) the component of the derivative instruments' gain or loss, if any, excluded from the assessment of hedge effectiveness, and a description of where the net gain or loss is reported in the statement of income or other statement of financial performance
- The amount of net gain or loss recognized in earnings when a hedged firm commitment no longer qualifies as a fair value hedge

Cash Flow Hedges

For derivative instruments that have been designated and have qualified as cash flow hedging instruments and for the related hedged transactions the following applies:

- The net gain or loss recognized in earnings during the reporting period representing (1) the amount of the hedges' ineffectiveness and (2) the component of the derivative instruments' gain or loss, if any, excluded from the assessment of hedge effectiveness, and a description of where the net gain or loss is reported in the statement of changes in net assets available for benefits
- Description of the transactions or other events that will result in the reclassification into earnings of gains and losses, and the estimated net amount of the existing gains or losses at the reporting date that is expected to be reclassified into earnings within the next twelve months
- The maximum length of time over which the entity is hedging its exposure to the variability in future cash flows for forecasted transactions, excluding those forecasted transactions related to the payment of variable interest on existing financial instruments
- The amount of gains and losses reclassified into earnings as a result of the discontinuance of cash flow hedges because it is probable that the original forecasted transactions will not occur

COMPARATIVE FINANCIAL STATEMENTS

As a plan's financial statements are generally presented in a comparative format to comply with the provisions of ERISA, the disclosures required above for items covered by the statement of net assets available for benefits would need to cover both the current plan year and the prior plan year, while disclosures required for items covering the statement of changes in net assets available for benefits would need to cover only the current year (unless comparative statements of changes in net assets available for benefits are presented).

DEFINED BENEFIT PENSION PLANS WITH 401(h) FEATURES

Certain defined benefit pension plans include a component for postretirement medical benefits pursuant to the provisions of Section 401(h) of the IRC. This particular section allows employers to fund a portion of their postretirement medical benefit obligations through a 401(h) account included within their defined benefit pension plans, subject to certain limitations and restrictions.

The funding of the 401(h) feature may be accomplished through the transfer of excess pension plan assets or through additional contributions to the 401(h) account by the plan sponsor. The assets which are transferred to the 401(h) account and the related investment income earned on those assets are only permitted to be used to pay the qualified current retiree health benefits for the taxable year of the transfer. Any assets that are transferred to the 401(h) account but that are not used to pay eligible health benefits during the year of the asset transfer must be transferred out from the defined benefit pension plan and treated as a reversion to the employer, which is subject to a 20% excise tax imposed by the IRS. Additionally, the IRC permits employers to allocate up to 25% of total contributions made to the defined benefit pension plan, to be used for the 401(h) account. If the entire amount of such contributions allocated to the 401(h) account is not used during the year, they may be accumulated for future retiree medical expenses in the 401(h) account. The assets allocated to the 401(h) account may only be used to pay current retiree health benefits, which are the obligation of a separate health and welfare plan administered by the employer; the assets may not be used to pay the pension obligations of the defined benefit plan.

During 1999, the AICPA issued Statement of Position 99-2, *Accounting for and Reporting of Postretirement Medical Benefit 401(h) Features of Defined Benefit Pension Plans*, to clarify the accounting and reporting of 401(h) features of defined benefit pension plans for both the defined benefit pension plan and the health and welfare plan. SOP 99-2 requires the following for a defined benefit pension plan:

- Defined benefit pension plans need to record the aggregate amount of net assets held in a 401(h) account related to health and welfare plan obligations for retirees as both assets and liabilities on the face of the statement of net assets available for pension benefits in order to arrive at net assets available for pension benefits
- 401(h) account assets used to fund health benefits, and the changes in those assets, should be reported in the financial statements of the health and welfare benefit plan. Benefit obligations related to the 401(h) account are also required to be reflected in the health and welfare plan's financial statements, if any
- Defined benefit pension plans need to disclose the fact the 401(h) account assets are available only to pay retirees' health benefits
- Health and welfare benefit plans should disclose in the notes to the financial statements the fact that retiree health benefits are funded partially through a 401(h) account of the defined benefit pension plan
- The statement of changes in net assets for the defined benefit pension plan should show only the changes in net assets of the defined benefit pension

plan and not any of the components of the changes in the net assets in the 401(h) account. The only amounts that should be reported in the statement of changes in net assets for the defined benefit plan are qualified transfers to the 401(h) account and/or any unused or unspent amounts (including allocated income) in the 401(h) account at the end of the year that were qualified transfers of excess pension plan assets that should have been but were not transferred back to the defined benefit pension plan.

ERISA requires that the 401(h) assets be reported as assets of the defined benefit pension plan. In addition, ERISA requires a plan's financial statements to include a note explaining differences between amounts reported in the financial statements and the amounts reported in the Form 5500. Because ERISA requires 401(h) accounts to be reported in the financial statements of the defined benefit pension plan, a reconciliation of the net assets reported in the financial statements to those reported in the Form 5500 is required. The reconciliation should be accompanied by a discussion of the 401(h) account, explaining clearly that the assets in the 401(h) account are not available to pay pension benefits.

This SOP is effective for financial statements for plan years beginning after December 15, 1998, although earlier application is encouraged. Chapter 13, Financial Statements and Disclosures, provides an example of illustrative financial statements and disclosures for a defined benefit pension plan with 401(h) account features. Also, see Chapter 9, Accounting, Auditing, and Reporting for Health and Welfare Plans, for additional information.

CASH-BALANCE PLANS

One of the specialized types of defined benefit pension plans which has become popular in recent years is the cash-balance plan. A cash-balance plan is a defined benefit plan that maintains hypothetical "accounts" for participants. The plan sponsor credits a participant's account with a certain number of dollars each plan year and promises earnings at a specified rate. Interest on the amount contributed is credited at a stated rate, which is often different from the plan's actual rate of investment return. The interest rate may be modified prospectively, as long as there are no reductions in the participant's benefit accrued to date. The formula for determining the amount of the actual contribution to be credited as a "contribution" to participants' accounts may be varied from year to year, if the plan sponsor properly amends the plan prior to the beginning of the year and provides notice to participants. The principal advantage of a cash-balance plan is the ability of participants to watch their hypothetical account balances grow (similar to a defined contribution pension plan) while providing certainty as to the interest to be credited to participants. With the cash-balance defined benefit pensions plans, participants bear no investment risk. The plan sponsor bears the risk that the plan's actual rate of return may fall below the stated rate of interest to be credited to participants' accounts.

In many cases, plan sponsors are introducing cash-balance plans as new benefit plans to employees while in other cases, plan sponsors are converting traditional defined benefit pension plans to cash-balance plans. When a traditional defined benefit pension plan is converted to a cash-balance plan, the plan remains a defined benefit pension plan, the benefit formula changes, but the accumulated plan benefit obligation may not significantly change, depending upon the age of the plan's participants. The concepts included within this chapter regarding the accounting, auditing, and reporting for defined benefit pension plans also apply to cash-balance plans.

9 ACCOUNTING, AUDITING, AND REPORTING FOR HEALTH AND WELFARE PLANS

INTRODUCTION

Health and welfare plans provide various benefits to plan participants. As mentioned in Chapter 2, Types of Plans, such benefits include, but are not limited to, medical, prescription drugs, dental, vision and psychiatric benefits, dependent care, life insurance, accidental death or dismemberment insurance, apprenticeships, tuition assistance, day care, and legal services. Health and welfare plans may be either defined benefit plans or defined contribution plans. The benefits provided by the plan and other provisions of the plan are included in the plan document. This chapter will provide a discussion of the accounting and auditing concepts involved with health and welfare plans.

COMPARISON OF DEFINED BENEFIT AND DEFINED CONTRIBUTION HEALTH AND WELFARE PLANS

Defined benefit health and welfare plans differ from defined contribution health and welfare plans in that a defined benefit plan provides a specific benefit to plan participants. For example, a defined benefit health and welfare plan may provide participants with 80% coverage of certain medical expenses, or the plan may provide for the payment of a specified amount to plan participants or their beneficiaries upon the occurrence of an event, for example, death benefits. Medical expenses under a defined benefit plan may be paid in one of three ways: directly to the plan participant, to an insurance company, or to the service provider on behalf of the plan participant. Some plan obligations of defined benefit health and welfare plans are calculated through an actuarial valuation; for example, most postretirement obligations and, in some cases, estimates of claims incurred but not reported (IBNR) and postemployment obligations. Defined contribution health and welfare plans provide each participant with an individual account into which the participant makes contributions and the employer may provide contributions. For example, a defined contribution plan may allow participants to contribute a specified amount monthly to the plan to be available for payment of qualified medical expenses. In a defined contribution plan, the plan's obligations are limited to the total of the balances of the participant accounts as the benefits to be paid for each participant are limited to the amounts contributed to the participant's individual account. The plan assets represent the total of the balances of the participant accounts, plus any applicable receivables.

Employers may choose to use insurance to provide for all or a portion of the benefits of a defined benefit plan. For plans offering benefits provided through insurance, the amounts contributed to the trust of a funded or partially funded plan are premium payments to be paid to the insurance company. The plan obligation related to the insured benefits is the premium payable. For insured benefits there are no IBNR, or postretirement or postemployment obligations, as the insurance company assumes the risk of loss in exchange for the plan's payment of premiums to the insurance company; therefore, the obligation to provide benefits is the insurance company's. Insurance is generally not used to provide benefits for a defined contribution health and welfare plan.

OPERATION AND ADMINISTRATION

Health and welfare plans may be sponsored by one employer, a single-employer plan, or they may be sponsored by more than one employer, either a multiemployer or multiple-employer plan, depending on the existence of collective bargaining agreements which relate to multiemployer plans. Plans that are established by companies under common control qualify as single-employer plans. A multiple-employer welfare arrangement (MEWA) is defined by ERISA as an "employee welfare benefit plan or other arrangement (other than an employee welfare benefit plan) which is established or maintained for the purpose of offering or providing welfare plan benefits to the employees of two or more employers (including one or more self-employed individuals), or to their beneficiaries, except that such term does not include any such plan or other arrangements which is established or maintained under or pursuant to one or more agreements which the Secretary of Labor finds to be collective bargaining agreements, by a rural electric cooperative, or by a rural telephone cooperative association." MEWAs may be established by a group of employers joining together, generally to purchase group health insurance, often using self-funded arrangements.

Plan Document

Health and welfare plans are typically established pursuant to a legal document entitled the plan instrument or plan document. The plan document provides information regarding the various provisions of the plan, such as employees covered, eligibility requirements, contributions required by participants, definition of the benefits provided under the plan, and the procedures for payment of claims. The plan document also identifies the individual(s) who is(are) responsible for the operation and administration of the plan (otherwise known as the plan fiduciary). The plan fiduciary is usually an officer or employee of the plan sponsor, such as the vice president of human resources or the chief financial officer, who generally reports to the board of directors or senior management. The fiduciary's primary responsibilities include operating the plan in accordance with the provisions of the plan document and applicable laws such as ERISA and the IRC and making policy decisions as they relate to the management of the plan's assets, payment of benefits, and other plan provisions. Plan documents are required by ERISA to be in writing and may take the format of a prototype plan, which is an industry-standard plan document customized by many plan sponsors to address the specifics of the particular plan.

Alternatively, the plan document may be one written specifically for the plan by plan management.

Funding the Plan

Health and welfare plans may be established to be self-funded plans, insured plans, or a combination of the two. In a self-funded plan, the plan sponsor retains the financial risk for claim payments. In an insured plan, the plan sponsor transfers this risk to one or more insurance companies. Self-funded plans are funded by the plan sponsor, both the plan sponsor and participants, and, at times, by participants only. Plan sponsors of self-funded plans may use a trust to fund the plan, such as an IRC Section 501(c)(9) Voluntary Employee Benefit Association (VEBA) trust. When using a VEBA trust, contributions by the plan sponsor and/or participants are deposited and amounts are withdrawn as necessary to pay claims directly or to reimburse the third-party administrator for payment of claims. As discussed later in the chapter, stop-loss insurance is often purchased by employers with self-funded plans, to limit the financial exposure for claims. In some cases, plan sponsors do utilize pass-through trusts, which are used only to receive contributions and pay claims; these trusts do not hold any assets at the end of the plan year. As a result, the existence of such trusts may be difficult to determine. However, the use of a trust by the plan does trigger an audit requirement for the plan.

Cafeteria Plans and Flexible Spending Accounts

Many plan sponsors have an IRC Section 125 Cafeteria Plan, which they sponsor either as part of or in addition to other health and welfare plans. This plan (referred to as "cafeteria plan") allows a participant the opportunity to contribute on a pretax basis through payroll deductions to a health and welfare plan for qualified benefits. Employees may elect to not participate in the plan and therefore continue to receive compensation, without pretax deductions for contributions to a health and welfare plan. Through a cafeteria plan, participants may receive various qualified nontaxable health and welfare benefits (payment of a participant's portion of premiums into a group insurance plan and the use of flexible spending accounts). The qualified benefits--for example, the payment of medical or dental benefits--are not included in the participant's taxable income. The cafeteria plan can be implemented in conjunction with a health and welfare plan or can itself be a fringe-benefit plan.

One popular type of IRC Section 125 plan is a flexible spending account (FSA) arrangement. In a flexible spending account arrangement, participants elect to make pretax contributions throughout the year, which total the amount of qualified expenses that they expect to incur. The contributions are made through payroll deductions, and reimbursement of the allowable expenses is made from the account directly to the participant. Generally, there are two types of flexible spending arrangements: health care and dependent care. Each type of flexible spending account is established separately (i.e., accounts for different types of benefits may not be combined).

A health care spending account reimburses participants for medical expenses, such as deductibles, copays, and other out-of-pocket expenses not covered by the medical plan. A health care spending account may also reimburse the participant for such items as eyeglasses and contact lenses. Premiums for individual health insurance policies, however, are not considered qualifying expenses. A dependent care spending account reimburses participants for the cost of qualified expenses, often for day care for dependent children. In both cases, the participant elects to contribute an annual amount to the account based on an estimate of expenses. After the participant incurs qualifying expenses, reimbursement from the account may be requested. The length of time after the end of the plan year that claims may be submitted for reimbursement is established by the plan sponsor and is often sixty to ninety days following the plan year-end. The balance that remains at the end of the reimbursement period, if any, is then forfeited by the participant and can be used to offset administrative expenses or other defined expenses, as allowed by IRC Section 125. Under the concept of immediate availability, the amount of the participant's annual election must be made available on the first day of the plan year for health FSAs. Therefore, if during the year the amount of expenses incurred exceeds the amount of participant contributions that have accumulated at that point during the year, the plan sponsor is required to fund the plan to provide for incurred expenses. The maximum amount that the plan sponsor would be required to fund, however, is the remaining amount that will be collected from the participant during the year. Exposure exists for employers to the extent that a participant may incur expenses exceeding his/her contributions and be reimbursed for the amount, then leave the employment of the company before all of the participant's annual contributions are made.

For example, a participant in a health flexible spending account plan made an annual election to contribute a total of $2,080 ($40 per week x 52 weeks). In April she incurred qualified expenses of $1,000. Although her account balance was $640 ($40 per week x 16 weeks), she would be reimbursed for the amount of the entire claim. If she left the employment of the employer shortly after receiving her reimbursement, the excess $320 reimbursed to her would not be recoverable from her individually but would be offset by forfeitures, if any, made by participants who have remaining balances in their account at the end of the year, as previously discussed.

Flexible spending accounts may be used to provide for the reimbursement of co-insurance amounts paid by participants. For example, if a health and welfare plan provides for 75% payment of the claim amounts and participants are required to pay the remaining 25% of the claim amounts, a flexible spending account could be established to reimburse participants for payments required to be paid by them at the time the claim is due.

FUNDING

In an insured health and welfare plan, the plan benefits are provided through insurance purchased by the plan from an insurance company. Insured plans may involve several types of funding arrangements. Plans that receive participant contributions and hold them in a trust--including self-funded, insured, or combination plans--may be required to be audited, depending on their size. The various funding arrangements and audit requirements are discussed later within this chapter.

ERISA generally requires that the assets of all employee benefit plans, including welfare plans, be held in a trust. However, as stated in ERISA Technical Release 92-01, the DOL is not enforcing ERISA's general requirement regarding the establishment of a trust to hold plan assets, including contributions from participants, for Section 125 Cafeteria Plans and other welfare plans that meet any of the following criteria:

> *Benefits are paid solely from the general assets of the employer (or employee organization) maintaining the plan; or Benefits are provided exclusively through insurance contracts or through a health maintenance organization (HMO), the premiums for which are paid directly by the employer (or employee organization) from its general assets and partly from contributions from its employees (or members), provided that contributions by participants are forwarded to the insurance company or HMO by the employer (or employee organization) within three months of receipt; or*
>
> *Benefits are paid partly from the general assets of the sponsor and partly through insurance contracts or through a qualified HMO [as stipulated above].*

To maximize the tax deductibility of health care expenses, an IRC Section 501(c)(9) Voluntary Employee Benefit Association (VEBA) trust may be established to fund some or all of the obligations of a welfare benefit plan. A VEBA allows an employer that self-insures part or all of its health programs to obtain an accelerated tax deduction by partially prefunding the plan. Employers may deduct their VEBA contribution, to a maximum amount defined by the IRC Section 419(a), in the year the contribution is made rather than in the year in which the benefits are incurred or paid. VEBAs may be used to fund current, postretirement, or postemployment health and welfare benefits and must be established pursuant to the IRC. In many cases, however, employers avoid establishing VEBAs due to the complexity of the tax rules related to deductibility of health care expenses.

Health plans are typically funded through various types of arrangements with insurance companies. The type of arrangement that the plan has with an insurance company generally determines the extent of the plan's assets and its benefit obligations. There is a variety of types of insurance arrangements available to provide for plan benefits and, in each case, specific benefits are covered by the insurance company. The following discussion of insurance funding arrangements, cost-sharing structures, and medical plan delivery systems relate to plans which provide various types of health benefits.

Insurance Funding Arrangements

There is a variety of insurance arrangements available to provide for plan benefits and in each case specific benefits are covered by the insurance company. However, in some cases, the only services provided by the insurance company are plan administration services. Some of the arrangements discussed below provide benefits to participants of only one plan and some of the arrangements are established by the insurance company to provide benefits to participants of multiple plans that are unrelated (e.g., not a multiemployer plan). Insurance arrangements are typically categorized by who has the obligation to pay plan benefits and how plan benefits and expenses are funded.

Health and welfare plans may include a combination of the following arrangements and features. These various "funding arrangements" result in various types of assets and liabilities for financial statement reporting purposes, depending on whether the plan sponsor or the insurance company assumes the plan's financial risk. The party that assumes the risk records the obligations for claims payable at the date of the financial statements and an estimate of the amount of claims which have been incurred (that is, the medical service has been provided to the participant) but not submitted for payment at the date of the financial statements. These claims are considered to be incurred but not reported (IBNR) claims.

Health and welfare plans have a variety of unique accounting and reporting requirements related to their benefit obligations and plan assets. The contracts and arrangements that health and welfare plans have with insurance companies should be reviewed and analyzed to identify the type of arrangement in effect and the resulting types of assets and obligations applicable for the plan. Following is a discussion of the various types of insurance funding arrangements.

Group insurance arrangements. Group insurance arrangements are arrangements that provide benefits to participants of two or more unrelated plans, fully insures the benefits of one or more welfare plans of each participating employer, and uses a trust to hold the insurance contracts and remit the payment of premiums to the insurance company. The party responsible for funding the arrangement, and for assuming risks associated with the arrangement, will depend upon the type of arrangement that has been established for the plan. Summarized below are the various types of insurance funding arrangements which may be structured as group insurance arrangements by the plan sponsor.

Fully insured pooled arrangement. Generally, the only obligation of the plan under a fully insured pooled arrangement is the payment of the insurance premium. The insurance company pools the experience of the plan with that of other similar arrangements and fully assumes the financial risk of adverse experience. A plan may be fully insured or a portion of the benefits may be fully insured (and the remaining portion self-funded). One example is a plan that provides life insurance benefits through a fully insured pooled arrangement and medical benefits through a self-funded arrangement. In fully insured pooled arrangements, premiums are calculated based primarily upon demographic factors of the group; therefore, the amount of incurred claims in one year does not affect future premium increases. Premiums, which are for current year coverage only, are typically paid monthly, and claims are filed with the insurance company as they are incurred, at which time the insurance company pays the claim. A plan with this type of arrangement generally would not have plan assets, such as deposits or other reserves, held by the insurance company.

Fully insured experience-rated arrangement. Under a fully insured experience-rated arrangement, the insurance company fully assumes the plan's financial risk, including the payment of any claims payable and incurred but not reported claims, in the event of contract termination. The premium charged to the plan under an experience-rated arrangement is determined based on the historical claims experience of the plan. The insurance company still pays the claim, but tracks the benefit payments for the plan. A typical delivery system for fully insured experience-rated arrangements are preferred provider organizations or comprehensive indemnity plans (described later in the chapter). If the total of the benefit payments and administrative costs to serve the plan exceed the premium of the plan, the loss is generally borne by the insurance company, but often future premiums are affected. This scenario does not result in the recording of an asset or obligation by the plan. Occasionally, the insurance contract stipulates that the loss may be charged to the plan over future years until it has been recovered, resulting in a benefit obligation for the plan. For example, if total benefit payments for a given plan year is $10 million and administrative expenses equal $2 million, the total cost of the plan to the insurance company would be $12 million. If premiums collected for the plan year totaled $11 million, the insurance company would have incurred expenses related to the plan of $1 million in excess of the premium collected. A loss incurred by the insurance company, as previously described, would be included as a benefit obligation if such amount can be reasonably estimated and only if it is contractually allowable for the amount to be considered in setting future premiums or applied against future experience-rating refunds. If an amount is not included as a benefit obligation because the above criteria are not met, the financial statements should at least include disclosure of the existence of the excess claims, if known. Under these contracts, if the benefit payments and administrative costs of the plan are less than the premium payments, the plan may be entitled to a refund or credit against the next period's premium. This amount is usually called a "premium stabilization reserve" and is generally considered a plan asset. Other receivables or deposits with the insurance company may exist which could be considered to be plan assets. If amounts held by the insurance company are forfeitable in the event of contract termination, the effect on their recognition as a plan asset should be considered.

Self-funded with stop-loss insurance arrangement. Under this arrangement, the plan pays a predetermined amount for administrative services to a third party to pay claims as they are incurred and reported. The plan sponsor therefore assumes the plan's financial risk up to the stop-loss insurance limits. The stop-loss insurance provision limits the plan's obligation for each participant's or dependent's claims to an annual fixed dollar amount, for example, $100,000 (usually called specific stop-loss insurance), and/or limits the plan's total obligation to a percentage of a pre-established claims level, for example, 125% of expected claims (aggregate stop-loss insurance). Excesses over the fixed dollar limit or the preestablished percentage are borne by the insurance company. Claims are generally paid by the plan to the insurance company through a zero-balance plan-sponsor bank account that the insurance company has authority to access and draw upon periodically throughout the plan year as claims are incurred and processed. This type of arrangement generally results in no insurance-related assets for the plan. Because the plan sponsor assumes the plan's financial risk, various benefit obligations are reported including health claims payable, IBNR, and postemployment and postretirement liabilities.

Minimum premium plan arrangement. This arrangement is a hybrid of the fully insured experience-rated and the self-funded with stop-loss arrangements. Typically, the minimum premium plan contract is filed within each state as a fully insured contract, but operates very similarly to the self-funded with stop-loss arrangement. Much like the self-funded with stop-loss arrangement, the minimum premium plan arrangement provides for a predetermined payment for administrative services to the insurance carrier, and the subsequent payment of claims by the plan sponsor (or trust) as they are incurred and reported. One main difference between the self-funded with stop-loss arrangement is that the administrative expenses, network access fees, and insurance premiums are combined to formulate one "minimum premium" payable each billing cycle (for example, $50 per employee and $80 per dependent per month). Another major difference is that the insurance carrier makes final determination on payment of claims based on the plan document (not the plan sponsor). An example of how a minimum premium plan operates is that the plan sponsor pays the fixed "minimum premium" each month that includes all administrative costs of the plan. All claims within and up to the established thresholds are paid by the insurance company, often from the plan sponsor's bank account. A minimum premium plan arrangement differs from the fully insured experience-rated arrangement in that the minimum premium plan arrangement establishes a dollar threshold (similar to stop-loss) to determine the dollar amount of benefits that will be paid by the plan. All claims within and up to the established thresholds are paid by the insurance company and reimbursed by the plan. The plan therefore records benefit obligations, including health claims payable, IBNR, and postemployment and postretirement obligations. The obligation amounts are determined by the insurance company. The insurance company bears the responsibility for the payment of all claims in excess of this preestablished threshold. With this type of arrangement, the insurance company may require a deposit or reserve to be held by the insurance company for reimbursement of claims paid after termination of the contract, and these amounts may result in plan assets. Conversely, if the payment is not required until the termination of the contract, an obligation should be recorded by the plan.

Self-insured (administrative services only) arrangement. This arrangement is similar to the self-funded with stop-loss arrangement, except that there are no insurance provisions in place. Under an administrative service arrangement all obligations of the plan are borne by the plan. The insurance company provides only administrative services to the plan, such as claims processing and recordkeeping. This type of arrangement also generally results in no insurance-related plan assets but, as with the self-funded with stop-loss arrangement, because the plan sponsor assumes the plan's financial risk, various benefit obligations are reported including health claims payable, IBNR, and postemployment and postretirement liabilities.

In addition to the preestablished thresholds of claims or premium amounts as discussed above, plans often establish maximum annual or lifetime benefit claims to be paid to each participant. The types of arrangements that previously discussed are generally annual arrangements with the insurance company that cover annual premiums and claims incurred by current employees, COBRA participants, and retirees.

The type of insurance arrangement that the plan has with the insurance company will determine whether an amount should be recorded as a deposit with an insurance company or as a receivable due from an insurance company. Any deposits that are required by the insurance company should be reported as plan assets until they are used to satisfy an obligation of the plan. Reserves that are held by the insurance company should also be reported as plan assets only if the contract allows for return to plan sponsor (or trust) of such reserves and if truly expected to be an asset of the plan. Also, if the insurance arrangement allows for the plan to receive a refund of the excess of the premiums paid by the plan over the benefits that were paid and the administrative costs of the plan, a receivable due from the insurance company at the end of the plan year should be recorded, if the amount of the refund can be reasonably estimated and if the likelihood of receipt is probable. Historical experience is often required before recording such amounts.

Cost-Sharing Structure/Benefit Plan Design

Employers must decide which type of cost-sharing structure/benefit plan design to establish including determining the type of insurance funding arrangement. Cost sharing refers to how the costs of the benefits provided are split between the participant and the plan sponsor. Most cost-sharing structures can be grouped into one of two general categories that are referred to in this chapter as **front-end cost sharing** and **back-end utilization cost sharing**. The simplest method of front-end cost sharing is to collect from the participant an allocated portion of the insurance premium or premium equivalents, if self-funded or self-insured. The portion of the premium that is borne by the participant will vary from plan to plan. This method of cost sharing may be called premium cost splitting.

Back-end utilization cost sharing requires the participant to pay a deductible, coinsurance, or copays prior to being eligible to receive the benefits offered by the plan. The amount of the deductible will also vary from plan to plan. In a coinsurance arrangement, the participant is responsible for a defined percentage of the claim costs, and the plan sponsor will be responsible for the remaining percentage of claim costs. The percentage that the participant is responsible for will often vary dependent upon the arrangement, type of service that is being provided, or the provider. Also, under a coinsurance arrangement, a participant may be required to pay a deductible prior to being eligible to receive the benefits. For example, an arrangement may provide for the participant to pay 20% of health claim costs incurred, with the plan sponsor paying the remaining 80% of the claim cost. However, the 20/80 split may not be effective until the participant has met an annual deductible of $200. In a copay situation, the participant is responsible for a set dollar amount based upon the health service provided. In this type of arrangement, the participant may be responsible for paying $10 for general medical visits and the plan sponsor would pay the remainder of the fee. This type of arrangement is common in plans that use health maintenance organizations as a service provider. In both a coinsurance arrangement and a copay arrangement, there are typically annual caps, in excess of the deductibles, on the amount that the participant is responsible for paying in any one year.

As previously discussed, health and welfare plans generally include several cost-sharing features. For example, an insured plan may utilize both premium cost splitting and deductibles that result in the participant bearing some of the cost of the plan and the plan sponsor and insurance company bearing others. The chart that follows (Exhibit 1) lists common health care costs, which entity bears the cost, the timing of the payment, and the resulting effect on the plan's benefit obligations.

Medical Plan Delivery Systems

There are several types of medical plans, but the most prevalent are Health Maintenance Organizations (HMOs), Point-of-Service (POS) plans, Preferred Provider Organizations (PPOs), and Comprehensive Indemnity plans. Each has characteristics that make it unique from the others, but there are also similarities among the systems. Plans that use these delivery systems often utilize premium cost splitting to offset the plan sponsor's premium cost.

HMO. An HMO is defined as an organization that provides a full range of health services to an enrolled population (generally through employer sponsored plans) within a defined geographic region in return for a prepaid fixed premium for all services provided. HMOs typically rely upon the copay method of cost sharing. HMO plans require that all medical services be directed by the participant's selected primary care physician (PCP). Any medical care that is not directed by the PCP is often not eligible for reimbursement through the plan, unless in an emergency situation. Although HMO plans achieve greater potential cost effectiveness than other plans, there are more limitations to access of care for the participants. HMO plans are typically funded through fully insured or minimum premium arrangements.

POS. A POS is a plan that typically combines an HMO plan with a non-network/non-PCP approved benefit option. Essentially, participants have a choice

Exhibit 1: Types of Health Care Costs

Health care cost	*Cost borne by*	*Timing of payment*	*Responsibility for related obligations*
Premium cost splitting (e.g., participant pays $15 per pay period, employer pays remaining premium amount). Premium cost splitting is not a plan benefit.	Participant and plan sponsor	Participant--generally withheld from compensation each pay period Plan sponsor--generally paid monthly to insurance company.	Premium--plan obligations Claims--insurance company, therefore no plan benefit obligation
Deductible (e.g., $300 annually). A deductible is not a plan benefit; therefore, it is never a plan benefit obligation.	Participant	Occurrence of claims, to the annual maximum	Participant--no plan obligation
Coinsurance (e.g., 20% of claim cost paid by participant/80% of cost paid by plan sponsor). Coinsurance is not a plan benefit.	Participant and plan sponsor	Occurrence of claim or time of claim processing	Participant portion--no plan benefit obligation Plan sponsor portion--plan obligation This information is currently accurate; however, the plan really does have an obligation for both portions (participant and plan sponsor). There is a proposed change in the accounting guidance which will require presentation of the gross obligation and the participant portion will be backed out.
Copay (e.g., $10 per doctor visit). A copay is not a plan benefit; therefore, it is never a plan benefit obligation.	Participant	Occurrence of claim	Participant--no plan obligation
Claim costs for self-insured plans with stop-loss coverage. Represents a plan benefit.	Plan sponsor to stop-loss threshold; insurance company in excess of stop-loss threshold	Time of claim processing	Claims to stop-loss level--plan obligation Claims in excess of stop-loss threshold--insurance company obligation, no plan obligation Premiums for stop-loss coverage--plan obligation
Premium costs for self-insured plan with stop-loss coverage. Represents a plan benefit.	Generally plan sponsor	Plan sponsor--generally paid monthly	Plan sponsor--plan obligation
Claim costs for insured plans. Represents a plan benefit.	Insurance company	Time of claim processing	Insurance company--no plan obligation

of using the HMO benefit or accessing care directly without utilizing the selected PCP. If a participant selects to use the designated PCP for delivery of care, a higher benefit amount is paid (usually 100% with varying copays on selected services). However, unlike the HMO plan, a participant may elect to access care directly (i.e., to see a specialist) and still have coverage for the services at a reduced benefit amount. This non-network/non-approved benefit usually has a deductible and co-insurance feature. The term "point-of-service" was coined because participants choose their method of accessing care and, therefore, their benefit level at the point in time when they receive service. Because POS plans are usually provided on an HMO platform, they utilize fully insured or, at times, minimum premium funding arrangements.

PPO. A PPO is a network of hospitals and doctors organized to provide a range of health care services for previously negotiated fees/discounts specified in a formal network contract and performed in an agreed-upon manner. PPO plans typically include copays, deductibles, and coinsurance cost-sharing methods with greater incentive (i.e., lower deductibles and coinsurance percentage) for using the PPO network. The discounted provider fee structure allows for substantial cost savings to the plan, while the absence of a "gatekeeper" PCP allows for greater participant control over access to care. PPO plans can be fully insured, minimum premium, or self-funded in terms of funding the claims and fixed expenses of the plan.

Comprehensive indemnity. Comprehensive indemnity arrangements provide health care services to participants, generally through reimbursement of claims, paid by the participant and submitted to the insurance company. These plans typically require a participant to pay a deductible and coinsurance before reimbursement is made. Participants have freedom of choice of providers since there is no network panel of providers that must be used in order to receive benefits. Plans that fall into this category include major medical, medical/surgical, managed indemnity, and the traditional Blue Cross and Blue Shield plans. Comprehensive indemnity plans were in existence long before the emergence of HMO, PPO, or POS plans. Although these plans provide the most choice and ease of access to care for participants, they usually cost the employer significantly more than other managed care plans (e.g., HMO and PPO plans). Comprehensive indemnity plans can be fully insured, minimum premium, or self-funded programs.

REPORTING FOR HEALTH AND WELFARE PLANS

Statement of Position (SOP) 92-6, *Accounting and Reporting by Health and Welfare Benefit Plans,* establishes the accounting and reporting for health and welfare plans. SOP 92-6 was issued in August 1992 and was effective for financial statements of single-employer plans with more than 500 participants prepared for plan years beginning after December 15, 1992. For financial statements of single-employer plans with less then 500 participants, the statement was effective for financial statements for plan years beginning after December 15, 1994. The SOP was effective for financial statements of multiemployer plans prepared for plan years beginning after December 15, 1995. However, the Department of Labor (DOL) provided plans with enforcement relief from adopting the provisions of SOP 92-6 (relating to postretirement benefit obligation information only) for plan years 1996 through 1999.

SOP 92-6 states

> *The primary objective of the financial statements of a defined-benefit health and welfare plan is to provide financial information that is useful in assessing the plan's present and future ability to pay its benefit obligations when due. To accomplish this objective, a plan's financial statements should provide information about:*
>
> - *Plan resources and the manner in which the stewardship responsibility for those resources has been discharged*
> - *Benefit obligations*
> - *The results of transactions and events that affect the information about those resources and obligations, and*
> - *Other factors necessary for users to understand the information provided.*

According to SOP 92-6

> *The objective of financial reporting by a defined-contribution health and welfare plan is to provide financial information that is useful in assessing the plan's present and future ability to pay its benefit obligations when due. To accomplish that objective, a plan's financial statements should provide information about:*
>
> - *Plan resources and the manner in which the stewardship responsibility for those resources has been discharged*
> - *The results of transactions and events that affect the information about those resources, and*
> - *Other factors necessary for users to understand the information provided.*

A defined contribution health and welfare plan's obligations are generally limited to the total of the participants' accounts; therefore, no benefit obligations are included in the financial statements. However, in a flexible spending arrangement, the excess of the participants' annual elections over the eligible expenses incurred is recorded as a liability at year-end and payable as outlined in the plan document.

Generally, financial statements of health and welfare plans should be prepared in accordance with generally accepted accounting principles (GAAP). However, the DOL accepts financial statements prepared on an other comprehensive basis of accounting, such as the modified cash basis. In modified cash-basis financial statements, investments are recorded at fair value and additions to net assets available for benefits are recognized when cash is received, and deductions are recognized when amounts are paid, except for the recognition of unrealized gains and/or losses on investments at the end of the plan year. Also, modified cash-basis financial statements must disclose the benefit obligation information required to be presented in GAAP basis financial statements, including health claims payable, IBNR, postretirement and postemployment obligations, as applicable, and changes in the benefit obligations. When plan financial statements are prepared on an other comprehensive basis of accounting, Statement on Auditing Standards (SAS) 62, *Special Reports,* should be followed as well as the Auditing Interpretation of SAS 62, AU 9623.88, which provides guidance in evaluating the adequacy of disclosures in the financial statements. See Chapter 10, Other Accounting and Auditing Considerations, for additional information regarding the use of other comprehensive bases of accounting.

The financial statements of all health and welfare plans should include the following:

- Statements of net assets available for benefits as of the end of the current plan year and the prior plan year-end
- A statement of changes in net assets available for benefits for the current plan year

In addition, financial statements of defined benefit health and welfare plans should include the following information in either one or more financial statements:

- Statements of the plan's benefit obligations as of the end of the current plan year and the prior plan year-end
- A statement of the effects, if significant, of certain factors affecting the change in the plan's benefit obligations for the current plan year. (There has been a proposed change to SOP 92-6 which would allow this information to be presented in the footnotes to the plan's financial statements, similar to the presentation of the changes in accumulated plan benefit obligations for a defined benefit pension plan, which are permitted to be disclosed in the footnotes to the plan's financial statements.)

Postretirement obligations should be segregated and reported as follows in the statement of plan benefit obligations:

- Obligations for current retirees
- Obligations for other participants fully eligible for benefits
- Participants not yet fully eligible for benefits

The changes in plan benefit obligations that are presented in the statements of changes in plan benefit obligations should include all significant factors that contributed to the changes and may be grouped into the changes related to the following three categories:

1. Claims and premiums currently payable for participants and dependents
2. Claims for current benefit coverage incurred but not reported
3. Postretirement benefit obligations

The items that affect the change in claims and premiums currently payable for participants and dependents are the payment of claims throughout the plan year-end and claims that have been approved for payment but that had not been paid as of the plan's year-end. The change in claims for current benefit coverage incurred but not reported is reported as either an increase or a decrease in the amount of claims payable. Many items affect the reported change in postretirement benefit obligations. Such items may consist of, but are not limited to, benefits accumulated, benefit payments, change in the discount rate, interest cost, changes in the plan itself (e.g., the effect of changes in plan provisions, plan mergers or other plan amendments), and other changes in the assumptions utilized in the actuarial valuation.

At a minimum, the financial statements should include the changes in benefit obligations resulting from plan amendments, changes in the nature of the plan, and changes in actuarial assumptions. In addition, any other significant factors that contributed to the change in the benefit obligation should be presented. When there are changes in actuarial assumptions, such changes are considered changes in accounting estimates and previously reported amounts should not be restated. Benefit payments that are included in the statement of changes in benefit obligations should generally equal the amount of benefit payments included in the statement of changes in net assets, and therefore, should only include those amounts paid by the plan and not the benefit payments made by the insurance company under an insured arrangement.

Due to the nature of defined contribution health and welfare plans, the reporting requirements for benefit obligations are not applicable for these plans. Although Statement of Financial Accounting Standards (SFAS) 35, *Accounting and Reporting by Defined Benefit Pension Plans,* does not apply to health and welfare plans, the valuation of plan assets and certain financial statement disclosures required by SOP 92-6 are similar to those required by SFAS 35. SFAS 106, *Employers' Accounting for Postretirement Benefits Other Than Pensions,* and SFAS 112, *Employers' Accounting for Postemployment Benefits,* provides guidance for the plan sponsor's accounting and reporting, and therefore are not applicable to health and welfare plan reports. However, the guidance conveyed in SOP 92-6 includes similar concepts of SFAS 106 and SFAS 112, such as the recognition of plan obligations and plan sponsor liabilities, respectively.

FILING AND AUDIT REQUIREMENTS

ERISA established the reporting requirements for employee benefit plans, including health and welfare plans. Health and welfare plans are generally subject to annual IRS filings, unless they are exempt from the filing requirement under the criteria discussed below. Beginning with the 1999 Form 5500, all plans that must file an annual report will be required to complete a two-page form and the applicable supplemental schedules (see Chapter 11, Form 5500). The filing requirements of a plan are determined based on the number of participants at the beginning of the plan year. For purposes of this determination, participants include employees or former employees (or their beneficiaries) eligible to receive a benefit under the plan. Dependents are therefore not considered to be participants. Generally, plans with greater than 100 participants at the beginning of the plan year have more extensive reporting requirements than plans with fewer than 100 participants (see Chapter 11, Form 5500). However, an exception is available for plans that have between 80 and 120 plan participants as of the beginning of the plan year. The exception allows those plans an option to file the same type of Form 5500 as in the prior year. For example, if a plan that filed a Form 5500 C/R as a small plan in the prior year has 110 participants at the beginning of the current plan year and 130 participants at the end of the plan year, the plan would be allowed to file as a small plan for the current year and would be required to file as a large plan in the following year (due to 130 participants at the beginning of the plan year). Also, plans with 100 or more participants at the beginning of the plan year (large plan filers) are required to be audited, unless they meet the exemption criteria discussed below.

Health and welfare plans that meet the following criteria are exempt from **both** the Form 5500 filing requirement and the related audit requirement, as discussed in the AICPA audit and accounting guide, *Audits of Employee Benefit Plans*:

> *(a) Plans that are unfunded or fully insured and provide benefits only to a select group of management or highly compensated employees; or*
>
> *(b) Plans that have less than 100 participants as of the beginning of the plan year, and*
>
> *(1) (a) Pay benefits solely from the general assets of the employer or employee organization maintaining the plan, or*
>
> *(b) Provide benefits exclusively through insurance contracts or policies issued by a qualified insurance company or through a qualified HMO, the premiums of which are paid directly out of the general assets of the employer or employee organization, or partly from general assets and partly from employee or employee organization (member) contributions provided that employee contributions to the insurance company are forwarded by the employer or employee organization within three months of receipt; and*
>
> *(2) In the case of insured plans, pay any employee refunds to employees within three months of receipt.*

Health and welfare plans that meet the following criteria are exempt from the audit requirement, regardless of the number of plan participants at the beginning of the plan year, but are still required to file a Form 5500:

> *(a) (1) Pay benefits solely from the general assets of the employer or employee organization maintaining the plan, or*
>
> *(2) Provide benefits exclusively through insurance contracts or policies issued by a qualified insurance company or through a qualified HMO, the premiums of which are paid directly out of the general assets of the employer or employee organization, or partly from general assets and partly from employee or [employee organization] member contributions, or*

(3) Provide benefits partly from the general assets of the employer or employee organization and partly through insurance provided that, for (2) or (3), employee contributions are forwarded to the insurance company within three months of receipt; and

(b) In the case of plans that provide for them, pay any employee refunds to employees within three months of receipt.

Both criteria must be met to qualify for the audit exemption. Plans which have established trusts to hold the assets of the health and welfare plans are required to be audited under ERISA (i.e., benefits are paid from other than the sources in (a) above). As discussed previously, pursuant to ERISA Technical Release 92-01, the DOL is not enforcing ERISA's general requirement regarding the establishment of a trust to hold plan assets, therefore, the audit exemption is common. For example, many cafeteria plans or other contributory plans are not required to be audited if a trust is not used to hold participant or sponsor contributions.

The audit requirement pertains to the financial statements of the plan, and not the financial statements of the trust. If the assets of the trust represent the assets of more than one plan, each plan that has assets included in the trust is subject to the audit requirement.

STATEMENT OF NET ASSETS AVAILABLE FOR BENEFITS

As required by ERISA, a health and welfare plan's financial statements are required to include a comparative statement of net assets available for benefits and, at a minimum, the current year's statement of changes in net assets available for benefits. The statement of net assets available for benefits details the assets and liabilities of the plan measured as of the end of the plan year. It is comparable to the balance sheet of the plan sponsor in that it presents the plan's net assets (assets minus liabilities) at a particular point in time (plan year-end); however, all obligations related to the plan are not included in the calculation of net assets. The obligations for benefits are additional amounts that are either included on the face of the statement of net assets, with a subtotal of total benefit obligations, or on a separate statement of benefit obligations. Health and welfare plan liabilities differ from plan obligations--plan liabilities are generally current amounts owed as a result of the operation of the plan for items other than benefits. Plan obligations are amounts, often estimated, that a plan is required to pay in the future for benefits, as a result of the provisions of the plan document. These obligations are to plan participants or on behalf of plan participants for the benefits offered under the plan. The net assets provide a basis to determine the funding of the plan, which can be compared with the benefit obligations of the plan (presented separately from the net assets), to determine the plan's present and future ability to pay its benefit obligations when they are due. It is important to remember that since many plans are essentially unfunded, there may be significant deficiencies in the funding status of the plan. Disclosure of how the plan sponsor intends to "fund" these deficiencies should be included in the footnotes to the plan's financial statements.

The statement of net assets available for benefits includes amounts for investments (often highly liquid), contributions and investment income receivable, deposits with and receivables from insurance companies, accruals for administrative expenses and receivables and accruals related to investment transactions settling after year-end. Depending on the tax status of the plan, income taxes payable may also be a liability of the plan, typically as a result of the trust earning unrelated business income, such as interest income or other income earned on balances invested in excess of certain limits (called "qualified asset account limits"), as specified by IRC Section 419A. Also, multiemployer plans may invest in certain other investments (e.g., limited partnerships) that may result in taxable income.

The accounting and auditing of investments has previously been discussed in this guide in Chapter 6, Investments. Investments comprise the majority of the assets available for benefits for most health and welfare plans. The following will discuss the accounting and auditing treatment of the other assets and liabilities that may appear in a health and welfare plan's statement of net assets available for benefits. Financial statement presentation will be illustrated in Chapter 13, Financial Statements and Disclosures.

CONTRIBUTIONS RECEIVABLE

Contributions receivable represent amounts which are due from either the plan sponsor for a single-employer plan, plan sponsors for a multiple-employer plan, the group of employers for a multiemployer sponsored plan, plan participants (if the plan is a contributory plan), or other entities such as federal or state agencies for grants. The amount that should be recorded as a contribution receivable should include amounts that represent formal commitments as well as contributions that are required to be paid to the plan subject to legal or contractual obligations. For employee contributions receivable, the amounts may represent amounts that were withheld from the wages of employees for contributions to the plan prior to the plan's year-end but which were not deposited into the plan's trust until the following plan year. According to the provisions of SOP 92–6, employer contributions receivable are generally recorded subject to a formal commitment, and the evidence constituting a "formal commitment" may consist of any or all of the following:

> *(a) a resolution by the employer's governing board approving a specified contribution, (b) a consistent pattern of making payments after the plan's year-end pursuant to an established funding policy that attributes such subsequent payments to the preceding plan year, (c) a deduction of a contribution for federal tax purposes for periods ending on or before the reporting date, or (d) the employer's recognition as of the reporting date of a contribution payable to the plan. However, the existence of an accrued liability in the employer's statement of financial position or a plan's benefit obligations exceeding its net assets available for benefit obligations does not, by itself, provide sufficient support for recognition of a contribution receivable by the plan.*

For federal tax purposes, a deduction may be taken on a corporate tax return for health and welfare contributions accrued at year-end for amounts related to the year and made by the due date of the company's tax return (including extensions). For example, for a company with a December 31 year-end who has extended its tax return deadline until September 15 of the following year, the company can take as deductions for the year subject to filing, contributions made by September 15 of the following year.

The existence of any or all of the situations previously described would warrant the recording of an employer contribution receivable on the plan's financial statements. One other account which should be considered in relation to contributions receivable is the applicability of an allowance for uncollectible receivables. For example, to the extent that there has been a pattern of contributions that have proven to be uncollectible by the plan in the past, this may necessitate that a reserve be recorded on the plan's financial statements. This situation is likely to be more prevalent with multiemployer sponsored plans or in cases where the financial stability of the plan sponsor is questionable.

Audit Objective

The audit objective for contributions receivable is to determine that only amounts which represent valid employee and/or employer receivables are recorded by the plan as of the end of the plan year.

Audit Procedures

To test employer contributions receivable, the auditor should review the contribution provisions of the plan document and verify compliance with the plan instrument (i.e., criteria that must be met for an employer and/or employee to make a contribution). The auditor should compare the amount of the employer contribution recorded in the plan's trustee report to the amount approved by the board of directors (or board of trustees for a multiemployer plan) of the plan sponsor, if the contribution requires board approval. That approval should be documented in the board minutes. Alternatively, given the period of time after the plan's year-end in which audit procedures are performed, the auditor may test subsequent payments by the employer to the plan. For employee contributions receivable, the auditor should inquire about the timing of employee contributions made to the plan. As with employer contributions, the auditor may test the subsequent receipts of employee contributions to determine if any contribution amounts received after year-end represented contributions attributable to the plan year under audit. In many cases, the existence of an employee contribution receivable amount on the plan's financial statements will depend upon the timing of the plan sponsor's payroll close to the plan's year-end. In addition to the above, the plan auditor should evaluate the collectibility of any amounts reported as contributions receivable at the end of the plan year. If a portion of the receivables are deemed to be uncollectible, an allowance for doubtful accounts should also be recorded on the plan's financial statements. As mentioned above, this situation most commonly occurs with multiemployer sponsored plans.

If the auditor also performs an audit of the plan sponsor, it is often efficient while performing audit procedures on the payroll system to test the total amount of contributions made to the plan and to reconcile such amounts to the plan's trustee records.

PARTICIPANT ELIGIBILITY

The auditor should include participant eligibility testing when auditing health and welfare plans, to ensure that participants have satisfied the appropriate criteria for participation in the plan, as established in the plan document. Participant eligibility testing may be performed while auditing participant contributions, if any, and benefit payments (addressed later in this chapter). The criteria for eligibility often include the following: the employee must be employed by the plan sponsor for a defined amount of time, or be an eligible former employee or retiree of the plan sponsor; the participant may have to be employed by the plan sponsor until the plan's next entry date; and the participant must complete an election form. For defined contribution health and welfare plans, an individual account record must exist for the participant, based upon the election made to participate in the plan.

Auditors should test participant eligibility either while testing internal controls for the plan (discussed earlier in Chapter 5, Internal Control), while testing participant contributions made to a contributory plan, or while testing benefit payments. If eligibility is tested in conjunction with detail testing of contributions or benefit payments, the same selections may be used to result in audit efficiencies by reducing the total number of selections to be subjected to testing.

For participant eligibility testing, auditors should review information from the plan sponsor's payroll and personnel files to determine the length of time the participant has been employed by the plan sponsor, whether the participant is an active employee, and whether the participant satisfies any other conditions stipulated by the plan document for participation, including completion of an election form, if required. For plans which provide postemployment or postretirement benefits, auditors should review information from the plan sponsor's records of terminated and retired employees. For defined contribution health and welfare plans, auditors should review the recordkeeping statements in order to determine whether an individual account record has been established for the participant.

In addition, for a multiemployer sponsored health and welfare plan, the auditor should review information from the plan administrator's files to determine that the participant has satisfied the appropriate conditions for participation in the plan, such as belonging to the appropriate union, length of service, and age.

For a plan that utilizes a voice response system (VRS) or the Internet for processing participant transactions and elections, testing of participant eligibility should not be affected by a voice response feature. For defined benefit health and welfare plans, the administrator of the VRS should be able to provide records of VRS activities, by participant (e.g., changes in medical coverages elected, addition of a dependent to a medical plan). For defined contribution health and welfare plans, the recordkeeper should be able to provide evidence of individual account records for eligible participants.

Audit Objectives

The objectives of testing participant eligibility are to provide the auditor with a reasonable basis to conclude that (1) all employee personnel that are eligible to participate in the plan are given the opportunity to participate and (2) those eligible personnel who choose to participate are contributing to the plan (for contributory plans) and, for defined contribution health and welfare plans, have an individual account included in the listing of the plan's individual account records.

The elements of participant eligibility that should be tested include

- Basic demographic data, such as name, birth date, and date of hire with the company (or rehire date if there was a leave of absence), which is required to determine eligibility pursuant to the provisions of the plan document
- Review of the plan's recordkeeping system to determine existence of an individual account record for selections (for defined contribution health and welfare plans)

Audit Procedures

Consider the following audit procedures when testing participant eligibility:

- Review applicable sections of the plan document to determine the criteria established for eligibility to participate in the plan
- Make selections of active employees from the plan sponsor's payroll records and, for plans which provide postemployment and postretirement benefits, make selections of former employees from the plan sponsor's records and review personnel files for eligibility data, as well as changes to this data such as salary information, rate changes, termination notices, hire date, and birth date
- Review recordkeeping system for the existence of an individual account record for the individual selected for testing (for defined contribution health and welfare plans)

OTHER ASSETS

Other assets of a health and welfare plan may include investment income receivable, receivables from broker for sales of investments not settled, deposits with insurance companies and premium stabilization reserves. As described in the section on insurance funding arrangements, plan assets may result from the arrangement established with the insurance company. Careful consideration of whether there has been a transfer of risk and the effect of the arrangement on the existence of plan assets is necessary; for example, if, under a minimum premium plan or similar arrangement, the insurance company may require a deposit or reserve to be held by the insurance company for reimbursement of claims paid after termination of the contract, these amounts may result in plan assets. Under a fully insured experience-rated or similar arrangement, the insurance contract stipulates that the loss may be charged to the plan over future years until it has been recovered. Typically, if the benefit payments and administrative costs of the plan are less than the premium payments, the plan may be entitled to a refund or credit against the next period's premium, which may result in a plan having a premium stabilization reserve, receivable, or deposit with the insurance company. Also, in the case of multiemployer plans, the plan may hold operating assets, such as buildings, equipment, and furniture. These assets should be reported at book value (historical cost less accumulated depreciation) in the plan's financial statements. However, in the Form 5500, these operating assets should be reported at fair market value. For additional information regarding operating assets, see Chapter 6, Investments.

Audit Objective

The audit objective for other assets is to determine that only amounts that are valid plan assets are recorded by the plan as of the end of the plan year.

Audit Procedures

Consider the following audit procedures when testing other assets:

- Obtain a listing of all accrued investment income amounts held as of the plan's year-end and make a selection of accrued investment income amounts (e.g., accrued dividends, interest) for testing. The auditor may test the selections by examining subsequent receipts or other records supporting the amounts, the timing of the selected accruals, and whether such amounts represent valid accruals at the plan's year-end.
- Consider the existence of sales of investments that are pending receipt for investments that are sold near the plan's year-end but for which the transaction did not settle until after year-end. Review trust statements for the first months of the following plan year to determine if there were amounts received for sales of investments with trade dates before year-end.
- Obtain a schedule of deposits and premium stabilization reserves held by the insurance company at year-end and a schedule of experience-rating refunds (sometimes called dividends) at year-end, if applicable, and reconcile the schedules to the plan's final accounting records.
- Determine whether deposits reported at year-end have been recorded in the proper amount in accordance with the provisions of the insurance contract. Also determine that the deposits are required to be maintained to be applied against future possible losses in excess of current premiums, thereby testing that they are plan assets.
- Determine whether premium stabilization reserves reported at year-end have been recorded in the proper amount in accordance with the provisions

of the insurance contract. Also determine that premium stabilization reserves have exceeded the total of claims paid and other charges and are intended to be refunded or used to reduce future premium payments, thereby testing that they are plan assets.

- Determine whether experience-rating refunds reported as plan assets at year-end have been properly recorded at the proper amount. Consider whether experience-rating refunds are specifically provided for by the insurance contract, and whether any refunds recorded are probable as to being due and reasonably estimable based on policy year experience as to premiums paid, paid claims, required reserves, and insurance company fees.
- Determine that operating assets reported, if any, exist and are in use by the plan. Test additions made during the year for validity and recording. Also, test dispositions, including any gains or losses realized on the transactions, and depreciation recorded for the period.

ACCRUED LIABILITIES

The most common types of liabilities which may be recorded on a health and welfare plan's financial statements are liabilities for administrative expenses payable, for securities purchased by the plan which had not yet settled by the plan's year-end, and for income taxes payable. Accruals for benefits (i.e., claims and premiums) are not considered accrued liabilities but rather benefit obligations and are described later in this chapter. All benefit obligations must be presented together in the plan's financial statements. The types of administrative expenses that may be paid for by a plan (and therefore should be considered for accrual) include trustee, accounting, and actuarial fees. Based upon the types of administrative expenses incurred by the plan, an accrual may be required to be recorded as of the date of the plan's financial statements, which would represent an accrual for expenses incurred by the plan prior to the end of the plan year but not paid until the following year. See discussion earlier in this chapter of when income taxes payable may be applicable for a plan.

Audit Objective

The audit objective relative to accrued liabilities is to determine that all liabilities of the plan at the end of the plan year, except benefit-related liabilities, have been recorded in the plan's statement of net assets available for benefits.

Audit Procedures

In order to audit the plan's liabilities at the end of the plan year, the plan auditor should perform the following:

- Review trust statements for the first and/or second months of the following plan year to determine if there were any investment purchases that settled at the beginning of the following plan year which represented liabilities at the end of the plan year currently under audit

- Review the supporting documentation for administrative expenses (generally during the first two months of the following plan year) to determine if any amounts paid represented administrative expenses that were incurred by the plan during the plan year currently under audit which should be recorded as liabilities at the end of the plan year
- Perform any other subsequent disbursements testing procedures deemed necessary

STATEMENT OF CHANGES IN NET ASSETS AVAILABLE FOR BENEFITS

The statement of changes in net assets available for benefits shows the activity that has occurred in the net assets of the health and welfare plan during the year. The statement of changes in net assets available for benefits is similar to the plan sponsor's income statement, except that the effect of accruals for benefits are not included. The statement of changes in net assets available for benefits includes amounts for investment income and expenses, contributions to the plan (employer and participant) and benefits paid from the plan, as well as other transactions recorded by the plan during the year. The changes in the plan's benefit obligations are not included in the calculation of the changes in net assets but are presented as changes in benefit obligations. The plan's statement of net assets and statement of changes in net assets are structured similarly for a health and welfare plan as for defined contribution and defined benefit pension plans. Presentation of a health and welfare plan's benefit obligations and changes in benefit obligations is discussed later in this chapter.

INVESTMENT INCOME

Investment income includes interest, dividends, rental income, and other earnings paid on investments that are or were held by the plan during the plan year. It also includes realized and unrealized gains and losses on those investments. Realized gains and losses result when an investment is bought at one price and later sold at a different price. If the selling price is higher than the purchase price, the plan realizes a gain. If the selling price is lower, the plan realizes a loss. In addition, at the end of the plan year, most investments held at year-end will be priced at fair market value. If the ending market value of an investment held at the plan's year-end is higher than the fair market value at the beginning of the year (or when purchased, if bought during the current plan year), then an unrealized gain results--unrealized because the investment is still held by the plan at year-end and has not been sold. If the ending market value is lower than the fair market value at the beginning of the year, then an unrealized loss results.

Audit Objectives

The audit objectives (for a full-scope audit only) for investment income are to provide assurance that earnings from the investment vehicles of the plan have been properly recorded in all material respects and appropriately allocated to the individual participant records. Generally accepted accounting principles require that the statement of changes in net assets available for benefits be presented in enough detail to identify the significant changes during the year. These generally should include

- Unrealized appreciation/depreciation, or unrealized gains and losses on investments during the year. The amount of unrealized gains and losses on investments represents the increase or decrease in the fair value of investments from the beginning of the plan year to the end of the plan year.
- Realized gains and losses generated from the sale of investments during the year. The amount of realized gains and losses is calculated as the difference between the proceeds from the sales of investments and the original (or historical) cost of such investments.

  NOTE: In some cases, the unrealized gains and losses and the realized gains and losses are combined for financial statement purposes and grouped in a category entitled the net appreciation/depreciation in fair value of investments. The Form 5500 requires that the unrealized and realized gains and losses be reported separately.
- Investment income, which includes interest, dividends, rental income, and other types of income (exclusive of unrealized appreciation/depreciation and realized gains and losses). For certain pooled-type investments, investment income should be presented as net investment gain/loss. This net investment gain/loss includes the net appreciation/depreciation on the pooled-type investments. (Note that this is consistent with the presentation required in Form 5500.)
- For a company that places assets relating to some or all of their plans in a master trust, the method used to allocate investment income to each plan is usually stated in the trust agreement. Each plan has an undivided interest in the assets of the trust, and ownership is represented by a record of proportionate dollar interest or by units of participation. The auditor should examine how ownership is attributed to the individual plans to ensure that the allocation method is reasonable and that it agrees with the provisions of the plan document.

Audit Procedures

When testing investment income in a full-scope audit, it may be more efficient to perform substantive analytical procedures or tests in total as compared to performing detailed testing procedures of individual investment purchases and sales transactions. The auditor may calculate the amount of income for a class of securities based upon published indices and compare this amount to the actual amount of investment income recorded. For some investments, it may be more appropriate to perform detail testing procedures. The following represents suggested analytical and detail audit procedures that may be used to audit investment income.

NOTE: The average rate of return that the auditor calculates may differ from the independent source if investment fees are netted against investment income. See the discussion of investment fees below.

1. Obtain from the trustee a schedule of investments showing beginning and ending balances, investment income, net unrealized gains or losses, and realized gains or losses. This information should have been obtained in connection with the audit of the statement of net assets available for benefits.
2. To perform analytical review procedures instead of, or in addition to, detail tests, consider performing the following procedures to test investment income:

   - Segregate investments by significant type--government securities, equities, fixed income securities, mutual funds, by type (i.e., growth fund vs. money-market fund) or temporary investments. It may be necessary to aggregate the investments by other than investment type in order to arrive at a reasonable expectation. Some other aggregations which may be considered include (1) by period (quarterly or monthly), or (2) by trust account or group of trust accounts.
   - Determine the average investment balance for each significant type by adding the beginning and ending investment balances together and dividing by two. This simple average may need to be refined (to adjust for the effects of contributions/distributions) to quarterly or monthly amounts if the activity during the year is not reasonably uniform.
   - Divide the investment income earned on each type of investment by its average investment balance, which will result in an average rate of return on that investment.
   - Develop separate expectations of investment income for the particular investment based on independent published sources. Note that for most of the indices listed below, quoted returns are often for the total return of the investment (i.e., investment income plus unrealized appreciation/ depreciation **plus** realized gains and losses less investment expenses incurred). Information regarding the indices, and the investment components included, should be available when accessing the sources below. Some examples of independent published sources--where to look for investment income data for selected types of investments--follow:

     Equity Investments
     Wall Street Journal
     Standard & Poor's 500 Stock Index
     Wilshire 5000 Stock Index
     Dow Jones Industrial Average
     Wilshire Target Large Company Growth

Wilshire Target Large Company Value
Wilshire Internet

Fixed-Income Investments
Moody's Bond Record
Various Shearson Lehman or Merrill Lynch Indices
Interest rates stated on the securities

Mutual Fund Investments
Wall Street Journal
Various Lipper Indices

Temporary Investments
Donoghue's 12-month Yield Index

- Compare the average amount calculated for the investment type to the expected amount. Obtain and corroborate an explanation from the plan administrator or trustee for any significant discrepancies.

3. To perform tests of details, obtain from the trustee a listing of all investment purchases and sales (i.e., proceeds and realized gains/losses) during the year. Consider the following procedures:
   - Perform tests of details to test both net realized gains or losses and investment income (e.g., interest and dividends) by making a selection of investment purchases/sales during the year. Reconcile the beginning of the year investment balance (at fair value) to the prior year working papers. Compare purchase/selling prices to published market price ranges on the applicable trade dates (the date an agreement is made to buy or sell the investment). Depending on the nature of the investment, obtain an independent source to compare the purchase/selling price. Compare interest, dividends, and net investment gain/loss received (e.g., for mutual funds) to an independent source (see list above). A business library will typically carry reference books that detail dividends declared and paid. This information may also be obtained from the Internet. The interest rate is generally stated on the investment instrument.
   - Examine brokers' advices, cash records, or other supporting documentation for the quantity, description, and date of acquisition/disposition of the investment. Note that often a trustee may be making large block purchases or sales for a number of plans. Information should exist that identifies investment amounts by plan.
   - In the event that brokers' advices or independent cash records are not available, confirm the purchase/sale with the broker.

NOTE: For many pooled investment vehicles (mutual funds, common collective trusts, or pooled separate accounts), quoted returns are often for total return (i.e., investment income plus unrealized appreciation/depreciation plus realized gains and losses less investment expenses incurred). In those cases, testing net investment gain/loss in total may be more efficient.

4. Test the calculation of the realized gain or loss on the transaction and agree the realized gain or loss to the listing of investment sales made during the year. Determine whether the method used for calculating the realized gain or loss on the transaction is in accordance with the DOL's rules and regulations (e.g., realized gains and losses should be based on beginning of year market values rather than historical cost).
5. Recalculate the unrealized gain/loss portion of the net appreciation or depreciation in fair value of investments. Obtain the beginning of the year market value of the selected investment. Add any purchases of that security and subtract any sales. (For the sales number, use the market value for that security from the beginning of the year, not the actual proceeds received.) This will result in the ending fair value of the investment. Compare this balance to the ending fair value recorded for that security on the trustee report. If the recorded fair value is higher, the investment has an unrealized gain. If the recorded value is lower, the investment has an unrealized loss. Compare the total appreciation/depreciation with the amount recorded by the trustee and evaluate any differences.
6. For investments in non-readily-marketable securities, recalculate the unrealized gains/losses during the year by referring to the fair value of the securities at the end of the prior plan year and the end of the current plan year. Any realized gains/losses generated from the sale of the securities should be tested by recomputing such gains/losses as proceeds from the sale less the original cost. In addition, actual income generated from such investments, such as dividend income from limited partnerships or capital distributions, should be audited through referring to independent sources, such as the tax filing for the limited partnership or audited financial statements, if available.

INVESTMENT FEES

The following discussion of investment fees relates only to full-scope audits.

Fees that are assessed by parties involved in the plan for the purchase or sale of securities--brokerage fees for investment advice or commission fees--are considered to be investment expenses. Investment expenses can be (1) assessed as a percentage of the purchase or selling price of the investment being traded, (2) a flat fee charged per transaction, or (3) a flat fee for asset management or percentage of managed assets charged on a per-month basis. Some trustees/brokers show the investment fee on a separate invoice or as a separate total on the brokers' advice. However, it is common practice to either net the brokerage fee with proceeds of the sale or deduct the fee automatically on a periodic basis (e.g., monthly) from the plan account. In each of these two examples, the investment fee is not readily available.

A mutual fund may charge certain distribution costs, such as advertising, promotion, and sales incentives to shareholders. These fees are called 12b-1 fees. The name comes from the Securities and Exchange Commission Rule 12b-1, established in 1980 and updated in 1993. The 12b-1 fee typically ranges from .25% to 8.5% of the invested fund balance. The 12b-1 fees are charged primarily in cases where the funds are sold through brokers, insurance agents, and financial planners. A no-load fund is a mutual fund that charges no sales fees to its shareholders. Individuals wishing to invest their money in a no-load mutual fund buy shares directly from the company who offers the fund, rather than through a broker.

The plan document may address investment fees. The auditor should determine the method used by the trustee/broker to assess fees by discussing this with the plan administrator. Inquiries should also be made of the plan administrator as to how investment fees are monitored. If fees are netted (normally done for mutual funds and common/commingled trust funds), it will be difficult to test this amount, as the fees will be shown on the trustee statement netted together with the investment income amount. However, if the investment return is substantially below other comparable indices, it may be worth pursuing with the plan administrator and the trustee. If amounts are not netted, test as necessary the investment expenses for a sample selection to determine that the amounts are properly assessed.

When assets are invested in securities/funds in which investment fees are netted against investment income on the statement of changes in net assets available for benefits, the investment income line should be shown as

Investment income (net of investment expenses)	$ x,xxx

If assets include investments with insurance companies (or other accounts where investment fees are not netted), determine that the investment fees assessed on these investments agrees with the investment fee stated in the investment contract. To do so, the auditor should examine the statement received from the insurance company which details the plan's investments in the insurance contracts during the year and also summarizes the investment fees charged to the plan during the year. The actual fees and the investment fee rate should be compared to the rate stated in the investment contract should be compared and significant discrepancies should be investigated with the plan administrator.

LIMITED-SCOPE AUDITS

When the plan administrator has elected to have a limited-scope audit performed, agree the investment income amounts certified on the trustee report(s) with the financial information reported on the plan's financial statements. In the event that the trustee/custodian has failed to report accrued investment income in the plan's trust reports, when such accrued investment income should be reported on the plan's financial statements, the auditor should perform appropriate audit procedures to determine the amount of the accrued investment income. In addition, such amounts would be excluded from the amounts certified by the trustee/custodian in the standard footnote disclosure used for limited-scope audits. See Chapter 13, Financial Statements and Disclosures, for an example of a plan's footnote disclosures for limited-scope audits.

CONTRIBUTIONS

Contributions received during the plan year may be segregated between employer contributions, employee contributions, and other contributions. The contributions recorded (as segregated by employer, employee, and other contributions) would also include the impact of accruals recorded for contributions not yet received by the end of the plan year and the reversal of any accrued contributions recorded as of the end of the prior plan year. For contributory plans the plan document, employee handbook and other information prepared by the plan sponsor records the rates charged to employees for various medical and other health and welfare coverages. The auditor should read the plan document, employee election forms, and other information to determine the extent of employee contributions to expect for the plan. Often the participant contribution levels are established and employer contributions are made to fund the remainder of the costs of the plan.

Audit Objectives

The audit objectives for contributions received from employers are to provide assurance that amounts received have been determined and recorded in accordance with the plan documents or minutes of the board. In health and welfare plans it is not uncommon to fund on a current basis--that is, as claims are presented for payment. Also, the auditor should ensure that employer contributions are properly recorded in the financial statements in conformity with generally accepted accounting principles. (Note that contributions receivable were covered previously in this chapter.)

The audit objectives for contributions received from participants are to provide assurance that amounts received have been determined and recorded in accordance with the plan document. Also, the auditor must ensure that employee contributions are properly recorded in the financial statements in conformity with generally accepted accounting principles and with the election of the plan participants (e.g., coverage for single with no dependents, family coverage). The auditor should determine that employee contributions are being deposited with the trustee or custodian of plan assets on a timely basis and in accordance with the plan's policies and procedures.

The DOL has established regulations related to the timing of deposit of employee contributions into the trust of a funded plan. As described in DOL Reg. 2510.3-102, an employer must

> *segregate employee contributions from its general assets as soon as practicable [for deposit into the trust of a funded plan], but in no event more than (a) ninety days after the contributions are paid by employees or withheld from their wages for a welfare benefit plan or (b) the 15th business day following the end of the month in which amounts are contributed by employees or withheld from their wages for a pension benefit plan.*

Audit Procedures

The following audit procedures apply to employer contributions for single-employer and multiemployer plans as well as employee contributions.

Employer contributions--single-employer plans and multiple-employer plans. To ensure the auditing objectives are met, the auditor should obtain directly from the plan sponsor a schedule of all employer contributions made to the plan. Select a sample from the list and perform the following:

- Consider confirming directly with the plan sponsor the amounts contributed to the plan, both already received and those that are receivable at year-end
- Obtain from the plan sponsor a reconciliation of the expense amounts recorded in the plan sponsor's accounting records to the plan's financial statement amounts for employer contributions

If the plan is a multiple-employer sponsored plan, the procedures listed above should be performed for each of the participating employers of the plan.

Employer contributions--multiemployer plans. For multiemployer plans, obtain a list of participating employers and determine that it is all-inclusive by examining appropriate plan documents (e.g., a collective bargaining agreement) and perform the following:

- Obtain a schedule of contributions received or receivable (usually provided by the administrator or trustee) and note that contributions are made by the employers from the list of participating employers
- Test the schedule of contributions to ensure that it is mathematically correct and that the contribution rate stated in the appropriate document(s) was used
- Consider confirming directly with the contributors the amounts contributed to the plan, both already received and those that are receivable at year-end

Employee contributions. For employee contributions, the auditor should perform the following:

- Obtain a schedule of contributions received or receivable from participants and reconcile the totals to the plan's financial accounting records.
- Review the participant election forms to understand the coverage options and related participant cost for each option. Evaluate the procedures employed by the plan sponsor or recordkeeper to ensure that elections are appropriate and applied consistently. Review the SAS 70 report for the recordkeeper, if applicable.
- Determine whether any withholdings (for employee contributions to the plan) that were authorized by the participant were withheld and deposited into the plan's trust as soon as practicable. Determine the plan's policy regarding the timing of deposits to the trustee for employee contributions. DOL regulations require them to be made as soon as those contributions can

be segregated by the plan sponsor, but no later than ninety days after the contributions are paid by employees or withheld from their wages. (To the extent monies are held by the sponsor and not deposited in a timely manner, this represents a prohibited transaction which should be reported on Schedule 27(e) of the old Form 5500 and Schedule G of the new Form 5500. This situation is considered to be a prohibited transaction because it is determined to be either a use of plan assets for the benefit of the employer or a prohibited extension of credit [a loan] to the employer. In extreme circumstances, it may constitute an embezzlement of plan assets.)

- Either detail test selected transactions or perform substantive analytical review to test the amount.
  - To detail test transactions, select contributions from the schedule received and trace the amounts contributed to the payroll records and the participant's coverage election form to determine whether the amount of the withholding was authorized by the participant and appropriately withheld. Compare the amount to the cost-sharing information for the plan year.
  - To test amounts by performing substantive analytical review procedures, develop an expectation of the contributions by using prior year activity, specified levels of participants' contributions per the cost-sharing information, number of plan participants, and payroll cycle. Compare the expectation to the actual amount of contributions received and recorded and obtain and corroborate explanations for any significant differences through examination of supporting documents. The auditor should recognize that unless the plan population is fairly stable it is often difficult to develop an independent expectation. Consideration of the challenges related to the calculation of an expectation for the specific plan being audited should be made when determining the preferred testing approach.

INDIVIDUAL PARTICIPANT ACCOUNTS-- DEFINED CONTRIBUTION HEALTH AND WELFARE PLANS

For a defined contribution health and welfare plan, individual participant accounts should also be tested. Because audits of defined contribution health and welfare plans are uncommon, suggested audit procedures are not described in this chapter. Consider procedures described in Chapter 7, Accounting, Auditing, and Reporting for Defined Contribution Pension Plans, for these audits.

BENEFIT PAYMENTS

As the caption suggests, this line item includes the amounts paid for claims and insurance premiums, which together represent benefits provided to participants and their dependents and beneficiaries during the course of the plan year.

Audit Objectives

The audit objectives for procedures applied to benefit payments are to provide the auditor with a reasonable basis to determine

- That all claim payments are made in accordance with applicable plan provisions
- That insurance payments are made in accordance with the insurance contracts
- That the payments are made to, or on behalf of, only those persons who are entitled to receive those benefits. Persons entitled to receive benefits may include active employees, employees who have terminated or retired from the company, their dependents or their designated beneficiary(ies), depending on the populations covered by the plan.
- That transactions are recorded in the proper account, amount and period.

Audit Procedures--Self-Funded Plans

Audit procedures that may be considered in testing benefit claims in self-funded plans include

- Obtain plan's benefit claim records showing total benefits paid to or on behalf of each participant during the year and reconcile the totals to the plan's final accounting records. Test the benefit payment recorded through test of details, analytical procedures, or a combination, as described below.
- If benefit payments are determined or made by a third-party service provider, obtain an understanding of the internal control procedures, either by obtaining a SAS 70 service auditor's report or by applying appropriate auditing procedures to the third-party administrator.

Test of details. When considering the type of testing to perform, the auditor should recognize that obtaining claim data is often difficult, due to its sensitive nature. The plan sponsor or claims administrator may require the auditor to sign a confidentiality agreement in order to obtain the data. When performing test of details, make a selection of recorded benefit payments and, for each selection, obtain the benefit application and perform the following:

1. Examine service provider statements or other evidence of service rendered or occurrence of event (e.g., statement from health benefit provider for medical claims, death certificate for life insurance claim)
2. Evaluate the individual's eligibility to receive payments by examining the benefit election form and dependent designation and appropriate evidence of age and employment history data, comparing employment dates and other applicable items
3. Recompute benefit payments based on the plan instrument provisions, the benefit option elected, applicable other coverage, pertinent service or salary history, and deductible or coinsurance limits

4. Determine that the third-party administrator, plan sponsor, or other claim processor has performed procedures for coordination of benefits (i.e., the payment of claims is "shared" due to the participant's coverage under another insurance company or plan), if any, to ensure that the plan has paid for the appropriate portion of the benefit
5. Determine that the amount paid for the claim represented an amount within the range of customary and normal charges for the type of service rendered. Information regarding the range of customary and normal charges to be paid for claims should be available through the plan sponsor, the insurance company, or third-party administrator.
6. Either obtain and examine canceled benefit payment checks or benefit application forms signed by the participant, or confirm payment of benefits with selected participant and compare participant signatures from the benefit application forms or the confirmation to the annual benefit election form or other appropriate documents.

Analytical procedures.

- Develop an expectation of the amount of benefit payments. The auditor should recognize that the development of an independent expectation is often quite difficult, due to the nature of benefits provided by health and welfare plans. To develop an expectation, the auditor should consider data related to benefit payments in prior periods, effect of plan amendments on benefit amounts, number of individuals expected to receive benefit payments, and changes in the form of distribution (e.g., changes in deductibles). Also, for plans with stop-loss coverage, the auditor should consider if catastrophic claims are covered by the plan and should inquire about the number of claims for the period. Catastrophic claims are claims that exceed specific stop loss levels or other defined thresholds. If the amount of the catastrophic claims and/or the reimbursement of the catastrophic claims are included in or deducted from the benefit payment amounts to be compared to the auditor's expectation, significant differences will exist. An understanding of the effect of these claims, if any, is important in auditing benefit payments.
- Compare the expectation to recorded amounts and obtain and corroborate explanations through examination of supporting documents for significant differences.

Other considerations.

- Evaluate whether procedures exist for determining the continued eligibility of participants or beneficiaries to receive benefits, to assure that individuals are removed from the benefit rolls upon death or termination of eligibility and that payments made to individuals over an unusually long number of years are still appropriate

- Evaluate whether procedures exist for investigating long-outstanding benefit checks
- Evaluate whether procedures exist for detecting duplicate payments of claims
- If benefit payments are determined or made by a third-party service provider, obtain an understanding of the internal control procedures of the third party (including procedures in place by the third party to detect duplicate payments of claims and to determine that claims submitted for payment are covered by the terns of the plan) either by obtaining a SAS 70 report or by applying appropriate auditing procedures to the third-party administrator. Consider using the third-party administrator's auditors or internal auditors to perform the procedures.

Insured Plans

Audit procedures that may be considered in testing benefit payments for insured plans include

- Obtain the plan's disbursement records showing total premiums remitted to the insurance company during the year, including the effect of retroactive premiums and dividends, if any, and agree or reconcile the totals to the plan's final accounting records
- Make a selection of recorded premium payments and, for each premium computation selected, obtain the related participant eligibility records and perform the following:
    - Compare the number of eligible participants, as shown by the eligibility records, to the premium computation
    - Compare applicable premium rates to the insurance contract
    - Trace a sample of participants listed in the premium computation list to the eligibility records
    - Investigate the reasons for significant changes in premium amounts from year to year, if applicable
- For retroactive premiums and dividends, compare the amounts recorded as receivable and received during the year to supporting documentation from the insurance company evidencing the nature of the amounts and the plan year for which the amount is paid. For amounts receivable at year-end, test for collectibility by agreeing the amount to the amount received subsequent to year-end.

ADMINISTRATIVE EXPENSES

This line item includes the amount of administrative expenses paid by the plan during the year, including any amounts accrued on the statement of net assets available for benefits at the end of the plan year and the corresponding reversal of any accruals for administrative expenses that were recorded at the end of the prior year.

For further information regarding the types of administrative expenses which may be paid by a plan, see the discussion in the previous section on accrued liabilities.

Audit Objectives

The audit objectives for procedures applied to administrative expenses are to provide the auditor with a reasonable basis to determine

- That all administrative expenses paid by the plan are made in accordance with applicable plan provisions
- That transactions are recorded in the proper account, amount, and period

Audit Procedures

When auditing administrative expenses paid by the plan, although substantive analytical review procedures may be performed, perhaps the most efficient type of testing is detail testing whereby the auditor makes a sample selection of administrative expenses paid by the plan and examines supporting documentation, such as copies of invoices and canceled checks to determine that the expense paid was a valid expense for the plan. As mentioned previously, the types of administrative expenses incurred by a health and welfare plan may include trustee and accounting fees, internal costs, and actuarial fees for plans with postretirement obligations. As a matter of practicality, the amount of administrative expenses incurred by a plan during the plan year is not generally a significant amount in comparison to the plan's net assets available for benefits. As such, when planning audit procedures with respect to administrative expenses, the auditor should consider the materiality of the administrative expenses line item to determine the most efficient approach for testing purposes.

TRANSFERS IN/TRANSFERS OUT

The transfer of assets into or from a health and welfare plan may result from a plan merger, plan termination (when the terminated plan is replaced by another plan), or, for plan sponsors who sponsor multiple plans for multiple locations, from the transfer of participants from one location to another. In these cases, the plan assets and the related benefit obligations related to the transferring participants are transferred from one plan to another plan.

Audit Objectives

The audit objectives for procedures applied to transfers are to provide the auditor with a reasonable basis to determine that the transfer of plan assets is recorded at the fair market value of the assets at the transfer date and that the benefit obligations related to such participants also transferred as appropriate.

Audit Procedures

When auditing transfers to or from the plan, the plan auditor should make selections for testing purposes to determine that the plan assets were transferred at the fair market value of the assets as of the transfer date. In addition, the auditor should determine that the benefit obligations related to the transfer were appropriately reflected in the plan's statement of benefit obligations.

STATEMENTS OF BENEFIT OBLIGATIONS AND STATEMENT OF CHANGES IN BENEFIT OBLIGATIONS

SOP 92-6 requires that the benefit obligations and, if significant, the changes in benefit obligations of the plan should also be included in the financial statements of a health and welfare plan. This information may be presented either in separate financial statements or as a part of the statement of net assets available for benefits and statement of changes in net assets available for benefits. ERISA requires the plan's statement of net assets available for benefits to be presented in comparative form; therefore, the benefit obligations at the end of the plan year and the previous plan year should be presented, while the changes in benefit obligations may be presented for the current year only. The statement of benefit obligations details the benefit-related liabilities of the plan measured as of the end of the plan year. The statement of benefit obligations includes amounts for claims and premiums payable, the liability for claims that are incurred but not reported, accumulated eligibility credits, and postretirement obligations for plans that provide postretirement benefits. The statement of changes in benefit obligations outlines the activity that has occurred in the benefit obligations of the health and welfare plan during the year. Specifically, the change in the claims payable (i.e., the claims that have been reported and approved for payment less the claims paid), the change in the estimate of claims incurred but not reported, and the changes in the postretirement obligation are included in the statement of changes in benefit obligations. In order to determine the level of funding of the plan, the statement of benefit obligations would need to be compared to the statement of net assets available for benefits.

The following provides a description of the accounts that would typically be recorded on the statement of benefit obligations and the statement of changes in benefit obligations. Following the description of the account is a summary of audit objectives and suggested audit procedures.

BENEFIT OBLIGATIONS

Benefit obligations of a plan include all obligations of the plan that are related to the plan's provision of benefits to participants. Examples of benefit obligations are claims currently due, premiums due, claims incurred but not reported and postretirement and postemployment benefit obligations (such as accumulated eligibility credits for supplemental unemployment benefits). Benefit obligations should be recorded at their actuarial present value as determined at the end of the plan year.

In addition, approved plan amendments are to be considered in the calculation of the postretirement and postemployment benefit obligations. For example, the effect of an amendment that changes the benefit that retirees will receive, effective after the plan's year-end, should be considered in the obligation calculation.

The following represents a summary of the types of benefit obligations and how such amounts would be reported on a plan's statement of benefit obligations:

- Claims currently due and claims incurred but not reported that are paid by the insurance company (i.e., the plan is fully insured) should be excluded from the financial statements of the plan.
- For insured plans, benefit obligations should include premiums due as well as postretirement obligations.
- Postretirement obligations are amounts that are calculated to be the actuarial present value of amounts to be paid in the future for current retirees and for active employees that will be eligible for benefits after retirement from employment at the plan sponsor. Currently, a plan sponsor cannot insure postretirement benefit obligations, except for the payments related to the current year.
- Postemployment obligations are amounts that are calculated to represent the actuarial present value of claims to be paid in the future for employees that will currently be eligible for benefits upon termination of employment (e.g., through disability or termination) for the period of time as specified within the plan document. Postemployment benefit obligations would be reported as a separate line item within the plan's statement of benefit obligations typically in the form of accumulated eligibility credits.
- If the plan is a self-funded plan, claims currently due for all plan participants, dependents, and beneficiaries--and incurred but not reported (IBNR) claims for active participants--should be recorded on the plan's financial statements as well as postretirement obligations, if applicable. IBNR claims for retired participants are generally excluded from the "claims currently due" line item since they are considered in the calculation of the plan's total postretirement benefit obligation. If the retiree claims incurred but not reported are not included in the calculation of the postretirement benefit obligation, the amount should be included in the IBNR line item.

Audit Objective

Overall, the audit objective for the area of benefit obligations is to determine that all benefit-related liabilities of the plan at the end of the plan year have been recorded as plan obligations. The focus of the discussion below is obligations for health benefits provided by a health plan; however, benefit obligations may exist in all types of health and welfare plans. Obligations related to postemployment benefits and accumulated eligibility credits provided, for example, for supplemental unemployment benefits, are discussed later in this chapter.

PREMIUMS AND HEALTH CLAIMS PAYABLE

Audit Objectives

The audit objective for health claims payable in **self-funded plans** is to determine whether all claims reported to the plan administrator, but not paid as of year-end, are recorded as obligations of the plan.

The audit objectives for premiums and health claims payable for **insured plans** are to determine whether the proper dollar amount of premiums has been remitted to the insurance company and whether any obligation for unpaid insurance premiums has been properly recorded. Because fully insured plans are not required to be audited, these objectives are applicable when a plan is partially insured and partially funded (for example, a self-funded with stop-loss insurance arrangement or a plan that is insured for life insurance benefits but self-funded for health benefits).

Audit Procedures

Self-funded plans. Consider using the following audit procedures in testing benefit obligations for premiums and health claims payable for self-funded plans:

- Obtain an understanding of the methods used to determine claims reported but not paid.
- Obtain the trial balance of claims reported to the plan but not paid. Test the summarization and the reconciliation of the total to the plan's final accounting records. Consider the lag time between the reporting and payment of a claim for reasonableness.
- Make a selection of claims paid from subsequent claims disbursement records during a period of approximately two to three months following the date of the claims trial balance and (1) trace selected claims paid to service provider statements and/or other supporting documents, and (2) determine whether those selected claims paid that indicate an obligation as of the trial balance date are recorded in the trial balance or in the reconciliation to the plan's final accounting records.

Insured plans. Consider using the following audit procedures for insured plans:

- Obtain information regarding premiums payable to the insurance company and reconcile the information to the plan's final accounting records.
- Determine whether premiums payable at year-end have been recorded at the proper amount by reviewing the basis for computation of the payable and trace the amount to a subsequent payment.
- Review the insurance contract to determine that the payable is in accordance with the contract provisions: (1) if the insurance contract requires payment of additional premiums when the loss ratio exceeds a specified percentage, determine whether circumstances exist requiring an additional payable for estimated additional premiums and whether any such amount

has been included in benefit obligations of the plan; or (2) if the insurance contract provides for experience rating adjustments, determine whether a premium deficit has resulted and that any such deficit has been included as a benefit obligation when either it is probable that the deficit will be applied against the amounts of future premiums or future experience rating refunds or the amount can be reasonably estimated; and (3) consider if the contract requires an amount to be paid upon termination of the contract or at the end of the contract's term and determine if the appropriate amount has been included as a benefit obligation.

INCURRED BUT NOT REPORTED OBLIGATION (IBNR)

Audit Objective

The audit objective for claims incurred but not reported is to determine that the estimates of the amounts are reasonable and that all obligations of the plan at year-end are included in one of the line items of the statement of benefit obligations.

Audit Procedures

An understanding of the development of the IBNR estimate is important; however, if the audit is being performed substantially after year-end, consider reviewing the actual claims reported and paid in the subsequent year for the year under audit. Obtain this information from the third-party administrator, if applicable, or from the plan sponsor. Consider the historical lag time for claim occurrence, reporting, and payment and evaluate the IBNR estimate considering the amount of claims paid and the estimate of claims still not paid (or not reported or paid) for the year under audit. If it is not feasible to review the actual claims amounts, the audit procedures that may be considered in testing the benefit obligations for IBNR for self-funded plans include the following:

- Obtain information regarding claims incurred but not reported (including actuarial reports, if applicable). Often for plans that provide postretirement benefits the IBNR estimates relate only to the active employees as the postretirement obligation may include IBNR estimates for retirees.
- Reconcile the information to the plan's final accounting records.
- Obtain an understanding of the methods (including the definition of catastrophic claims and how they are handled), assumptions (e.g., discount rate, cost assumptions, lag period), and employee groups covered and benefit coverages (including cost-sharing provisions) used in developing the IBNR estimate and consistency of their application.
- Determine whether claims incurred but not reported are measured at the present value of estimated ultimate cost to the plan of settling the claims. Estimated ultimate cost should reflect the plan's obligation to pay claims to or for the participants, beyond the financial statement date as stipulated by the plan document.

- Document how changes in benefit coverages or employee groups covered are communicated to the actuary or insurance company.
- Compare the summary of benefit coverages included in the actuarial valuation report to pertinent provisions in the plan document and to any amendments, as applicable.
- Compare the summary of employee groups covered included in the actuarial valuation report to supporting documentation maintained by plan management, as applicable.
- Conclude on the reasonability of the methods, assumptions, employee groups covered, and benefit coverages used in developing the IBNR estimate.

POSTRETIREMENT BENEFIT OBLIGATIONS/ACTUARIAL DATA

Some health and welfare plans provide for the payment of future health insurance premiums or health care claims for retirees. Depending on the provisions of the plan, the benefits may begin upon termination of service, or eligibility for benefits may be deferred until the participant reaches a defined age. Plans that provide for the payment of future health care claims are more common; however, plans that provide for the payment of future health insurance premiums also exist and the postretirement benefit obligation for these plans is based on the projection of the cost of future premiums.

SOP 92-6 describes the requirements for measuring and reporting the postretirement obligations for health and welfare benefit plans. The postretirement benefit obligation represents the actuarial present value of the claims, which are to be paid to, or on behalf of, the participants of the plan after they retire. The amount is the measurement of the obligation for retirees and for active employees based on their credited service to date and considering the date they will become eligible to receive benefits.

The postretirement obligations are provided by an actuary and should include benefit obligations for the following categories of plan participants:

- Current retirees
- Other participants fully eligible for benefits
- Participants not yet fully eligible for benefits

In general, the determination of the amount of postretirement obligations should be dependent upon the provisions included in the plan document. The obligation should include amounts expected to be paid to or on behalf of the participant's beneficiaries and dependents, as well as to the participant. The measurement of the plan's postretirement benefit obligation should be as of the end of the plan year; however, a measurement date not more than three months prior to that date may be used, if it is used consistently from year to year.

In measuring the postretirement obligation, the assumptions related to the following items must be considered:

- Discount rate, which is determined based upon the rate of return on plan assets
- The expected timing and amount of future postretirement benefit payments considering various factors including per capita claims cost by age, health care cost-trend rates, current medicare reimbursement rates, retirement age, dependency status, and mortality
- The probability of payment considering variables such as turnover, retirement age, dependency status, and mortality
- For contributory plans, participation rates

The information which is to be presented regarding the changes in the postretirement benefit obligations from the end of the prior year should include the following information to the extent applicable for the plan's circumstances. The presentation of information regarding changes in the postretirement benefit obligations is not required unless the components resulting in the change in the postretirement benefit obligations are significant.

- The impact of plan amendments (For example, a plan could be amended to increase the amount of participant or surviving spouse contributions required by the plan. The impact of such a change needs to be quantified by the actuary to determine the decrease in the plan's postretirement benefit obligations.)
- Changes in actuarial assumptions (For example, to the extent that a change is made to the average retirement age from 65 to 62, that change would increase the plan's postretirement benefit obligations.) Also changes to assumptions may be the result of changes in the health care cost-trend rate.
- Changes in the nature of the plan (e.g., due to spin-off or merger of the plan or plan sponsor)
- Benefits earned (or accumulated) during the year by active employees. This line item will include the impact of another year of benefits earned by active employees of the plan sponsor and also the impact of actuarial gains and losses resulting from actual experience of participants relating to mortality and turnover, which may differ from the initial expectations of the actuary. In essence, this line item performs a "true-up" of actuarial estimates to actual plan experience.

Audit Objective

The audit objective for a plan's postretirement benefit obligations is the determination of whether the obligation reasonably presents the amount that the plan is obligated to pay for the future benefits for retirees.

Audit Procedures

The primary focus for an auditor when auditing the postretirement benefit obligations presented by the plan within its financial statements is the information prepared by the actuary. As mentioned earlier, for purposes of developing the postretirement benefit obligations for the plan, an actuary should be engaged by the plan. The remaining procedures discussed below are applicable for actuarial information or valuations prepared as of either the beginning or end of the plan year. The procedures listed below are applicable for either full-scope audits or limited-scope audits.

Engaging a specialist. One of the first considerations to be made by the auditor are the requirements with respect to the use of specialists in an audit engagement. Actuaries are considered to be specialists as defined by SAS 73, *Using the Work of a Specialist.* According to the provisions of SAS 73, when a specialist is used by a plan, the auditor should perform procedures to evaluate the specialist's qualifications, reputation, and relationship to the client. In this regard, the auditor should consider obtaining a letter from the actuary regarding their independence from the plan and the plan sponsor. The auditor should document in the audit working papers the basis for conclusions that support reliance on the use of the actuary's work and its propriety as audit evidence. Considerations of the actuary's professional qualifications should include whether the actuary is an "enrolled actuary" as defined by ERISA 3041 and 3042 and whether the actuary is a member of the American Academy of Actuaries or a fellow in the Society of Actuaries. In addition, in accordance with the provisions of SAS 85, as amended by SAS 89, if the work of a specialist has been used by an entity, the auditor should include additional representations from management relating to that use. The following represents an example of the item to be included in the management representation letter:

> We agree with the findings of the actuary in evaluating the plan's postretirement benefit obligations and have adequately considered the qualifications of the actuary in determining the amounts and disclosures used in the financial statements and underlying accounting records. We did not give or cause any instructions to be given to specialists with respect to the values or amounts derived in an attempt to bias their work, and we are not otherwise aware of any matters that had an impact on the independence or objectivity of the actuary.

The actuarial valuation. A typical actuarial valuation or other report includes a variety of information to be used by the auditor. For instance, the actuary will determine the postretirement benefit obligations for the plan. The auditor should reconcile this information with the plan's financial statements to determine that the plan has correctly reported the postretirement benefit obligation information within the plan's financial statements. This procedure may be accomplished through a confirmation that requests the actuary to send to the auditor a copy of what has previously been prepared for the plan sponsor--often a valuation report or similar documentation of the calculation of the obligation, its components, and the assumptions considered in the calculation. Also, the auditor should obtain directly from the actuary a reconciliation of the plan's postretirement benefit obligation to that obligation amount reported and audited at the sponsor level pursuant to SFAS 106 and test significant discrepant items.

In order for the auditor to determine that the actuary has all of the relevant information regarding the plan and that the actuary demonstrates an adequate understanding of the provisions of the plan to enable the actuary to prepare the postretirement benefit obligation information, the auditor will want to review the section of the actuarial valuation which contains the summary of plan provisions. Within this section, the actuary will highlight key provisions of the plan, that are critical to its operation, such as the date of last plan amendment, participants covered by the plan, and date of plan's inception. In order to ensure that the summary of plan provisions as reported by the actuary is accurate, the auditor should compare such information to the plan document and any relevant plan amendments for consistency. In addition, to the extent that the auditor has been made aware of amendments that have been executed by plan management, the auditor should determine that the actuary has received information regarding the amendment. This can be accomplished by reviewing the summary of plan provisions, and specifically, the date listed as the date of the latest plan amendment. The auditor may also review the sections within the plan document that have changed to ensure that the actuary has appropriately reflected the impact of such amendments in the summary of plan provisions.

The actuarial valuation will also include census information regarding the plan which provides a summary of the total number of active and retired participants as of the benefit information date. In addition, although not generally provided with the actuarial valuation, the auditor may request from the actuary the detailed demographic information for the plan which will list detailed information for each group of plan participants such as their hire date, date of birth, date of retirement, average salary, and coverages elected. In order to determine that the actuary has taken into consideration the complete population for the plan, the auditor may perform either procedure 1 or procedure 2 listed below relative to the census data and demographic data depending upon the auditor's assessment of how effective the communication between the plan sponsor and the actuary has been on these matters. (Note that procedures 3 and 4 listed below should be performed by auditors in any case.)

1. For each of the significant components: (actives and retirees, including dependents and beneficiaries) the auditor should independently obtain information from the plan sponsor (such as from the payroll system and benefit payment register) to determine the number of actives and retirees as of the benefit information date. If the number of beneficiaries and dependents is not readily accessible by the plan sponsor, the auditor should consider ways to reasonably estimate the number of each in order to test the information used by the actuary. The auditor should then compare the information to that reported by the actuary to determine consistency in the census data.
2. The auditor may also perform detailed testing procedures relative to the demographic data by making a selection of participants from the plan sponsor's personnel files and agreeing relevant information such as birth date, hire date, and coverages to the detailed demographic information received

from the actuary. The auditor should then perform the same procedures but by making the initial selections from the actuary's detailed demographic data and agreeing back to the plan sponsor's personnel files to determine consistency of information between the two sources. Furthermore, s/he should trace through the demographic information indicated for each selection that appears to be a new participant or a participant who has changed his or her classification, to verify the propriety of the participant's eligibility status, birth date, hire date, or any other factors that could impact postretirement benefits. For participants who do not appear to be new to the plan, trace the demographic information to the prior year actuarial listing of demographic information or to personnel records to verify no changes in eligibility status, birth date, and other such factors.

3. The auditor should also periodically review the actuarial assumptions used by the actuary to determine that they are still appropriate, particularly if there have been significant changes in the plan's provisions, eligibility, and investment assets or if there have been any other such changes which may warrant a revision of the actuarial assumptions.
4. Any exceptions identified in the procedures performed above should be quantified and brought to the attention of the plan sponsor and to the actuary for clarification and resolution. In addition, the auditor should evaluate the exceptions and determine the effect of such exceptions upon postretirement benefit obligation.

In addition to testing the demographic data used by the actuary to estimate the postretirement benefit obligation, the auditor should test the significant assumptions used by the actuary in measuring the postretirement benefit obligation. Procedures to consider for the significant assumptions are the following:

1. Test the information utilized by the actuary in determining the health care cost data assumption. The health care cost data includes per capita claims cost by age, health care cost-trend rates, and current medicare reimbursement rates. The auditor should understand the data used by the actuary to develop the assumptions including the historical pattern of claims by age (i.e., claims curve) or comparable data. Generally a health care specialist develops the health care data assumption.
2. Test the reasonableness of the discount rate utilized by the actuary. The effect of the discount rate on the postretirement obligation is the result of the effect of the value of money over time on the obligation, when considering the estimated amounts and the timing of future claim payments and other costs. When performing this test also consider the prevailing interest rates on high-quality, fixed income investments currently available, whose cash flows match the timing and amount of expected benefit payments in the market at the end of the plan year. To the extent that the discount rate utilized by the actuary does not fall within a close range of the market rates, the

auditor should investigate this situation with the plan administrator and the actuary.

With respect to the information included within the changes in the postretirement benefit obligations from the prior year, the auditor should perform the following procedures. (Note that with respect to the line items presented below, while the actuary is a specialist used to determine the postretirement benefit obligations, ultimately, the auditors are required to take responsibility for amounts included in the plan's financial statements and should be comfortable with all amounts presented in the financial statements which relate to the plan's postretirement benefit obligations.)

1. For amounts listed as benefit payments, the auditor should agree such amounts to the amount of benefit payments reported in the plan's statement of changes in net assets available for benefits, or to support for the amount if the benefit payment amount includes payments for actives as well as retirees.
2. For the changes in actuarial assumptions line item, while the auditor may not be able to quantify or recompute the amount appearing as the impact of a change in an actuarial assumption, the auditor should review the summary of actuarial assumptions, which appears as part of the actuarial valuation, and compare this to the summary included in the prior year's actuarial valuation. The auditor should note whether there have been changes to the actuarial assumptions and, if so, if there is a related amount in the changes in the postretirement benefit obligation for the incorporation of the new assumption into the measurement of the obligation. For changes in the discount rate and health care cost data, as discussed above, amounts should be included in the changes in postretirement obligations. The auditor should determine that each of the significant changes in actuarial assumptions appears reasonable given the circumstances for the plan. An absence of a change in assumptions likewise suggests the absence of an amount appearing as a change in actuarial assumptions.
3. Consider whether any plan amendments were contractually agreed to during the period. Similar to the previous discussion, the auditor may not be able to recompute the amount listed as a plan amendment; however, based upon the knowledge obtained about the plan during the course of the audit, the auditor should determine whether any plan amendments have been effective or adopted which would affect the postretirement benefit obligation for the plan. In certain cases, depending upon the nature of the plan amendment, the auditor may be able to estimate the impact that an amendment will have upon the postretirement benefit obligations.
4. The increase for interest due to the decrease in the discount period can normally be computed by the auditor by multiplying the beginning-of-the-year actuarial present value of postretirement benefit obligation, or the average

of the beginning-of-year and end-of-year benefit obligation, by the assumed discount rate.

5. For amounts appearing as benefits earned (or accumulated)--net, the auditor should determine the general reasonability of the amount based upon the general knowledge of the plan and through review of additional information included within the actuarial valuation, which may discuss the actual plan experience during the year covered by the actuarial valuation. The actual experience of the plan as determined for the year and compared to the estimate for the year is reflected in the benefits accumulated line item generally in the form of actuarial gains and losses. For example, to the extent that a plan realizes an actual return on plan investments which exceeds the estimated return by the actuary, this would result in an actuarial gain for the plan which would lower the plan's accumulated plan benefit obligations.
6. For other amounts which may appear in the reconciliation of postretirement benefit obligations, such as transfers due to plan mergers, the auditor should assess the reasonability of the amounts listed based upon activities of the plan during the year.

Any discrepancies found while performing the procedures listed above should be discussed with the appropriate levels of plan management to be resolved to the satisfaction of the auditor.

POSTEMPLOYMENT BENEFIT OBLIGATIONS

Postemployment benefit obligations include health and welfare and other benefits that are expected to be paid to or on behalf of former or inactive employees, after employment and before retirement. These benefits include salary continuation, disability, training, supplemental disability and health and insurance coverages. In many cases, union contracts require that plan sponsors fund such benefits by contributing a specified amount of money per hour worked by union employees to provide for certain benefits such as unemployment benefits and vacation pay. Postemployment benefits may be paid to the former employee, their beneficiaries, and covered dependents and are considered obligations if the employee has rendered the required service, the benefit is vested, payment is probable, and the amount can be reasonably determined. The benefits may be paid upon the termination of the employee's employment (e.g., through disability or termination) or may be designed to be paid over time, in which case the obligation may be calculated actuarially. Principal actuarial assumptions should address, if applicable, discount rates, the timing and amount of postemployment benefit payments, and mortality.

SFAS 112, *Employers' Accounting for Postemployment Benefits: An Amendment of FASB Statements 5 and 43,* established the accounting standards for employers who provide postemployment benefits. Defined benefit health and welfare plans, which encompasses postemployment benefits, should present the obligations related to postemployment benefits as described in this statement, measuring the obligations in the same way as the obligations in general are measured and include them in the plan sponsor's financial statements. The statement requires that if the postemployment benefit meets the conditions as stated in SFAS 43, *Accounting for Compensated Absences*, the employer should account for the benefit in accordance with SFAS 43, which states

> *An employer shall accrue a liability for employee's compensation for future absences if **all** of the following conditions are met:*
>
> - *The employer's obligation relating to employees' rights to receive compensation for future absences is attributable to employees' services already rendered,*
> - *The obligation related to rights that vest or accumulate*
> - *Payment of the compensation is probable, and*
> - *The amount can be reasonable estimated.*

If postemployment benefits do not meet these stated conditions, SFAS 112 states that they should be accounted for in accordance with SFAS 5, *Accounting for Contingencies,* which states

> *An estimated loss from a loss contingency (as defined in paragraph 1 [of SFAS 5]) shall be accrued by a charge to income if **both** of the following conditions are met:*
>
> 1. *Information available prior to issuance of the financial statements indicates that it is probable that an asset had been impaired or a liability had been incurred at the date of the financial statements. It is implicit in this condition that it must be probable that one or more future events will occur confirming the fact of the loss.*
> 2. *The amount of loss can be reasonably estimated.*

SFAS 112 requires that if the postemployment benefit is not accrued because it is not able to be estimated, the footnotes to the plan's financial statements should disclose this fact.

Audit Objective

The audit objective for a plan's postemployment benefit obligations is the determination of whether the obligation reasonably presents the amount that the plan is obligated to pay for the future benefits.

Audit Procedures

An actuary may or may not be involved in the calculation of the postemployment benefit obligations presented by the plan within its financial statements, depending on the type and structure of the benefit. If actuarial calculations are necessary, like with the postretirement benefit obligation, a primary focus for an auditor is the information prepared by the actuary. As part of the audit process, the auditor should independently receive a copy of the actuarial valuation. The procedures listed above for auditing postretirement obligations related to the actuarial information are also applicable for postemployment benefit obligations and should be considered for either full-scope audits or limited-scope audits, including testing of the actuarial assumptions for health care cost data, for plans offering postemployment health care benefits, and for discount rate assumptions.

For plans which have nonactuarially determined postemployment benefit obligations, the following procedures should be considered. An understanding of the development of the postemployment benefit obligation is important; however, if the postemployment obligation is to be paid over a short period of time (for example, severance medical benefits offered through a health and welfare plan), and the audit is being performed substantially after year-end, consider reviewing actual amounts paid for the benefits subsequent to year-end. Obtain the information from the third-party administrator, if applicable, or from the plan sponsor. If it is not feasible to review the actual amounts paid, consider the following audit procedures in testing the postemployment benefit obligations:

- Obtain information regarding the postemployment benefit obligations, including a reconciliation of the information to the plan's final accounting records and calculations supporting the amounts recorded.
- Review assumptions made by management for purposes of calculating the obligations for reasonableness.
- Test the mathematical accuracy of the postemployment calculation schedule.
- For each of the significant components eligible to receive the postemployment benefit, including active and inactive employees and dependents and beneficiaries, obtain information from the plan sponsor (such as from the payroll system, benefit payment register, etc.) to determine the number of covered employees as of the benefit information date. Test the obligation recorded with test of details, analytical procedures, or a combination.

Test of details. Make a selection of individuals from the plan sponsor's personnel files and perform the following:

1. Determine the employee's eligibility for the benefit and test the calculation of the obligation for appropriate inclusion or exclusion of the employee.
2. Test the demographic data used in the calculation by agreeing relevant information such as birth date, hire date, health coverages, and pay rate to the calculation of the obligation.
3. Perform procedures 1 and 2 again by making the selections from the census data used to calculate the postemployment obligation. Agree the data to the plan sponsor's personnel files to determine consistency of information.

Analytical procedures.

- Develop an expectation of the postemployment obligation by considering the historical costs and/or claim rates, current premium rates or other related cost or expected cost of benefits related to the type of benefit offered (e.g., health claims, vacation payments, or supplemental unemployment payments) per eligible participant.

- Compare the expectation to recorded obligation amount and obtain and corroborate explanations for significant differences.

With respect to the information included within the changes in the postemployment benefit obligations from the prior year, the auditor should consider the following procedures:

- For amounts listed as benefit payments, the auditor should agree such amount to the amount of benefit payments included in the plan's statement of changes in net assets available for benefits, or to support for the amount if the benefit payment amount includes payments for actives as well as retirees
- Consider whether any plan amendments were contractually agreed to during the period and their impact on the postemployment benefit obligation.
- For other changes in the postemployment benefit obligation assess the reasonableness of the amounts reflected in the plan financial statement as changes in the postemployment benefit obligations.

Any discrepancies identified during the performance of the procedures listed above should be discussed with the appropriate levels of plan management to be resolved to the satisfaction of the auditor.

ACCUMULATED ELIGIBILITY CREDITS

Another postemployment benefit obligation presented on the statement of benefit obligations is accumulated eligibility credits. Accumulated eligibility credits are applicable primarily to multiemployer plans or single-employer plans that cover collectively bargained employees and represent "other obligations for current benefit coverage" at the end of the plan year. Eligibility credits arise when the plan provides for postemployment medical coverage or salary for participants who have accumulated a sufficient number of eligibility credits or hours (often measured quarterly). In many cases, the plan sponsor will contribute to the plan a certain amount of money per hour worked by the employee to fund such postemployment benefits. The number of eligibility credits accumulated during the preceding period determine the participant's eligibility for coverage paid by the employer during the postemployment period. This feature results in coverage for participants who are not currently active employees. This amount represents an obligation of the plan because the accumulated credits are the result of a service that has already been provided and for which employer contributions have already been received. For insured plans, the amount of the obligation can be estimated using the current insurance premium rates and the number of accumulated eligibility credits, adjusted for items that will influence the ultimate amount payable (e.g., mortality, expected turnover, and other considerations, based on the provisions of the plan). If a participant has not accumulated the required number of eligibility credits for full coverage, a pro rata amount of eligibility credits may be calculated for the participant, if provided in the plan document. Finally, in some cases, plans exist which may provide for participant contributions to fund a portion of the benefits to retain coverage that would otherwise be unavailable to them, or the plan may be structured as a contributory plan.

Audit Procedures

Consider the following audit procedures when testing benefit obligations for accumulated eligibility credits:

- Obtain the plan's information regarding accumulated eligibility credits and agree or reconcile the totals to the plan's final accounting records. Test the obligation recorded with test of details, analytical procedures or a combination of both.
- Obtain information from the actuary (for plans that use an actuary to estimate obligations) regarding the census data and the calculation through a confirmation. Reconcile the number of participants and the accumulated eligibility credits from the plan sponsor's records to the actuary's information. Then, review the actuary's information to test whether the plan provisions related to accumulated eligibility credits appear to have been applied correctly.

Test of details. Make a selection of individuals from the employee eligibility records and perform the following:

- Review the participants' eligibility records to determine the hours worked by the employee during the plan year, the participant's salary, years employed by the plan sponsor, and any other relevant data
- Obtain the amount of the employer contribution for the participant
- Test the mathematical accuracy of the amount contributed for the participant by recomputing the amount of the accumulated credits by applying current insurance premium rates to accumulated eligibility credits or by applying the average cost of benefits per eligible participant
- If the plan includes "self-pay" provisions (i.e., participants may contribute to the plan to retain coverage if eligibility credits are not sufficient for a period of time, or the plan may be a contributory plan), consider effect of participant contributions on the obligation

Analytical procedures.

- Develop an independent expectation of the amount of accumulated eligibility credits by considering the balance of accumulated eligibility credits in the prior periods, current insurance premium rates or the average cost of benefits per eligible participant, and historical usage of the credits by eligible participants (including consideration of historical employee turnover and mortality and consideration of the reasonableness of the assumptions for the current period). Note that the obligation for accumulated eligibility

credits needs to be appropriately discounted for purposes of presentation on the plan's statement of benefit obligations.
- Compare the expectation to recorded obligation amount and obtain and corroborate explanations for significant differences.

The procedures listed above represent suggested approaches for auditing the accounts of a health and welfare plan. Consideration should also be given to the concepts discussed in the chapters on Planning, Internal Control, Investments, Other Accounting and Auditing Considerations, Auditors' Reports, and Financial Statements and Disclosures, since the material presented within those chapters is important and applicable to health and welfare plans. Chapter 12, Auditors' Reports, includes examples of auditors' reports and Chapter 13, Financial Statements and Disclosures, includes illustrative financial statements and sample footnote disclosures which are relevant to health and welfare plans.

OTHER FINANCIAL STATEMENT DISCLOSURES

In addition to the information regarding benefit obligations and net assets of the plan, the plan's financial statements should include a discussion of additional matters in accordance with the provisions of SOP 92-6. These additional disclosures would include the following:

1. A brief discussion of the provisions of the plan document including, but not limited to, a description of: the employees covered by the plan; benefits provided under the plan; description of employee contributions, if applicable; and name of plan trustee and/or custodian. Alternatively, the footnotes may include a note which refers readers to the plan document for a summary of the plan's provisions, as opposed to discussing the provisions within the footnotes. It is unusual, however, to not include some basic information regarding the plan within the plan's footnote disclosures.
2. The plan should disclose significant accounting policies, such as its use of estimates in determining amounts included within the financial statements, any concentrations of risks of investments, and if significant costs of administering the plan are paid by the plan sponsor.
3. For plans which are contributory (contributions made by employees), the plan should disclose the method for determining employee contributions.
4. A discussion of the methods used to determine the fair value of investments held by the plan should be included. This would include all investments held by the plan, including insurance contracts and those for which an active market exists for the investment and those which are not readily marketable.
5. To the extent that the plan invests in allocated contracts (not considered to be plan assets), disclosure should be made of the amount of such assets held by the plan as well as the plan's policy regarding the purchase of these types of contracts from insurance companies. Any dividend income related

to these allocated contracts should be disclosed, although it is permissible to net the amount of administrative expenses paid to the insurance companies for administering the contracts against the amount of dividend income earned.

6. The plan's financial statements should separately disclose any single investment which exceeds 5% of net assets available for benefits as of the end of the plan year. To the extent that the investment is already listed separately in the statement of net assets available for benefits, the investment is not required to be disclosed again in the footnotes.
7. The plan's financial statements should disclose the net appreciation (depreciation) in fair value of investments by major class of investment, such as equities or fixed-income securities, as well as segregating the net appreciation (depreciation) generated by investments whose fair value is determined by quoted market prices (such as an investment in a mutual fund) from the amount generated by investments whose fair value is estimated (such as a limited partnership or real estate).
8. If the plan invests in a master trust along with other employee benefit plans of the plan sponsor, the financial statements should include the following disclosures: a general description of the types of investments held by the master trust (e.g., equity, debt, fixed income) and the amounts of such assets at the end of the year; the components of investment income earned by the master trust during the year (e.g., interest, dividends, net appreciation/depreciation); the plan's percentage of the total master trust's investments at the end of the year; and a discussion of the method used by the master trust to allocate investments and investment income to the participating plans.
9. A discussion of the significant actuarial assumptions used by the actuary in determining the plan's benefit obligations.
10. To the extent that a change has been made in the assumptions used by the actuary during the current year as compared to those used in the prior year, such changes should also be disclosed.
11. The assumed health care cost-trend rate used to measure the expected cost of benefits covered by the plan for the next year. A general description of the assumed trend rates thereafter, including the direction and pattern of change, the ultimate trend rate, and when that rate is expected to be achieved.
12. For health and welfare benefit plans which provide postretirement health care benefits, the effect on the postretirement benefit obligation of a one-percentage-point increase in the assumed health care cost-trend rates for each future year.
13. Modification of the existing cost-sharing provisions of the plan and the nature of any commitment to increase benefits provided by the plan, including their effect on the plan's financial statements.

14. Additional changes in circumstances which may significantly affect a plan's benefit obligations would be significant plan amendments or the partial or full termination of a plan.
15. A discussion of the plan's funding policy and any changes that were made in the policy during the year.
16. The federal tax status of the plan, including information regarding the tax-exempt status of the trust pursuant to the IRC. Information regarding whether a plan has or has not received a favorable determination letter is not required to be disclosed under generally accepted accounting principles, but is required by ERISA.
17. From a tax perspective, to the extent that a plan has entered into a voluntary compliance program sponsored by either the DOL or the IRS, consideration should be given to the disclosure of such a fact as well as plan management's assessment as to the potential impact upon the plan. In addition, consideration should be given to potential modifications which may need to be made to the independent auditors' report relative to the plan's tax-qualified status.
18. A description of significant plan amendments which have been adopted during the year and disclosure of the expected impact of such amendments upon the plan's financial statements. The expected impact of such amendments should be available, as it would be a rare plan sponsor who would accept an amendment to a plan without knowing the cost of the plan amendment.
19. A description of the general priorities upon termination of the plan.
20. A discussion of any unusual events or transactions occurring after the latest benefit information date but before the issuance of the plan's financial statements that might affect the usefulness of the financial statements in determining the ability of the plan to pay its benefits in the future. Such types of events may include plan mergers, plan terminations, or significant plan amendments which increase the amount of benefits payable under the plan. Disclosure should be made of the expected impact of such events upon the plan's financial statements, and if not yet determinable, such a fact should be explained, including the reason why an impact cannot yet be determined.
21. In the event that the plan has entered into any nonexempt transactions during the year (i.e., prohibited transactions)--and to the extent that such transactions are material to the plan's financial statements--disclosure should be made of a description of such transactions and the corrective action being taken by the plan sponsor in relation to the transactions. This information is also required to be reported in the supplemental schedules which are part of the plan's Form 5500 filing.
22. If the plan engaged in significant transactions during the year with a related party, a description of the nature and amount of the transactions should be

included in the footnotes to the plan's financial statements. In addition, any employer securities held by the plan should be disclosed in the footnotes to the plan's financial statements.

ADDITIONAL DISCLOSURES FOR FULLY BENEFIT-RESPONSIVE INVESTMENT CONTRACTS

For fully benefit-responsive investment contracts that are described in SOP 94-4, *Reporting of Investment Contracts Held by Health and Welfare Benefit Plans and Defined Contribution Pension Plans,* the following disclosures must also be made (in the aggregate):

- The average yield for each period for which a statement of net assets available for benefits is presented. This information is available from the investment company.
- The crediting interest rate as of the date of each statement of net assets available for benefits presented. Again, this rate is available from the investment company.
- The amount of valuation reserves recorded to adjust contract amounts (for example, due to problems with the creditworthiness of the contract issuer or the third-party guarantor).
- The fair values of fully benefit-responsive investment contracts reported at contract value on the statement of net assets available for benefits. Note, however, that SFAS 126, *Exemption From Certain Required Disclosures About Financial Instruments for Certain Nonpublic Entities*, provides that plans which satisfy all of the following criteria are not required to disclose the fair value of fully benefit-responsive investment contracts: (1) The plan is a nonpublic entity (in other words, a Form 11-k filing is not required for the plan); (2) The plan's total assets are less than $100 million on the date of the plan's financial statements, and (3) The plan has no instrument that, in whole or in part, is accounted for as a derivative instrument under SFAS 133, *Accounting for Derivative Instruments and Hedging Activities*, during the reporting period.

SFAS 105, 107, AND 119

Any additional disclosure requirements pursuant to SFAS 107, *Disclosures About Fair Value of Financial Instruments*, should be included within the plan's financial statements. SFAS 107 requires the disclosure of the fair value of financial instruments for which it is practicable to estimate that value. In addition, any significant assumptions that were utilized to establish the fair value must be disclosed. SFAS 107 states

> *If it is not practicable for an entity to estimate the fair value of a financial instrument or a class of financial instruments, the following should be disclosed:*

- *Information pertinent to estimating the fair value of that financial instrument or class of financial instruments, such as the carrying amount, effective interest rate, and maturity, and*
- *The reasons why it is not practicable to estimate fair value.*

See previous description regarding the effect of the issuance of SFAS 126 on the required disclosures under SFAS 107. Also, the fair-value disclosures are not required for plan obligations, including postretirement obligations.

SFAS 105, *Disclosure of Information About Financial Instruments With Off-Balance-Sheet Risk and Financial Instruments With Concentrations of Credit Risk,* established requirements for all entities to disclose information principally about financial instruments with off-balance-sheet risk of accounting loss. SFAS 119, *Disclosure About Derivative Financial Instruments and Fair Value of Financial Instruments*, was issued in October 1994 and superseded SFAS 105. SFAS 119 expanded on the applicability of the disclosure requirements mandated by SFAS 105. The disclosure requirements established by SFAS 105 were as follows:

- The face, contract, or notional principal amount
- The nature and terms of the instruments and a discussion of their credit and market risk, cash requirements, and related accounting policies
- The accounting loss the entity would incur if any party to the financial instrument failed completely to perform according to the terms of the contract and if the collateral or other security, if any, for the amount due proved to be of no value to the entity
- The entity's policy for requiring collateral or other security on financial instruments it accepts and a description of collateral on instruments presently held

SFAS 105 also added disclosure requirements related to information about significant concentrations of credit risk from an individual counterparty or groups of counterparties for all financial instruments. The following are disclosure requirements related to concentrations:

- Information about the activity, region, or economic characteristic that identifies the concentration
- The amount of the accounting loss due to credit risk the entity would incur if parties to the financial instruments that make up the concentration failed completely to perform according to the terms of the contracts and if the collateral or other security, if any, for the amount due proved to be of no value to the entity
- The entity's policy of requiring collateral or other security to support financial instruments subject to credit risk, information about the entity's access to that collateral or other security, and the nature and a brief description of the collateral or other security supporting those financial instruments

SFAS 105 provided an exemption of the previously described disclosure requirements for the following:

- Insurance contracts, other than financial guarantees and investment contracts
- Unconditional purchase obligations
- Employers' and plans' obligations for pension benefits, postretirement health care and life insurance benefits, employee stock option and stock purchase plans, and other forms of deferred compensation arrangements
- Financial instruments of a pension plan, including plan assets, when subject to the accounting and reporting requirements of SFAS 87, *Employers' Accounting for Pensions*
- Substantively extinguished debt subject to the disclosure requirements of SFAS 76, *Extinguishment of Debt,* and any assets held in trust in connection with an in-substance defeasance of that debt.
- SFAS 119 requires disclosures about derivative financial instruments--futures, forward, swap, and option contracts; and other financial instruments with similar characteristics, such as interest rate caps or floors and fixed-rate loan commitments. SFAS 119 established additional disclosure requirements about amounts, nature, and terms of derivative financial instruments that were not subject to the disclosure requirements under SFAS 105 because they did not result in off-balance-sheet risk of accounting loss. This statement also requires that a distinction be made between financial instruments held or issued for trading purposes and financial instruments held or issued for purposes other than trading. For options held and other derivative financial instruments not included in the scope of SFAS 105, an entity is required to disclose either in the body of the financial statements or in the accompanying notes the following information by category of financial instrument:
    - The face or contract amount (or notional principal amount if there is no face or contract amount), and
    - The nature and terms, including, at a minimum, a discussion of the (1) the credit and market risk of those instruments, (2) the cash requirements of those instruments, and (3) the related accounting policy pursuant to the requirements of APB Opinion 22, *Disclosure of Accounting Policies.*

Additional disclosure requirements based on the classification of the financial instrument (i.e., held or issued for trading purposes or held and issued for purposes other than trading) were also established with SFAS 119.

ADDITIONAL DISCLOSURES FOR DERIVATIVES

SFAS 133 was issued in June 1998 and it establishes accounting and reporting standards for these derivative instruments and hedging activities. The application date of SFAS 133 was delayed to plan years beginning after June 15, 2000, via the issuance of SFAS 137, *Accounting for Derivative Instruments and Hedging Activities--Deferral of the Effective Date of FASB Statement 133.* In accordance with SFAS 133, the following additional disclosures should be made when a plan invests in the purchase or sale of derivative instruments:

Fair Value Hedges

Fair value hedges are instruments that hedge the exposure to changes in fair value of an asset or liability. For derivative instruments, as well as nonderivative instruments that may give rise to foreign currency transaction gains or losses that have been designated and have qualified as fair value hedging instruments and for the related hedged items the following applies:

- The net gain or loss recognized in earnings during the reporting period representing (1) the amount of the hedges' ineffectiveness and (2) the component of the derivative instruments' gain or loss, if any, excluded from the assessment of hedge effectiveness, and a description of where the net gain or loss is reported in the statement of changes in net assets available for benefits.
- The amount of net gain or loss recognized in earnings when a hedged firm commitment no longer qualifies as a fair value hedge.

Cash Flow Hedges

For derivative instruments that have been designated and have qualified as cash flow hedging instruments and for the related hedged transactions the following applies:

- The net gain or loss recognized in earnings during the reporting period representing (1) the amount of the hedges' ineffectiveness and (2) the component of the derivative instruments' gain or loss, if any, excluded from the assessment of hedge effectiveness, and a description of where the net gain or loss is reported in the statement of changes in net assets available for benefits.
- A description of the transactions or other events that will result in the reclassification into earnings of gains and losses, and the estimated net amount of the existing gains or losses at the reporting date that is expected to be reclassified into earnings within the next twelve months.
- The maximum length of time over which the entity is hedging its exposure to the variability in future cash flows for forecasted transactions, excluding those forecasted transactions related to the payment of variable interest on existing financial instruments.
- The amount of gains and losses reclassified into earnings as a result of the discontinuance of cash flow hedges because it is probable that the original forecasted transactions will not occur.

COMPARATIVE FINANCIAL STATEMENTS

As a plan's financial statements are generally presented in a comparative format to comply with the provisions of ERISA, the disclosures required above for items covered by the statement of net assets available for benefits would need to cover both the current plan year and the prior plan year, while disclosures required for items covering the statement of changes in net assets available for benefits would need to cover only the current year (unless comparative statements of changes in net assets available for benefits are presented).

HEALTH AND WELFARE PLANS WITH 401(h) FEATURES

SOP 99-2, *Accounting for and Reporting of Postretirement Medical Benefit (401(h)) Features of Defined Benefit Pension Plans,* specifies the accounting for and disclosure of 401(h) features of defined benefit pension plans and health and welfare benefit plans. The following effects on health and welfare plans are specified in the SOP, namely:

- The assets in the 401(h) account that are used to fund health benefits of retirees, and the changes in those assets, are to be reported in the financial statements of the health and welfare benefit plan. Benefit obligations related to the 401(h) account are also required to be reflected in the health and welfare plan financial statements.
- The financial statements of health and welfare benefit plans must disclose the fact that the retiree health benefits are funded partially through a 401(h) account of the defined benefit pension plan.

The SOP provides specific guidance regarding the presentation of 401(h) account assets in the financial statements of defined benefit pension plans as well. See Chapter 8, Accounting, Auditing, and Reporting for Defined Benefit Pension Plans, for discussion of the accounting and reporting requirements for a defined benefit pension plan with 401(h) accounts.

The SOP specifies that the 401(h) account assets used to fund health benefits, and the changes in those assets, be reported in the financial statements of the health and welfare benefit plan. This requirement may be satisfied in one of two ways. The information may be presented as a single line item on the face of the statements or included in individual line items. When the information is presented in individual line items, information related to the 401(h) amounts included in the individual line items must be disclosed in the footnotes to the financial statements. The presentation of these amounts within the statement of changes in net assets available for benefits, whether as a single line item on the face of the statement or included in individual line items, should be consistent with the presentation included in the statement of net assets assets available for benefits. The SOP specifies also that the 401(h) benefit obligations and all claims paid through the 401(h) account be reported in the health and welfare benefit plan's statements of benefit obligations and changes in benefit obligations, respectively. In addition, the SOP requires the following to be disclosed in the notes to the financial statements:

- The significant components of net assets and changes in net assets of the 401(h) account
- The fact that retiree health benefits are funded partially through a 401(h) account of the defined benefit pension plan
- The fact that the assets in the 401(h) account are available only to pay retiree health benefits

As discussed in Chapter 8, Accounting, Auditing, and Reporting for Defined Benefit Pension Plans, the defined benefit pension plan must record the aggregate amount of net assets held in a 401(h) account related to health and welfare plan obligations for retirees as both assets and liabilities. For regulatory filing purposes, however, ERISA requires that the 401(h) assets be reported as assets of the defined benefit pension plan and not as assets of the health and welfare benefit plan. ERISA requires disclosure in the footnotes of a plan's financial statements of the differences between amounts reported in the financial statements and the amounts reported in the Form 5500. As a result, a reconciliation of the net assets reported in the health and welfare plan financial statements to those reported in the Form 5500 is required.

This SOP is effective for financial statements for plan years beginning after December 15, 1998, although earlier application is encouraged. See Chapter 13, Financial Statements and Disclosures, for example financial statements for both health and welfare plans and defined benefit pension plans with 401(h) features.

10 OTHER ACCOUNTING AND AUDITING CONSIDERATIONS

INTRODUCTION

In addition to planning, internal controls, and substantive testing, the auditor must give consideration to tax status, party-in-interest transactions, commitments and contingencies, subsequent events, management and legal representations, plan mergers and terminations, and initial audits of existing plans.

TAX STATUS

Generally, the financial statements of defined contribution pension plans, defined benefit pension plans and health and welfare plans do not record any income tax liability or provision for income tax expense, since each plan should be designed and operated in accordance with the Internal Revenue Code (IRC) requirements to maintain its qualified tax-exempt status. With the majority of plans, plan management requests a determination letter from the Internal Revenue Service (IRS) which states that as of a certain date and point in time, the plan document has been found to be in accordance with the appropriate IRC requirements to qualify for tax-exempt status. (For plans whose plan document is created from a standardized prototype, the plans may rely on the determination letter received by the prototype's sponsor. In these cases, the determination letter will be issued to the prototype's sponsor.)

While a plan may have received a favorable determination letter from the IRS, this is not a guarantee that the plan is qualified. Plan documents must be amended from time to time to comply with changes in IRC requirements for plan design. For a plan to continue to maintain its qualified status, the majority of plans must comply on an annual basis with certain operating tests, such as tests of coverage, anti-discrimination, and maximum benefit limitation. Examples of the more common types of tests are discussed below.

The auditor should consider performing the following procedures when reviewing the plan's tax status. The auditor should evaluate whether the trust continues to be tax-exempt under the IRC and whether there have been any events noted during the course of the audit (e.g., violations of tax laws) that could jeopardize the plan's qualified tax-exempt status:

- Read a copy of the plan's determination letter. The IRC does not require that a plan obtain a determination letter. However, obtaining a determination letter is advisable, as it provides confirmation that the plan and its related trust qualify for tax-exempt status. The determination letter is based on facts and conditions as stated in the request. An amendment that changes the facts and conditions stated in the request may invalidate the determination letter. If the plan has not obtained a determination letter, the auditor should consider obtaining an opinion regarding the plan's tax status from legal counsel.
- If a favorable determination letter has been obtained and there have been significant amendments since the date of the determination letter, the auditor should consider obtaining an opinion regarding the plan's tax status from legal counsel.
- Obtain and read copies of annual compliance testing performed to ensure that the plan is operating in such a manner as to maintain its tax-exempt status. Examples of such compliance tests would include
    - **Actual contribution percentage (ACP) test.** The contribution percentage (includes both employer matching and after-tax employee contributions) for highly compensated employees may not exceed the actual contribution percentage for non-highly-compensated employees by more than 1.25 times or the contribution percentages for highly compensated employees may not exceed 2% of the contribution percentages for non-highly-compensated employees. Applies to 401(k) plans only.
    - **Actual deferral percentage (ADP) test.** The deferral percentage for highly compensated employees may not exceed the deferral percentage for non-highly-compensated employees by more than 1.25 times or 2 times up to a maximum differential of 2% of contribution percentages for the highly compensated employees as compared to the non-highly-compensated employees.
    - **Top-heavy test.** 60% of plan assets may not be allocated to key employees as defined by the IRS (typically owners and top management). This applies to 401(k) plans only.
    - **Minimum coverage test (IRC 410(b)).** The percentage of non-highly-compensated employees covered in a plan must be at least 70% of the percentage of highly compensated employees covered.
    - **IRC 415 test.** This test limits the maximum contribution for a defined contribution pension plan for each individual to the lesser of 25% of pay or $30,000.

NOTE: With respect to each of the tests listed above, if the auditor has determined that the plan has adequate procedures in place with respect to the calculations of the tests, the auditor is not required to retest any of the amounts above.

- Obtain written representations from plan management regarding the plan's compliance with laws and regulations.
- Obtain copies of any voluntary compliance filings with the IRS and review the status of any corrective actions.
- If the plan has lost its tax-exempt status, the auditor should determine whether the plan has appropriately recorded any income tax liability and expense for any realized investment income earned by the plan and has disclosed that matter in accordance with generally accepted accounting principles (consider SFAS 5 requirements in this scenario). In addition, the auditor should determine whether a receivable from the plan sponsor should be recorded on the plan's financial statements if the plan has any income tax exposure.

As previously discussed in Chapter 1, Background of Employee Benefit Plans, and Chapter 3, Employee Retirement Income Security Act of 1974, the IRS offers various types of compliance programs, which allow plan sponsors to report defects and propose corrective actions for the plans. The types of defects which may adversely affect the qualification of a plan may be classified into one of three categories.

1. Plan document failure. A plan document failure means that a plan provision (or absence of a plan provision) that, on its face, violates the requirements of IRC Section 401(a) or 403(b). For example, the failure of a plan to be amended to reflect a new qualification requirement within the plan's applicable remedial amendment period as defined by the IRC is a plan document failure.
2. Operational failure. An operational failure is a qualification failure that arises solely from the failure to follow plan provisions.
3. Demographic failure. A demographic failure is a failure to satisfy the requirements of IRC Sections 401(a)(4), 401(a)(26) or 410(b) that is not an operational failure. The correction of a demographic failure generally requires a substantive corrective amendment to the plan adding more benefits or increasing existing benefits to participants.

IRS Compliance Programs

The following represents a summary of various IRS compliance programs that can preserve a plan's tax-qualified status by correcting any of the types of defects mentioned above. The IRS compliance programs listed below have been rolled into the Employee Plans Compliance Resolution System (EPCRS), which was created as a result of IRS Revenue Procedure 98-22.

1. Administrative Policy Regarding Self-Correction (APRSC) This program allows plan sponsors to self correct certain operational errors without filing an application with the IRS. Plans must have a favorable determination letter to participate in the program. In addition, to be eligible for APRSC, the plan sponsor must have established practices and procedures to promote overall compliance with requirements of IRS Sections 401(a) and 403(b). Correction by plan amendment is not permitted in APRSC, and the APRSC program is not available for qualification failures relating to the diversion or misuse of plan assets. Finally, Section 403(b) plans (discussed in Chapter 7, Accounting, Auditing, and Reporting for Defined Contribution Pension Plans) are not eligible for APRSC if operational failures exist involving contributions in excess of the 415 limit and the maximum exclusion allowance. The violation can be self-corrected by the end of the second plan year following the failure.
2. Voluntary Compliance Resolution Program (VCR Program) This program allows for plan sponsors to submit a plan of action for correcting operational defects of plans. Plans must have a favorable determination letter and not be under audit to participate in this program. Correction by plan amendment is not permitted in VCR. The VCR program is not available for qualification failures relating to the diversion or misuse of plan assets. The IRS will issue a compliance statement after it is satisfied with the proposed corrective action(s). The plan sponsor must correct the operational defects for all years detailed in the VCR application in accordance with the compliance statement.
3. Standardized VCR Procedure (SVP) This program is available for certain types of violations, such as the failure of ADP and ACP testing in a 401(k) plan and the failure to distribute excess deferrals. The plan sponsor must submit a notification letter to the IRS identifying which IRS-approved correction methods will be used.
4. Voluntary Closing Agreement Program (CAP) This program is available to plan sponsors who are not eligible for the VCR Program. Plan sponsors who have exhibited repeated or deliberate disregard for the terms of the plan document are eligible to participate in this program if the plan is not under audit or has not been notified of an impending audit.

If the plan sponsor is participating in a compliance program, the auditor should (1) obtain tailored representations in the management representation letter, and (2) ensure that pertinent information regarding the compliance application and related corrective action is disclosed in the footnotes to the plan's financial statements.

PARTY-IN-INTEREST TRANSACTIONS

As discussed in Chapter 3, ERISA prohibits plans from engaging in transactions with parties-in-interest because of the potential for abuse. Although similar to related parties as defined in SFAS 57, the definition of parties-in-interest is much broader. Parties-in-interest, as defined in Section 3(14) of ERISA, include but are not limited to the following:

- Fiduciaries (e.g., plan administrator, officer, trustee)
- Employees (e.g., participants) of the plan
- Any person who provides services to the plan (e.g., accountant, attorney, trustee, actuary, investment manager)
- An employer whose employees are covered by the plan (e.g., plan sponsor)
- An employee association (e.g., labor union, trade association) whose members are covered by the plan
- Relatives of such persons described above

Prohibited transactions are nonexempt transactions with parties-in-interest. A fiduciary with respect to a plan shall not cause the plan to engage in a transaction, if the fiduciary knows or should know that such transactions constitute a direct or indirect

- Sale or exchange, or leasing, of any property
- Lending of money or other extension of credit
- Furnishing of goods, services, or facilities
- Transfer to, or use by, or for the benefit of a party-in-interest, of any assets of the plan
- Acquisition, on behalf of the plan, of any employer security or employer real property in violation of a 10% limit

Certain transactions are statutorily exempted under Section 408 of ERISA and are not deemed to be prohibited transactions. Such exemptions include the following:

- A plan's investment in mutual funds or common trust funds that are issued by the plan's trustee.
- Individual account balances held by the plan sponsor's employees are exempt party-in-interest transactions.
- A 401(k) plan or employee stock ownership plan is permitted to provide employer matching contributions in the form of employer securities.
- The payment of fees to other service providers of the plan from plan assets is usually acceptable provided that the fees charged are reasonable.
- A bank is permitted to serve as the trustee for an employee benefit plan which it sponsors for its employees.
- Loans made by the plan to parties-in-interest who are participants or beneficiaries of the plan if such loans: (1) are available to all participants and beneficiaries on a reasonably equivalent basis, (2) are not made available to highly compensated employees in an amount greater than the amount made available to other employees, (3) are made in accordance with provisions

regarding such loans as set forth in the plan document, (4) bear a reasonable interest rate, and (5) are adequately secured.

- A loan to an employee stock ownership plan if: (1) such loan is primarily for the benefit of participants and beneficiaries of the plan and (2) such loan is at a reasonable interest rate.
- Any transaction between a plan and a common/collective trust fund or pooled investment fund maintained by a party-in-interest that is a bank or trust company supervised by a state or federal agency if: (1) the transaction is a sale or purchase of an interest in the fund, (2) the bank or trust company receives only reasonable compensation, and (3) the transaction is permitted by the plan document, trust agreement, or by a fiduciary who has the authority to manage and control the plan's assets.
- A merger of multiemployer plans or the transfer of assets or liabilities between multiemployer plans determined by the Pension Benefit Guaranty Corporation (PBGC) to satisfy the requirements of ERISA Section 4231.
- In certain cases plan documents provide for the payment of plan expenses from plan assets which may result in payments being made to the plan sponsor. For example, the salary and benefits costs of employees of the plan sponsor who provide services to the plan, such as accounting and administration, might be charged to the plan. These cases are not very prevalent particularly with single-employer sponsored benefit plans, as the IRS has imposed strict restrictions on the types of "internal" costs which may be paid by the plan to the plan sponsor.

The auditor should be alert to what constitutes a prohibited transaction while performing audit procedures. Procedures that the auditor may perform to determine the existence of and to identify party-in-interest transactions include but are not limited to the following:

- Evaluate the plan administrator's procedures for identifying and properly accounting for party-in-interest transactions
- Request or prepare a listing of all known parties-in-interest and inquire whether there were any transactions with these parties during the period
- Review the minutes of the meetings of the board of trustees or retirement committee of the plan
- Inquire of the plan administrator as to whether any prohibited transactions have been identified
- Review accounting records for large, unusual, or nonrecurring transactions or balances
- Review filings of the plan with the Department of Labor (DOL) and other regulatory agencies for the names and information about parties-in-interest
- Review conflict-of-interest statements obtained by the plan from plan officials

- Consider whether transactions are occurring but are not being given accounting recognition such as receiving or providing services at no charge
- Review the extent and nature of business transacted with the plan's major investees, suppliers, borrowers, lessees, and lenders for indications of previously undisclosed relationships.

For any identified party-in-interest transactions, the auditor should consider performing the following:

- Obtain an understanding of the business purpose of the transaction
- Discuss the transaction with the plan's legal counsel and obtain a written opinion about whether it is a prohibited transaction. If the transaction is a prohibited transaction consider whether the transaction is an illegal act, and if so, the implications to the plan.

Identified, nonexempt party-in-interest transactions should be reported on the Schedule of Nonexempt Transactions without regard to their materiality. It is often helpful to add a note on the Schedule of Nonexempt Transactions describing the status of the nonexempt party-in-interest transaction (i.e., whether the plan sponsor has corrected the situation that gave rise to the transaction). In addition, the IRS imposes a 15% excise tax on prohibited transactions that are required to be reported on IRS Form 5330, Return of Excise Taxes Related to Employee Benefit Plans. When a prohibited transaction is identified, this form should be completed, and the plan sponsor must pay the required excise tax.

If the nonexempt party-in-interest transaction has not been disclosed in the supplemental schedule, and if the auditor concludes that the noted transaction is immaterial to the plan, then the auditor's report should be modified to include a paragraph disclosing the transaction. If the auditor deems the transaction material to the plan, the auditor should express a qualified or adverse opinion on the supplementary schedule. For example of such auditors' reports, see Chapter 12, Auditors' Reports.

COMMITMENTS AND CONTINGENCIES

The plan sponsor's responsibility is to ensure that all potential contingencies are recorded and disclosed in the financial statements. When auditing an employee benefit plan, the auditor should be concerned with the following areas:

- Violations that could affect the tax status of the plan
- Prohibited party-in-interest transactions
- Reportable events to either the PBGC or the DOL
- Disputed claims made by participants against the plan

To the extent that any of the matters listed above are identified to exist for the plan, the plan's financial statements should record any receivables from the plan sponsor which may be appropriate and include disclosures in the footnotes to the plan's financial statements to describe the situations and the corrective actions to be taken by plan management. For prohibited party-in-interest transactions, such amounts are also required to be disclosed in a supplemental schedule to the Form 5500 filing. (See the previous discussion regarding party-in-interest transactions.) For additional information regarding a plan's tax status, see the discussion on tax status.

Suggested procedures include the following:

- Review and evaluate the client's policies and procedures for identifying, evaluating and accounting for potential litigation, claims, and assessments
- Examine documents in the client's possession concerning litigation, claims, and assessments, including correspondence and invoices from attorneys
- Consider sending letters of audit inquiry to any outside or in-house legal counsel whose services were retained during the year

In many circumstances, the plan will not have consulted either in-house counsel or an outside attorney. In this situation is not necessary to send a letter of audit inquiry to legal counsel. The auditor should tailor the applicable management representations to reflect the fact that legal counsel was not retained during the period under audit.

Exhibit 1 is an illustrative legal letter of inquiry which was excerpted from the AICPA accounting and auditing guide, *Audits of Employee Benefit Plans.*

Exhibit 1

[*Date*]

[*Name and address of attorney*]

Dear [*attorney*]:

In connection with an audit of the financial statements of ABC Employee Benefit Plan, as of December 31, 20X1, and for the year then ended, management of the plan has prepared and furnished to our independent auditors, [n*ame of CPA firm*] a description and evaluation of certain contingencies (including those set forth below) involving matters with respect to which you have been engaged and to which you have devoted substantive attention on behalf of the plan in the form of legal consultation or representation. These contingencies are regarded by management of the plan as material [*management may indicate the materiality limit used, if an understanding has been reached for this purpose*]. Your response to the specific requests for certain information, set forth below, should include matters that existed at [*financial statement date*] as well as new matters during the period from that date to the specified effective date of your response.

Pending or Threatened Litigation (excluding unasserted claims):

Please furnish to our auditors information regarding all pending or threatened litigation, claims, and assessments your firm is handling on our behalf and to which you have devoted substantial attention. Such information should include the following: (1) the nature of the litigation, (2) the progress of the case to date, (3) the manner in which management is responding or intends to respond to the litigation (e.g., to contest the case vigorously or to seek an out-of-court settlement), and (4) an evaluation of the likelihood of an unfavorable outcome and an estimate, if one can be made, of the amount or range of potential loss.

Unasserted Claims or Assessments:

We have represented to our auditors that there are no unasserted possible claims that you have advised us are probable of assertion and must be disclosed in accordance with Statement of Financial Accounting Standards.

We have also represented to our auditors that none of the following events have occurred during the year under audit:

- Breach of fiduciary responsibilities
- Nonexempt party-in-interest transactions and other transactions prohibited by ERISA
- Loans or leases in default and reportable to the DOL
- Events reportable to the PBGC
- Events that may jeopardize the plan's tax qualification status
- Legal actions brought by the plan on behalf of plan participants and beneficiaries
- Review or inquiry by the DOL, the IRS, or other regulatory agency of the plan's activities or filings since the last audit.

We understand that, in the course of performing legal services for us with respect to a matter recognized to involve either (1) an unasserted possible claim or assessment or (2) one of the above-noted matters that may require financial statement disclosure, whenever you have formed a professional opinion that we should disclose or consider disclosing such possible claim or assessment or other above-noted matter, as a matter of professional responsibility to us, you will so advise us and will consult with us concerning the question of such disclosure and the applicable requirements of Statement of Financial Accounting Standards 5, Department of Labor Rules and Regulations for Reporting and Disclosure, Internal Revenue Code and ERISA.

Please specifically identify the nature of, and reasons for, any limitation on your response.

Also, please furnish our auditors with the amount of any unpaid fees due as of [*financial statement date*] for services rendered through that date.

Yours truly,

____

By [*Name of Plan management*]

Upon receipt on the letters of audit inquiry, the auditor should evaluate the matters covered in each attorney's written responses to determine whether any disclosures or accruals for commitments and contingencies are required under generally accepted accounting principles. In this regard, the auditor should follow the guidance in SFAS 5, *Commitments and Contingencies*. The auditor should also document in the working papers the basis for conclusions reached in the decisions made to disclose and/or accrue amounts for commitments and contingencies.

SUBSEQUENT EVENTS

The **subsequent events** auditing procedures for employee benefit plans are similar to those performed for audits of other entities. If there is a delay (generally more than two weeks) between the last day of fieldwork and the date the auditor actually issues the report on the plan's financial statements, the auditor should update subsequent events procedures from the last day of the plan year to the last day of fieldwork and also through the report issuance date. Following are typical audit procedures that should be applied for all engagements:

- Review the latest available interim financial statements of the plan, if available, or subsequent trustee statements and investigate any unusual fluctuations
- Review minutes of plan committee meetings and plan sponsor board meetings held through the completion of fieldwork
- Obtain a client representation letter
- Inquire of the plan administrator or the plan sponsor about the existence of subsequent events including matters such as the following:
  - Amendments to the plan or trust agreement
  - Audits and reviews by the IRS, the DOL, or other regulatory agencies
  - Material changes in the investment or funding policy of the plan
  - Significant changes in plan participation (e.g., layoffs, sale of division) which may result in the partial termination of a plan. (Note that in cases of partial plan terminations, participants become fully vested in their accrued benefits.)
  - Changes in the nature of the plan (e.g., merger with another plan, plan spin-off, or an acquisition)
  - Changes in actuarial assumptions to be used by the plan for future financial reporting (Note that to the extent that the change in actuarial assumptions significantly affected accumulated plan benefits for a defined benefit pension plan or benefit obligations for a health and welfare plan, the impact should be disclosed in the footnotes to the plan's financial statements.)
  - Change in recordkeeper, trustee, custodian, and/or actuaries
  - Changes in plan commitments or contingent liabilities
  - Significant transactions entered into by the plan sponsor that may impact the plan

After completing the subsequent events procedures, the auditor should evaluate the information obtained from this process and determine whether any matters require disclosure or accrual in the plan's financial statements. The auditor's working papers should document the basis for the conclusions reached.

MANAGEMENT REPRESENTATIONS

The auditor should obtain written representations from plan officials, to include the plan administrator, who is responsible for the plan's investment and management functions. In addition to the plan administrator's signature, the auditor may also consider obtaining the signatures of the following officials based on specific circumstances: chief financial officer, the chief human resources officer, a member of the board of trustees, or a union official for a multiemployer plan. The representation letter should cover all financial statements and periods included in the auditors' report. It should be typed on the plan sponsor's letterhead and dated as of the independent auditors' report date. The representation letter should be tailored to meet specific circumstances of the engagement. Note, the guidance for management representation letters is found in SAS 85, *Management Representations*. During late 1999, SAS 89 was issued which amended SAS 85 to require auditors to obtain written representations from management regarding plan management's belief that the effects of any uncorrected financial statement misstatements identified by the auditor are immaterial to the plan's financial statements taken as a whole. Representations 3 and F in the sample letter are in response to SAS 89.

Exhibit 2 shows an example management representation letter for a full-scope audit of a defined benefit pension plan which is based upon the example provided in the AICPA audit and accounting guide, *Audits of Employee Benefit Plans*.

Exhibit 2

Date

To [*Independent Accountant*]

We are providing this letter in connection with your audits[1] of the financial statements and supplemental schedules of ABC Company Benefit Plan (the plan) as of December 31, 20X1 and 20X0, and for the year ended December 31, 20X1. We understand that your audits were made for the purpose of expressing an opinion as to whether the financial statements present fairly, in all material respects, the financial status[2] and changes in financial status[2] of the plan in conformity with generally accepted accounting principles, and whether the supplemental schedules are fairly stated in all material respects in relation to the basic financial statements taken as a whole.

---

[1]*For limited scope engagements, substitute the following for the first paragraph of this letter:*

> *We understand that, at our instruction, you did not perform any audit procedures with respect to investment-related information prepared and certified to by [Name of Institution(s)] the trustee(s)/custodian, for the ABC Company Plan, as of December 31, 20X1 and 20X0 and for the years then ended, in accordance with the Department of Labor's Rules and Regulations for Reporting and Disclosure under the Employee Retirement Income Security Act of 1974 (29 CFR 2520.103-8), other than comparing such information to the financial statements and supplemental schedules. Because of the significance of the information which you did not audit, we understand that you will not express an opinion on the financial statements and schedules taken as a whole. We confirm that we are responsible for the fair presentation in the plan's financial statements of net assets available for benefits and changes therein, in conformity with generally accepted accounting principles and for the fair presentation of the accompanying supplemental schedules in conformity with the Department of Labor's Rules and Regulations for Reporting and Disclosure under ERISA.*
>
> *In connection with your limited scope audit of the ABC Retirement Plan, we confirm, to the...*

[2]*Defined contribution pension and health and welfare plans replace "financial status" with "net assets."*

Certain representations in this letter are described as being limited to matters that are material, solely for purposes of preparing this letter individually or collectively in the aggregate, involving potential amounts of more than $XXX[3]. These amounts are not intended to represent the materiality threshold for financial reporting and disclosure purposes. Notwithstanding this, items are considered material, regardless of size, if they involve an omission or misstatement of accounting information that, in the light of surrounding circumstances, makes it probable that the judgment of a reasonable person relying on the information would be changed or influenced by the omission or misstatement.

We confirm, to the best of our knowledge and belief as *of [date of auditor's report]*, the following representations made to you during your audit.

1. We are responsible for the fair presentation in the plan's financial statements of financial status[1] and changes in financial status[1] in conformity with generally accepted accounting principles [or other comprehensive basis of accounting] and for the fair presentation of the accompanying supplemental schedules in conformity with the Department of Labor's Rules and Regulations for Reporting and Disclosure under the Employee Retirement Income Security Act of 1974. The financial statements and related footnotes are fairly presented in conformity with generally accepted accounting principles [or other comprehensive basis of accounting] and the notes include all disclosures required by laws and regulations to which the plan is subject.
2. We have made available to you all
   a. Financial records and related data.
   b. All minutes of the meetings [*name of plan administrative committee or trustee*] or summaries of actions of recent meetings for which minutes have not yet been prepared.
   c. Amendments made to the plan instrument, the trust agreement, or insurance contracts (as applicable) during the year, including amendments to comply with applicable laws.
3. We believe the effects of any uncorrected financial statement misstatements aggregated by you during the current audit engagement and pertaining to the latest period presented are immaterial, both individually and in the aggregate, to the financial statements taken as a whole. A summary of such uncorrected misstatements has been attached as Appendix A.
4. There have been no
   a. Communications from regulatory agencies concerning noncompliance with, or deficiencies in, financial reporting practices that could have an effect on the plan's financial statements in the event of noncompliance.
   b. Fraud involving management or employees who have significant roles in the plan's internal control.

[1] *See footnote 1 on page 263.*

[3] *The overall materiality level for the financial statement audit should not be used. The understanding reached on materiality limits with management, for purposes of their representation letter, should be sufficiently low to take into consideration known errors and undetected errors (allowance for detection risk).*

   c. Fraud involving other employees that could have a material effect on the financial statements.

5. We have no
   a. Plans or intentions that may materially affect the carrying value or classification of the plan's assets and liabilities.
   b. Intentions to terminate the plan.
6. The following have been properly recorded or disclosed in the financial statements:
   a. Related-party transactions, including transactions with parties-in-interest, as defined in ERISA section 3(14) and regulations thereunder, including sales, purchases, loans, transfers, leasing arrangements, and guarantees, and amounts receivable from or payable to related parties.
   b. Guarantees, whether written or oral, under which the plan is contingently liable to a bank or other lending institution.
   c. All significant estimates and material concentrations known to management that are to be disclosed in accordance with AICPA Statement of Position 94-6, *Disclosure of Certain Significant Risks and Uncertainties*. [We understand that the significant estimates covered by this disclosure are estimates at the balance sheet date that are reasonably possible of changing materially within the next year. Concentrations refer to the nature and type of investments held by the plan, or markets for which events could occur which would significantly disrupt normal finances within the next year.]
7. There are no
   a. Violations or possible violations of laws or regulations whose effects would be considered for disclosure in the financial statements or as a basis for recording a loss contingency.
   b. Unasserted claims or assessments that our lawyer has advised us are probable of assertion and must be disclosed in accordance with Financial Accounting Standards Board (FASB) Statement 5, *Accounting for Contingencies*.
   c. Other liabilities or gain or loss contingencies that are required to be accrued or disclosed by FASB Statement 5.
   d. Transactions that have not been properly recorded in the accounting records underlying the financial statements, except as listed in Appendix A.
   e. Other matters (e.g., breach of fiduciary responsibilities, nonexempt transactions, loans or loans in default, events reportable to the PBGC, or events that may jeopardize the tax status) that legal counsel have advised us that must be disclosed.
8. There were no omissions from the participants' data provided to the plan's actuary for the purpose of determining the actuarial present value of accumulated plan benefits (for health and welfare plans: liability for claims incurred but not reported, postretirement benefit obligations and other actuarially determined amounts) and other actuarially determined amounts in the financial statements.
9. The plan administrator agrees with the actuarial methods and assumptions used by the actuary for funding purposes and for determining the actuarial present

value of accumulated plan benefits (for health and welfare plans: liability for claims incurred but not reported, postretirement benefit obligations and other actuarially determined benefit amounts). We did not give any, nor cause any, instructions to be given to the plan's actuary with respect to values or amounts derived in an attempt to bias their work, and we are not aware of any matters that have impacted the independence or objectivity of the plan's actuary.

10. There have been no changes in [or the following have been properly recorded or disclosed in the financial statements]:
    a. The actuarial methods or assumptions used in calculating amounts recorded or disclosed in the financial statements.
    b. Plan provisions between the actuarial valuation date and the date of this letter.
11. The plan has complied with all aspects of debt and other contractual agreements that would have a material effect on the financial statements in the event of noncompliance.
12. The methods and significant assumptions used to estimate fair values of financial instruments are as follows: [*describe methods and significant assumptions used to estimate fair values of financial instruments*]. The methods and significant assumptions used result in a measure of fair value appropriate for financial measurement and disclosure purposes.
13. Financial instruments with off-balance-sheet risk and financial instruments with concentrations of credit risk have been properly recorded or disclosed in the financial statements.
14. All required filings of plan [trust] documents with the appropriate agencies have been made.
15. The plan (and the trust established under the plan) is qualified under the appropriate section of the Internal Revenue Code and intends to continue as a qualified plan (and trust). The plan's sponsor(s) has operated the plan and trust or insurance contract in a manner that did not jeopardize this tax status.
16. The plan has complied with the DOL's regulations concerning the timely remittance of participants' contributions to trusts containing assets for the plan.
17. The plan has complied with the fidelity bonding requirements of ERISA.
18. The plan has satisfactory title to owned assets, [*state exceptions, if any*] and all liens, encumbrances, or security interest requiring disclosure in the financial statements have been properly disclosed.
19. There are no
    a. Nonexempt party-in-interest transactions (as defined in ERISA section 3(1) and regulations under that section) that were not disclosed in the supplemental schedules or financial statements.
    b. Investments in default or considered to be uncollectible that were not disclosed in the supplemental schedules.
    c. Reportable transactions (as defined in ERISA section 103(b)(3)(h) and regulations under that section) that were not disclosed in the supplemental schedules.
20. We have apprised you of all communications, whether written or oral, with regulatory agencies concerning the operation of the plan.

21. There were no reviews or inquiries by the DOL, IRS, or other regulatory agency of the plan's activities or filings since the last audit.
22. The plan has complied with all aspects of contractual agreements that, in the event of noncompliance, would have an effect on the plan's financial statements.
23. No events have occurred subsequent to the balance sheet date and through the date of this letter that would require adjustment to or disclosure in the aforementioned financial statements.

The following representations would be obtained only when applicable.

A. The plan sponsor has not completed the process of evaluating the impact that will result from adopting Statement of Financial Accounting Standards No. XXX/Statement of Position YYY, [*Title*], as discussed in Note X. The plan sponsor is therefore unable to disclose the impact that adopting Statement of Financial Accounting Standards No. XXX/Statement of Position YYY will have on the plan's financial status[2] and changes in its financial status[2] when such statement is adopted.
B. Note X to the financial statements discloses all of the facts (i.e., significant conditions and events and management's plans) of which we are aware that are relevant to the plan and/or plan sponsor's ability to continue as a going concern.
C. We are not aware of any intentions on the part of the plan sponsor to terminate benefit responsive investment contracts held by the plan.
D. The plan is responsible for determining and maintaining the adequacy of the allowance for doubtful notes, loans, and accounts receivable, as well as estimates used to determine such amounts. Plan management believes the allowance(s) is [*are*] adequate to absorb currently estimated bad debts in the account balances(s).
E. Unusual or infrequent events or transactions, including plan amendments, occurring after the latest benefit information date but before issuance of the plan's financial statements that might affect the usefulness of the plan's financial statements when assessing the plan's present and future ability to pay benefits.
F. [When the auditor detects errors in a sample:]
We understand [*name of account*] was tested using statistical or other sampling techniques and that certain errors in recording [*identify account*] as of [*specify year-end*] were found by you in the sample items selected. The effect of the known errors identified has been included in the summary of uncorrected misstatements attached to this letter as Appendix A. We also understand that to estimate the total amount of errors in [*identify account*], a mathematical projection of the known errors has been computed, which results in [*specify impact; e.g., a potential additional $x,xxx of unrecorded income*] at [*specify year-end*]. Only additional testing and verification by either the pan or you would produce a more accurate estimate of [*identify account*]. Such potential additional unrecorded amounts are not included

[2] *See footnote 2 on page 263.*

as part of Appendix A. Based on our judgment of the materiality of your mathematically projected potential error, we believe the effects of such potential unrecorded errors, as well as the effects when considered with the items in Appendix A, are immaterial to the financial statements taken as a whole.

____
[*Name of Plan Administrator and Title*]

PLAN MERGERS

Company mergers and acquisitions often result in the merger of the benefit plans of the plan sponsors. In addition, plan sponsors may elect to merge various employee benefit plans which they sponsor in order to reduce administrative costs and to consolidate benefit plans with similar features. For health and welfare plans, many plan mergers occur due to the wrapper features which cover multiple health and welfare plans sponsored by the plan sponsor. The auditor's responsibility is to test whether the assets are properly transferred into the merged plan and, if applicable, whether the benefit obligation for a defined benefit pension plan and/or a health and welfare plan is recorded appropriately in the surviving plan.

For defined contribution pension plans, defined benefit pension plans, and health and welfare plans, both the cost and the market value of the assets recorded by the trustee prior to the merger should be reconciled to the respective values recorded by the trustee subsequent to the merger. Occasionally, the new trustee will record the cost of the plan's assets at market value on the date of the transfer. In this situation, the auditor should confirm that the correct number of shares or units was properly recorded for each asset. Also, a sample of individual account balances should be tested to ensure that the value of the assets in each individual's account was transferred properly for defined contribution pension plans.

For defined benefit pension plans and health and welfare plans, the merger may require certain actuarial adjustments if the plans employed different actuarial assumptions and methodologies. The auditor should discuss any adjustment with the plan's actuary and review the actuarial report to ensure that there are adequate disclosures in the financial statements. For plans that are being merged into a surviving plan and have not been audited, the auditor should consider testing demographic information (i.e., hire date, birth date, sex) and payroll data (i.e., hours worked) to test whether participants were eligible to participate in the plan. For plans that have been audited prior to the merger, the auditor may not be required to test demographic information; however, the auditor might consider inquiring of the prior auditors if there had been any issues with the demographic testing and reviewing the appropriate workpapers of the predecessor auditors as suggested by SAS 84, *Communications Between Predecessor and Successor Auditors*.

The auditor should read the plan amendment(s) and other related documentation related to the merger to ensure that the effective merger date is properly reflected in the financial statements. Listed below is an example of a footnote disclosure to describe a plan merger situation.

> On December 31, 20X1, the ABC Company Retirement Plan was merged into the Plan. The terms and conditions of the ABC Company Retirement Plan and the Plan as in effect separately prior to the merger continue as such under the merged plan. The net assets of the ABC Company Retirement Plan amounting to approximately $25 million and the accumulated plan benefit obligations of approximately $20 million were transferred into the Plan as the close of business on December 31, 20X1.

For purposes of accounting for the plan merger, to the extent that the transfer of plan assets to the surviving plan is imminent, the merging plan should record a transfer payable line item on the statement of net assets available for benefits reflecting that net assets equal zero. In this case, the plan should still record investments on the plan's financial statements, and the Schedule of Assets Held for Investment Purposes would also be required. In the event that the transfer of assets does not occur shortly after the plan's year end, the plan should continue to report net assets available for benefits on the plan's financial statements, which would also require the preparation of the Schedule of Assets Held for Investment Purposes. The DOL does not view plan mergers to be final until the assets have completely transferred to the surviving plan. In many cases, merged benefit plans will continue to require audits for periods after the plan's effective merger date when there are delays in transferring the plan's assets to the surviving plan. An exception exists when the surviving plan legally has two trusts (i.e., one relating to the merging plan and one relating to the surviving plan) and benefit payments can be paid from the assets of either trust, in which case the plan's merger date is the effective date of the merger not the asset transfer date. A plan's final Form 5500 is due to be filed with the DOL seven months following the month end in which the plan's assets are completely transferred.

TERMINATING PLANS

A terminating plan is a plan for which a termination decision has been made, regardless of whether the terminating plan will be replaced by a new plan to be offered by the plan sponsor. If the decision to terminate the plan is made prior to year-end, the plan's financial statements must be presented on the liquidation basis of accounting. The auditors' report should disclose the change in the basis of accounting and the termination event. If the decision to terminate a plan is made after the plan's year-end, the auditors' report is not affected, however, a description of the termination should be included in the financial statements.

If the plan is being terminated but merged into another plan, the plan's financial statements should not be prepared on the liquidation basis of accounting.

Generally, the liquidation basis of accounting requires that the plan's financial statements present net assets at their current market values. Typically, changing to the liquidation basis of accounting has little to no effect on the recorded values of the plan's assets since they are already carried at fair market value. Exceptions could include guaranteed investment contracts and insurance contracts, which may be carried at contract value, and often impose fees for early termination. Other exceptions may be large blocks of stocks which might not be readily disposed of at their quoted market price such as for an employee stock ownership plan or non-readily-marketable securities.

For a defined benefit pension plan, accumulated plan benefits should be determined on the liquidation basis of accounting, which may differ considerably from the actuarial present value of accumulated plan benefits for an ongoing plan (e.g., less service time reduces the amount of the benefit obligation; however, the termination of the plan requires full vesting of all benefits which increases the amount of the benefit obligation). Since all employees are 100% vested in their accrued benefits once a plan is terminated, there may not be sufficient plan assets to fund the benefit obligation. In this situation, absent a distressed termination, the plan sponsor will have to fund the plan in order to meet the required benefit obligations.

When a decision is made to terminate an employee benefit plan, all plan participants must be given fifteen days notice before further accruals of benefits or future contributions to the plan are ceased (see the exception below for defined benefit pension plans). The decision to terminate a plan should be made as a corporate resolution by the board of directors or other governing body and an amendment may be approved to document the plan's termination. (Note that for profit sharing plans, the fifteen-day notice is not required because the contribution to the profit sharing plan is discretionary, not required, by the plan sponsor.) For defined benefit pension plans, interested parties must be given an additional sixty to ninety days notice (in addition to the fifteen-day notice requirement) prior to the date that benefit accruals cease. Interested parties include all plan participants, beneficiaries of deceased participants, alternate payees under qualified domestic orders, and any union that represents the plan.

If the plan is **not** a defined benefit pension plan, there are no other requirements that need to be satisfied in order to terminate the plan; however it is strongly recommended that the plan sponsor request IRS approval of the termination. To obtain approval from the IRS, the plan sponsor should file Form 5310, Application for Determination for Terminating Plan. There is no specific requirement as to when this application must be filed. It is suggested, however, that the application be filed during the plan year in which the decision was made to terminate the plan. Generally, approval for plan terminations occurs three to six months after submission of the application to the IRS.

The information that is required to be submitted along with the Form 5310 is listed on page 6 of the form. This information includes data regarding nondiscrimination issues, eligibility, benefits, and number of participants. A copy of the current plan document, along with all amendments made subsequent to the writing of the current plan document, must also be submitted. If the plan has an IRS determination letter, it too must be submitted.

In addition to the above, Form 8717, User Fee for Employee Plan Determination Letter Request, must be submitted along with the appropriate fee, which is currently $225. If the plan administrator elects, Form 2848, Power of Attorney, may also be submitted. This form permits an attorney, accounting firm, consulting firm, or other entity listed on the power of attorney form to act as an agent of the plan to answer questions that the IRS may raise during their review of the application for termination.

After a letter is received from the IRS stating that they have reviewed and approved the plan being considered for termination, assets of the plan should be distributed to plan participants and beneficiaries as soon as possible within twelve months of receipt of the letter. It is advisable **not** to distribute assets until the letter is received, so as to ensure that the plan has operated within legal parameters regarding the termination.

If the plan being considered for termination is a defined benefit pension plan, generally the plan must also notify the PBGC. To notify the PBGC, the plan sponsor should file Form 500, PBGC Standard Termination Notice. The plan should submit Form 5310 to the IRS by the time a submission is made to the PBGC. The PBGC does not send a response back to the plan to indicate their approval of the termination. Basically, the absence of notification from the PBGC indicates approval of the plan termination.

In terms of plan terminations, there are generally two types of terminations--those for plans which are fully funded and distressed terminations. A plan that is fully funded is one in which the net assets available for benefits exceed the plan's accumulated plan benefit obligations. A distressed termination is one in which the plan's sponsor is in liquidation, in bankruptcy, or insolvency proceedings or has filed for Chapter 11 bankruptcy and the costs of providing pension coverage have become unreasonably burdensome to the plan sponsor. In the case of a distressed termination, the PBGC may become involved to make benefit payments to participants.

In general, upon full or partial termination of a defined benefit or defined contribution pension plan, participants become 100% vested in their accrued benefits as of the termination date. A partial termination occurs, generally, when 20% or more the plan's participants are terminated either at a point in time or over a period of one year. This situation could occur in connection with a plant closing, significant layoffs due to deteriorating business conditions or the sale of a division.

In connection with the termination of a plan, additional financial statement disclosures should include the following:

- A statement that the plan is terminated
- An effective date for the freezing of benefit accruals for defined benefit pension plans
- A description of the method of payment of benefits to participants
- The timing of benefit payments to participants

If benefits are frozen and a wasting trust is established (i.e., the plan remains in existence until all accrued benefits are paid), then the disclosures as noted above must be made in all subsequent financial statements until the assets have been disbursed. A frozen plan is one in which benefits have ceased to accrue (frozen benefits) while contributions may still be required to be made to the plan (in the case of underfunded plans). Frozen plans which exceed 100 participants at the beginning of the plan year continue to require audits which primarily would be focused upon the audits of benefit payments and investments (for a full-scope audit). Audits of frozen plans continue to be required until the number of participants falls below 100 at the beginning of a plan year.

Additional considerations which should be given by the auditor may include, but are not limited to, the following:

- Test benefit payments to ensure that they have been made in accordance with applicable plan provisions
- Consult legal and tax experts to discuss any issues with terminating the plan
- Inquire as to whether the plan administrator has filed the appropriate forms with the IRS and PBGC (for defined benefit pension plans) to request approval for the plan termination
- Review the actuarial valuation for defined benefit pension plans and health and welfare plans which should be prepared on the liquidation basis of accounting, and perform the types of procedures that normally would be performed on the actuarial valuation. For a discussion of such procedures, see Chapter 8, Accounting, Auditing, and Reporting for Defined Benefit Pension Plans and Chapter 9, Accounting, Auditing, and Reporting for Health and Welfare Plans. In addition, the auditor should review the summary of actuarial assumptions used by the actuary and determine that the assumptions appear reasonable and have been changed to accommodate for the liquidation basis of accounting.

Occasionally in conjunction with the termination of a defined benefit pension plan, there will be plan assets in excess of the projected benefit obligation. The auditor should refer to the plan document or amendment for the treatment of the excess amount. Typically, plan assets in excess of the projected benefit obligation are distributed to the plan's participants on a pro rata basis. In general, with defined contribution pension plans, there are no excess assets as participants are paid the value of their account balances and defined contribution pension plans do not hold unallocated assets. With health and welfare plans, any excess of plan assets over benefit obligations would be used to pay benefits to participants.

If the disbursement of the assets of a terminated plan is imminent, the plan should record a transfer payable line item in the statement of net assets available for benefits such that net assets available for benefits equal zero. In this case, the plan should still record investments on the plan's financial statements, and the Schedule of Assets Held for Investment Purposes would be required. In the event that the distribution of assets does not occur shortly after the plan's year-end, the plan should continue to report net assets available for benefits on the plan's financial statements, which would also require the preparation of the Schedule of Assets Held for Investment Purposes. The DOL does not view plan terminations to be final until all of the plan assets have been distributed and the trust is left with a zero balance for plan assets. In many cases, terminated benefit plans will continue to require audits for periods after the plan's effective termination date when there are delays in distributing the plan's assets. A plan's final Form 5500 is due to be filed with the DOL seven months following the month end in which the plan's assets have been completely distributed.

INITIAL AUDITS OF EXISTING PLANS

An initial audit of an existing plan is required in the first year that the number of eligible participants exceeds 100 at the beginning of the plan year. If the plan was not audited in the prior year, the auditor should perform procedures to obtain reasonable assurance that the accounting principles used by the plan in the current and the prior year are consistent.

ERISA requires that audited plan financial statements present a comparative statement of net assets available for benefits, unless this is the first year of existence for the plan. When comparative statements are presented, the current year's financial statements should be audited, while the prior year's financial statements may be either audited, compiled, or reviewed. The only exception to this is for a defined contribution pension plan which is required to file a Form 11-K with the SEC. In this case, the prior year's financial statements will need to be audited as the SEC will not accept unaudited financial statements for the prior year.

In the cases where the plan's prior year financial statements are either reviewed or compiled, the auditor should issue a review report or compilation report on the plan's prior year financial statements. In the current year auditor report, the auditor should include an explanatory paragraph which describes that either a review or compilation was performed for the prior year financial statements. Chapter 12, Auditors' Reports, provides examples of the modifications to be made to the auditors' reports in these circumstances and also provides examples of a review report and compilation report.

Following are typical audit procedures that could be applied for initial audits of existing plans:

- Audit work is necessary to test the opening account balances for net assets available for benefits. If a limited-scope audit is performed, the auditors should confirm the opening balances with the trustee of plan assets. If a full-scope audit is performed, the auditor should confirm the opening balances and perform additional procedures to audit the plan's beginning net assets. Such additional procedures may include taking the audited net assets at the end of the year, subtracting the audited investment purchases

during the plan year, adding the audited investment sales during the year and subtracting the audited investment income earned by the plan to arrive at the plan's beginning net assets. The auditor may also make a selection of investments held by the plan at the beginning of the year and audit the fair value of such investments. See Chapter 6, Investments, for a summary of audit procedures which may be applied to investments.
- For a sample of plan participants in a defined contribution pension plan and health and welfare plans, agree beginning of year account balances to the trustee statement, recordkeeper's detail, or participants' statements.
- For a defined benefit pension plan, reconcile information contained in the actuarial report regarding number of plan participants to independent information maintained by the plan sponsor for the different categories of plan participants.

OTHER BASIS OF ACCOUNTING

ERISA allows for a plan's financial statements to be presented on a basis of accounting other than generally accepted accounting principles. SAS 62, *Special Reports*, as amended by SAS 77, provides guidance on financial statements prepared on a comprehensive basis of accounting other than generally accepted accounting principles. In addition, an auditing interpretation of SAS 62, AU 9623.88, provides guidance in evaluating the adequacy of disclosures in financial statements, which are prepared on an other comprehensive basis of accounting. The method of accounting should be described in the footnotes and stated in the independent auditors' report. An example of a method of accounting other than generally accepted accounting principles would be the modified cash basis of accounting. Under the modified cash basis of accounting, investments are adjusted to fair value; however, adjustments to record accruals and receivables are not recorded. Note that the use of the pure cash basis of accounting is not accepted by the DOL because investments would not be presented at fair value under that method. According to the provisions of SAS 62 as amended by SAS 77, when reporting on financial statements prepared in conformity with a basis of accounting other than generally accepted accounting principles, the auditor should determine whether the financial statements and the footnotes include all informative disclosures that are appropriate in the circumstances. For example, if a health and welfare plan's financial statements are prepared on the modified cash basis of accounting, the plan will not include a statement of benefit obligations; however, the footnotes to the plan's financial statements are required to include all of the information regarding benefit obligations as required by SOP 92-6.

GOING CONCERN CONSIDERATIONS

In connection with the audit of an employee benefit plan, the auditor should assess the plan sponsor's ability to continue as a going concern. If there is a question about the plan sponsor's ability to continue as a "going concern" for the foreseeable future, the auditor should review management's plans and its effective implementation of these plans. If it appears likely that the plan sponsor will be unable to meet its funding obligations to the plan (i.e., employer match, funding a defined benefit pension plan or health and welfare plan), the auditor should assess whether an allowance should be recorded against the employer contribution receivable amount. In the case of health and welfare plans, if the plan sponsor is facing a going concern situation, the plan can normally be terminated. For defined contribution pension plans, unless the plan sponsor contributions to the plan are mandatory, which is not generally the case since the majority of employer contributions are discretionary, there is very little impact upon the plan if the plan sponsor is in a going concern situation. For defined benefit pension plans which are fully funded, once again there is generally little impact upon the plan.

The greatest impact upon a plan is for a defined benefit pension plan that is not fully funded and where the employer is still required to make contributions to the plan. In this case, the fact that the plan sponsor may not be able to continue as a going concern or may not be able to make contributions to the plan should be disclosed in the footnotes to the plan's financial statements. If substantial doubt exists and there will be a material impact on the plan, the auditor should (1) include an explanatory paragraph in the auditors' report and (2) include appropriate footnote disclosure of the conditions and events that led to this conclusion as well as any mitigating factors. When additional disclosures are made relating to the company's ability to continue as a going concern, the management representation letter should include a statement that the plan sponsor has disclosed all pertinent facts in the plan's financial statements.

11 THE FORM 5500

INTRODUCTION

The Form 5500 is an annual report developed jointly by the Internal Revenue Service (IRS), the Department of Labor (DOL), and the Pension Benefit Guaranty Corporation (PBGC). Its purpose is to summarize certain data for each employee benefit plan and report that data to the respective governmental authorities. These agencies have revised the Form 5500 and the new form is being used for plan years beginning during 1999. This chapter will present a discussion of plans that are required to file a Form 5500 and those that have no such filing requirement. The new Form 5500 will be discussed; a summary of the old Form 5500 will be presented for informational purposes, and a summary of major changes to the Form 5500 will be discussed. Finally, Exhibit 1 has been included at the end of this chapter which summarizes when Form 5500 filings and audits are required for various employee benefit plans.

TYPES OF PLANS

Plan administrators must generally file a Form 5500 for each of the following types of plans (see Exhibit 1 for a summary of situations in which Form 5500 filings are not required).

Pension Benefit Plans

A pension benefit plan is an employee benefit plan that is covered by the Employee Retirement Income Security Act (ERISA). The return is due whether or not the plan is qualified and even if (1) benefits no longer accrue and/or (2) contributions were not made this plan year. A frozen plan (also called a wasting trust) is one in which participants no longer accrue benefits but the plan will remain in existence as long as necessary to pay benefits that have already accrued.

Pension plans that are required to file a return include defined benefit pension plans and defined contribution pension plans. Some types of defined benefit and defined contribution pension plans include cash-balance, profit-sharing, stock bonus, and money purchase plans. (See Chapter 7, Accounting, Auditing, and Reporting for Defined Contribution Pension Plans, and Chapter 8, Accounting, Auditing, and Reporting for Defined Benefit Pension Plans, for further discussion.)

Health and Welfare Benefit Plans

A health and welfare benefit plan is a plan that provides benefits such as medical, dental, life insurance, apprenticeship and training, scholarship funds, severance pay, and disability. (See Chapter 9, Accounting, Auditing, and Reporting for Health and Welfare Plans, for further discussion.)

403(b) Plans (Defined Contribution Pension Plan)

403(b) plans are retirement savings arrangements sponsored by nonprofit organizations (e.g., hospitals and private colleges) and public schools that are established under Internal Revenue Code (IRC) 403(b). They are defined contribution pension plans with individual salary deferral limits which are similar, but not identical, to 401(k) plans. Contributions may be made by employees (through salary deferral) and through employer contributions.

Certain 403(b) plans are required to file the Form 5500. Under current ERISA regulations, plans which use a tax-deferred annuity arrangement exclusively or invest in mutual funds are required to complete only certain line items of the Form 5500. (See Chapter 7, Accounting, Auditing, and Reporting for Defined Contribution Pension Plans, for further discussion.)

Employee Stock Ownership Plans (ESOP) (Defined Contribution Pension Plan)

An ESOP is a unique type of defined contribution pension plan. It is exempt from the prohibited transaction requirement as it is permitted to concentrate its plan investments in qualifying employer securities, which are frequently not publicly traded. ESOPs also have the ability to borrow money that is guaranteed by the plan sponsor (in the case of leveraged ESOPs). (See Chapter 7, Accounting, Auditing, and Reporting for Defined Contribution Pension Plans, for further discussion.)

PLANS THAT DO NOT HAVE TO FILE A RETURN

Employee benefit plans that are not required to file a return include

- Welfare benefit plans that cover less than 100 participants as of the beginning of the plan year and are unfunded, fully insured, or a combination of both
- Unfunded defined benefit pension plans or unfunded or insured welfare benefit plans: (1) whose benefits go only to a select group of management or highly compensated employees and (2) that meet DOL regulation 29 CFR 2520.104-23 or 29 CFR 2520.104-24, which provides an exemption for welfare plans for certain selected employees

- Plans which are maintained only to comply with workers' compensation, unemployment compensation, or disability insurance laws
- Unfunded excess benefit plans (e.g., plans using rabbi trusts, which are not considered to hold plan assets)
- Welfare benefit plans maintained outside the United States primarily for persons substantially all of whom (the plan participants) are nonresident aliens
- Pension benefit plans maintained outside the United States if it is a qualified foreign plan
- Annuity arrangements
- Simplified employee pensions (SEPs) described in IRC Section 408(k) that conform to the alternative method of compliance described in 29 CFR 2520.104-48 or -49. A SEP is a pension plan that meets certain minimum qualifications regarding eligibility and employer contributions.
- Savings Incentive Match Plans for Employees of Small Employers (SIMPLE) that involve SIMPLE IRAs
- Church plans not electing coverage under IRC Section 410(d)
- Governmental plans
- Welfare benefit plans that participate in a group insurance arrangement that files a return/report Form 5500 on behalf of the welfare benefit plan
- Apprenticeship or training plans that meet all of the conditions specified in 29 CFR 2520.104-22
- Day care centers as specified in CFR 2520.104-25
- Certain dues-financed welfare and pension plans that meet the requirements of 29 CFR 2520.104-26 and 2520.104-27

The IRS is responsible for ensuring compliance with the IRC. The IRC sets rules for operating a tax-qualified pension plan, which includes funding and vesting requirements.

Both sponsors and participants can receive special tax benefits from a tax-qualified pension plan. For example, the sponsor may be eligible to deduct as corporate expenses the amounts contributed to a tax-qualified plan. Likewise, a participant who contributes to a 401(k) defined contribution pension plan is not assessed federal income tax on those monies contributed to the plan until the monies are withdrawn.

The DOL has the responsibility to enforce Title I of ERISA, which, in part, establishes the rights of the participants and the duties of the fiduciaries. The Pension and Welfare Benefits Administration (PWBA), which is an agency of the DOL, is responsible for enforcing the rules that discuss appropriate conduct of plan managers, the investment of plan money, the reporting and disclosure of plan information, and rights of the participants.

The PBGC is a nonprofit corporation which is part of the DOL. The PBGC guarantees the payment of certain pension benefits of defined benefit pension plans that are terminated and have insufficient money in the plan to pay benefits to its participants.

THE FORM 5500 FILING DEADLINE

The deadline for filing the Form 5500 is seven months after the plan year-end. An extension of time for filing the report can be requested from the IRS by filing Form 5558, Application for Extension of Time to File Certain Employee Plan Returns, prior to the original due date. This extension, when properly completed and signed, automatically provides an additional two-and-a-half months to satisfy the filing requirement. Since this is an automatic extension approval, the IRS will not return a copy of the request. When the return is filed, a photocopy of the extension request must be included in the filing. (On the new Form 5500, the box in Part 1, item D must be checked when an application for an extension of time was filed.) The plan administrator has the fiduciary responsibility to ensure the Form 5500 is completed properly and submitted on a timely basis.

An automatic extension to file the Form 5500 until the due date of the sponsor's federal income tax return is automatically granted if all of the following conditions are met:

- The plan year and the employer's tax year are the same
- The employer has been granted an extension of time to file its federal income tax return to a date later than the normal due date for filing the Form 5500
- A copy of the IRS extension of time to file the federal income tax return is attached to the Form 5500 when it is filed with the IRS

The Form 5500 is permitted to be filed electronically or through magnetic media (magnetic tapes or floppy disks). If the plan administrator chooses to file electronically or through magnetic media, Form 8453-E, Employee Benefit Plan Declaration and Signature for Electronic/Magnetic Media Filing, must also be filed.

A copy of the audited financial statements for the employee benefit plan must be submitted along with the Form 5500, which is filed with the IRS by the plan administrator.

AGREEMENT OF FINANCIAL STATEMENTS TO FORM 5500

Before issuing the audit report, the auditor should determine whether the amounts presented in the financial statements agree to those reported on the Form 5500. If there are any differences in the amounts included in the audited financial statements from those reported on the Form 5500, other than differences in grouping the investments, those differences must be disclosed in the footnotes to the financial statements. The DOL may reject a Form 5500 filing that does not properly reconcile variances between the audited financial statements and what is reported on the Form 5500.

Financial Statements/Auditors' Report Issued Prior to Form 5500

If the financial statements and auditors' report is issued prior to the auditor's review of the Form 5500, the auditor should inform the plan administrator that the financial statements and auditors' report are not to be attached to the Form 5500 filing until the auditor reviews the Form 5500. If differences between the financial statements and the Form 5500 are noted, the notes to the financial statements must be updated to include an explanation of the differences, and the report should be reissued and dual-dated with respect to the note explaining the differences.

THE NEW FORM 5500

As discussed earlier, the IRS, the DOL, and the PBGC are developing a new Form 5500 which will be effective for plan years beginning in 1999. This form will replace the current Form 5500 and the Form 5500-C/R. The new form can best be compared to the Form 1040 for individual taxpayers because it has a one-page main form with basic information to identify the plan. The one-page main form also includes a checklist that guides the preparer to select up to thirteen detailed schedules that must be filed if that particular item is applicable to the filer's specific type of plan. This format will allow the filer to customize the Form 5500 filing by including only the main form and those additional schedules that are applicable to the plan.

At the same time that the new form was being developed, the agencies were also developing a new computerized system which will be used to process the new Form 5500. It is called EFAST (the ERISA Filing Acceptance System). EFAST is expected to reduce the cost of filing the report by the pension plans as well as reducing costs for the agencies associated with receiving and processing the Form 5500.

In addition, the new Form 5500 will use computer scannable forms and electronic filing technologies to help reduce costs. During this transition phase, the DOL is permitting the old Form 5500 to be used for 1999 Form 5500 filings.

The following is a brief description of the new form and the schedules that may be required to be attached:

- Form 5500. This form provides information about the plan itself--namely, the type of plan; the name of the plan; the plan sponsor; plan administrator; the name, address, and employee identification number of the preparer; and a checklist to determine what additional schedules are required to be attached. This includes investments with insurance companies such as guaranteed investment contracts (GICs).
- Schedule A. This form provides information on contracts with insurance companies. A separate Schedule A must be completed and filed for each and every insurance contract in which the plan invests (similar to old Form 5500).

- Schedule B. Actuarial information for all defined benefit pension plans that are subject to minimum funding standards must be reported on this form (similar to old Form 5500).
- Schedule C. Schedule C lists service provider information for the forty highest paid service providers. Service providers whose compensation for all services to the plan during the plan year which did not exceed $5,000 may be omitted (similar to the old Schedule C).
- Schedule D. All Direct Filing Entities (DFEs) and those who participate in certain pooled investment/insurance arrangements must file this form. These arrangements include MTIAs (master trust investment accounts), CCTs (bank common or collective trusts), PSAs (pooled separate accounts), and 103-12 IES (103-12 investment entities).
- Schedule E. This form is to be used to report annual information relating to an ESOP (similar to the old Form 5500).
- Schedule F. Fringe benefit plans will use Schedule F to file information regarding their plan (similar to the old Form 5500).
- Schedule G. Schedule G will report information on nonexempt transactions and loans, leases and fixed-income investments in default. The Schedule G will be required to be used to report the information required. The information required by this Schedule is similar to the information included in the Schedules 27(b), 27(c), and 27(e) of the old Form 5500.

  NOTE: The information required by old Items 27(a) and 27(d) are to be included as part of the new Form 5500 as attachments to the Form 5500. The information required by these schedules is discussed later in this chapter.

- Schedule H. This is where the financial statements and related information for large plans (generally 100 or more participants) must be reported (similar to Items 31 and 32 of the old Form 5500).
- Schedule I. For small plans (generally less than 100 participants) this is where the financial statements and related information must be reported (similar to Items 27 and 28 of the old Form 5500).
- Schedule P. Large and small pension plans must file Schedule P to start the running of the IRS statute of limitations for a trust which is exempt from tax. A plan wants the IRS statute of limitations (typically three years) to start running in the event a problem with the plan is found by the IRS. In most instances, once the three-year statute of limitations has expired, the IRS considers that plan year closed and they will not go back and reopen it. Thus, if a similar problem may have existed in a closed year, the IRS would probably let it go and not seek to correct it in a closed year (similar to the old Form 5500). (There is no statute of limitations with respect to the DOL. The DOL can and sometimes goes back to 1988 when the Office of the Chief Accountant started.)

- Schedule SSA. Information that is required by the Social Security Administration. Separated participants who have rights to future benefits under this plan must be reported on Schedule SSA. (This form is similar to the current Form 5500.)

THE OLD FORM 5500

The following provides a general description of the information needed to complete the old Form 5500. The description of the information required by the supplemental schedules (old Item 27) has been revised; the basic structure of the supplemental schedules has remained unchanged.

Page 1, questions 1-6d. These questions ask general informational questions to determine the plan year, if this return is an amended return, the first return, or the final return. It asks the name and address of the plan sponsor and the plan administrator and the sponsor's EIN (employer identification number). It also asks the name of the plan and the type of plan that it is (e.g., welfare benefit, pension benefit, or fringe benefit). At the bottom of the page, the plan sponsor and the plan administrator must sign and date the return. (Same information is included in the new Form 5500.)

Page 2, questions 6e-14. These questions inquire as to all applicable investment arrangements; the number of participants in the plan, including active, retired or separated, and deceased; plan amendments; plan termination; plan merger or consolidation; the funding arrangement; if the plan is under a collective bargaining agreement; and if benefits are paid by an insurance company or a similar organization. (Similar to Part II of the new Form 5500, question 6, 7, and 9a and 9b.)

Page 3, questions 15-21. These questions deal with minimum funding standards; limits on annual compensation; distributions; special elections by the plan (e.g., a change in the actuarial funding method); and questions on the discrimination tests. (Similar to Schedule R, Part II, and Schedule B, Part 1,5i of the new Form 5500.)

Page 4, questions 22-27. Questions on page 4 include "hard-to-value investments"; other qualified pension benefit plans offered by the sponsor; third parties involved in the plan; exemption from the annual audit requirement; information on the supplemental schedules (see next part of this chapter). (Similar to Schedules B and C of the new Form 5500.)

Page 5, questions 28-30. Some of the questions asked on page 5 of the Form 5500 include the purchase of whole life insurance contracts; fidelity bonds; and if the plan is covered under PBGC termination insurance. (Similar to Schedule H, Part I, of the new Form 5500.)

Page 6, questions 31 and 32. These questions address the summary of the plan's financial information. These pages show the net assets of the plan (balance sheet) and the income and expenses, (income statement) for the plan year being reported on this Form 5500. (Similar to Schedule H, Part II, of the new Form 5500.)

Supplemental Schedules

When applicable, the following schedules must be attached to the Form 5500 which is filed with the IRS by the plan administrator.

Line 27(a)--Schedule of Assets Held for Investment Purposes. This schedule lists the assets held in the plan for investment purposes. The following information should be included:

- Identity of the issue, borrower, lessor, or similar party
- Description of the investment (including the maturity date, rate of interest, collateral, par or maturity value)
- Cost (the original or acquisition cost of the asset)
- Current value

Participant loans may be aggregated and presented with a general description of terms and interest rates. If a person is known to be a party-in-interest to the plan, place an asterisk to the left of that line which indicates the party-in-interest. (This schedule is part of Schedule H of the new Form 5500.)

Line 27(a)--Schedule of Assets Held for Investment Purposes Which Were Both Acquired and Disposed of Within the Plan Year. On Schedule 27(a), include the following:

- Identity of the issue, borrower, lessor or similar party
- Description of the investment (including the maturity date, rate of interest, collateral, par or maturity value)
- Costs of acquisitions
- Proceeds of dispositions (sales)

Note that this schedule is rarely filed because of the variety of investments that are exempt from being reported on this schedule. The original purpose of this schedule was to identify the churning of investments. The exemptions include the following:

- Debt obligations of the United States
- Interests issued by a company registered under the Investment Company Act of 1940
- Bank certificates of deposit with a maturity of not more than one year
- Commercial paper with a maturity of not more than nine months, if it is (1) ranked in the highest category by at least two nationally recognized statistical rating services and (2) issued by a company required to file reports with the SEC under Section 13 of the Securities Exchange Act of 1934
- Participations in a bank common or collective trust
- Participations in an insurance company pooled separate account
- Securities purchased from a person registered as a broker/dealer under the Securities Exchange Act of 1934 and listed on a national securities exchange registered under Section 6 of that Act or quoted on NASDAQ
- Any investment assets reported in any of the other supplemental schedules (27(b) through 27(e))

This schedule is part of Schedule H of the new Form 5500.

Line 27(b)--Schedule of Loans or Fixed Income Obligations. This schedule lists loans or fixed income obligations for which unpaid amounts are overdue. All loans which were renegotiated during the year must be included on this schedule. Include the following information on line 27(b):

- Identify and address of obligor
- Original amount of loan
- Principal received during the plan year
- Interest received during the plan year
- Unpaid balance at the end of the year
- A detailed description of the loan, including dates of making and maturity, interest rate, the type and value of collateral, any renegotiation of the loan, and the terms of the renegotiation along with other material items
- Principal amount overdue
- Interest amount overdue

This schedule is part of Schedule G of the new Form 5500.

Line 27(c)--Schedule of Leases in Default or Classified as Uncollectible. Include the following information on line 27(c).

- Identity of lessor/lessee
- Relationship to plan, employer, employee organization, or other party-in-interest
- Terms and description (type of property; location and date it was purchased; terms regarding rent, taxes, insurance, repairs, expenses, renewal options, and date property was leased)
- Original cost
- Current value at time of the lease
- Gross rental receipts during the plan year
- Expenses paid during the plan year
- Net receipts
- Amount in arrears

As with line 27(a), if a person is known to be a party-in-interest to the plan, place an asterisk to the left of that line which shows the party-in-interest. This schedule is part of Schedule G of the new Form 5500.

Line 27(d)--Schedule of Reportable Transactions. This schedule lists investments which were purchased or sold during the year whose value at the time of the transaction exceeds 5% of the current value of plan assets at the beginning of the plan year. For a plan in its first year of existence--in other words, the current value of plan assets at the beginning of the plan year equals zero, use the initial contribution amount multiplied by the 5% as the benchmark for reportable transactions. For plan years beginning in 1999 which are in their first year of existence, the threshold is calculated as 5% multiplied by the current value of plan assets at the end of the first plan year. For line 27(d), include the following:

- Identify of party involved
- Description of asset (including interest rate and maturity in the case of a loan)
- Purchase price
- Selling price
- Lease rental
- Expenses incurred with transaction
- Cost of asset (original or acquisition cost)
- Current value of asset on transaction date
- Net gain or (loss)

This schedule is part of Schedule H of the new Form 5500.

Line 27(e) or Line 27(f)--Schedule of Nonexempt Transactions. This schedule lists any and all prohibited transactions that occurred during the plan year regardless of the dollar value of the transactions. The following information should be shown:

- Identity of party involved
- Relationship to plan, employer, or other party-in-interest
- Description of transactions, including maturity date, rate of interest, collateral, par or maturity value
- Purchase price
- Selling price
- Lease rental
- Expenses incurred in connection with the transaction
- Cost of asset (original or acquisition cost)
- Current value of asset
- Net gain or (loss) on each transaction

This schedule is part of Schedule G of the new Form 5500.

IRS Form 5330 may have to be filed and a 15% excise tax on the transaction may have to be paid by the plan sponsor which is a tax imposed by the IRS on all prohibited transactions.

ADDITIONAL FORM 5500 SCHEDULES

The following schedules may be required to be filed with the IRS as an attachment to the Form 5500 if applicable.

Schedule C, Service Provider and Trustee Information. Schedule C lists all entities who provided services to the plan and received in excess of $5,000 in compensation for such services. Service providers whose compensation for all services to the plan during the plan year which did not exceed $5,000 may be omitted. (This schedule is similar to Schedule C of the new Form 5500.)

Schedule E, ESOP Annual Information. This Schedule E is to be used to report annual information relating to an ESOP. (This schedule is similar to Schedule E of the new Form 5500.)

Schedule F, Fringe Benefit Plan Annual Information Return. Fringe benefit plans will use Schedule F to file information regarding their plan. (This schedule is similar to Schedule F of the new Form 5500.)

Schedule G, Financial Schedules. Schedule G includes the information required by Item 27 (all supplemental schedules). If the plan's audited financial statements include the schedules required by Item 27 (which they are required to include), then Schedule G does not need to be completed. In other words, two copies of the supplemental schedules are not required for a Form 5500 filing.

Schedule P, Annual Return of Fiduciary of Employee Benefit Trust. Large and small pension plans must file Schedule P to start the running of the IRS statute of limitations for a trust which is exempt from tax. A large plan is generally one that has 100 or more participants. (This schedule is similar to Schedule P of the new Form 5500.)

Schedule SSA, Annual Registration Statement Identifying Separated Participants With Deferred Vested Benefits. Information that is required by the Social Security Administration. Separated participants who have rights to future benefits under the plan must be reported on Schedule SSA. (This schedule is similar to Schedule SSA of the new Form 5500.)

SUMMARY OF SIGNIFICANT CHANGES TO THE FORM 5500

In addition to the changes to the basic structure of the Form 5500, the following represents a summary of the more significant changes to information required by the Form 5500.

Schedule of Assets Held for Investment Purposes. Information regarding the cost of investments (i.e., historical cost) is no longer required to be presented for participant-directed investments. Examples of participant directed investments include, for a 401(k) savings plan, investment options selected by participants in which to direct their investments. Self-directed account features of defined contribution pension plans (discussed in Chapter 7, Accounting, Auditing, and Reporting for Defined Contribution Pension Plans) are also considered to be participant-directed investments.

Schedule of Reportable Transactions. Participant-directed transactions (such as the transfer of investment funds in a 401(k) savings plans) are no longer required to be reported in the Schedule of Reportable Transactions.

In a plan's initial year, the 5% threshold for the Schedule of Reportable Transactions should be based upon the plan's ending balance of net assets available for benefits.

Schedule D--(Direct Filing Entity/Participating Plan Information). This schedule was created as part of an overall effort to standardize the reporting format for all filers and to standardize the way information is filed about insurance company pooled separate accounts (PSAs), bank common or collective trusts (CCTs), master trust investment accounts (MTIAs), 103-12 investment entities, and group insurance arrangements (GIAs) all of which are known as direct filing entities. Essentially, all direct filing entities are required to file certain information with the DOL via the use of Schedule D. In the case of CCTs or PSAs, in the event that such entities elect to not file a Form 5500 as a direct filing entity, the plans which hold investments in either the CCT or PSA will be required to include in their Form 5500 filing, detailed information regarding the assets of the CCT or PSA and the plan's respective share of such assets such as the plan's pro-rata share of assets of the CCT or PSA which would need to be reported in the plans's Schedule of Assets Held for Investment Purposes. In these cases, the reporting by an individual plan will be a more cumbersome process.

Schedule A--Insurance Information. Information required by this schedule will now be permitted to be reported on an insurance contract or policy year basis.

Schedule C--Service Provider Information. This schedule will be limited to the top forty paid service providers and will require explanations of service provider terminations only for accountants and enrolled actuaries. Plan trustees are no longer required to be identified on an annual basis.

FINAL RETURN/REPORT FOR A TERMINATED PLAN

For a terminated plan, once all assets have been distributed to the participants, their beneficiaries, or to another employee benefit plan--or for a welfare benefit plan, when all liabilities which may be paid out of that benefit plan are satisfied--check the "final return/report" box at the top of the form for the Form 5500 filed for that plan. Since all the monies have been distributed, this year of complete distribution is the final year that a Form 5500 will be required to be filed for that plan. For a defined benefit pension plan covered by the PBGC, a PBGC Form 1 must be filed and a premium must be paid until the end of the plan year in which the assets are distributed or brought under the control of the PBGC. For an overfunded defined benefit pension plan, the excess over the amounts that are paid to provide benefits to the participants is refunded back to the sponsor. If, at the end of a plan year, amounts still remain to be paid to participants or to be transferred into another plan, some assets of the terminating plan still remain and the final Form 5500 cannot be filed. A Form 5500 will be filed for the current plan year (and for all future years) until the assets of the plan equal zero. The final return/report is due seven months from the end of the month in which all the assets are distributed. The same extensions that apply to an annual Form 5500 also apply to the final Form 5500 filing.

Exhibit 1: Summary of ERISA filing requirements

	5500 or currently 5500CR	*Audit required*
Welfare[3] w/ <100 Participants		
Unfunded[2]	No	No
Funded by insurance	No	No
Uninsured medical plan funded by employer and after-tax employee contributions	Yes	No
Cafeteria plan		
Funded through employer or plan sponsor	Yes	No
Funded through trust	Yes	No
Welfare[3] for select group of management or HCEs[1]--unfunded or fully funded (see below)	No (4)	No
Welfare[3] w/ >100		
Unfunded[2]	Yes	No
Funded by insurance	Yes	No
Uninsured medical funded by employer and after-tax employee contributions	Yes	Yes
Cafeteria plan		
Funded through employer or plan sponsor general assets	Yes	No
Funded through trust	Yes	Yes
Defined benefit or defined contribution pension w/ <100		
Qualified plan funded through trust	Yes	No
Fully insured qualified plan	Yes	No
Unfunded plan for select group of management or HCEs[1]--unfunded or fully funded (see below)	No (4)	No
Defined benefit or defined contribution pension w/ >100		
Qualified plan funded through trust	Yes	Yes
Fully insured qualified plan	Yes	No

1 *HCEs represent highly compensated employees.*

2 *An unfunded plan represents one in which all benefits/claims are paid from the general assets of the plan sponsor.*

3 *The above chart does not contemplate any health and welfare plan holding the stock of a public company.*

4 *A Form 5500 is not required to be filed for a plan covering highly compensated employees (a top heavy plan) as long as in the initial year of the plan an election was made by the plan sponsor to not file the Form 5500 on an annual basis for the plan.*

12 AUDITORS' REPORTS

INTRODUCTION

This chapter provides examples of various types of auditors' reports for defined benefit pension and health and welfare plans, defined contribution pension and health and welfare plans, and related trusts. The type of report to be issued depends on the type of opinion to be rendered (unqualified, qualified, adverse, or disclaimer), the type of plan audited (defined benefit or defined contribution pension or health and welfare), and the scope of work performed (full-scope or limited-scope).

This chapter also includes examples of the standard audit report, modified reports with explanatory paragraphs, qualified opinion reports, adverse opinion reports, disclaimer of opinion reports, the limited-scope audit report, and a sample report for a plan whose financial statements have been prepared on a comprehensive basis of accounting other than generally accepted accounting principles.

The DOL generally rejects Form 5500 filings that include auditors' reports that express either a qualified opinion, adverse opinion, or disclaimer of opinion other than the disclaimer of opinion as permitted by 29 CFR 2520.103-8 of the Department of Labor's Rules and Regulations for Reporting and Disclosure under ERISA (see Limited-Scope Audit Report section later in this chapter for further discussion). If the DOL does reject a Form 5500 filing due to the qualification of the auditors' report, they will send a letter to the plan administrator indicating that the plan's Form 5500 filing has been rejected and giving the plan a period of time (usually forty-five days) to correct the deficiencies. The plan must then correct the deficiencies to the auditor's satisfaction which should then enable the auditor to issue an unqualified opinion on the plan's financial statements within the period of time given by the DOL. The plan must then submit an amended Form 5500 filing with the unqualified auditors' opinion attached.

ERISA and DOL Regulations require that additional information be presented in supplemental schedules accompanying the financial statements in a format prescribed by the instructions to the Form 5500. For additional information regarding the Form 5500 and the supplemental schedules, see Chapter 11, The Form 5500. This additional information is required to be presented in supplemental schedules and reported on by the auditor even if the same information is included in the financial statements (see the section on supplemental schedules later in this chapter for further discussion).

REQUIREMENTS FOR AUDITORS' REPORTS AND PLAN FINANCIAL STATEMENTS

Statement on Auditing Standards 58, *Reports on Audited Financial Statements,* identifies the basic elements of the report as the following:

- A title that includes the word "independent"
- A statement that the financial statements identified in the report were audited
- A statement that the financial statements are the responsibility of the plan's management and that the auditor's responsibility is to express an opinion on the financial statements based on the audit
- A statement that the audit was conducted in accordance with generally accepted auditing standards
- A statement that generally accepted auditing standards require that the auditor plan and perform the audit to obtain reasonable assurance about whether the financial statements are free of material misstatement
- A statement that an audit includes the processes of
    - Examining, on a test basis, evidence supporting the amounts and disclosures in the financial statements
    - Assessing the accounting principles used and significant estimates made by management
    - Evaluating the overall financial statement presentation
- A statement that the auditor believes that the audit provides a reasonable basis for the opinion
- An opinion as to whether the financial statements present fairly, in all material respects, the plan's net assets available for benefits (or financial status) as of the date of the statements of net assets available for benefits and the changes in net assets available for benefits (or financial status) for the period then ended in conformity with generally accepted accounting principles
- The manual or printed signature of the auditor's firm
- The date of the audit report

Generally, the auditors' report should be addressed to the plan administrator or trustees whose financial statements are subject to audit and to the plan's participants. The name of the plan should be the same as is shown in the plan document and Form 5500. ERISA requires that the auditors' report be manually signed and indicate the city and state where issued. The Form 5500 is permitted to be filed electronically or through magnetic media. If the Form 5500 is filed electronically, Form 8453E, Employee Benefit Plan Declaration and Signature for electronic magnetic media, must also be filed to waive the requirement for a manually signed auditors' report.

The report should identify any auditing procedures that were omitted and the reasons for the omission and should clearly express any identified exceptions. ERISA requires that the statement of net assets available for benefits be comparative, other than in the initial year, while the statement of changes in net assets available for benefits is required to be presented at a minimum for the most current year. However, if a defined benefit pension plan presents information regarding its accumulated plan benefits as of the beginning of the year, comparative statements of changes in net assets available for benefits must be presented. The comparative statements must be presented in order to match the plan's assets and changes for the year with its accumulated plan benefit obligations and changes in the benefit obligations for the year.

SUPPLEMENTAL SCHEDULES

The following section discusses the reporting requirements for the various supplemental schedules.

Reporting Requirements

ERISA and DOL regulations require additional information to be presented for the current year-end under audit in certain supplemental schedules along with the financial statements and related footnotes. ERISA requires that all supplemental schedules be covered by the auditors' report. According to the revised Form 5500, the information required to be reported by three of the supplemental schedules--the Schedule of Loans or Fixed Income Obligations, the Schedule of Leases in Default or Classified as Uncollectible, and the Schedule of Nonexempt Transactions--have been incorporated into Schedule G of Form 5500. The information required by the Schedule of Assets Held for Investment Purposes (old item 27a) and the Schedule of Reportable Transactions (old item 27d) is to be provided as part of the Form 5500 filing as part of Schedule H. The supplemental schedules generally required to be covered by the auditors' report include

1. **Schedule of Assets Held for Investment Purposes**--includes all assets held for investment purposes at the end of the plan year. Each investment should be separately identified by issue, maturity date, rate of interest, collateral, par or maturity value, cost and current value, and loan repayment schedule. Note that cost information is only required to be presented for

non-participant-directed investments. Participant loans should also be included on this schedule along with the interest rates charged and the range of maturity dates on outstanding loans. For plans (usually defined contribution pension plans) with investments in self-directed accounts, each of the individual investments comprising the self-directed accounts is required to be reported as a separate line item within this schedule. See Chapter 6, Investments, and Chapter 11, The Form 5500, for additional information.

2. **Schedule of Assets Held for Investment Purposes**--Schedule of investments that were both acquired and disposed of within the plan year--including all assets acquired and disposed of during the plan year as defined by 29 CFR 2520.103-11. This schedule should include all of the same information as discussed in 1. above. Note that this schedule is very rarely filed since many securities are exempt from inclusion in this schedule. For additional information, see Chapter 11, The Form 5500.
3. **Schedule of Loans or Fixed Income Obligations**--includes loans or fixed income obligations which were in default or deemed uncollectible at the end of the plan year, including obligations in which required periodic payments have not been received on the due date (note that participant loans in default that are secured by the participant's account balance in the plan are no longer required to be reported in this schedule).
4. **Schedule of Leases in Default or Classified as Uncollectible**--includes all leases that were in default or deemed uncollectible at the end of the plan year, including leases in which required periodic payments have not been received on the due date.
5. **Schedule of Reportable Transactions**--includes all reportable transactions made during the year as defined by CFR 2520.103-6. Note that transactions that represent participant-directed (or -initiated) transactions are no longer required to be presented on this supplemental schedule. Generally, reportable transactions are defined as any single transaction or series of transactions during the plan year in excess of 5% of the current value of plan assets at the beginning of the plan year.
6. **Schedule of Nonexempt Transactions**--includes transactions with persons known to be parties-in-interest, excluding certain transactions as listed in 29 CFR 2520.103-10(b)(3)(ii).

SAS 29, *Reporting on Information Accompanying the Basic Financial Statements in Auditor-Submitted Documents*, provides guidance on reporting on those supplemental schedules in the auditors' report. Basically, the report should identify the supplemental schedules, state that the audit has been performed for the purpose of forming an opinion on the basic financial statements taken as a whole, and state that the schedules are presented for the purpose of additional analysis and are not a required part of the basic financial statements. The report should also include either an opinion or a disclaimer of opinion on whether the supplemental schedules are fairly stated in all material respects in relation to the basic financial statements taken as a whole, depending on whether the schedules were subjected to auditing procedures. Although not required by SAS 29, auditors may wish to add a statement that the supplemental schedules are the responsibility of the plan's management.

Full-Scope Audit (Unqualified Opinion)

The following illustrative paragraph should be added to the auditors' report after the opinion paragraph if supplemental schedules are presented with basic financial statements which have been subjected to full-scope audit procedures. This example assumes that the supplemental schedules accompanying the financial statements are the (1) Schedule of Assets Held for Investment Purposes and the (2) Schedule of Reportable Transactions. These two supplemental schedules almost always accompany the basic financial statements.

> Our audits were performed for the purpose of forming an opinion on the basic financial statements taken as a whole. The supplemental schedules of (1) assets held for investment purposes as of December 31, 20X1, and (2) reportable transactions for the year ended December 31, 20X1, are presented for the purpose of additional analysis and are not a required part of the basic financial statements but are supplemental information required by the Department of Labor's Rules and Regulations for Reporting and Disclosure under the Employee Retirement Income Security Act of 1974. These supplemental schedules are the responsibility of the Plan's management. The supplemental schedules have been subjected to the auditing procedures applied in the audit of the basic 20X1 financial statements and, in our opinion, are fairly stated in all material respects in relation to those basic financial statements taken as a whole.

Plan Invests in a Master Trust

If a plan invests only in a master trust, none of the supplemental schedules would need to accompany the basic financial statements and, therefore, the preceding illustrative paragraph would not need to be added to the auditors' report. All of the relevant supplemental schedules would be included as part of the master trust filing.

If a plan invests in a master trust as well as other investments outside of a master trust, the supplemental schedules, as well as the illustrative paragraph above, would be required, and should include in the Schedule of Assets Held for Investment Purposes, one line item presentation for the investment in the master trust to report the investment, the cost, and fair value of the investment in the master trust.

Limited-Scope Audit

If a limited-scope audit report is presented, the illustrative paragraph on supplemental schedules shown above should not be added to the report. However, the third paragraph of the limited-scope report should be modified to state that the information included in the financial statements and supplemental schedules are presented in compliance with the Department of Labor's Rules and Regulations for Reporting and Disclosure under the Employee Retirement Income Security Act of 1974. This example report is a negotiated report between the accounting profession and the DOL as this report "reads like a piecemeal opinion," which is not acceptable under generally accepted accounting principles. The following illustrative paragraph is the third paragraph of a limited-scope report in which the auditor disclaims an opinion on the financial statements and supplemental schedules taken as a whole:

> Because of the significance of the information that we did not audit, we are unable to, and do not, express an opinion on the accompanying financial statements and supplemental schedules taken as a whole. The form and content of the information included in the financial statements and supplemental schedules, other than that derived from the information certified by the trustee or custodian, have been audited by us in accordance with generally accepted auditing standards and, in our opinion, are presented in compliance with the Department of Labor's Rules and Regulations for Reporting and Disclosure under the Employee Retirement Income Security Act of 1974.

DEFINED BENEFIT PENSION PLAN--FULL-SCOPE AUDIT

Reporting Requirements

SFAS 35 and ERISA require that the annual financial statements of a defined benefit pension plan include

- Statements of net assets available for benefits (ERISA requires this statement to be comparative)
- Statement(s) of changes in net assets available for benefits

In addition, either the plan's financial statements or footnotes need to include information regarding the plan's accumulated plan benefit obligations and changes in accumulated plan benefit obligations.

In an auditors' report which expresses an unqualified opinion on the financial statements of a defined benefit pension plan wherein the accumulated plan benefit obligation information is presented as of the end of the plan year, the auditor expresses an opinion that the plan's financial statements present fairly, in all material respects, its financial status and the changes therein in conformity with GAAP for the current year and that its net assets available for benefits for the prior year are presented fairly in conformity with GAAP.

NOTE: This example above presumes that the plan's financial statements present a comparative statement of net assets available for benefits and a single-year statement of changes in net assets available for benefits.

A defined benefit pension plan's financial status refers to its financial position. The term financial status was coined because the plan's accumulated benefits are classified as obligations versus liabilities. This dates back to when SFAS 35, *Accounting and Reporting by Defined Benefit Pension Plans,* was issued. In other words, it represents the plan's resources to pay benefits (net assets available for benefits) compared to the liability for payments of benefits (accumulated plan benefits).

Since the primary objective of the financial statements is to provide information that is useful in assessing the plan's present and future ability to pay benefits when due--or to present the financial status of the plan--it is necessary to include information regarding net assets available for benefits and changes therein and the actuarial present value of accumulated plan benefits and changes therein. In order to present an accurate picture of the financial status of a plan, information regarding its net assets available for benefits and its accumulated plan benefits must be presented as of the same date (end-of-year benefit information is the preferred method). Alternatively, SFAS 35 permits plans to present beginning-of-year benefit information because the end-of-year benefit information may not be available on a timely basis. Although based on the extended time period in which plans have to file their annual report on Form 5500, the lack of timely information is not usually an issue. If beginning-of-year information is presented, the financial status of the plan will be presented only as of the end of the preceding year. Therefore, a plan's financial statements will not present its financial status as of its current year-end and, accordingly, the opinion paragraph of the report should not make reference to the fair presentation of the plan's financial status with respect to the current year but instead should refer to the plan's net assets available for benefits and changes therein. When beginning-of-year information is presented, comparative statements of changes in net assets available for benefits must also be presented in order to present the plan's financial status as of the prior year.

SFAS 35 allows defined benefit pension plans to present information regarding the actuarial present value of accumulated plan benefits and significant changes therein either on the face of one or more financial statements, in one or more separate statements or, in the accompanying notes. Each category of information must be presented in its entirety in whatever location is chosen. If such information is not presented in a separate statement but is presented in the footnotes, the introductory paragraph of the report should refer only to the financial statements that are presented (i.e., statement of net assets available for benefits and the changes therein); however, the opinion paragraph would still refer to the financial status of the plan. In order for the actuarial present value of accumulated plan benefits to be presented on the face of the statement of net assets available for benefits or the statement of changes in net assets available for benefits, the information must be as of the same date or for the same period as the financial statement on which it is presented.

End-of-Year Benefit Information, Full-Scope Audit, Unqualified Opinion

The following illustrates a table of contents of a defined benefit pension plan and an auditors' report, which expresses an unqualified opinion on the financial statements of a defined benefit pension plan with information presented in a separate statement of accumulated plan benefits rather than in the footnote form, as of the end of the year. Since most plans subject to ERISA are required to include the Supplemental Schedule of Assets Held for Investment Purposes and Supplemental Schedule of Reportable Transactions, there is also an illustrative paragraph after the opinion paragraph that should be included when those supplemental schedules are presented with the basic financial statements and have been subjected to full-scope audit procedures (for a discussion of the supplemental schedules, see Chapter 11, The Form 5500).

ABC Company Defined Benefit Pension Plan Table of Contents

Independent Auditors' Report

To the ABC Company Defined Benefit Pension Plan and Participants:

We have audited the accompanying financial statements of the ABC Company Defined Benefit Pension Plan as of December 31, 20X1 and 20X0, and for the year ended December 31, 20X1, as listed in the Table of Contents. These financial statements are the responsibility of the Plan's management. Our responsibility is to express an opinion on these financial statements based on our audits.

We conducted our audits in accordance with generally accepted auditing standards. Those standards require that we plan and perform the audit to obtain reasonable assurance about whether the financial statements are free of material misstatement. An audit includes examining, on a test basis, evidence supporting the amounts and disclosures in the financial statements. An audit also includes assessing the accounting principles used and significant estimates made by management as well as evaluating the overall financial statement presentation. We believe that our audits provide a reasonable basis for our opinion.

In our opinion, the financial statements referred to above present fairly, in all material respects, the financial status of the Plan as of December 31, 20X1 and 20X0, and the changes in its financial status for the year ended December 31, 20X1, in conformity with generally accepted accounting principles.

Our audits were performed for the purpose of forming an opinion on the basic financial statements taken as a whole. The supplemental schedules listed in the Table of Contents are presented for the purpose of additional analysis and are not a required part of the basic financial statements but are supplemental information required by the Department of Labor's Rules and Regulations for Reporting and Disclosure under the Employee Retirement Income Security Act of 1974. These supplemental schedules are the responsibility of the Plan's management.

The supplemental schedules have been subjected to the auditing procedures applied in the audit of the basic 20X1 financial statements and, in our opinion, are fairly stated in all material respects in relation to the basic financial statements taken as a whole.

[Signature]

[Date]

Beginning-of-Year Benefit Information, Full-Scope Audit, Unqualified Opinion

The following illustrative report expresses a standard unqualified opinion on financial statements of a defined benefit pension plan, which has prepared a separate statement of accumulated plan benefits rather than alternative footnote disclosure, as of the beginning of the year. A table of contents was not prepared in this example. Also, this example assumes supplemental schedules have been attached.

Independent Auditors' Report

To the ABC Company Defined Benefit Pension Plan and Participants:

We have audited the accompanying statements of net assets available for benefits of the ABC Company Defined Benefit Pension Plan as of December 31, 20X1 and 20X0, and the related statements of changes in net assets available for benefits for the years then ended and the statement of accumulated plan benefits as of December 31, 20X0, and the related statement of changes in accumulated plan benefits for the year then ended. These financial statements are the responsibility of the Plan's management. Our responsibility is to express an opinion on these financial statements based on our audits.

We conducted our audits in accordance with generally accepted auditing standards. Those standards require that we plan and perform the audit to obtain reasonable assurance about whether the financial statements are free of material misstatement. An audit includes examining, on a test basis, evidence supporting the amounts and disclosures in the financial statements. An audit also includes assessing the accounting principles used and significant estimates made by management, as well as evaluating the overall financial statement presentation. We believe that our audits provide a reasonable basis for our opinion.

In our opinion, the financial statements referred to above present fairly, in all material respects, the Plan's net assets available for benefits as of December 31, 20X1, and the changes therein for the year then ended and its financial status as of December 31, 20X0, and the changes therein for the year then ended, in conformity with generally accepted accounting principles.

Our audits were performed for the purpose of forming an opinion on the basic financial statements taken as a whole. The supplemental schedules of (1) assets held for investment purposes as of December 31, 20X1, and (2) reportable transactions for the year ended December 31, 20X1, are presented for the purpose of additional analysis and are not a required part of the basic financial statements but are supplemental information required by the Department of Labor's Rules and Regulations for Reporting and Disclosure under the Employee Retirement Income Security Act of 1974. These supplemental schedules are the responsibility of the Plan's management. The supplemental schedules have been subjected to the auditing procedures applied in the audit of the basic 20X1 financial statements and, in our opinion, are fairly stated in all material respects in relation to the basic financial statements taken as a whole.

[Signature]

[Date]

Beginning-of-Year Benefit Information, Full-Scope Audit, Unqualified Opinion

The following illustrative report expresses a standard unqualified opinion on financial statements of a defined benefit pension plan which has presented the accumulated plan benefit information in the footnotes to the plan's financial statements.

A table of contents was not prepared in this example. Also, this example assumes supplemental schedules have been attached.

Independent Auditors' Report

To the ABC Company Defined Benefit Pension Plan and Participants:

We have audited the accompanying statements of net assets available for benefits of the ABC Company Defined Benefit Pension Plan as of December 31, 20X1 and 20X0, and the related statements of changes in net assets available for benefits for the years then ended. These financial statements are the responsibility of the Plan's management. Our responsibility is to express an opinion on those financial statements based on our audits.

We conducted our audits in accordance with generally accepted auditing standards. Those standards require that we plan and perform the audit to obtain reasonable assurance about whether the financial statements are free of material misstatement. An audit includes examining, on a test basis, evidence supporting the amounts and disclosures in the financial statements. An audit also includes assessing the accounting principles used and significant estimates made by management as well as evaluating the overall financial statement presentation. We believe that our audits provide a reasonable basis for our opinion.

In our opinion, the financial statements referred to above present fairly, in all material respects, the Plan's net assets available for benefits as of December 31, 20X1, and the changes therein for the year then ended and its financial status as of December 31, 20X0, and the changes therein for the year then ended, in conformity with generally accepted accounting principles.

Our audits were performed for the purpose of forming an opinion on the basic financial statements taken as a whole. The supplemental schedules of (1) assets held for investment purposes as of December 31, 20X1, and (2) reportable transactions for the year ended December 31, 20X1, are presented for the purpose of additional analysis and are not a required part of the basic financial statements but are supplemental information required by the Department of Labor's Rules and Regulations for Reporting and Disclosure under the Employee Retirement Income Security Act of 1974. These supplemental schedules are the responsibility of the Plan's management. The supplemental schedules have been subjected to the auditing procedures applied in the audit of the basic 20X1 financial statements and, in our opinion, are fairly stated in all material respects in relation to the basic financial statements taken as a whole.

DEFINED CONTRIBUTION PENSION PLAN--FULL-SCOPE AUDIT

Reporting Requirements

The annual financial statements of a defined contribution pension plan should include the following:

- Statements of net assets available for benefits
- Statement(s) of changes in net assets available for benefits

According to the provisions of AICPA SOP 99-3, a defined contribution pension plan is not required to present plan investments by general type or investment program for participant-directed investments in the statement of net assets available for benefits or the statement of changes in net assets available for benefits.

However, the plan is required to identify non-participant-directed investments and the significant components of the changes in net assets relating to the non-participant-directed investments in the footnotes to the financial statements or on the face of the plan's financial statements. The plan should also identify, in the footnotes to the financial statements or on the face of the plan's financial statements, all investments that represent 5% or more of the plan's net assets and also any non-participant-directed investments which exceed 5% of the total amount of non-participant-directed assets. The plan's net appreciation/depreciation in fair value of investments by major class of investments (e.g., equities, fixed-income securities) also needs to be presented and would most likely be in the footnotes to the financial statements.

The following illustrative auditors' reports give examples of how the auditors' report should look if the plan was audited in total without "by-fund" information presented, if the plan was audited in total with "by-fund" information presented, and if the plan was audited "by fund and in total." The following examples have been presented for plans that continue to report by-fund information for participant-directed and non-participant-directed investments on the face of the financial statements. In the past, participant-directed funds needed to be included either on the face of the plan's financial statements or within the footnotes; as such, these examples are presented for purposes of plans that continue to report such information on the face of the plan's financial statements.

Full-Scope Audit, Unqualified Opinion, Plan Audited in Total (Not by Fund)

The following is an illustrative table of contents and auditors' report that expresses a standard unqualified opinion on the financial statements of a defined contribution pension plan with supplemental schedules attached. In this case, the plan's financial statements include comparative statements of net assets available for benefits and a single-year presentation of the statement of changes in net assets available for benefits which is consistent with the Form 5500 requirements.

ABC Company Defined Contribution Pension Plan Table of Contents

Title	*Page no.*
Independent Auditors' Report	1
Financial Statements:	
Statement of Net Assets Available for Benefits as of December 31, 20X1 and 20X0	2
Statement of Changes in Net Assets Available for Benefits for the Year Ended December 31, 20X1	3
Notes to Financial Statements	4
Supplemental Schedules:	
Schedule of Assets Held for Investment Purposes as of December 31, 20X1 (old Schedule 27a)	8
Schedule of Loans or Fixed Income Obligations December 31, 20X1 (old Schedule 27d)	9

Independent Auditors' Report

To the ABC Company Defined Contribution Pension Plan and Participants:

We have audited the accompanying financial statements of the ABC Company Defined Contribution Pension Plan as of December 31, 20X1 and 20X0, and for the year ended December 31, 20X1, as listed in the Table of Contents. These financial statements are the responsibility of the Plan's management. Our responsibility is to express an opinion on these financial statements based on our audits.

We conducted our audits in accordance with generally accepted auditing standards. These standards require that we plan and perform the audit to obtain reasonable assurance about whether the financial statements are free of material misstatement. An audit includes examining, on a test basis, evidence supporting the amounts and disclosures in the financial statements. An audit also includes assessing the accounting principles used and significant estimates made by management as well as evaluating the overall financial statement presentation. We believe that our audits provide a reasonable basis for our opinion.

In our opinion, the financial statements referred to above present fairly, in all material respects, the net assets available for benefits of the Plan as of December 31, 20X1 and 20X0, and the changes in net assets available for benefits for the year ended December 31, 20X1, in conformity with generally accepted accounting principles.

Our audits were performed for the purpose of forming an opinion on the basic financial statements taken as a whole. The supplemental schedules listed in the table of contents are presented for the purpose of additional analysis and are not a required part of the basic financial statements but are supplemental information required by the Department of Labor's Rules and Regulations for Reporting and Disclosure under the Employee Retirement Income Security Act of 1974. These supplemental schedules are the responsibility of the Plan's management. The supplemental schedules have been subjected to the auditing procedures applied in the audit of the basic 20X1 financial statements and, in our opinion, are fairly stated in all material respects in relation to those basic financial statements taken as a whole.

[Signature]

[Date]

By-Fund Information Presented on the Face of the Financial Statements as Supplemental Information

Even though this plan has been audited "in total" and not "by fund," the financial statements may still be presented with "by-fund" information on the face of the financial statements. In that case, the supplemental information presented on the face of the financial statements should be labeled as "supplemental information" and the last paragraph of the preceding illustrative auditors' report should be replaced with the following paragraph:

Our audits were performed for the purpose of forming an opinion on the basic financial statements taken as a whole. The supplemental schedules listed in the Table of Contents are presented for the purpose of additional analysis and are not a required part of the basic financial statements but are supplemental information required by the Department of Labor's Rules and Regulations for Reporting and Disclosure under the Employee Retirement Income Security Act of 1974. The supplemental information by fund in the statements of net assets available for benefits and the statement of changes in net assets available for benefits is presented for the purpose of additional analysis rather than to present the net assets available for benefits and changes in net assets available for benefits of the individual funds. The supplemental schedules and supplemental information by fund are the responsibility of the Plan's management.

Such supplemental schedules and supplemental information by fund have been subjected to the auditing procedures applied in our audit of the basic 20X1 financial statements and, in our opinion, are fairly stated in all material respects when considered in relation to those basic financial statements taken as a whole.

Full-Scope Audit, Unqualified Opinion, Plan Audited by Fund and in Total

The following illustrative report expresses a standard unqualified opinion on financial statements of a defined contribution pension plan with supplemental schedules attached. In this case, the plan's financial statements include comparative statements of net assets available for benefits, a single-year presentation of the statement of changes in net assets available for benefits and supplemental schedules accompany the basic financial statements. This plan was audited by fund and in total.

Independent Auditors' Report

To the ABC Company Defined Contribution Pension Plan and Participants:

We have audited, by fund and in total, the statements of net assets available for benefits of the ABC Company Defined Contribution Pension Plan as of December 31, 20X1 and 20X0, and the related statement of changes in net assets available for benefits for the year ended December 31, 20X1. These financial statements are the responsibility of the Plan's management. Our responsibility is to express an opinion on these financial statements based on our audits.

We conducted our audits in accordance with generally accepted auditing standards. These standards require that we plan and perform the audit to obtain reasonable assurance about whether the financial statements are free of material misstatement. An audit includes examining, on a test basis, evidence supporting the amounts and disclosures in the financial statements. An audit also includes assessing the accounting principles used and significant estimates made by management, as well as evaluating the overall financial statement presentation. We believe that our audits provide a reasonable basis for our opinion.

In our opinion, the financial statements referred to above present fairly, by fund and in total, in all material respects, the net assets available for benefits of the Plan as of December 31, 20X1, and 20X0, and the changes in net assets available for benefits for the year ended December 31, 20X1, in conformity with generally accepted accounting principles.

Our audits were performed for the purpose of forming an opinion on the basic financial statements taken as a whole. The supplemental schedules of (1) assets held for investment purposes as of December 31, 20X1, and (2) reportable transactions for the year ended December 31, 20X1, are presented for the purpose of additional analysis and are not a required part of the basic financial statements but are supplemental information required by the Department of Labor's Rules and Regulations for Reporting and Disclosure under the Employee Retirement Income Security Act of 1974. These supplemental schedules are the responsibility of the Plan's management. The supplemental schedules have been subjected to the auditing procedures applied in the audit of the basic 20X1 financial statements and, in our opinion, are fairly stated in all material respects in relation to those basic financial statements taken as a whole.

[Signature]

[Date]

DEFINED BENEFIT HEALTH AND WELFARE PLAN

Reporting Requirements

The reporting requirements for a defined benefit health and welfare plan are similar to those of a defined benefit pension plan. The annual financial statements of a defined benefit health and welfare plan should include the following:

- Statements of net assets available for plan benefits
- Statement(s) of changes in net assets available for plan benefits
- Statements of benefit obligations
- Statement(s) of changes in benefit obligations

The statements of benefit obligations and statement of changes in benefit obligations should be presented on the face of the financial statements, not in the accompanying notes. Note that if a proposed change is being contemplated with respect to the presentation of benefit obligations information, it would permit such information to be presented in the footnotes to the plan's financial statements. In order to obtain information regarding this proposed change and to follow up on any changes made, readers should refer to the AICPA website, www.aicpa.org. See Chapter 9, Accounting, Auditing, and Reporting for Health and Welfare Plans, for additional information.

In an auditors' report which expresses an unqualified opinion on the financial statements of a defined benefit health and welfare plan, the auditor expresses an opinion that the plan's financial statements present fairly, in all material respects, its financial status and the changes therein in conformity with GAAP for the current year, and that its net assets available for benefits for the prior year are presented fairly in conformity with GAAP for the prior year.

NOTE: This example presumes that the plan's financial statements present a comparative statement of net assets available for benefits and a single-year statement of changes in net assets available for benefits.

Statement of Position 92-6, *Accounting and Reporting by Health and Welfare Benefit Plans* (SOP 92-6), was effective for audits of financial statements of single-employer plans with more than 500 participants for plan years beginning after December 15, 1992, and for single-employer plans with less than 500 participants for plan years beginning after December 15, 1994. This SOP was effective for audits of financial statements of multiemployer plans for plan years beginning after December 15, 1995. The DOL, however, has taken a nonenforcement policy and will not reject qualified or adverse opinions on financial statements of multiemployer plans that have not complied with the postretirement benefit obligation provisions of SOP 92-6 for plan years beginning prior to January 1, 2000. For the multiemployer plans which adopt the provisions of SOP 92-6, they will be required to restate the prior year's financial statements in order to present comparative statements of benefit obligations. The impact of restating the prior year financial statements will need to be disclosed in the current year financial statements.

Full-Scope Audit, Unqualified Opinion

The following illustrative table of contents and auditors' report expresses a standard unqualified opinion on financial statements of a defined benefit health and welfare plan which has adopted SOP 92-6.

ABC Company Defined Benefit Health and Welfare Plan Table of Contents

Independent Auditors' Report

To the ABC Company Defined Benefit Health and Welfare Plan and Participants:

We have audited the accompanying financial statements of the ABC Company Defined Benefit Health and Welfare Plan as of December 31, 20X1 and 20X0, and for the year ended December 31, 20X1, as listed in the Table of Contents. These financial statements are the responsibility of the Plan's management. Our responsibility is to express an opinion on these financial statements based on our audits.

We conducted our audits in accordance with generally accepted auditing standards. Those standards require that we plan and perform the audit to obtain reasonable assurance about whether the financial statements are free of material misstatement. An audit includes examining, on a test basis, evidence supporting the amounts and disclosures in the financial statements. An audit also includes assessing the accounting principles used and significant estimates made by management as well as evaluating the overall financial statement presentation. We believe that our audits provide a reasonable basis for our opinion.

In our opinion, the financial statements referred to above present fairly, in all material respects, the financial status of the Plan as of December 31, 20X1 and 20X0, and the changes in its financial status for the year ended December 31, 20X1, in conformity with generally accepted accounting principles.

Our audits were performed for the purpose of forming an opinion on the basic financial statements taken as a whole. The supplemental schedules listed in the Table of Contents are presented for the purpose of additional analysis and are not a required part of the basic financial statements but are supplemental information required by the Department of Labor's Rules and Regulations for Reporting and Disclosure under the Employee Retirement Income Security Act of 1974. These supplemental schedules are the responsibility of the Plan's management.

The supplemental schedules have been subjected to the auditing procedures applied in the audit of the basic 20X1 financial statements and, in our opinion, are fairly stated in all material respects in relation to those basic financial statements taken as a whole.

[Signature]

[Date]

Adverse Opinion--Plans Not in Accordance With SOP 92-6

The following illustrative report expresses an adverse opinion on the financial statements of a defined benefit health and welfare plan because the financial statements do not present the postretirement benefit obligations in accordance with SOP 92-6. The AICPA has indicated that in most situations, the exclusion of postretirement benefits would be material to the plan's financial statements and pervasive, and therefore, an adverse auditors' report on the financial statements would be issued for the plan. Also, as SOP 92-6 has to be adopted in 2000, the situation described by this example is no longer expected to be prevalent. The statements of net assets available for benefits and benefit obligations are comparative, the statement of changes in net assets available for benefits and benefit obligations are for a single year and supplemental schedules accompany the financial statements. A table of contents was not prepared in this example.

A disclaimer of opinion is expressed on the supplemental schedules because an adverse opinion has been expressed on the basic financial statements. When an adverse or disclaimer of opinion is given on the basic financial statements, the auditor should not express an opinion on the accompanying supplemental schedules because it may appear to contradict the adverse or disclaimer of opinion on the basic financial statements.

Independent Auditors' Report

To the DEF Multiemployer Defined Benefit Health and Welfare Plan and Participants:

We have audited the accompanying statements of net assets available for benefits and of benefit obligations of DEF Multiemployer Defined Benefit Health and Welfare Plan as of December 31, 20X1 and 20X0, and the related statements of changes in net assets available for benefits and of changes in benefit obligations for the year ended December 31, 20X1. These financial statements are the responsibility of the Plan's management. Our responsibility is to express an opinion on these financial statements based on our audits.

We conducted our audits in accordance with generally accepted auditing standards. Those standards require that we plan and perform the audit to obtain reasonable assurance about whether the financial statements are free of material misstatement. An audit includes examining, on a test basis, evidence supporting the amounts and disclosures in the financial statements. An audit also includes assessing the accounting principles used and significant estimates made by management as well as evaluating the overall financial statement presentation. We believe that our audits provide a reasonable basis for our opinion.

As discussed in Note X to the financial statements, the Plan's financial statements do not present the plan's obligations to provide health and welfare benefits to participants after retirement (postretirement benefit obligations). Generally accepted accounting principles require that a plan's statement of benefit obligations and statement of changes in benefit obligations include the postretirement benefit obligations. The Plan administrator has not quantified the amount of, or change in, the Plan's postretirement benefit obligations, and in the absence of an actuarial determination, such amounts are not reasonably determinable. However, the effects of the omission of the postretirement benefit obligation information on the Plan's financial statements are presumed to be material.

In our opinion, because of the effects of the matters discussed in the preceding paragraphs, the financial statements referred to above do not present fairly, in conformity with generally accepted accounting principles, the financial status of the Plan as of December 31, 20X1, and the changes in its financial status for the year ended December 31, 20X1.

The supplemental schedules of (1) assets held for investment purposes as of December 31, 20X1 and (2) reportable transactions for the year ended December 31, 20X1, are presented for the purpose of additional analysis and are not a required part of the basic financial statement, but are supplemental information required by the Department of Labor's Rules and Regulations for Reporting and Disclosure under the Employee Retirement Income Security Act of 1974. These supplemental schedules are the responsibility of the Plan's management. The supplemental schedules have been subjected to the auditing procedures applied in the audit of the basic financial statements for the year ended December 31, 20X1; however, because the basic financial statements are not presented fairly in conformity with generally accepted accounting principles, we do not express an opinion on any of the supplemental schedules.

[Signature]

[Date]

DEFINED CONTRIBUTION HEALTH AND WELFARE PLAN

Reporting Requirements

The financial statements of a defined contribution health and welfare plan should include

- Statements of net assets available for benefits
- Statement(s) of changes in net assets available for benefits

Because a plan's obligation to provide benefits is limited to the amounts accumulated in an individual's account, information regarding benefit obligations is not applicable.

Full-Scope Audit, Unqualified Opinion

The following is an illustrative table of contents and auditors' report that expresses a standard unqualified opinion on the financial statements of a defined contribution health and welfare plan with supplemental schedules attached. In this case, the plan's financial statements include comparative statements of net assets available for benefits and a single-year presentation of the statement of changes in net assets available for benefits.

ABC Company Defined Contribution Health and Welfare Plan Table of Contents

Independent Auditors' Report

To the ABC Company Defined Contribution Health and Welfare Plan and Participants:

We have audited the accompanying financial statements of the ABC Company Defined Contribution Health and Welfare Benefit Plan as of December 31, 20X1 and 20X0, and for the year ended December 31, 20X1, as listed in the Table of Contents. These financial statements are the responsibility of the Plan's management. Our responsibility is to express an opinion on these financial statements based on our audits.

We conducted our audits in accordance with generally accepted auditing standards. Those standards require that we plan and perform the audit to obtain reasonable assurance about whether the financial statements are free of material misstatement. An audit includes examining, on a test basis, evidence supporting the amounts and disclosures in the financial statements. An audit also includes assessing the accounting principles used and significant estimates made by management as well as evaluating the overall financial statement presentation. We believe that our audits provide a reasonable basis for our opinion.

In our opinion, the financial statements referred to above present fairly, in all material respects, the net assets available for benefits of the Plan as of December 31, 20X1 and 20X0, and the changes in net assets available for benefits for the year ended December 31, 20X1, in conformity with generally accepted accounting principles.

Our audits were performed for the purpose of forming an opinion on the basic financial statements taken as a whole. The supplemental schedules listed in the Table of Contents are presented for the purpose of additional analysis and are not a required part of the basic financial statements but are supplementary information required by the Department of Labor's Rules and Regulations for Reporting and Disclosure under the Employee Retirement Income Security Act of 1974. These supplemental schedules are the responsibility of the Plan's management. The supplemental schedules have been subjected to the auditing procedures applied in the audit of the basic 20X1 financial statements and, in our opinion, are fairly stated in all material respects in relation to those basic financial statements taken as a whole.

[Signature]

[Date]

LIMITED-SCOPE AUDIT REPORT

The following provides an example of a limited-scope audit report, whereby the investment information is certified by a trustee or custodian.

A limited-scope audit report is issued when an auditor has not performed auditing procedures with respect to investments and net investment income certified by the plan's trustee. In order to qualify for the limited-scope audit, the trustee must be a bank, insurance company, or similar institution that is state or federally chartered, regulated, supervised, and subject to periodic examination by a state or federal agency. The trustee must certify that the information provided to the plan administrator is complete and accurate. Thus, the plan administrator restricts the scope of the audit to exclude investments, investment income, and investment expenses. A limited-scope audit may be performed on any type of plan (e.g., defined benefit pension, defined contribution pension, or health and welfare) as long as the proper certification is obtained. If a limited-scope audit has been performed, the auditor should disclaim an opinion on the financial statements unless investments are immaterial (e.g., some health and welfare plans).

The following illustrative report is an example of such a disclaimer of opinion; the basic format would be the same for all plan types.

Independent Auditors' Report

To the ABC Company Benefit Plan and Participants:

We were engaged to audit the accompanying statements of net assets available for benefits of ABC Company Benefit Plan as of December 31, 20X1 and 20X0, the related statement of changes in net assets available for benefits for the year ended December 31, 20X1, and the Supplemental Schedule of Assets Held for Investment Purposes as of December 31, 20X1, and the Schedule of Reportable Transactions for the year ended December 31, 20X1. These financial statements and supplemental schedules are the responsibility of the Plan's management.

As permitted by 29 CFR 2520.103-8 of the Department of Labor's Rules and Regulations for Reporting and Disclosure under the Employee Retirement Income Security Act of 1974, the plan administrator instructed us not to perform, and we did not perform, any auditing procedures with respect to the information summarized in Note X, which was certified by EFG Bank and HIJ Insurance Company, the trustees of the Plan, except for comparing such information with the related information included in the financial statements. We have been informed by the plan administrator that the trustees hold the Plan's investment assets and execute investment transactions. The plan administrator has obtained certifications from the trustees as of December 31, 20X1 and 20X0, and for the year ended December 31, 20X1, that the information provided to the plan administrator by the trustees is complete and accurate.

Because of the significance of the information that we did not audit, we are unable to, and do not, express an opinion on the accompanying financial statements taken as a whole. The form and content of the information included in the financial statements and supplemental schedules, other than that derived from the information certified by the trustees (or custodians), have been audited by us in accordance with generally accepted auditing standards and, in our opinion, are presented in compliance with the Department of Labor's Rules and Regulations for Reporting and Disclosure under the Employee Retirement Income Security Act of 1974.

[Signature]

[Date]

The footnotes to the plan's financial statements should summarize the financial information which was certified by the trustee/custodian. The following is an example of the format that may be used in the footnote:

Note X--Information Certified by the Trustee

The following is a summary of the unaudited information regarding the Plan as of December 31, 20X1 and 20X0, and for the year ended December 31, 20X1, included in the Plan's financial statements and supplemental schedules, that was prepared by or derived from information prepared by EFG Bank and HIJ Insurance Company, the trustees of the Plan, and furnished to the plan administrator. The plan administrator has obtained certifications from the trustees that such information is complete and accurate.

a. Investment information as indicated on the statements of net assets available for benefits as of December 31, 20X1 and 20X0

	20X1	*20X0*
ABC common stock	$xxx	$xxx
High-growth mutual fund	xxx	xxx
Income receivable	xx	xx

b. Investment income as indicated on the statement of changes in net assets available for benefits for the year ended December 31, 20X1

Net appreciation	$xxx
Dividend income	xxx

c. All information included in the supplemental Schedule of Assets Held for Investment Purposes as of December 31, 20X1
d. All information included in the supplemental Schedule of Reportable Transactions for the year ended December 31, 20X1

Plan investments not held by a trustee who qualifies for the limited-scope exemption, as set forth in the DOL regulations, should be subjected to appropriate full-scope audit procedures. If the plan had some investments held by a trustee who qualifies for the limited-scope exemption and some investments held by a trustee who does not qualify, the limited-scope audit report would be required if the amount of the plan's assets that are not audited (i.e., those assets covered by the trustee certification) are material to the plan's financial statements taken as a whole.

Full-Scope Audit in Current Year, Limited-Scope Audit in Prior Year

The plan administrator may elect not to limit the scope of the audit in the current year even though the scope of the audit in the prior year was limited in accordance with DOL regulations, or the custodian of plan assets may have changed from a bank to an institution that does not satisfy the DOL criteria to permit a limited-scope audit of the plan. The following illustrates a report on comparative financial statements of a defined benefit pension plan under those circumstances.

Independent Auditors' Report

To the ABC Company Defined Benefit Pension Plan and Participants:

We have audited the accompanying statements of net assets available for benefits of ABC Company Defined Benefit Pension Plan as of December 31, 20X1 and 20X0, and the related statement of changes in net assets available for benefits for the year ended December 31, 20X1, and the statements of accumulated plan benefits as of December 31, 20X1 and 20X0, and the related statement of changes in accumulated plan benefits for the year ended December 31, 20X1. These financial statements are the responsibility of the Plan's management. Our responsibility is to express an opinion on these financial statements based on our audits.

Except as explained in the following paragraph, we conducted our audits in accordance with generally accepted auditing standards. Those standards require that we plan and perform the audit to obtain reasonable assurance about whether the financial statements are free of material misstatement. An audit includes examining, on a test basis, evidence supporting the amounts and disclosures in the financial statements. An audit also includes assessing the accounting principles used and significant estimates made by management as well as evaluating the overall financial statement presentation. We believe that our audits provide a reasonable basis for our opinion.

As permitted by 29 CFR 2520.103-8 of the Department of Labor's Rules and Regulations for Reporting and Disclosure under the Employee Retirement Income Security Act of 1974, investment assets held by KLM Bank, the trustee (or custodian) of the Plan, and transactions in those assets were excluded from the scope of our audit of the Plan's 20X0 financial statements, except for comparing the information provided by the trustee (or custodian), which is summarized in Note X, with the related information included in the financial statements.

Because of the significance of the information that we did not audit, we are unable to, and do not, express an opinion on the Plan's financial statements as of December 31, 20X0. The form and content of the information included in the 20X0 financial statements, other than that derived from the information certified by the trustee (or custodian), have been audited by us and, in our opinion, are presented in compliance with the Department of Labor's Rules and Regulations for Reporting and Disclosure under the Employee Retirement Income Security Act of 1974.

In our opinion, the financial statements, referred to above, of ABC Company Defined Benefit Pension Plan as of December 31, 20X1, and for the year then ended present fairly, in all material respects, the financial status of ABC Company Defined Benefit Pension Plan as of December 31, 20X1, and changes in its financial status for the year then ended in conformity with generally accepted accounting principles.

Our audit of the Plan's financial statements as of and for the year ended December 31, 20X1, was made for the purpose of forming an opinion on the financial statements taken as a whole. The supplemental schedules of (1) assets held for investment purposes as of December 31, 20X1, and (2) reportable transactions for the year ended December 31, 20X1, are presented for the purpose of additional analysis and are not a required part of the basic financial statements, but are supplemental information required by the Department of Labor's Rules and Regulations for Reporting and Disclosure under the Employee Retirement Income Security Act of 1974. These supplemental schedules are the responsibility of the Plan's management. The supplemental schedules have been subjected to the auditing procedures applied in the audit of the basic 20X1 financial statements, and, in our opinion, are fairly stated in all material respects in relation to the basic financial statements taken as a whole.

[Signature]

[Date]

Limited-Scope Audit in Current Year, Full-Scope Audit in Prior Year

Similarly, a plan administrator may exclude from the auditor's examination the plan's assets held by banks or insurance companies in the current year, whereas the scope of the audit in the prior year was unrestricted, since comparative financial statements are required under ERISA. Under those circumstances, the auditor's report should refer to the date of the previously issued report on the prior year's financial statements of the plan in expressing an opinion on that information. The following illustrates a report on comparative financial statements in those circumstances.

Independent Auditors' Report

To the ABC Company Defined Contribution Pension Plan and Participants:

We were engaged to audit the accompanying statements of net assets available for benefits of ABC Company Defined Contribution Pension Plan as of December 31, 20X1 and 20X0, and the related statement of changes in net assets available for benefits for the year ended December 31, 20X1, and the supplemental Schedule of Assets Held for Investment Purposes as of December 31, 20X1, and the Schedule of Reportable Transactions for the year ended December 31, 20X1. These financial statements and supplemental schedules are the responsibility of the Plan's management.

As permitted by 29 CFR 2520.103-8 of the Department of Labor's Rules and Regulations for Reporting and Disclosure under the Employee Retirement Income Security Act of 1974, the plan administrator instructed us not to perform, and we did not perform, any auditing procedures with respect to the information summarized in Note X, which was certified by KLM Bank, the trustee (or custodian) of the Plan, except for comparing the information with the related information included in the 20X1 financial statements and the supplemental schedules.

We have been informed by the plan administrator that the trustee (or custodian) holds the Plan's investment assets and executes investment transactions. The plan administrator has obtained a certification from the trustee (or custodian) as of and for the year ended December 31, 20X1, that the information provided to the plan administrator by the trustee (or custodian) is complete and accurate.

Because of the significance of the information in the Plan's 20X1 financial statements that we did not audit, we are unable to, and do not, express an opinion on the accompanying financial statements and supplemental schedules as of and for the year ended December 31, 20X1. The form and content of the information included in the financial statements and supplemental schedules, other than that derived from the information certified by the trustee, have been audited by us in accordance with generally accepted auditing standards and, in our opinion, are presented in compliance with the Department of Labor's Rules and Regulations for Reporting and Disclosure under the Employee Retirement Income Security Act of 1974.

We have audited the statement of net assets available for benefits of ABC Company Defined Contribution Pension Plan as of December 31, 20X0, and in our report dated May 25, 20X1, we expressed our opinion that such financial statement presents fairly, in all material respects, the net assets available for benefits of ABC Company Defined Contribution Pension Plan as of December 31, 20X0, in conformity with generally accepted accounting principles.

NOTE: This paragraph referring to the statement of net assets available for benefits is required in this format as a comparative statement of changes in net assets available of benefits is not being presented with the current year's financial statements.

CHANGE IN AUDITOR

Prior Year Audited by Another Firm

If the auditor is issuing a report on comparative financial statements in which the auditor has only audited the financial statements of the current year but other auditors have audited the financial statements of the prior year, the auditor should refer to the report of the other auditors in the first paragraph of the report.

Both years full-scope audits. The following illustrative report should be used if the prior year's financial statements were audited by another firm and both the current and prior year audits were full-scope audits.

Independent Auditors' Report

To the ABC Company Defined Benefit Pension Plan and Participants:

We have audited the statement of net assets available for benefits of the ABC Company Defined Benefit Pension Plan as of December 31, 20X1, and the related statement of changes in net assets available for benefits for the year then ended. These financial statements are the responsibility of the Plan's management. Our responsibility is to express an opinion on these financial statements based on our audit. The financial statements of ABC Company Defined Benefit Pension Plan as of December 31, 20X0, were audited by other auditors whose report dated June 17, 20X1, expressed an unqualified opinion on those statements.

We conducted our audit in accordance with generally accepted auditing standards. Those standards require that we plan and perform the audit to obtain reasonable assurance about whether the financial statements are free of material misstatement.

An audit includes examining, on a test basis, evidence supporting the amounts and disclosures in the financial statements. An audit also includes assessing the accounting principles used and significant estimates made by management, as well as evaluating the overall financial statement presentation. We believe that our audit provides a reasonable basis for our opinion.

In our opinion, the financial statements referred to above present fairly, in all material respects, the financial status of the Plan as of December 31, 20X1, and the changes in its financial status for the year then ended in conformity with generally accepted accounting principles.

[Signature]

[Date]

Full-scope audit in prior year, limited-scope audit in current year. The following illustrative report should be used if the prior year's financial statements were audited by another firm, the prior year's audit was full-scope and the current year's audit was limited-scope.

Independent Auditors' Report

To the ABC Company Defined Benefit Pension Plan and Participants:

We were engaged to audit the accompanying statement of net assets available for benefits of the ABC Company Defined Benefit Pension Plan as of December 31, 20X1, and the related statement of changes in net assets available for benefits for the year then ended. These financial statements are the responsibility of the Plan's management. The financial statements of ABC Company Defined Benefit Pension Plan as of December 31, 20X0, were audited by other auditors whose report dated June 17, 20X1, expressed an unqualified opinion on those statements.

As permitted by 29 CFR 2520.103-8 of the Department of Labor's Rules and Regulations for Reporting and Disclosure under the Employee Retirement Income Security Act of 1974, the plan administrator instructed us not to perform, and we did not perform, any auditing procedures with respect to the information summarized in Note X, which was certified by FGH Bank, the trustee of the Plan, except for comparing such information with the related information included in the financial statements. We have been informed by the plan administrator that the trustee holds the Plan's investment assets and executes investment transactions. The plan administrator has obtained a certification from the trustee as of December 31, 20X1, and for the year then ended, that the information provided to the plan administrator by the trustee is complete and accurate.

Because of the significance of the information that we did not audit, we are unable to, and do not, express an opinion on the December 31, 20X1 financial statements taken as a whole. The form and content of the information included in the financial statements, other than that derived from the information certified by the trustee, have been audited by us in accordance with generally accepted auditing standards and, in our opinion, are presented in compliance with the Department of Labor's Rules and Regulations for Reporting and Disclosure under the Employee Retirement Income Security Act of 1974.

[Signature]

[Date]

SUPPLEMENTAL SCHEDULES

Departure From DOL Reporting and Disclosure Requirements

As shown in the illustrative paragraphs above, when a full-scope audit has been performed in accordance with generally accepted auditing standards and an unqualified opinion of the financial statements and supplemental schedules is issued, the report states that the schedules are fairly stated in all material respects in relation to the basic financial statements taken as a whole.

When a limited-scope audit has been performed and a disclaimer of opinion on the financial statements and supplemental schedules is issued, the report states that the supplemental schedules are presented in compliance with the DOL Regulations under ERISA.

During the audit, the auditor may become aware of a departure from the DOL filing requirements (such as required information in supplemental schedules) that is not a departure from generally accepted accounting principles. If information required to be presented on a supplemental schedule is omitted, or is inaccurate or inconsistent with the financial statements, the auditors' report needs to be either modified by adding an explanatory paragraph or by expressing a qualified or adverse opinion on the supplemental schedules. The following illustrative reports are examples of modifications that an auditor might consider to be necessary when a required schedule, or information thereon, is omitted, inaccurate, or materially inconsistent with the financial statements. In addition, the following table, which is derived from the AICPA audit guide, *Audits of Employee Benefit Plans,* illustrates the report modifications which should be made under various circumstances.

Exhibit 1: Report Modifications for Supplemental Schedule Deficiencies

	Report modification		
		Limited-scope audit	
Error, omission, or inconsistency	*Full-scope audit*	*Exception in information certified by trustee or custodian*	*Exception in information not certified by trustee or custodian but tested by auditor*
Required information omitted from schedule, for example, historical cost information for non-participant-directed investments	Explanatory paragraph	Explanatory paragraph	Qualified or adverse as to schedules
Required schedule omitted, for example, schedule of reportable transactions	Explanatory paragraph	Explanatory paragraph	Qualified or adverse as to schedules
Require schedule materially inconsistent with financial statements	Qualified or adverse as to schedules	Explanatory paragraph	Qualified or adverse as to schedules

Omission of required supplemental schedule or information thereon, full-scope audit, explanatory paragraph. The following illustrative report is an example of how an explanatory paragraph should be added to a full-scope auditors' report that has expressed an unqualified opinion on the financial statements because a required supplemental schedule or information required on a supplemental schedule has been omitted. In the event that the omitted required supplemental schedule is the Schedule of Nonexempt Transactions, this may result in the need to issue a qualified or adverse opinion on the plan's financial statements.

Independent Auditors' Report

To the ABC Company Defined Contribution Pension Plan and Participants:

We have audited the statements of net assets available for benefits of the ABC Company Defined Contribution Pension Plan as of December 31, 20X1 and 20X0, and the related statement of changes in net assets available for benefits for the year ended December 31, 20X1. These financial statements are the responsibility of the Plan's management. Our responsibility is to express an opinion on these financial statements based on our audits.

We conducted our audits in accordance with generally accepted auditing standards. These standards require that we plan and perform the audit to obtain reasonable assurance about whether the financial statements are free of material misstatement. An audit includes examining, on a test basis, evidence supporting the amounts and disclosures in the financial statements. An audit also includes assessing the accounting principles used and significant estimates made by management as well as evaluating the overall financial statement presentation. We believe that our audits provide a reasonable basis for our opinion.

In our opinion, the financial statements referred to above present fairly, in all material respects, the net assets available for benefits of the Plan as of December 31, 20X1 and 20X0, and the changes in net assets available for benefits for the year ended December 31, 20X1, in conformity with generally accepted accounting principles.

The Plan has not presented the schedule of reportable transactions (transactions in excess of 5% of the current value of plan assets at the beginning of the year). Disclosure of this information is required by the Department of Labor's Rules and Regulations for Reporting and Disclosure under the Employee Retirement Income Security Act of 1974.

Our audits were performed for the purpose of forming an opinion on the basic financial statements taken as a whole. The supplemental schedule of assets held for investment purposes as of December 31, 20X1, is presented for the purpose of additional analysis and is not a required part of the basic financial statements but is supplemental information required by the Department of Labor's Rules and Regulations for Reporting and Disclosure under the Employee Retirement Income Security Act of 1974. This supplemental schedule is the responsibility of the Plan's management. The supplemental schedule has been subjected to the auditing procedures applied in the audit of the basic 20X1 financial statements and, in our opinion, is fairly stated in all material respects in relation to the basic 20X1 financial statements taken as a whole.

[Signature]

[Date]

Omitted, Incomplete, or Materially Inconsistent Supplemental Schedule, Full-Scope Audit, Qualified Opinion on Schedules

The following illustrative report is an example of a qualified opinion on the supplemental schedules because the required supplemental Schedule of Assets Held for Investment Purposes does not include participant loans and is, therefore, incomplete, and the amount of the participant loans is significant to the plan's financial statements. Similarly, the same type of explanatory paragraph and "except for" language should be added to the auditors' report when a required supplemental schedule has been omitted or information in a supplemental schedule is materially inconsistent with the financial statements.

Independent Auditors' Report

To the ABC Company Defined Contribution Pension Plan and Participants:

We have audited the statements of net assets available for benefits of the ABC Company Defined Contribution Pension Plan as of December 31, 20X1 and 20X0, and the related statement of changes in net assets available for benefits for the year ended December 31, 20X1. These financial statements are the responsibility of the Plan's management. Our responsibility is to express an opinion on these financial statements based on our audits.

We conducted our audits in accordance with generally accepted auditing standards. These standards require that we plan and perform the audit to obtain reasonable assurance about whether the financial statements are free of material misstatement. An audit includes examining, on a test basis, evidence supporting the amounts and disclosures in the financial statements. An audit also includes assessing the accounting principles used and significant estimates made by management, as well as evaluating the overall financial statement presentation. We believe that our audits provide a reasonable basis for our opinion.

In our opinion, the financial statements referred to above present fairly, in all material respects, the net assets available for benefits of the Plan as of December 31, 20X1 and 20X0, and the changes in net assets available for benefits for the year ended December 31, 20X1, in conformity with generally accepted accounting principles.

The accompanying supplemental schedule of assets held for investment purposes does not disclose that the Plan had participant loans, which represented 30% of the plan's net assets available for benefits as of December 31, 20X1, which are considered assets held for investment purposes. Disclosure of this information is required by the Department of Labor's Rules and Regulations for Reporting and Disclosure under the Employee Retirement Income Security Act of 1974.

Our audits were performed for the purpose of forming an opinion on the basic financial statements taken as a whole. The supplemental schedules of (1) assets held for investment purposes as of December 31, 20X1, and (2) reportable transactions for the year ended December 31, 20X1, are presented for the purpose of additional analysis and are not a required part of the basic financial statements but are supplemental information required by the Department of Labor's Rules and Regulations for Reporting and Disclosure under the Employee Retirement Income Security Act of 1974. These supplemental schedules are the responsibility of the Plan's management. The supplemental schedules have been subjected to the auditing procedures applied in the audit of the basic 20X1 financial statements and, in our opinion, except for the omission of the information discussed in the preceding paragraph, are fairly stated in all material respects in relation to those basic financial statements taken as a whole.

[Signature]

[Date]

Omitted, Incomplete, or Materially Inconsistent Supplemental Schedule, Limited-Scope Audit, Exception in Information Certified by Trustee, Explanatory Paragraph

The following illustration is an example of the explanatory paragraph that should be added to a limited-scope auditors' report because the required supplemental schedule of reportable transactions has been omitted.

Similarly, the same type of explanatory paragraph should be added to the report if a required supplemental schedule is incomplete or materially inconsistent with the financial statements with respect to information certified by the trustee.

Independent Auditors' Report

To the ABC Company Defined Benefit Plan and Participants:

We were engaged to audit the accompanying statements of net assets available for benefits of ABC Company Defined Benefit Pension Plan as of December 31, 20X1 and 20X0, and the related statement of changes in net assets available for benefits for the year ended December 31, 20X1. These financial statements and supplemental schedules are the responsibility of the Plan's management.

As permitted by 29 CFR 2520.103-8 of the Department of Labor's Rules and Regulations for Reporting and Disclosure under the Employee Retirement Income Security Act of 1974, the plan administrator instructed us not to perform, and we did not perform, any auditing procedures with respect to the information summarized in Note X, which was certified by EFG Bank and HIJ Insurance Company, the trustees (or custodians) of the Plan, except for comparing such information with the related information included in the financial statements. We have been informed by the plan administrator that the trustees (or custodians) hold the Plan's investment assets and execute investment transactions. The plan administrator has obtained certifications from the trustees (or custodians) as of December 31, 20X1 and 20X0, and for the year ended December 31, 20X1, that the information provided to the plan administrator by the trustees (or custodians) is complete and accurate.

The Plan has not presented the schedule of reportable transactions (transactions in excess of 5% of the current value of plan assets at the beginning of the year). Disclosure of this information is required by the Department of Labor's Rules and Regulations for Reporting and Disclosure under the Employee Retirement Income Security Act of 1974.

Because of the significance of the information that we did not audit, we are unable to, and do not, express an opinion on the accompanying financial statements taken as a whole.

The form and content of the information included in the financial statements and supplemental schedules, other than that derived from the information certified by the trustees (or custodians), have been audited by us in accordance with generally accepted auditing standards and, in our opinion, except for the omission of the schedule described in the preceding paragraph, are presented in compliance with the Department of Labor's Rules and Regulations for Reporting and Disclosure under the Employee Retirement Income Security Act of 1974.

[Signature]

[Date]

Omitted, Incomplete, or Materially Inconsistent Supplemental Schedule, Limited-Scope Audit, Exception in Information Not Certified by Trustee, Qualified Opinion on Schedules

The following illustrative auditors' report is an example of a limited-scope report when the auditor must express a qualified opinion on the supplemental schedules because a required supplemental schedule has been omitted. In the following illustration, the plan has engaged in nonexempt transactions with parties-in-interest, which are not material to the plan's financial statements, and has not reported them on a supplemental schedule of nonexempt transactions as required by ERISA. The transaction has been appropriately disclosed in the footnotes to the plan's financial statements. Because the omitted schedule is not certified by the trustee or custodian, a qualified opinion should be issued on the applicable supplemental schedules. Note that the DOL is very likely to reject such a report.

The same explanatory paragraph and "except for" language should be used in a limited-scope audit report if uncertified information is omitted from a supplemental schedule or if uncertified information contained in a supplemental schedule is materially inconsistent with the financial statements.

Independent Auditors' Report

To the ABC Company Defined Benefit Pension Plan and Participants:

We were engaged to audit the accompanying statements of net assets available for benefits of ABC Company Defined Benefit Pension Plan as of December 31, 20X1 and 20X0, and the related statement of changes in net assets available for benefits for the year ended December 31, 20X1, and the Schedule of Assets Held for Investment Purposes as of December 31, 20X1, and the Schedule of Nonexempt Transactions for the year ended December 31, 20X1. These financial statements and the supplemental schedules are the responsibility of the Plan's management.

As permitted by 29 CFR 2520.103-8 of the Department of Labor's Rules and Regulations for Reporting and Disclosure under the Employee Retirement Income Security Act of 1974, the plan administrator instructed us not to perform, and we did not perform, any auditing procedures with respect to the information summarized in Note X, which was certified by EFG Bank and HIJ Insurance Company, the trustees (or custodians) of the Plan, except for comparing such information with the related information included in the financial statements. We have been informed by the plan administrator that the trustees (or custodians) hold the Plan's investment assets and execute investment transactions. The plan administrator has obtained certifications from the trustees (or custodians) as of December 31, 20X1 and 20X0, and for the year ended December 31, 20X1, that the information provided to the plan administrator by the trustees (or custodians) is complete and accurate.

The Plan has not presented the schedule of nonexempt transactions to disclose that the Plan issued a loan to the plan administrator in the amount of $50,000 in August 20X1. Disclosure of this information is required by the Department of Labor's Rules and Regulations for Reporting and Disclosure under the Employee Retirement Income Security Act of 1974.

Because of the significance of the information that we did not audit, we are unable to, and do not, express an opinion on the accompanying financial statements and supplemental schedules taken as a whole. The form and content of the information included in the financial statements and schedules, other than that derived from the information certified by the trustee, have been audited by us in accordance with generally accepted auditing standards and, in our opinion, except for the omission of the schedule of nonexempt transactions discussed in the preceding paragraph, are presented in compliance with the Department of Labor's Rules and Regulations for Reporting and Disclosure under the Employee Retirement Income Security Act of 1974.

[Signature]

[Date]

NONEXEMPT TRANSACTIONS INVOLVING A PARTY-IN-INTEREST

The DOL requires that all prohibited (nonexempt) transactions with parties-in-interest be reported on the supplemental schedule irrespective of the materiality of the transaction to the plan's financial statements.

When the auditor concludes that the plan has entered into a prohibited transaction with a party-in-interest, and the transaction has not been properly disclosed in the required supplemental schedule, the auditor should either express a qualified opinion or an adverse opinion on the supplemental schedule if the effect of the transaction is material to the financial statements, or modify his or her report on the supplemental schedule by adding an explanatory paragraph to disclose the omitted transaction if the effect of the transaction is not material to the financial statements. The issuance of either a qualified opinion or adverse opinion is a judgmental matter to be considered by the auditor.

Material Prohibited Transaction Properly Disclosed in Notes to Financial Statements but Not Properly Disclosed in the Supplemental Schedule--Qualified Opinion on Supplemental Schedules

When a material prohibited transaction with a party-in-interest is omitted from the supplemental schedules, the auditor should issue a qualified or adverse opinion on the supplemental schedules. The following illustrative auditors' report provides an example when the auditor concludes that his or her opinion on the supplemental schedules should be qualified. This example assumes that the material prohibited transaction has been disclosed in the plan's financial statements.

Independent Auditors' Report

To the ABC Company Defined Benefit Health and Welfare Plan and Participants:

We have audited the accompanying statements of net assets available for benefits and of benefit obligations of ABC Company Defined Benefit Health and Welfare Plan as of December 31, 20X1 and 20X0, and the related statements of changes in net assets available for benefits and of changes in benefit obligations for the year ended December 31, 20X1. These financial statements are the responsibility of the Plan's management. Our responsibility is to express an opinion on these financial statements based on our audits.

We conducted our audits in accordance with generally accepted auditing standards. Those standards require that we plan and perform the audit to obtain reasonable assurance about whether the financial statements are free of material misstatement. An audit includes examining, on a test basis, evidence supporting the amounts and disclosures in the financial statements. An audit also includes assessing the accounting principles used and significant estimates made by management as well as evaluating the overall financial statement presentation. We believe that our audits provide a reasonable basis for our opinion.

In our opinion, the financial statements referred to above present fairly, in all material respects, the financial status of the Plan as of December 31, 20X1 and 20X0, and the changes in its financial status for the year ended December 31, 20X1, in conformity with generally accepted accounting principles.

The plan has not presented the schedule of nonexempt transactions to disclose that the Plan issued a loan to the plan sponsor in the amount of $500,000 in February 20X1. Disclosure of this information is required by the Department of Labor's Rules and Regulations for Reporting and Disclosure under the Employee Retirement Income Security Act of 1974.

Our audits were performed for the purpose of forming an opinion on the financial statements taken as a whole. The supplemental schedules of (1) assets held for investments purposes as of December 31, 20X1, and (2) reportable transactions for the year ended December 31, 20X1, are presented for the purpose of additional analysis and are not a required part of the basic financial statements but are supplemental information required by the Department of Labor's Rules and Regulations for Reporting and Disclosure under the Employee Retirement Income Security Act of 1974. These supplemental schedules are the responsibility of the Plan's management. The supplemental schedules have been subjected to the auditing procedures applied in the audit of the basic 20X1 financial statements and, in our opinion, except for the omission of the schedule of nonexempt transactions discussed in the preceding paragraph, are fairly stated in all material respects in relation to those basic financial statements taken as a whole.

[Signature]

[Date]

NON-GAAP-BASIS FINANCIAL STATEMENTS

ERISA and DOL regulations permit a plan's financial statements included in its Form 5500 filing to be prepared on a comprehensive basis of accounting other than GAAP (OCBOA). If the plan's financial statements are prepared on an OCBOA, ERISA requires that the variances from GAAP be disclosed in the notes to the financial statements and that the plan's investments in securities be presented at fair value. Therefore, one of the most common types of OCBOA methods used in preparing plan financial statements is the modified cash basis of accounting. The modified cash basis of accounting is basically cash basis accounting except that investments are adjusted to fair value. Also, if the financial statements are prepared on an OCBOA, that accounting basis should be included in the title of the financial statements (e.g., "statement of net assets available for benefits--modified cash basis" and "statement of changes in net assets available for benefits--modified cash basis").

SAS 62, *Special Reports*, as amended by SAS 77, paragraphs 2 through 10, provides guidance on financial statements prepared in conformity with an OCBOA. The auditors' report on financial statements prepared on an OCBOA should include a paragraph that states the basis of presentation, refers to the note to the financial statements that describes the basis, and states that the basis of presentation is a comprehensive basis of accounting other than generally accepted accounting principles.

Financial statements prepared under the modified cash basis of accounting should still include accumulated plan benefits information (for defined benefit pension plans) and benefit obligations information (for defined benefit health and welfare plans) in order to disclose a fair presentation of the plan's financial position. This information may be presented either on the face of the financial statements or in the notes to the financial statements. If information regarding accumulated plan benefits (such as the amount of the plan's estimated accumulated plan benefits or accumulated benefit obligations, as applicable, and the amount of accumulated benefit obligations by type, for example, claims payable, IBNR, accumulated eligibility credits, and postretirement benefit obligations) is not disclosed, the auditor should comment in his or her report on the lack of such disclosures and should express a qualified or an adverse opinion on the financial statements. For additional information regarding non-GAAP-basis financial statements, see Chapter 10, Other Accounting and Auditing Considerations.

Financial Statements Prepared on Modified Cash Basis--Unqualified Opinion

The following is an illustration of an auditors' report on financial statements prepared on the modified cash basis of accounting.

Independent Auditors' Report

To the ABC Company Defined Benefit Pension Plan and Participants:

We have audited the accompanying statements of net assets available for benefits (modified cash basis) of ABC Company Defined Benefit Pension Plan as of December 31, 20X1 and 20X0, and the related statement of changes in net assets available for benefits (modified cash basis) for the year ended December 31, 20X1. These financial statements are the responsibility of the Plan's management. Our responsibility is to express an opinion on these financial statements based on our audits.

We conducted our audits in accordance with generally accepted auditing standards. Those standards require that we plan and perform the audit to obtain reasonable assurance about whether the financial statements are free of material misstatement. An audit includes examining, on a test basis, evidence supporting the amounts and disclosures in the financial statements.

An audit also includes assessing the accounting principles used and significant estimates made by management, as well as evaluating the overall financial statement presentation. We believe that our audits provide a reasonable basis for our opinion.

As described in Note X, these financial statements were prepared on a modified cash basis of accounting, which is a comprehensive basis of accounting other than generally accepted accounting principles.

In our opinion, the financial statements referred to above present fairly, in all material respects, the net assets available for benefits of the ABC Company Defined Benefit Pension

Plan as of December 31, 20X1 and 20X0, and the changes in its net assets available for benefits for the year ended December 20X1, on the basis of accounting described in Note X.

Our audits were performed for the purpose of forming an opinion on the financial statements taken as a whole. The supplemental schedules of (1) assets held for investment purposes as of December 31, 20X1, and (2) reportable transactions for the year ended December 31, 20X1, are presented for the purpose of additional analysis and are not a required part of the basic financial statements, but are supplemental information required by the Department of Labor's Rules and Regulations for Reporting and Disclosure under the Employee Retirement Income Security Act of 1974. These supplemental schedules are the responsibility of the Plan's management. The supplemental schedules have been subjected to the auditing procedures applied in the audit of the basic 20X1 financial statements and, in our opinion, are fairly stated in all material respects in relation to those basic financial statements taken as a whole.

[Signature]

[Date]

SAS 62, as amended by SAS 77, also states that when reporting on financial statements prepared in conformity with an OCBOA, the auditor should consider whether the financial statements (including the accompanying notes) include all informative disclosures that are appropriate for the basis of accounting used. The auditor should apply essentially the same criteria to financial statements prepared on an OCBOA as the auditor does to financial statements prepared in conformity with GAAP in order to form an opinion on whether the financial statements, including the accompanying notes, are informative of matters that may affect their use, understanding, and interpretation.

NON-READILY-MARKETABLE SECURITIES

ERISA defines current value as "fair market value where available and otherwise the fair value as determined in good faith by a trustee or a named fiduciary." Investments for which fair market value may not be readily determinable include such items as securities that are not readily marketable, private debt placements, and real estate investments.

An explanatory paragraph should be added to the auditors' report when (1) the financial statements include securities whose values were estimated by the plan (plan administrator or board of trustees) in the absence of readily available market values and (2) the range of possible values of those securities is significant. The following illustrative report is an example of how the auditors' report should be modified to include an explanatory paragraph regarding nonreadily marketable securities.

Non-Readily-Marketable Securities--Explanatory Paragraph

Independent Auditors' Report

To the ABC Company Defined Benefit Pension Plan and Participants:

We have audited the accompanying statements of net assets available for benefits and accumulated plan benefits of the ABC Company Defined Benefit Pension Plan as of December 31, 20X1 and 20X0, and the related statements of changes in net assets available for benefits and accumulated plan benefits for the year ended December 31, 20X1. These financial statements are the responsibility of the Plan's management. Our responsibility is to express an opinion on these financial statements based on our audits.

We conducted our audits in accordance with generally accepted auditing standards. Those standards require that we plan and perform the audit to obtain reasonable assurance about whether the financial statements are free of material misstatement. An audit includes examining, on a test basis, evidence supporting the amounts and disclosures in the financial statements. An audit also includes assessing the accounting principles used and significant estimates made by management, as well as evaluating the overall financial statement presentation. We believe that our audits provide a reasonable basis for our opinion.

In our opinion, the financial statements referred to above present fairly, in all material respects, the financial status of the plan as of December 31, 20X1 and 20X0, and the changes in its financial status for the year ended December 31, 20X1, in conformity with generally accepted accounting principles.

As discussed in Note X, the financial statements include securities valued at $265,000 and $330,000 (5.3 and 5.5% of net assets, respectively) as of December 31, 20X1 and 20X0, respectively, whose values have been estimated by the Board of Trustees in the absence of readily ascertainable market values. We have reviewed the procedures used by the Board of Trustees in arriving at its estimate of value of such securities and have inspected underlying documentation, and, in the circumstances, we believe the procedures are reasonable and the documentation is appropriate. However, because of the inherent uncertainty of valuation, those estimated values may differ significantly from the values that would have been used had a ready market for the securities existed, and the differences could be material.

Our audits were performed for the purpose of forming an opinion on the financial statements taken as a whole. The supplemental schedules of (1) assets held for investment purposes and (2) reportable transactions are presented for the purpose of additional analysis and are not a required part of the basic financial statements, but are supplemental information required by the Department of Labor's Rules and Regulations for Reporting and Disclosure under the Employee Retirement Income Security Act of 1974. These supplemental schedules are the responsibility of the Plan's management. That additional information has been subjected to the auditing procedures applied in the audit of the basic 20X1 financial statements, and in our opinion, is fairly stated in all material respects in relation to those basic financial statements taken as a whole.

[Signature]

[Date]

Non-Readily-Marketable Securities--Qualified Opinion

If the auditors' review discloses that the valuation procedures followed by the plan are inadequate or unreasonable, or if the underlying documentation does not appear to support the valuation, the auditor should consider the need to express a qualified opinion on the financial statements because of the departure from generally accepted accounting principles.

The following illustration provides an example of an auditors' report qualified for a departure from generally accepted accounting principles because of inadequate procedures to value investments. The illustration assumes that the auditor cannot reasonably determine the effects of the departure.

Independent Auditors' Report

To the ABC Company Employee Stock Ownership Plan and Participants:

We have audited the accompanying statements of net assets available for benefits of the ABC Company Employee Stock Ownership Plan as of December 31, 20X1 and 20X0, and the related statement of changes in net assets available for benefits for the year ended December 31, 20X1. These financial statements are the responsibility of the Plan's management. Our responsibility is to express an opinion on these financial statements based on our audits.

We conducted our audits in accordance with generally accepted auditing standards. Those standards require that we plan and perform the audit to obtain reasonable assurance about whether the financial statements are free of material misstatement. An audit includes examining, on a test basis, evidence supporting the amounts and disclosures in the financial statements. An audit also includes assessing the accounting principles used and significant estimates made by management as well as evaluating the overall financial statement presentation. We believe that our audits provide a reasonable basis for our opinion.

As discussed in Note X, investments amounting to $550,000 and $570,000 (10% and 12.1% of net assets available for benefits) as of December 31, 20X1 and 20X0, respectively, have been valued at estimated fair value as determined by the Board of Trustees. We have reviewed the procedures applied by the trustees in valuing the securities and have inspected the underlying documentation. In our opinion, those procedures are not adequate to determine the fair value of the investments in conformity with generally accepted accounting principles. The effect on the financial statements and supplemental schedules of not applying adequate procedures to determine the fair value of the securities is not readily determinable.

In our opinion, except for the effects of the procedures used by the Board of Trustees to determine the valuation of investments as described in the preceding paragraph, the financial statements referred to above present fairly, in all material respects, the net assets available for benefits of the ABC Company Employee Stock Ownership Plan as of December 31, 20X1, and the changes in its net assets available for benefits for the year then ended in conformity with generally accepted accounting principles.

Our audits were performed for the purpose of forming an opinion on the financial statements taken as a whole. The supplemental schedules of (1) assets held for investment purposes and (2) reportable transactions are presented for the purpose of additional analysis and are not a required part of the basic financial statements, but are supplemental information required by the Department of Labor's Rules and Regulations for Reporting and Disclosure under the Employee Retirement Income Security Act of 1974. These supplemental schedules are the responsibility of the Plan's management. That additional information has been subjected to the auditing procedures applied in the audit of the basic 20X1 financial statements, and in our opinion, except for the effects of the valuation of investments, as described above, the additional information is fairly stated in all material respects in relation to those basic financial statements taken as a whole.

[Signature]

[Date]

OTHER MODIFIED REPORTS

Terminating Plans

If the decision to terminate a plan is made before the end of the plan year, the plan's financial statements should be presented on the liquidation basis of accounting, and an explanatory paragraph should be added to the auditors' report. If the decision to terminate a plan is made after the plan's year-end, the footnotes to the plan's financial statements should describe the plan termination, but the financial statements are not required to be presented on the liquidation basis of accounting; however, a comment regarding the plan termination may be included in the independent auditors' report. For a discussion of audit requirements regarding terminating employee benefit plans, see Chapter 10, Other Accounting and Auditing Considerations.

The auditor may express an unqualified opinion on financial statements prepared on the liquidation basis of accounting, provided the basis has been properly applied and that adequate disclosures are made in the financial statements. The auditors' report normally should be modified by the addition of an explanatory paragraph that states that the plan is being terminated and that the financial statements (including the benefit information disclosures presented) have been prepared on a liquidation basis. If the financial statements are presented along with financial statements of a period prior to adoption of a liquidation basis that were prepared on the basis of generally accepted accounting principles for ongoing plans, the explanatory paragraph should state that the plan has changed the basis of accounting used to determine the amounts at which assets, liabilities, and benefit information are presented from the ongoing plan basis to a liquidation basis.

NOTE: If a plan termination occurs only due to a plan merger situation, no explanatory paragraphs are required to be added to the auditors' report.

Terminating before year-end, explanatory paragraph. The following illustrative explanatory paragraph should be added to the auditors' report when the decision to terminate the plan was made *before* the plan year-end. This explanatory paragraph would be the third paragraph of the auditors' report.

> As discussed in Note X to the financial statements, the Board of Directors of the ABC Company, the Plan's sponsor, voted on November 9, 20X1 to terminate the Plan. In accordance with generally accepted accounting principles, the Plan has changed its basis of accounting from the ongoing plan basis used in presenting the 20X0 financial statements to the liquidation basis used in presenting the 20X1 financial statements.

Terminating after year-end, explanatory paragraph. The following illustrative explanatory paragraph may be added to the auditors' report when the decision to terminate the plan was made *after* the plan year-end:

> As discussed in Note X to the Plan's financial statements, on March 15, 20X2, the Board of Directors announced their decision to terminate the Plan effective December 31, 20X2.

Plan Merger

If a decision has been made to merge a plan with another plan, a modification of the auditors' report is not required. However, the auditor may want to add an explanatory paragraph to the report to mention the merger. The plan merger should be discussed in the footnotes to the plan's financial statements. The following illustrative explanatory paragraph may be added to the auditors' report.

> As discussed in Note X, the Plan was merged into the GHI Company Benefit Plan effective February 10, 20X2.

Going Concern

SAS 59, *The Auditor's Consideration of an Entity's Ability to Continue as a Going Concern*, as amended by SAS 77, provides guidance on evaluating a plan's ability to continue as a going concern. Although employee benefit plans may not necessarily be affected by the plan sponsor's financial adversities, the auditor should address whether those difficulties will have an effect on the plan and, if so, what the impact may be.

Typically, defined contribution pension plans would not be affected by the plan sponsor's financial problems except for money purchase pension plans, which require employer contributions based on a fixed formula not related to profits. Defined benefit pension plans are more likely to be affected if the plan is not fully funded and, therefore, require employer contributions to be remitted to the plan. Plans that are fully funded are not likely to be affected by the plan sponsor's financial difficulties. The following is an illustrative example of such an auditors' report.

Independent Auditors' Report

To the ABC Company Defined Benefit Pension Plan and Participants:

We have audited the accompanying statements of net assets available for benefits and of accumulated plan benefits of ABC Company Defined Benefit Pension Plan as of December 31, 20X1 and 20X0, and the related statement of changes in net assets available for benefits and of changes in accumulated plan benefits for the year ended December 31, 20X1. These financial statements are the responsibility of the Plan's management. Our responsibility is to express an opinion on these financial statements based on our audits.

We conducted our audits in accordance with generally accepted auditing standards. Those standards require that we plan and perform the audit to obtain reasonable assurance about whether the financial statements are free of material misstatement. An audit includes examining, on a test basis, evidence supporting the amounts and disclosures in the financial statements. An audit also includes assessing the accounting principles used and significant estimates made by management, as well as evaluating the overall financial statement presentation. We believe that our audits provide a reasonable basis for our opinion.

In our opinion, the financial statements referred to above present fairly, in all material respects, the financial status of the Plan as of December 31, 20X1 and 20X0, and the changes in its financial status for the year ended December 31, 20X1, in conformity with generally accepted accounting principles.

As discussed in Note X to the financial statements, ABC Company (the plan sponsor) has filed for reorganization under the protection of Chapter 11 of the Federal Bankruptcy Code and, at December 31, 20X1, the Plan's net assets available for benefits were less than the actuarial present value of accumulated plan benefits. As a result of the Plan sponsor's bankruptcy filing, the continuation of the Plan is uncertain. The financial statements do not include any adjustments that might result from this uncertainty.

Our audits were performed for the purpose of forming an opinion on the financial statements taken as a whole. The supplemental schedules of (1) assets held for investments purposes as of December 31, 20X1, and (2) reportable transactions for the year ended December 31, 20X1, are presented for the purpose of additional analysis and are not a required part of the basic financial statements, but are supplemental information required by the Department of Labor's Rules and Regulations for Reporting and Disclosure under the Employee Retirement Income Security Act of 1974. These supplemental schedules are the responsibility of the Plan's management. The supplemental schedules have been subjected to the auditing procedures applied in the audit of the basic 20X1 financial statements and, in our opinion, are fairly stated in all material respects in relation to those basic financial statements taken as a whole.

[Signature]

[Date]

INITIAL AUDITS OF PLANS

Plan Inception During Current Year

For an initial audit of a plan that was created in the period the auditor is reporting on, the plan year should be from the inception of the plan until the end of the plan year. The following illustrative report is for a plan whose effective date was within the plan year on which the auditor is reporting.

Independent Auditors' Report

To the ABC Company Defined Contribution Pension Plan and Participants:

We have audited the accompanying statement of net assets available for benefits of the ABC Company Defined Contribution Pension Plan as of December 31, 20X1, and the related statement of changes in net assets available for benefits for the period from April 15, 20X1 (inception), to December 31, 20X1. These financial statements are the responsibility of the Plan's management. Our responsibility is to express an opinion on these financial statements based on our audit.

We conducted our audit in accordance with generally accepted auditing standards. These standards require that we plan and perform the audit to obtain reasonable assurance about whether the financial statements are free of material misstatement. An audit includes examining, on a test basis, evidence supporting the amounts and disclosures in the financial statements. An audit also includes assessing the accounting principles used and significant estimates made by management as well as evaluating the overall financial statement presentation. We believe that our audit provides a reasonable basis for our opinion.

In our opinion, the financial statements referred to above present fairly, in all material respects, the net assets available for benefits of the Plan as of December 31, 20X1, and the changes in net assets available for benefits for the period from April 15, 20X1 (inception), to December 31, 20X1, in conformity with generally accepted accounting principles.

Our audit was performed for the purpose of forming an opinion on the financial statements taken as a whole. The supplemental schedules of assets held for investment purposes as of December 31, 20X1, and reportable transactions for the period from April 15, 20X1 (inception), to December 31, 20X1, are presented for the purpose of additional analysis and are not a required part of the basic financial statements, but are supplemental information required by the Department of Labor's Rules and Regulations for Reporting and Disclosure under the Employee Retirement Income Security Act of 1974. These supplemental schedules are the responsibility of the Plan's management. The supplemental schedules have been subjected to the auditing procedures applied in the audit of the basic 20X1 financial statements and, in our opinion, are fairly stated in all material respects in relation to those basic financial statements taken as a whole.

[Signature]

[Date]

Plan Had Assets in Prior Year but Was Not Required to Have an Audit Performed in Prior Year

For initial audits of plans where the plan had assets in the prior year, ERISA requires the presentation of a comparative statement of net assets available for plan benefits. Therefore, the auditor must perform either an audit, review, or compilation of the prior year's financial statements. In these cases, the auditor needs to issue a separate review report or compilation report if a review or compilation is performed of the prior year's financial statements. If a review or compilation is performed, the prior year's statements should be clearly marked to indicate their status as either reviewed or compiled. In addition, the report on the current year should include an explanatory paragraph describing (1) the level of service performed in the prior period, (2) the date of the report on that service, (3) a description of any material modifications identified in the report, and (4) a statement that indicates that the scope of the service was less than an audit and does not provide the basis for expressing an opinion on the financial statements taken as a whole.

Review in Prior Year, Audit in Current Year

The following illustrative explanatory paragraph should be added to a report in which the auditor reviewed the prior year financial statements. In the event that a review was performed for the prior year financial statements, a separate review report needs to be issued. The example review report follows. This paragraph would be applicable for both a full-scope audit in the current year or a limited-scope audit:

> We have performed a review of the statement of net assets available for benefits of the Plan as of December 31, 20X0, and we issued a review report on the statement which was dated June 15, 20X2. The scope of the review was less than an audit and does not provide the basis for expressing an opinion on the 20X0 financial statements taken as a whole.

Review Report Issued on Prior Year Financial Statements

The following is an example of a review report issued on prior year financial statements.

Independent Accountants' Report

To the ABC Company Defined Contribution Pension Plan and Participants:

We have reviewed the accompanying statement of net assets available for benefits of ABC Company Defined Contribution Pension Plan as of December 31, 20X0, and the related statement of changes in net assets for the year then ended, in accordance with Statements on Standards for Accounting and Review Services issued by the American Institute of Certified Public Accountants. All information included in these financial statements is the representation of the plan management.

A review of plan financial statements consists principally of inquiries of the plan management and analytical procedures applied to financial data. It is substantially less in scope than an audit in accordance with generally accepted auditing standards, the objective of which is the expression of an opinion regarding the financial statements taken as a whole. Accordingly, we do not express such an opinion.

Based on our review, we are not aware of any material modifications that should be made to the accompanying financial statements in order for them to be in conformity with generally accepted accounting principles.

Compilation in Prior Year, Audit in Current Year

The following illustrative explanatory paragraph should be added to a report in which the auditor compiled the prior year financial statements. In the event that a compilation was performed for the prior year financial statements, a separate compilation report needs to be issued. The example compilation report follows. This paragraph would be applicable for both a full-scope audit in the current year or a limited-scope audit.

We have performed a compilation of the statement of net assets available for benefits of the plan as of December 31, 20X0, and the related statement of changes in net assets available for benefits for the year then ended. The scope of the compilation was less than an audit and does not provide the basis for expressing an opinion on the 20X0 financial statements taken as a whole.

Compilation Report Issued on Prior Year Financial Statements

When the auditor has compiled the prior-year financial statements, a separate compilation report should be issued. The following is an example of a compilation report issued on prior-year financial statements.

Independent Accountants' Report

To the ABC Company Defined Contribution Pension Plan and Participants:

We have compiled the accompanying statement of net assets available for benefits of ABC Company Defined Contribution Pension Plan as of December 31, 20X0, and the related statement of changes in net assets available for benefits for the year then ended, in accordance with Statements on Standards for Accounting and Review Services issued by the American Institute of Certified Public Accountants.

A compilation is limited to presenting in the form of financial statements information that is the representation of the plan whose financial statements are presented. We have not audited or reviewed the accompanying financial statements and, accordingly, do not express an opinion or any other form of assurance on them.

Auditor Unable to Test Opening Participant Account Balances

In an initial audit of a defined contribution pension plan, the auditor should perform tests of the plan's procedures for allocating contributions, income, and forfeitures to participants' individual accounts in prior years. It is possible that improper allocations of prior year contributions, income, and forfeitures could be material to the current year financial statements. If the auditor is unable to perform these tests for any reason, such as lost or inadequate records, it is considered a scope limitation and the auditor should issue a qualified or disclaimer of opinion. Due to the nature of the scope limitation, the reports on the plan's financial statements in succeeding years may indefinitely be qualified or disclaimed. Such a disclaimer or qualified opinion would not be accepted by the DOL for ERISA filings. Therefore, the client must make every effort to reconstruct the participant account balances from inception. The following illustrative report is an example of when the auditor has decided to issue a qualified opinion due to a scope limitation on opening participant account balances.

Independent Auditors' Report

To the ABC Company Defined Contribution Pension Plan and Participants:

We have audited the accompanying statements of net assets available for benefits of the ABC Company Defined Contribution Pension Plan as of December 31, 20X1 and 20X0, and the related statement of changes in net assets available for benefits for the year ended December 31, 20X1. These financial statements are the responsibility of the Plan's management. Our responsibility is to express an opinion on these financial statements based on our audits.

We conducted our audits in accordance with generally accepted auditing standards. These standards require that we plan and perform the audit to obtain reasonable assurance about whether the financial statements are free of material misstatement. An audit includes examining, on a test basis, evidence supporting the amounts and disclosures in the financial statements. An audit also includes assessing the accounting principles used and significant estimates made by management as well as evaluating the overall financial statement presentation. We believe that our audits provide a reasonable basis for our opinion.

Because of the inadequacy of the prior years' records, we were unable to perform auditing procedures with respect to the participants' individual account balances accumulated from inception of the plan and therefore are unable to form an opinion regarding the basis on which participants' equity is stated as of December 31, 20X1, or the propriety of the distributions to terminated participants during the year then ended.

In our opinion, except for the effect of such adjustments, if any, as might have been disclosed had we been able to apply certain auditing procedures as discussed in the preceding paragraph, the financial statements referred to above present fairly, in all material respects, the net assets available for benefits of the Plan as of December 31, 20X1 and 20X0, and the changes in net assets available for benefits for the year ended December 31, 20X1, in conformity with generally accepted accounting principles.

Our audit was performed for the purpose of forming an opinion on the financial statements taken as a whole. The supplemental schedules of assets held for investment purposes as of December 31, 20X1, and reportable transactions for the year ended December 31, 20X1, are presented for the purpose of additional analysis and are not a required part of the basic financial statements, but are supplemental information required by the Department of Labor's Rules and Regulations for Reporting and Disclosure under the Employee Retirement Income Security Act of 1974. These supplemental schedules are the responsibility of the Plan's management. The supplemental schedules have been subjected to the auditing procedures applied in the audit of the basic 20X1 financial statements and, in our opinion, are fairly stated in all material respects in relation to those basic financial statements taken as a whole.

[Signature]

[Date]

DEPARTURE FROM GENERALLY ACCEPTED ACCOUNTING PRINCIPLES

In certain instances, the auditor may determine that the plan's financial statements are not in compliance with generally accepted accounting principles because of inadequate disclosures or other deficiencies. For example, the financial statements of a defined benefit pension plan, prepared in conformity with generally accepted accounting principles, should include information regarding the actuarial present value of accumulated plan benefits and the effects, if significant, of certain factors affecting the year-to-year change in accumulated plan benefits. If the benefit information either is omitted or is not appropriately measured in conformity with SFAS 35, the auditor should express a qualified or adverse opinion on the plan's financial statements. As noted above in the section on non-GAAP-basis financial statements, even financial statements prepared on a comprehensive basis of accounting other than generally accepted accounting principles require disclosure of the accumulated plan benefits information. See the AICPA Audit Guide, Section 13.24-25 for additional information.

Inadequate Disclosure, Qualified Opinion

The following illustrative auditors' report is an example of when the auditor has determined that the plan's financial statements are not in conformity with GAAP due to the absence of information regarding investments exceeding 5% of net assets available for benefits at the end of the plan year.

Independent Auditors' Report

To the ABC Company Defined Contribution Pension Plan and Participants:

We have audited the accompanying statements of net assets available for benefits of the ABC Company Defined Contribution Pension Plan as of December 31, 20X1 and 20X0, and the related statement of changes in net assets available for benefits for the year ended December 31, 20X1. These financial statements are the responsibility of the Plan's management. Our responsibility is to express an opinion on these financial statements based on our audits.

We conducted our audits in accordance with generally accepted auditing standards. Those standards require that we plan and perform the audit to obtain reasonable assurance about whether the financial statements are free of material misstatement. An audit includes examining, on a test basis, evidence supporting the amounts and disclosures in the financial statements. An audit also includes assessing the accounting principles used and significant estimates made by management, as well as evaluating the overall financial statement presentation. We believe that our audits provide a reasonable basis for our opinion.

The Plan's financial statements do not include certain information regarding the investments which exceed 5% of net assets available for benefits as of December 31, 20X1 and 20X0, as required by generally accepted accounting principles. As such, the Plan's financial statements have not been prepared in conformity with generally accepted accounting principles.

In our opinion, except for the omission of the information discussed in the preceding paragraph, the financial statements referred to above present fairly, in all material respects, the net assets available for benefits of the Plan as of December 31, 20X1 and 20X0, and the changes in net assets available for benefits for the year ended December 31, 20X1, in conformity with generally accepted accounting principles.

[Signature]

[Date]

REFERENCE TO THE WORK OF OTHER AUDITORS OR SPECIALISTS

In certain circumstances, the auditor may use the work of other auditors or specialists to audit certain account balances of the plan. Some of the most common examples of situations in which the auditor would use the work of other auditors or specialists are

- Use of another auditor's independent auditors' report for the financial statements of a common/commingled trust fund or pooled separate account to audit the plan's investment in that trust vehicle
- Use of a service auditor's report (SAS 70) to assess a plan's control structure
- Use of an actuarial report to audit the plan's actuarial present value of accumulated plan benefits or benefit obligations and changes therein

In these cases, the plan auditor would still remain the principal auditor but the work of the other auditor or specialist may be used to assist in testing an account balance reported in the plan's financial statements or to obtain an understanding of the plan's internal controls related to an account balance. As the auditor for the plan needs to perform auditing procedures on all of the other accounts of the plan, no other auditor is in the position to express an opinion on the plan's financial statements. Therefore, the report of another auditor or specialist may be used as competent evidential matter, but there cannot be a meaningful division of responsibility for the plan's financial statements, and the plan auditor should not refer to the other auditor or specialist in his or her report under these circumstances.

SCOPE LIMITATION ON MULTIEMPLOYER PLANS

During an audit, the auditor may not receive all required information needed to test certain account balances. Therefore, the scope of the audit has been limited and the auditor should disclaim his/her opinion on the plan's financial statements. Historically, the DOL has rejected Form 5500 filings with disclaimer of opinions on the financial statements such as the illustrative disclaimer of opinion below.

Disclaimer of Opinion Due to Scope Limitation

The following is an example of the auditors' report disclaiming an opinion on the financial statements of a multiemployer defined benefit pension plan when the auditor has been unable to apply all the procedures considered necessary with regard to participants' data maintained by the sponsor companies. Since contributions and benefit payments are determined based on the participant data, this is a scope limitation and the auditor should disclaim an opinion on the financial statements.

Independent Auditors' Report

To the ABC Multiemployer Defined Benefit Pension Plan and Participants:

We were engaged to audit the statements of net assets available for benefits of ABC Multiemployer Defined Benefit Pension Plan as of December 31, 20X1 and 20X0, and the related statement of changes in net assets available for benefits for the year ended December 31, 20X1. These financial statements are the responsibility of the Plan's management.

The Plan's records and procedures are not adequate to assure the completeness of participants' data on which contributions and benefit payments are determined, and the Board of Trustees did not engage us to perform, and we did not perform, any other auditing procedures with respect to participants' data maintained by the sponsor companies or individual participants.

Because of the significance of the information that we did not audit, the scope of our work was not sufficient to enable us to express, and we do not express, an opinion on these financial statements.

[Signature]

[Date]

MASTER TRUSTS

When more than one plan is sponsored by a single employer or group of employers under common control, the plan sponsor may choose to combine the investment assets of those plans under common control into a combined trust account in which a bank serves as trustee or custodian. This is known as a **master trust**. Each plan owns an undivided interest in the net assets of the master trust usually measured in percentages or units. A master trust is established to hold and invest the assets of the plans. Therefore, contributions are remitted to the master trust to buy investments, and when an individual plan needs to pay benefits, the master trust will sell investments and transfer the funds to the plan. The plan will then pay benefits out of the plan. Plan benefits are not paid out of the master trust.

When a plan invests in a master trust, the plan's interest in the master trust is presented as a single line item on the statement(s) of net assets available for benefits. Similarly, the income from investment in the master trust is presented as a single line item on the statement(s) of changes in net assets available for benefits.

In the notes to the financial statements, the plan should present information on the master trust in which it invests (with the exception of defined contribution pension plans, according to the provisions of SOP 99-3--see Chapter 6, Investments, for additional information). Basically, the information on the master trust should be detailed enough to provide the major classes of investments of the master trust (e.g., corporate bonds, common stocks, or government securities) as of the date of the plan's statement(s) of net assets available for benefits.

Investment income detailed by type of income should also be disclosed (e.g., interest, dividends, and net appreciation) for the same periods as presented on the statement(s) of changes in net assets available for benefits. Also, the percentage of the plan's ownership in the master trust and a description of the basis of allocation of the master trust's net assets, investment income, and gains/losses between the plans participating in the master trust should also be disclosed in the notes to the financial statements.

Master trusts are not currently required by ERISA or the DOL to prepare financial statements, but they are required to file an annual report with the DOL similar to the Form 5500 with supplemental schedules. With the revised Form 5500, master trusts will be required to prepare financial statements as a direct filing entity (DFE). Therefore, the individual plans are not required to attach supplemental schedules to the plan financial statements if the plan only has investments in a master trust. If the plan has investments in a master trust and investments outside of the master trust, the supplemental schedules would be required.

In certain cases, the plan administrator may engage an independent auditor to report on the financial statements of a master trust. Users of the financial statements of the trust may not be aware of the distinction between the trust and the plan. Therefore, when reporting on such a trust, the auditors' report should explain that the financial statements of the trust do not purport to present the financial status or changes in financial status of the plan in accordance with generally accepted accounting principles and that the financial statements do not purport to satisfy the DOL reporting and disclosure requirements.

Unqualified Opinion

The following is an example of the auditors' report on the financial statements of a master trust.

Independent Auditors' Report

To the ABC Master Trust:

We have audited the accompanying statements of net assets of ABC Master Trust as of December 31, 20X1 and 20X0, and the related statement of changes in net assets and trust balance for the year ended December 31, 20X1. These financial statements are the responsibility of the Trust's management. Our responsibility is to express an opinion on these financial statements based on our audits.

We conducted our audits in accordance with generally accepted auditing standards. Those standards require that we plan and perform the audit to obtain reasonable assurance about whether the financial statements are free of material misstatement. An audit includes examining, on a test basis, evidence supporting the amounts and disclosures in the financial statements. An audit also includes assessing the accounting principles used and significant estimates made by management as well as evaluating the overall financial statement presentation. We believe that our audit provides a reasonable basis for our opinion.

In our opinion, the financial statements referred to above present fairly, in all material respects, the net assets of ABC Master Trust as of December 31, 20X1 and 20X0, and the changes in its net assets and trust balance for the year ended December 31, 20X1, in conformity with generally accepted accounting principles.

The accompanying statements are those of ABC Master Trust, which is established for various ABC Pension Plans; the statements do not purport to present the financial status of any of the ABC Pension Plans. The financial statements do not contain certain information on accumulated plan benefits and other disclosures necessary for a fair presentation of the financial status of the ABC Pension Plans in conformity with generally accepted accounting principles. Furthermore, these statements do not purport to satisfy the Department of Labor's Rules and Regulations for Reporting and Disclosure under the Employee Retirement Income Security Act of 1974 relating to the financial statements of the ABC Company employee benefit plans.

[Signature]

[Date]

REPORTS FILED PURSUANT TO THE SECURITIES AND EXCHANGE COMMISSION (SEC) FORM 11-K

Certain plans are required to file an annual report to the SEC on Form 11-K. Generally, if employee contributions are allowed to be used to purchase employer securities pursuant to the provisions of the plan, the Securities Exchange Act of 1934 requires that the audited financial statements of the employee benefit plan accompany the filing with the SEC on Form 11-K. As part of the Form 11-K filing, the plan's financial statements and related auditors' report and an independent auditors' consent must be provided. The independent auditors' consent is used to incorporate by reference the independent auditors' report on the plan's financial statements into the Registration Statement on Form S-8, which was used originally to register the shares of stock for the plan. This consent is required on an annual basis as provided by the SEC Form S-8 registration statements. The SEC does not accept limited-scope reports. Additionally, there is no limit as to the number of participants in a plan to trigger a Form 11-K filing. In other words, a plan which offers employer stock with less than 100 participants is required to file a Form 11-K.

ERISA Plans

The instructions to the Form 11-K indicate that if a plan is subject to the provisions of ERISA, then the plan's financial statements may be presented to include only the financial statements and supplemental schedules required by ERISA; namely, a comparative statement of net assets available for benefits and the most recent year's statement of changes in net assets available for benefits. Also remember that the DOL historically will not accept a qualified, adverse, or disclaimer of opinion; therefore, a plan that is required to file an annual report on both the Form 11-K with the SEC and the Form 5500 with the DOL will need an independent auditors' report expressing an unqualified opinion on the plan's financial statements to meet the requirements of both filings. The Form 11-K filings under this format must be filed with the SEC within 180 days following the plan's year-end (a 15-day extension is available). Because of the easier reporting requirements under this format, the majority of plans that are subject to ERISA and are required to file a Form 11-K adopt the reporting format prescribed by ERISA for purposes of such financial statements.

Regulation S-X Filing

Article 6A of Regulation S-X requires that for a Form 11-K filing, the plan's financial statements present a comparative statement of net assets available for benefits and three years of data for the statement of changes in net assets available for benefits. Under this method of filing, which is very rarely used, the footnote disclosures to the plan's financial statements would be for either two or three years depending on the type of disclosure (i.e., two years of disclosure for items involving the statement of net assets available for benefits and three years of disclosure for items involving the statement of changes in net assets available for benefits). In addition, the following schedules must also be presented: (1) Schedule I, Investments, (2) Schedule II, Allocation of Plan Assets and Liabilities to Investment Programs (that is, by-fund type of reporting), and (3) Schedule III, Allocation of Plan Income and Changes in Plan Equity to Investment Programs. The filing of the Form 11-K under this format is due ninety days after the plan's year-end.

Consent

This following is an illustrative consent which should be used in an Annual Report on Form 11-K when the auditors' report in the Form 11-K is being incorporated by reference in an effective registration statement on Form S-8. A Form S-8 is an SEC form which is used to register shares of an employer's publicly traded common stock for use by an employee benefit plan.

Independent Auditors' Consent

> We consent to the incorporation by reference in Registration Statement No. 99-99999 of ABC Company on Form S-8 of our report dated June 15, 20X2, appearing in this Annual Report on Form 11-K of ABC Company 401(k) savings plan for the year ended December 31, 20X1.
>
> [Signature]
>
> [Date]

AUDITORS' REPORT ATTACHED TO THE FORM 5500

Another option accepted by the DOL in filing the plan's annual report on Form 5500 is to attach the auditors' report directly to the completed Form 5500 instead of preparing separate plan financial statements. In this case, the statements of net assets available for benefits would be presented on Schedule H (for the 1999 Form 5500) and the statement of changes in net assets available for benefits would be presented on Schedule H (for the 1999 Form 5500). Notes to the financial statements would also be attached to the Form 5500 and a reference should be added to Schedule H (or applicable lines) which states "See Notes to Schedule H attached." Information regarding the actuarial present value of accumulated plan benefits and changes therein must be presented in the notes to the financial statements. If the actuarial present value of accumulated plan benefits and changes therein is presented as of the beginning of the plan's year, then the prior-year statement of changes in net assets available for benefits (Schedule H for 1999) should also be attached to the current year Form 5500 filing, and the auditors' report should be modified to address two complete years of financial information on Form 5500. Note that this approach can be extremely awkward and would not currently be acceptable for a defined benefit health and welfare plan.

The following illustrative auditors' report is an example of an unqualified opinion expressed on the financial statements of a defined benefit pension plan in Items 31 and 32 of the old Form 5500. It assumes that the independent auditors' report is attached to Form 5500 with accompanying notes to the financial statements (i.e., separate plan financial statements are not prepared). The following illustration also assumes that information regarding the actuarial present value of accumulated plan benefits and changes therein is presented as of the end of the plan's current year in a footnote disclosure.

Independent Auditors' Report

To the ABC Company Defined Benefit Pension Plan and Participants:

We have audited the statements of net assets available for benefits of the ABC Company Defined Benefit Pension Plan as of December 31, 20X1 and 20X0, as set forth in the accompanying Annual Return/Report of ABC Company Defined Benefit Pension Plan (Form 5500) (Item 31), and the statement of changes in net assets available for benefits for the year ended December 31, 20X1, (Item 32). These financial statements and supplemental schedules are the responsibility of the Plan's management. Our responsibility is to express an opinion on these financial statements based on our audits.

We conducted our audits in accordance with generally accepted auditing standards. Those standards require that we plan and perform the audit to obtain reasonable assurance about whether the financial statements are free of material misstatement.

An audit includes examining, on a test basis, evidence supporting the amounts and disclosures in the financial statements. An audit also includes assessing the accounting principles used and significant estimates made by management, as well as evaluating the overall financial statement presentation. We believe that our audits provide a reasonable basis for our opinion.

In our opinion, such financial statements present fairly, in all material respects, the financial status of the Plan as of December 31, 20X1, and the changes in its financial status for the year then ended and the information regarding the Plan's net assets available for benefits as of December 31, 20X0, in conformity with generally accepted accounting principles.

Our audits were conducted for the purpose of forming an opinion on the basic financial statements taken as a whole. The accompanying supplemental schedules of (1) assets held for investment purposes as of December 31, 20X1, and (2) reportable transactions for the year ended December 31, 20X1, are presented for the purpose of additional analysis and are not a required part of the basic financial statements, but are supplemental information required by the Department of Labor's Rules and Regulations for Reporting and Disclosure under the Employee Retirement Income Security Act of 1974. These schedules are the responsibility of the Plan's management. Such schedules have been subjected to the auditing procedures applied in our audit of the basic 20X1 financial statements and, in our opinion, are fairly stated in all material respects when considered in relation to those basic financial statements taken as a whole.

[Signature]

[Date]

MULTIPLE PLAN REPORTING

The DOL has indicated that it is acceptable to include the financial statements of more than one plan in one set of financial statements (totals of all plans should not be presented), provided the independent public accountant issues a separate opinion on each plan and all footnote disclosures and supplemental schedules are prepared for each plan. The plan sponsor must consider that the readers of the financial statements would have access to the information of more than one plan even if they participate in only one of the plans.

DISCREPANCIES BETWEEN THE FINANCIAL STATEMENTS AND THE FORM 5500 FILING

ERISA requires that a plan's financial statements include a note reconciling differences, if any, between amounts reported in the financial statements and the amounts reported in the Form 5500. The most common difference between the amounts reported on the financial statements and the Form 5500 is benefits payable, which may be reported on the Form 5500 but not on the financial statements. Also, sometimes the Form 5500 is prepared using the cash-basis method and the financial statements are prepared using the accrual basis of accounting. These differences should be shown as a reconciliation between net assets available for benefits per the financial statements and the net assets available for benefits per the Form 5500 in the notes to the financial statements. Also, in the same footnote a similar reconciliation should be shown between the corresponding account in the statement of changes in net assets available for benefits (such as benefits paid per the financial statements reconciled to benefits paid per the Form 5500).

In some cases, the plan's financial statements may be issued prior to the completion of the plan's Form 5500. If that is the case, the auditor should review the Form 5500 once completed. If the auditor identifies any differences, the auditors' report should be reissued, adding the financial statement footnote to reconcile between the financial statements and Form 5500 and dual-date the report with respect to the new footnote.

If the differences represent a material inconsistency in the preparation of the Form 5500, the auditor should consider revising his or her report to include an explanatory paragraph describing the material inconsistency, withholding the use of the auditors' report in the document, or withdrawing from the engagement.

13 FINANCIAL STATEMENTS AND DISCLOSURES

INTRODUCTION

The previous chapters of this guide have discussed various accounting and auditing concepts associated with employee benefit plans that are relevant in understanding the nature of the plans and in coordinating audits of such plans, as well as the different types of independent auditors' reports that might be issued for them (see Chapter 12, Auditors' Reports). The purpose of this chapter is to provide examples of financial statements and related footnote disclosures for defined benefit pension plans (including a set of financial statements for a multiemployer plan, which appears as the last example in this chapter), defined contribution pension plans, and health and welfare plans. Also, it is important to note that the financial statements, supplemental schedules, and footnote disclosures are only examples of more common types of financial statements and disclosures and are not meant to represent the only manner in which these documents may be prepared or described within a plan's financial statements. A section has been provided at the end of this chapter to provide examples of footnote disclosures that are not common but that may be encountered during an employee benefit plan engagement. In addition, note that examples of supplemental schedules have been included in Example B of the Defined Benefit Pension Plan financial statements and Example A of the Defined Contribution Pension Plan financial statements. In accordance with the provisions of Section 103 of ERISA, the financial statements presented below will include only a single-year presentation for the statement of changes in net assets available for benefits (except for the defined benefit pension plan presented with beginning of the year benefit information which requires a comparative statement of changes in net assets available for benefits). Lastly, the preparation of a plan's financial statements and related footnote disclosures is dependent upon the circumstances of the individual plan subject to audit.

DEFINED BENEFIT PENSION PLANS

This section will present examples of the following types of financial statements for defined benefit pension plans:

- Example A--Defined benefit pension plan with end-of-year benefit information presented as a separate financial statement--full-scope audit performed
- Example B--Defined benefit pension plan with beginning-of-year benefit information presented as a separate financial statement--limited-scope audit performed
- Example C--Defined benefit pension plan with end-of-year benefit information included in the footnotes to the plan's financial statements--full-scope audit performed
- Example D--Defined benefit pension plan with a 401(h) account feature

Example A: Defined Benefit Pension Plan With End-of-Year Benefit Information

ABC Company Retirement Plan
Statements of Net Assets Available for Benefits
December 31, 20X1 and 20X0

	20X1	*20X0*
Assets		
Investments:		
Investment in LM common stock	$1,100,000	$ 800,000
US government securities	200,000	100,000
Investment in HK insurance company	50,000	30,000
Corporate bonds	150,000	80,000
Total investments	1,500,000	1,010,000
Receivables:		
Employer contributions receivable	100,000	50,000
Employer contributions receivable	70,000	30,000
Sales pending settlement	10,000	5,000
Accrued interest income	5,000	5,000
Total receivables	185,000	90,000
Total assets	1,685,000	1,100,000
Liabilities		
Administrative expenses payable	20,000	20,000
Purchases pending settlement	100,000	50,000
Total liabilities	120,000	70,000
Net assets available for benefits	$1,565,000	$1,030,000

See notes to financial statements.

ABC Company Retirement Plan
Statement of Changes in Net Assets Available for Benefits
Year Ended December 31, 20X1

Additions:	
Interest	$100,000
Dividends	15,000
Net appreciation in fair value of investments	80,000
Total investment income	195,000

Employer contributions	470,000
Total additions	665,000
Deductions:	
Benefit payments	100,000
Administrative expenses	30,000
Total deductions	130,000
Net increase	535,000
Net assets available for benefits, beginning of year	1,030,000
Net assets available for benefits, end of year	$1,565,000

See notes to financial statements.

ABC Company Retirement Plan
Statement of Accumulated Plan Benefits
December 31, 20X1 and 20X0

	20X1	*20X0*
Actuarial present value of accumulated plan benefits		
Vested benefits:		
Participants currently receiving benefit payments	$2,000,000	$1,800,000
Other participants	200,000	150,000
Total vested benefits	2,200,000	1,950,000
Nonvested benefits	300,000	250,000
Total actuarial present value of accumulated plan benefits	$2,500,000	$2,200,000

See notes to financial statements.

ABC Company Retirement Plan
Statement of Changes in Accumulated Plan Benefits
Year Ended December 31, 20X1

Actuarial present value of accumulated plan benefits, beginning of year	$2,200,000
Increase (decrease) during the year attributable to:	
Increase in interest due to decrease in the discount period	96,000
Benefits accumulated--net	304,000
Benefits paid	(100,000)
Net increase	300,000
Actuarial present value of accumulated plan benefits, end of year	$2,500,000

See notes to financial statements.

ABC Company Retirement Plan
Notes to Financial Statements
Years Ended December 31, 20X1 and 20X0

1. **Description of Plan**

The following brief description of the ABC Company Retirement Plan (the "Plan") is provided for general information purposes only. Participants should refer to the Plan document for more complete information.

a. **General**--The Plan is a noncontributory defined benefit pension plan which provides for normal retirement, early retirement, and disability benefits covering all hourly employees of ABC Company (the "Company"). XYZ Bank serves as the trustee of the Plan, and together with several investment managers, manages the Plan's investments. The Plan is subject to the provisions of the Employee Retirement Income Security Act of 1974 (ERISA).

b. **Pension benefits**--Participants become fully vested after seven years of vesting service based upon the vesting schedule, as defined by the Plan. There is no partial vesting of benefits. Benefits are payable in the form of a joint-and-survivor annuity or single-life annuity. The amount of benefits payable upon retirement is contingent upon the number of years of service and the benefit rate in effect at the time of retirement.

2. **Summary of significant accounting policies**

a. **Basis of accounting**--The financial statements of the Plan were prepared on the accrual basis of accounting.

b. **Valuation of investments**--The Plan's investments are presented at fair value, which has been determined based on quoted market prices for the investments. The Plan's insurance contract with HK Insurance Company is valued at fair value by discounting the related cash flows based on current yields of similar instruments with similar maturities. Purchases and sales of securities are recorded on a trade-date basis. Interest income is recorded on the accrual basis. Dividends are recorded on the ex-dividend date.

c. **Expenses of the plan**--Plan expenses are paid solely by the Plan as provided by the Plan document.

d. **Actuarial present value of accumulated plan benefits**--Accumulated plan benefits are those future periodic payments, including lump-sum distributions, that are attributable under the Plan's provisions to the service employees have rendered. Accumulated plan benefits include benefits expected to be paid to (1) retired or terminated employees or their beneficiaries, (2) beneficiaries of employees who have died, and (3) present employees or their beneficiaries. The actuarial present value of accumulated plan benefits has been determined by an independent actuary, and is an amount which results from applying actuarial assumptions to adjust the accumulated plan benefits to reflect the time value of money (through discounts for interest) and the probability of payment (by means of decrements such as for death, disability, withdrawal, or retirement) between the actuarial valuation date and the expected date of payment. The effect of plan amendments on accumulated plan benefits is recognized in the year in which such amendments are adopted.

The more significant assumptions underlying the actuarial computations as of December 31, 20X1, and 20X0 are as follows:

Retirement	*Investment Return*	*Mortality*
Average retirement age--65	8.25% per annum, compounded annually	1983 Group Annuity Mortality Table

The foregoing actuarial assumptions are based on the presumption that the Plan will continue. Were the Plan to terminate, different actuarial assumptions and other factors might be applicable in determining the actuarial present value of accumulated plan benefits.

3. **Use of estimates and risks**

The preparation of financial statements in conformity with generally accepted accounting principles requires management to make estimates and assumptions that affect the reported amounts of assets, liabilities, accumulated plan benefit information and disclosure of contingent assets and liabilities at the date of the financial statements. Actual results could differ from those estimates.

The Plan utilizes various investment instruments including US government securities, corporate debt instruments, corporate stocks, and insurance contracts. Investment securities, in general, are exposed to various risks, such as interest rate, credit, and overall market volatility. Due to the level of risk associated with certain investment securities, it is reasonably possible that changes in the values of investment securities will occur in the near term and that such changes could materially affect the amounts reported in the statements of net assets available for plan benefits.

4. **Funding policy**

Contributions to provide benefits under the Plan are made solely by the Company. The Company's funding policy is to make cash contributions to the Plan in amounts computed by the Plan's actuary, using the entry-age-normal cost method. This method and the actuarial assumptions referred to above have been designed to provide sufficient funds to pay benefits as they become payable under the Plan. The Company met the minimum funding requirements of the ERISA in 20X1 and 20X0.

5. **Net appreciation in fair value of investments**

During 20X1, the Plan's investments generated net appreciation in the fair value of investments as follows:

Investments at fair value as determined by quoted market prices:	
Investment in LM common stock	$40,000
US government securities	20,000
Corporate bonds	10,000
	70,000
Investments at estimated fair value:	
Investment in insurance company contract	10,000
Total	$80,000

6. **Plan termination**

In the event the Plan is terminated, the net assets of the Plan will be allocated for payment of Plan benefits to the participants in an order of priority determined in accordance with ERISA, applicable regulations thereunder, and the Plan document.

Certain benefits under the Plan are insured by the Pension Benefit Guaranty Corporation (PBGC) if the Plan terminates. Generally, the PBGC guarantees most vested normal age retirement benefits, early retirement benefits, and certain disability and survivor's pensions. However, the PBGC does not guarantee all types of benefits under the Plan, and the amount of benefit protection is subject to certain limitations. Vested benefits under the Plan are guaranteed at the level in effect on the date of the Plan's termination, subject to a statutory ceiling on the amount of an individual's monthly benefit.

Whether all participants receive their benefits, should the Plan be terminated at some future time, will depend on the sufficiency, at that time, of the Plan's net assets to provide those benefits, the priority of those benefits to be paid, and the level and type of benefits guaranteed by the PBGC at that time. Some benefits may be fully or partially provided for by the then-existing assets and the PBGC guaranty while other benefits may not be provided for at all.

7. **Tax status**

The Company has not yet requested a determination letter for the Plan. However, the Company believes that the Plan currently is designed and being operated in compliance with the applicable requirements of the IRC and that, therefore, the Plan continues to qualify under Section 401(a) and the related trust continues to be tax-exempt as of December 31, 20X1. Therefore, no provision for income taxes has been included in the Plan's financial statements.

8. **Plan amendments**

Effective January 1, 20X2, the Plan was amended to provide for an increase in the monthly benefits payable to participants retiring on or after June 1, 20X1, from $20 per year of credited service to $25 per year of credited service. The Plan's actuary has estimated that the amendment will increase accumulated plan benefits by approximately $300,000.

The Plan was not amended during 20X1 or 20X0.

9. **Party-in-interest transactions**

The Plan has not considered Company contributions to the Plan or benefits accrued or paid by the Plan for participants as party-in-interest transactions.

Example B: Defined Benefit Pension Plan With Beginning-of-Year Benefit Information

ABC Company Retirement Plan
Statements of Net Assets Available for Benefits
December 31, 20X1 and 20X0

	20X1	*20X0*
Assets		
Investments:		
Investment in ABC Master Trust	$1,000,000	$750,000
Investment in money market fund	100,000	50,000
Total investments	1,100,000	800,000
Receivable-employer contributions receivable	100,000	50,000
Total assets	1,200,000	850,000
Liabilities		
Administrative expenses payable	20,000	20,000
Net assets available for benefits	$1,180,000	$830,000

See notes to financial statements.

ABC Company Retirement Plan
Statements of Changes in Net Assets Available for Benefits
Years Ended December 31, 20X1 and 20X0

	20X1	*20X0*
Additions:		
Net investment gain from the ABC Master Trust	$ 248,500	$ 140,000
Interest	8,000	7,000
Total investment income	256,500	147,000
Employer contributions	208,500	103,000
Total additions	465,000	250,000
Deductions:		
Benefit payments	85,000	80,000
Administrative expenses	30,000	27,000
Total deductions	115,000	107,000

Net increase	350,000	143,000
Net assets available for benefits, beginning of year	830,000	687,000
Net assets available for benefits, end of year	$1,180,000	$830,000

See notes to financial statements.

ABC Company Retirement Plan
Statement of Accumulated Plan Benefits
December 31, 20X0

Actuarial present value of accumulated plan benefits	
Vested benefits:	
Participants currently receiving benefit payments	$1,000,000
Other participants	200,000
Total vested benefits	1,200,000
Nonvested benefits	300,000
Total actuarial present value of accumulated plan benefits	$1,500,000

See notes to financial statements.

ABC Company Retirement Plan
Statement of Changes in Accumulated Plan Benefits
Year Ended December 31, 20X0

Actuarial present value of accumulated plan benefits, beginning of year	$1,200,000
Increase (decrease) during the year attributable to:	
Increase in interest due to decrease in the discount period	96,000
Benefits accumulated--net	114,000
Benefits paid	(80,000)
Changes in actuarial assumptions	50,000
Plan amendments	120,000
Net increase	300,000
Actuarial present value of accumulated plan benefits, end of year	$1,500,000

See notes to financial statements.

ABC Company Retirement Plan
Notes to Financial Statements
Years Ended December 31, 20X1 and 20X0

1. **Description of Plan**

The following brief description of the ABC Company Retirement Plan (the "Plan") is provided for general information purposes only. Participants should refer to the Plan document for more complete information.

a. **General**--The Plan is a noncontributory, defined benefit pension plan which provides for normal retirement, early retirement, and disability benefits covering all salaried employees of ABC Company (the "Company"). XYZ Bank serves as the trustee of the Plan and, together with several investment managers, manages the Plan's investments. Substantially all of the Plan's assets are invested in the ABC Master Trust along with the assets of the ABC Company Retirement Plan for Hourly Employees. The Plan's other assets consist of an investment in a money market fund. The Plan is subject to the provisions of the Employee Retirement Income Security Act of 1974 (ERISA).

b. **Pension benefits**--Participants become fully vested after five years of vesting service, as defined by the Plan. There is no partial vesting of benefits. Benefits are payable in the form of a joint-and-survivor annuity or single-life annuity. The amount of benefits payable upon retirement is contingent upon the number of years of service, the participants' salary history, and the benefit rate in effect at the time of retirement.

2. **Summary of significant accounting policies**
   a. **Basis of accounting**--The financial statements of the Plan were prepared on the accrual basis of accounting.
   b. **Valuation of investments**--The Plan's interest in the master trust represents its investment in the ABC Company Master Trust Fund (the "Master Trust"). The Plan's investment in the Master Trust is presented at fair value, which has been determined based on the fair value of the underlying investments of the Master Trust. The Plan's investment in the money market fund represents its investment in the XYZ Bank Money Market Fund, which is presented at fair value.
   c. **Expenses of the plan**--Plan expenses are paid by the Plan or by the Company as provided by the Plan document.
   d. **Actuarial present value of accumulated plan benefits**--Accumulated plan benefits are those future periodic payments, including lump-sum distributions, that are attributable under the Plan's provisions to the service employees have rendered. Accumulated plan benefits include benefits expected to be paid to (1) retired or terminated employees or their beneficiaries, (2) beneficiaries of employees who have died, and (3) present employees or their beneficiaries. The actuarial present value of accumulated plan benefits has been determined by an independent actuary, and is that amount which results from applying actuarial assumptions to adjust the accumulated plan benefits to reflect the time value of money (through discounts for interest) and the probability of payment (by means of decrements such as for death, disability, withdrawal, or retirement) between the actuarial valuation date and the expected date of payment. The effect of Plan amendments on accumulated plan benefits is recognized in the year in which such amendments are effective. During 20X0, certain amendments to the Plan became effective which increased accumulated plan benefits by $120,000. See Note 9 for additional information.

      The more significant assumptions underlying the actuarial computations as of December 31, 20X0, are as follows:

Retirement	*Investment Return*	*Mortality*
Average retirement age--65 (December 31, 1999--63)	8% per annum, compounded annually	1983 Group Annuity Mortality Table, set back 2-5 years for females

      The impact of the change in the actuarial assumption, was to increase the Plan's accumulated plan benefits by $50,000. The foregoing actuarial assumptions are based on the presumption that the Plan will continue. Were the Plan to terminate, different actuarial assumptions and other factors might be applicable in determining the actuarial present value of accumulated plan benefits.

3. **Use of estimates and risks**

   The preparation of financial statements in conformity with generally accepted accounting principles requires management to make estimates and assumptions that affect the reported amounts of assets, liabilities, accumulated plan benefit information, and disclosure of contingent assets and liabilities at the date of the financial statements. Actual results could differ from those estimates.

The Plan utilizes, through participation in the Master Trust and other investments, various investment instruments including short-term investments, US government securities, corporate debt instruments, corporate stocks, pooled separate accounts, and common/collective trust accounts. Investment securities, in general, are exposed to various risks, such as interest rate, credit, and overall market volatility. Due to the level of risk associated with certain investment securities, it is reasonably possible that changes in the values of investment securities will occur in the near term and that such changes could materially affect the amounts reported in the statements of net assets available for plan benefits.

4. **Investment in the ABC Company Master Trust**

The Plan's investment assets held in a trust account at XYZ Bank consist of an interest in an investment account of the Master Trust Fund, a master trust established by the Company and administered by XYZ Bank. Use of the Master Trust permits the commingling of the trust assets of the Plan and the ABC Company Retirement Plan for Hourly Employees for investment and administrative purposes. Although assets are commingled in the Master Trust, XYZ Bank maintains supporting records for the purpose of allocating the net gain of the investment accounts to the two participating plans.

The assets held by the Master Trust are valued at fair value at the end of each month. If available, quoted market prices are used to value investments. In instances wherein quoted market prices are not available, the fair value of investments is estimated primarily by independent investment brokerage firms and insurance companies. The net investment income of the investment assets is allocated by XYZ Bank to each participating plan based on the relationship of the interest of each trust to the total of the interests of the participating plans.

The net assets of the Master Trust at December 31, 20X1 and 20X0 are summarized as follows:

	20X1	*20X0*
US government securities	$ 500,000	$ 300,000
EFG common stock	200,000	100,000
HIJ insurance company contracts	100,000	75,000
XYZ bank pooled separate account	100,000	150,000
Real estate	100,000	200,000
KLM preferred stock	300,000	250,000
Certificates of deposit	100,000	75,000
Total net assets	$1,400,000	$1,150,000

The net investment income of the Master Trust for the years ended December 31, 20X1 and 20X0, is summarized as follows:

	20X1	*20X0*
Interest	$ 50,000	$ 40,000
Dividends	70,000	35,000
Net investment gain from pooled separate accounts	80,000	55,000
Net appreciation in fair value of investments	160,000	93,000
Administrative expenses	(10,000)	(8,000)
Net investment income	$350,000	$215,000

The Plan's interest in the Master Trust as a percentage of net assets of the Master Trust was approximately 71% and 65% at December 31, 20X1 and 20X0, respectively.

5. **Funding policy**

Contributions to provide benefits under the Plan are made solely by the Company. The Company's funding policy is to make cash contributions to the Plan in amounts computed by the Plan's actuary using the unit credit actuarial cost method. This method and the actuarial assumptions referred to above have been designed to provide sufficient funds to pay benefits as they become payable under the Plan. The Company met the minimum funding requirements of ERISA in both 20X1 and 20X0.

6. **Information certified by the custodian (unaudited)**

The following is a summary of the unaudited information included in the Plan's financial statements and supplemental schedules derived from information prepared by XYZ Bank, the trustee of the Plan's investment assets, and furnished to the plan administrator for the years ended December 31, 20X1, and 20X0. The plan administrator has obtained certifications from the trustee that the following information is complete and accurate:

	20X1	*20X0*
Statements of Net Assets Available for Benefits:		
Value of interest in Master Trust	$1,000,000	$750,000
Interest bearing cash	100,000	50,000
Statements of Changes in Net Assets Available for Benefits:		
Net investment gain from ABC Master Trust	248,500	140,000
Interest income	8,000	7,000

All information included in the supplemental schedules.

7. **Plan termination**

In the event the Plan is terminated, the net assets of the Plan will be allocated for payment of Plan benefits to the participants in an order of priority determined in accordance with ERISA, applicable regulations thereunder and the Plan document.

Certain benefits under the Plan are insured by the Pension Benefit Guaranty Corporation (PBGC) if the Plan terminates. Generally, the PBGC guarantees most vested normal age retirement benefits, early retirement benefits, and certain disability and survivor's pensions. However, the PBGC does not guarantee all types of benefits under the Plan, and the amount of benefit protection is subject to certain limitations. Vested benefits under the Plan are guaranteed at the level in effect on the date of the Plan's termination, subject to a statutory ceiling on the amount of an individual's monthly benefit.

Whether all participants receive their benefits, should the Plan be terminated at some future time, will depend on the sufficiency, at that time, of the Plan's net assets to provide those benefits, the priority of those benefits to be paid, and the level and type of benefits guaranteed by the PBGC at that time. Some benefits may be fully or partially provided for by the then-existing assets and the PBGC guaranty while other benefits may not be provided for at all.

8. **Tax status**

The Internal Revenue Service (IRS) has determined and informed the Company by a letter dated June 30, 20X0, that the Plan and related trust are designed in accordance with applicable sections of the Internal Revenue Code (IRC). The Plan has been amended since receiving the determination letter. The Company believes that the Plan currently is designed and being operated in compliance with the applicable requirements of the IRC and that, therefore, the Plan continues to qualify under Section 401(a) and the related trust continues to be tax-exempt as of December 31, 20X1. Therefore, no provision for income taxes has been included in the Plan's financial statements.

9. **Plan amendments**

Effective June 1, 20X1, the Plan was amended to provide for an increase in the monthly benefits payable to participants retiring on or after June 1, 20X2, from $20 per year of credited service to $25 per year of credited service. The Plan's actuary estimates that the amendment will increase accumulated plan benefits by approximately $250,000.

Effective January 1, 20X0, the Plan was amended to provide for an increase in the monthly benefit rate payable to participants from $19 per year of credited service to $20 per year of credited service. The effect of this amendment increased accumulated plan benefits by $120,000.

10. **Party-in-interest transactions**

The Plan has not considered Company contributions to the Plan or benefits accrued or paid by the Plan for participants as party-in-interest transactions.

NOTE: The following pages illustrate the Schedule of Assets Held for Investment Purposes (formerly Item 27a of the Form 5500) and the Schedule of Reportable Transactions (formerly Item 27d of the Form 5500) for the Plan. For purposes of the Schedule of Reportable Transactions, only the transactions of the money market fund are presented. The reportable transactions for the Master Trust are included in the supplemental schedules included as part of the Master Trust filing (Schedule D) of the new Form 5500 made directly to the Department of Labor (DOL).

ABC Company Retirement Plan
Schedule of Assets Held for Investment Purposes
December 31, 20X1

Column A	Column B Identity of issuer borrower, lessor, or similar party	Column C Description of investment, including maturity date, rate of interest, collateral, or maturity value	Column D Cost	Column E Fair value
	XYZ Bank*	Investment in ABC Master Trust	$800,000	1,000,000
	XYZ Bank*	XYZ Bank Money Market Fund	100,000	100,000
			$900,000	$1,100,000

* *Party-in-interest*

ABC Company Retirement Plan
Schedule of Reportable Transactions
Series of Transactions, When Aggregated, Exceeding 5% of Beginning Plan Assets
Year Ended December 31, 20X1

Column A *Identity of party involved*	*Column B* *Description of asset*	*Column C* *Purchases*	*Column D* *Sales*	*Column G* *Cost of asset*	*Column H* *Current value of asset on transaction date*	*Column I* *Net gain (loss)*
	XYZ Bank money market fund	$600,000		$600,000	$600,000	
	XYZ Bank money market fund		550,000	550,000	550,000	

Example C: Defined Benefit Pension Plan With End-of-Year Benefit Information Presented in the Footnotes

ABC Company Retirement Plan
Statements of Net Assets Available for Benefits
December 31, 20X1 and 20X0

	20X1	*20X0*
Assets		
Investments:		
Investment in XYZ Trust Company Mutual Fund	$1,000,000	$750,000
Investment in real estate	100,000	50,000
Total investments	1,100,000	800,000
Receivable-employer contributions receivable	100,000	50,000
Total assets	1,200,000	850,000
Liabilities		
Administrative expenses payable	20,000	20,000
Net assets available for benefits	$1,180,000	$830,000

See notes to financial statements.

ABC Company Retirement Plan
Statement of Changes in Net Assets Available for Benefits
Year Ended December 31, 20X1

Additions:	
Net investment gain from registered investment company	$250,000
Net appreciation in fair value of real estate	15,000
Total investment income	265,000
Employer contributions	200,000
Total additions	465,000
Deductions:	
Benefit payments	85,000
Administrative expenses	30,000
Total deductions	115,000
Net increase	350,000
Net assets available for benefits, beginning of year	830,000
Net assets available for benefits, end of year	$1,180,000

See notes to financial statements.

ABC Company Retirement Plan
Notes to Financial Statements
Years Ended December 31, 20X1 and 20X0

1. **Description of Plan**

   The following brief description of the ABC Company Retirement Plan (the "Plan") is provided for general information purposes only. Participants should refer to the Plan document for more complete information.

   a. **General**--The Plan is a noncontributory, defined benefit pension plan which provides for normal retirement, early retirement, and disability benefits covering all hourly employees of ABC Company (the "Company"). XYZ Bank serves as the trustee of the Plan, and together with several investment managers, manages the Plan's investments. The Plan is subject to the provisions of the Employee Retirement Income Security Act of 1974 (ERISA).

b. **Pension benefits**--Participants become fully vested after five years of vesting service, as defined by the Plan. There is no partial vesting of benefits. Benefits are payable in the form of a joint-and-survivor annuity or single-life annuity. The amount of benefits payable upon retirement is contingent upon the number of years of service and the benefit rate in effect at the time of retirement.

2. **Summary of significant accounting policies**

a. **Basis of accounting**--The financial statements of the Plan were prepared on the accrual basis of accounting.

b. **Valuation of investments**--The Plan's interest in the mutual fund represents its investment in the DEF Trust Company. The Plan's investment in the mutual fund is presented at fair value, which has been determined based on the fair value of the underlying investments of the mutual fund. The investment in real estate is valued at estimated fair value based upon an independent appraisal of the property as of the end of the plan year.

c. **Expenses of the plan**--Plan expenses are paid by the Plan or by the Company as provided by the Plan document.

d. **Actuarial present value of accumulated plan benefits**--Accumulated plan benefits are those future periodic payments, including lump-sum distributions, that are attributable under the Plan's provisions to the service employees have rendered. Accumulated plan benefits include benefits expected to be paid to (1) retired or terminated employees or their beneficiaries, (2) beneficiaries of employees who have died, and (3) present employees or their beneficiaries. The actuarial present value of accumulated plan benefits has been determined by an independent actuary, and is an amount which results from applying actuarial assumptions to adjust the accumulated plan benefits to reflect the time value of money (through discounts for interest) and the probability of payment (by means of decrements such as for death, disability, withdrawal, or retirement) between the actuarial valuation date and the expected date of payment. The effect of Plan amendments on accumulated plan benefits is recognized in the year in which such amendments are effective.

During 20X1 certain amendments to the Plan became effective which increased accumulated plan benefits by approximately $250,000. See Note 7 for a discussion of the amendments.

The more significant assumptions underlying the actuarial computations as of December 31, 20X1 and 20X0, are as follows:

Retirement	*Investment Return*	*Mortality*
Average retirement age-65	8.25% per annum, compounded annually	1983 Group Annuity Mortality Table

The foregoing actuarial assumptions are based on the presumption that the Plan will continue. Were the Plan to terminate, different actuarial assumptions and other factors might be applicable in determining the actuarial present value of accumulated plan benefits.

At December 31, 20X1, the actuarial present value of accumulated plan benefits was as follows:

Vested Benefits:	
Participants currently receiving benefit payments	$1,000,000
Other participants	200,000
Total vested benefits	1,200,000
Nonvested benefits	300,000
Total actuarial present value of accumulated plan benefits	$1,500,000

The changes in the actuarial present value of accumulated plan benefits for the year ended December 31, 20X1, are as follows:

Actuarial present value of accumulated plan benefits, beginning of year	$1,200,000
Increase (decrease) during the year attributable to:	
Increase in interest due to decrease in the discount period	96,000
Benefits accumulated--net	39,000
Benefits paid	(85,000)
Changes in actuarial assumptions	50,000
Plan amendments	250,000
Net increase	300,000
Actuarial present value of accumulated plan benefits, end of year	$1,500,000

3. **Use of estimates and risks**

The preparation of financial statements in conformity with generally accepted accounting principles requires management to make estimates and assumptions that affect the reported amounts of assets, liabilities, accumulated plan benefit information, and disclosure of contingent assets and liabilities at the date of the financial statements. Actual results could differ from those estimates.

The Plan utilizes, through participation in the DEF Trust Company Mutual Fund, various investment instruments including short-term investments, US government securities, corporate debt instruments, corporate stocks, pooled separate accounts and real estate. Investment securities, in general, are exposed to various risks, such as interest rate, credit, and overall market volatility. Due to the level of risk associated with certain investment securities, it is reasonably possible that changes in the values of investment securities will occur in the near term and that such changes could materially affect the amounts reported in the statements of net assets available for plan benefits.

4. **Funding policy**

Contributions to provide benefits under the Plan are made solely by the Company. The Company's funding policy is to make cash contributions to the Plan in amounts computed by the Plan's actuary, using the unit-credit-actuarial cost method. This method and the actuarial assumptions referred to above have been designed to provide sufficient funds to pay benefits as they become payable under the Plan. The Company met the minimum funding requirements of ERISA in both 20X1 and 20X0.

5. **Plan termination**

In the event the Plan is terminated, the net assets of the Plan will be allocated for payment of Plan benefits to the participants in an order of priority determined in accordance with ERISA, applicable regulations thereunder, and the Plan document.

Certain benefits under the Plan are insured by the Pension Benefit Guaranty Corporation (PBGC) if the Plan terminates. Generally, the PBGC guarantees most vested normal age retirement benefits, early retirement benefits, and certain disability and survivor's pensions. However, the PBGC does not guarantee all types of benefits under the Plan, and the amount of benefit protection is subject to certain limitations. Vested benefits under the Plan are guaranteed at the level in effect on the date of the Plan's termination, subject to a statutory ceiling on the amount of an individual's monthly benefit.

Whether all participants receive their benefits, should the Plan be terminated at some future time, will depend on the sufficiency, at that time, of the Plan's net assets to provide those benefits, the priority of those benefits to be paid, and the level and type of benefits guaranteed by the PBGC at that time. Some benefits may be fully or partially provided for by the then-existing assets and the PBGC guaranty while other benefits may not be provided for at all.

6. **Tax status**

   The Internal Revenue Service has determined and informed the Company by a letter dated June 30, 20X0, that the Plan and related trust are designed in accordance with applicable sections of the Internal Revenue Code (IRC). The Plan has been amended since receiving the determination letter. The Plan was not timely amended to bring it into compliance with the requirements of the Tax Reform Act of 1986. The Company voluntarily requested to correct the defect under the Closing Agreement Program of the Internal Revenue Service. Under this program, the Company and the Internal Revenue Service entered into a signed closing agreement in which the Internal Revenue Service concluded that it will treat the Plan as having been amended for the purposes of the Tax Reform Act of 1986. The penalty assessed by the IRS for this violation was paid by the Company.

7. **Plan amendments**

   Effective June 1, 20X1, the Plan was amended to provide for an increase in the monthly benefits payable to participants retiring on or after June 1, 20X1, from $20 per year of credited service to $25 per year of credited service. The Plan's actuary estimates that the amendment will increase accumulated plan benefits by approximately $250,000. Such amendment is reflected in the accumulated plan benefits information as of December 31, 20X1.

   Effective January 1, 20X0, the Plan was amended to provide for an increase in the monthly benefit rate payable to participants from $19 per year of credited service to $20 per year of credited service. Such amendment was reflected in the accumulated plan benefits information as of December 31, 20X0.

8. **Subsequent event**

   On June 1, 20X2, the Company announced that the Plan will be merged with the ABC Retirement Plan for Salaried Employees effective December 31, 20X2. The benefits provided under the provisions of the Plan will continue to remain effective under the merged plan.

9. **Party-in-interest transactions**

   The Plan has not considered Company contributions to the Plan or benefits accrued or paid by the Plan for participants as party-in-interest transactions.

Example D: Defined Benefit Pension Plan With a 401(h) Feature

The following presents an example of a set of financial statements for a defined benefit pension plan with a 401(h) account feature. The example is excerpted from the

AICPA's *Audit of Employee Benefits Plans*. The footnotes to the plan's financial statements provide only those footnotes unique to the 401(h) feature.

C&H Company Pension Plan
Statement of Net Assets Available for Pension Benefits

	December 31, 20X1	20X0
Assets		
Investments at fair value (Note A):		
Plan interest in C&H Master Trust	$2,000,000	$1,660,000
C&H Company common stock	600,000	800,000
Investment contract with insurance company	850,000	800,000
Corporate bonds and debentures	3,000,000	3,170,000
US government securities	300,000	200,000
Mortgages	480,000	460,000
Money market fund	270,000	240,000
Total investments	7,500,000	7,330,000
Net assets held in 401(h) account (Note H)	1,072,000	966,000
Receivables:		
Employer's contribution	20,000	10,000
Securities sold	310,000	175,000
Accrued interest and dividends	70,000	70,000
Total receivables	400,000	255,000
Cash	180,000	80,000
Total assets	9,152,000	8,631,000
Liabilities		
Due to broker for securities purchased	--	400,000
Accounts payable	70,000	60,000
Accrued expenses	70,000	25,000
Amounts related to obligation of 401(h) account	1,072,000	966,000
Total liabilities	1,212,000	1,451,000
Net assets available for pension benefits	$7,940,000	$7,180,000

The accompanying notes are an integral part of the financial statements.

C&H Company Pension Plan
Statement of Changes in Net Assets Available for Pension Benefits

	Year ended December 31, 20X1
Investment income:	
Net appreciation in fair value of investments	$233,000
Interest	293,000
Dividends	4,000
	530,000
Less investment expenses	30,000
	500,000
Plan interest in C&H Master Trust investment income	117,000
	617,000
Contributions:	
Employer	740,000
Employees	450,000
	1,190,000
Total additions	1,807,000

Benefits paid directly to participants	740,000
Purchases of annuity contracts	257,000
	997,000
Administrative expenses	50,000
Total deductions	1,047,000
Net increase	760,000
Net assets available for pension benefits, beginning of year	7,180,000
Net assets available for pension benefits, end of year	$7,940,000

The accompanying notes are an integral part of the financial statements.

Notes To Financial Statements

A. **401 (h) Account**

Effective January 1, 19X0, the Plan was amended to include a medical benefit component in addition to the normal retirement benefits in order to fund a portion of the postretirement obligations for retirees and their beneficiaries in accordance with Section 401(h) of the Internal Revenue Code (IRC). A separate account has been established and maintained in the Plan for the net assets related to the medical benefit component (401(h) account). In accordance with IRC Section 401(h), the Plan's investments in the 401(h) account may not be used for, or diverted to, any purpose other than providing health benefits for retirees and their beneficiaries. Any assets transferred to the 401(h) account from the defined benefit pension plan in a qualified transfer of excess pension plan assets (and any income allocable thereto) that are not used during the plan year must be transferred out of the account to the pension plan. The related obligations for health benefits are not included in this Plan's obligations in the statement of accumulated plan benefits but are reflected as obligations in the financial statements of the C&H health and welfare benefit plan. Plan participants do not contribute to the 401(h) account. Employer contributions or qualified transfers to the 401(h) account are determined annually and are at the discretion of the Plan Sponsor. Certain of the Plan's net assets are restricted to fund a portion of postretirement health benefits for retirees and their beneficiaries in accordance with IRC Section 401(h).

H. **Reconciliation of financial statements to Form 5500***

The following is a reconciliation of net assets available for pension benefits per the financial statements to the Form 5500:

	December 31,	
	20X1	*20X0*
Net assets available for pension benefits per the financial statements	$7,940,000	$7,180,000
Net assets held in 401(h) account included as assets in Form 5500	1,072,000	966,000
Net assets available for benefits per Form 5500	$9,012,000	$8,146,000

The net assets of the 401(h) account included in Form 5500 are not available to pay pension benefits but can be used only to pay retiree health benefits.

**The reconciliation of amounts reported in the plan's financial statements to amounts reported in Form 5500 is required by ERISA.*

The following is a reconciliation of the changes in net assets per the financial statements to Form 5500:

	For the year ended December 31, 20X1		
	Amounts per financial statements	*401(h) account*	*Amounts per Form 5500*
Net appreciation in fair value of investments	$233,000	$ 10,800	$243,800
Interest income	293,000	80,200	373,200
Employer contributions	740,000	40,000	780,000
Benefits paid to retirees	740,000	10,000	750,000
Administrative expenses	50,000	15,000	65,000

DEFINED CONTRIBUTION PENSION PLANS

This section provides examples of the following types of financial statements for defined contribution pension plans:

- Example A--defined contribution 401(k) plan--full-scope audit performed
- Example B--defined contribution employee stock ownership plan--(leveraged ESOP)--full-scope audit performed

The financial statements for the defined contribution pension plans have been presented in conformity with the provisions of AICPA Statement of Position 99-3, *Accounting for and Reporting of Certain Defined Contribution Benefit Plan Investments and Other Disclosure Matters,* which is discussed in Chapter 6, Investments.

Example A: Defined Contribution 401(k) Plan

ABC Company 401(k) Savings Plan
Statements of Net Assets Available for Benefits
December 31, 20X1 and 20X0

	20X1	*20X0*
Assets		
Investments:		
Participant loans	$ 100,000	$ 70,000
Investments in ABC common stock	900,000	430,000
Other investments	2,000,000	1,000,000
Total investments	3,000,000	1,500,000
Receivables:		
Employer contributions receivable	100,000	50,000
Employee contributions receivable	75,000	35,000
Total receivables	175,000	85,000
Total assets	3,175,000	1,585,000
Liabilities		
Administrative expenses payable	20,000	20,000
Excess contributions refundable	10,000	5,000
Total liabilities	30,000	25,000
Net assets available for benefits	$3,145,000	$1,560,000

See notes to financial statements.

NOTE: The participant loans presented above represent participant-directed investments. They have been reflected as a separate line item only for emphasis. The participant loans can be grouped into the other investments line item.

ABC Company 401(k) Savings Plan
Statement of Changes in Net Assets Available for Benefits
Year Ended December 31, 20X1

Additions:	
Interest	$ 50,000
Dividends	185,000
Net appreciation in fair value of investments	400,000
Total investment income	635,000
Contributions:	
Participant contributions	800,000
Employer contributions	365,000
Total contributions	1,165,000
Total additions	1,800,000
Deductions:	
Benefit payments	165,000
Administrative expenses	50,000
Total deductions	215,000
Net increase	1,585,000
Net assets available for benefits, beginning of year	1,560,000
Net assets available for benefits, end of year	$3,145,000

See notes to financial statements.

ABC Company 401(k) Savings Plan
Notes to Financial Statements
Years Ended December 31, 20X1 and 20X0

1. **Description of Plan**

   a. **General**--The following brief description of the ABC Company 401(k) Savings Plan (the "Plan") is provided for general information purposes only. Participants should refer to the Plan document for additional information.

   The Plan is a contributory defined contribution pension plan covering substantially all salaried and hourly employees of ABC Company (the "Company") who have completed one year of service and have attained the age of twenty-one. The Plan is subject to the provisions of the Employee Retirement Income Security Act of 1974 (ERISA).

   b. **Contributions**--Participants may make pre-tax contributions to the Plan ranging from 1% to 10% of their annual compensation. The Company matches 50% of the participant's contributions. The Company's matching contributions are made in the form of ABC Company Common Stock. All contributions are subject to the limitations under the IRC, which permitted a maximum contribution of $10,000 to the Plan during both 20X1 and 20X0.

   Participants may elect to have amounts credited to their investment account in one or more of the Plan's investment funds in increments of 10%. DEF Bank is the trustee of the Plan's assets.

The Company may also make discretionary contributions to the Plan. Discretionary contributions are allocated to participants based upon the ratio of the participant's annual compensation to total compensation for all participants. The discretionary contributions would be made in the form of ABC Common Stock. No discretionary contributions were made to the Plan by the Company during the years ended December 31, 20X1, or 20X0.

c. **Vesting**--Participants are vested in their salary deferral contributions plus earnings thereon at all times. Vesting in the Company contributions and earnings thereon is based on years of service as follows:

Years of service	*Vested percentage*
Less than 1	0%
1	20%
2	40%
3	60%
4	80%
5	100%

d. **Forfeitures**--Forfeitures of nonvested Company matching and discretionary contributions are used to reduce future Company contributions to the Plan. During 20X1 and 20X0, forfeitures of Company contributions of approximately $35,000 and $28,000, respectively, were used to reduce Company contributions to the Plan.

e. **Participant loans**--Participants may obtain a loan in an amount as defined in the Plan (not less than $1,000 and not greater than $50,000 or 50% of the participant's vested balance) from the balance of the participant's account. Interest is charged at a rate equal to interest rates charged by commercial lending institutions for similar loans. The loans can be repaid through payroll deductions over periods ranging from 12 to 60 months or up to 120 months for the purchase of a primary residence. Payments of principal and interest are credited to the participant's account. Participants may have only one outstanding loan at a time.

2. **Summary of significant accounting policies**

a. **Valuation of investments**--The plan's investments, except the investments in the guaranteed investment contracts, are valued at fair value based upon the quoted market prices of the underlying securities within each fund at December 31, 20X1 and 20X0. The investments in the guaranteed investment contracts are presented at contract value as Plan management has determined that the investment contracts are fully benefit responsive in accordance with the AICPA Statement of Position 94-4, *Reporting of Investment Contracts Held by Health and Welfare Benefit Plans and Defined Contribution Pension Plans.* Contract value represents the accumulated contributions plus accrued net earnings, less distributions. The fair value of the investment in the guaranteed investment contract was approximately $250,000 and $100,000 at December 31, 20X1 and 20X0, respectively.

NOTE: According to the provisions of SFAS 126, disclosure of the fair value of the guaranteed investment contracts is not required in this example. However, the fair value disclosure has been added for illustrative purposes only.

The crediting interest rate of the investment contracts held by the guaranteed investment contracts at December 31, 20X1 and 20X0, was 7.5% and 7.8%, respectively. For the years ended December 31, 20X1 and 20X0, the average return for the guaranteed investment contracts was 7.3% and 7.6%, respectively. The interest rates on the guaranteed investment contracts are reset on an annual basis.

b. **Use of estimates**--The preparation of the financial statements in conformity with generally accepted accounting principles requires Plan management to make estimates and assumptions that affect the reported amounts of Plan assets and liabilities at the date of the financial statements and the disclosure of contingent assets and liabilities. Actual results could differ from those estimates.

The Plan utilizes various investment instruments including short-term investments, US government securities, corporate debt instruments, corporate stocks, pooled separate accounts, and common/collective trust accounts. Investment securities, in general, are exposed to various risks such as interest rate, credit, and overall market volatility. Due to the level of risk associated with certain investment securities, it is reasonably possible that changes in the values of investment securities will occur in the near term and that such changes could materially affect the amounts reported in the statements of net assets available for plan benefits.

3. **Benefit claims payable**

At December 31, 20X1, and 20X0, net assets available for benefits included $35,600 and $25,800, respectively, for distributions to participants who have withdrawn from the Plan prior to the end of the plan year.

4. **Excess contributions refundable**

At December 31, 20X1, and 20X0, liabilities of $10,000 and $5,000, respectively, are recorded for amounts refundable by the Plan to participants for contributions made in excess of amounts allowed by the IRS.

5. **Investments exceeding 5% of net assets available for benefits**

The following represents a summary of the investments which exceeded 5% of net assets available for benefits at December 31, 20X1, and 20X0:

	20X1	*20X0*
Participant-directed accounts:		
Investment in KLJ Equity Fund	$1,000,000	$500,000
Investment in guaranteed investment contracts	225,000	90,000
Investment in TUH International Fund	600,000	200,000
Non-participant-directed accounts:		
ABC common stock	900,000	430,000

6. **Net appreciation in fair value of investments**

During 20X1, the Plan's investments generated net appreciation in the fair value of investments as follows:

	20X0
Investments at fair values as determined by quoted market prices:	
Participant-directed accounts:	
Investment in KLJ Equity Fund	$200,000
Investment in TUH International Fund	100,000
Non-participant-directed accounts:	
ABC common stock	100,000
Total	$400,000

7. **Supplemental fund information**

The following represents information regarding the increases and decreases in net assets available for benefits for the year ended December 31, 20X1, attributable to the investment in ABC Common Stock.

Employer contributions	$400,000
Net appreciation in fair value of investments	100,000
Benefit payments	30,000

8. **Tax status**

The IRS has determined and informed the Company by a letter dated June 30, 20X0, that the Plan and related trust are designed in accordance with applicable sections of the IRC. The Company believes that the Plan currently is designed and being operated in compliance with the applicable requirements of the IRC and that, therefore, the Plan continues to qualify under Section 401(a) and the related trust continues to be tax exempt as of December 31, 20X1. Therefore, no provision for income taxes has been included in the Plan's financial statements.

9. **Plan termination**

The Company has the right under the Plan to discontinue its contributions and to terminate the Plan, subject to the provisions set forth in ERISA. In the event of any termination of the Plan, or upon complete or partial discontinuance of contributions, the accounts of each affected participant shall remain fully vested.

10. **Party-in-interest transaction**

The Plan has not considered Company contributions to the Plan or benefits accrued or paid by the Plan for participants as party-in-interest transactions.

11. **Prohibited transaction**

During 20X1, the Company failed to remit certain employee salary deferral contributions in the amount of approximately $50,000 to the trustee, DEF Bank, in accordance with the DOL's rules regarding the timeliness of depositing such employee contributions. The amounts were originally contributed by participants during April 20X1 and subsequently deposited with the trustee during August 20X1. The Company has completed their evaluation of the amount of investment income, which would have been earned by the participants on those contributions during the period from April 20X1 to August 20X1. The Company made an additional contribution to the Plan during 20X2 to the participants' accounts in the amount of $26,000, which represented the amount of investment income that was earned by their contributions during the affected period.

NOTE: An example of the required supplemental schedule to be filed as part of the Plan's Form 5500 filing follows this page.

ABC Company 401(k) Savings Plan
Schedule of Assets Held for Investment Purposes
December 31, 20X1

Column A	*Column B* *Identity of issuer borrower, lessor, or similar party*	*Column C* *Description of investment, including maturity date, rate of interest, collateral, or maturity value*	*Column D* *Cost*	*Column E* *Fair value*
	ABC Company*	ABC common stock, 18,000 shares	$ 700,000	$900,000
	KLJ Bank	KLJ equity fund, 15,000 shares	700,000	1,000,000
	MNO Insurance Company	Guaranteed investment contracts	225,000	250,000
	TUH Trust Company	TUH International Fund, 14,000 shares	500,000	600,000
	DEF Bank*	Money market fund	175,000	175,000
	Various participants*	Participant loans, with interest rates ranging form 8.5% to 11% and maturities of 12 months to 120 months	100,000	100,000
			$2,400,000	$3,025,000

* *Party-in-Interest*

ABC Company 401(k) Savings Plan
Schedule G--Part I
Schedule of Loans or Fixed Income Obligations

Column A	*Column B*	*Column C*	*Column D*	*Column E*	*Column F*	*Column G*	*Column H*	*Column I*
	Identity and address of obligor	Original amount of loan	Amt. received during year principal/interest		Unpaid balance at end of year	Detailed description of loan, including dates of making and maturity, interest rate, the type and value of collateral, any renegotiations of the loan, the terms of the renegotiation, and other material items.	Amount principal	Overdue interest
	Various Participants	$10,000	--	--	$7,000	Various participant loans with maturities to 20X7; interest rates ranging from 8.5% to 10.0%	$7,000	$1,000

NOTE: In this case, the participant loans were not secured by the remaining balance in the participants' accounts; therefore, this schedule is required to be completed for the loans in default. If such loans are secured by the balance, this schedule would no longer be required under the new Form 5500.

ABC Company 401(k) Savings Plan
Schedule G--Part III
Schedule of Nonexempt Transactions
Year Ended December 31, 20X1

Identity of party involved	*Relationship to plan, employer or other party-in-interest*	*Description of transactions including date, rate of interest, collateral, par or maturity value*	*Purchase price*	*Selling price*	*Cost of asset*	*Current value of asset*
ABC Company	Plan sponsor	During 20X1, ABC Company failed to remit $50,000 of employee salary deferral contributions to the trustee on a timely basis. The amounts were originally contributed by employees in April 20X1 and deposited with the trustee in August 20X1. ABC Company made a contribution to the Plan during 20X2 in the amount of $16,000 for investment earnings, which were earned by participants from April 20X1 to the date the additional contribution was made by ABC Company.	--	--	$50,000	$50,000

Example B: Defined Contribution Employee Stock Ownership Plan--Leveraged

ABC Company Employee Stock Ownership Plan
Statements of Net Assets Available for Benefits
December 31, 20X1 and 20X0

	20X1			*20X0*		
	Allocated	*Unallocated*	*Total*	*Allocated*	*Unallocated*	*Total*
Assets						
Investments:						
Investment in ABC common stock	$34,890,000	$57,430,000	$92,320,000	$24,568,000	$47,015,000	$71,583,000
Receivables:						
Employer contributions		8,607,000	8,607,000		7,062,000	7,062,000
Dividends & interest	570,000	459,000	1,029,000	280,000	3,000	283,000
Cash & cash equivalents	156,000	863,000	1,019,000	101,000	448,000	549,000
Total assets	35,616,000	67,359,000	102,975,000	24,949,000	54,528,000	79,477,000
Liabilities						
Interest payable		1,396,000	1,396,000		1,033,000	1,033,000
Loan payable		73,970,000	3,970,000		80,000,000	80,000,000
Total liabilities		75,366,000	75,366,000		81,033,000	81,033,000
Net assets available (deficit) for benefits	$35,616,000	$(8,007,000)	$27,609,000	$24,949,000	$(26,505,000)	$(1,556,000)

The columns reflected in the example are appropriate for the presentation of a leveraged ESOP. For a nonleveraged ESOP, the presentation would reflect only the total column without the segregation between allocated and unallocated.

Allocated and unallocated designations distinguish between assets that belong to plan participants and those that are still available as collateral for the ESOP loan. Under ERISA, the lender has access to the securities held by the plan that represent unallocated employer contributions to service the debt, and any earnings on those amounts. Earnings on temporary cash investments also are available to the lender.

An accrued employer contribution for current or future debt service is, therefore, reflected on the statement of net assets available for benefits and the statement of changes in net assets available for benefits in the unallocated column. In contrast, an employer contribution accrued to fund distributions to terminated participants is reflected in the allocated column.

This distinction is not reflected in the participant account balances when reporting to the participant under ERISA. Contributions accrued for future debt service are allocated to the accounts of plan participants.

ABC Company Employee Stock Ownership Plan
Statement of Changes in Net Assets Available for Benefits
Year Ended December 31, 20X1

	Allocated	*Unallocated*	*Total*
Additions:			
Net appreciation in fair value of investments	$9,205,000	$15,052,000	$24,257,000
Dividends	1,380,000	2,184,000	3,564,000
Interest	31,000	58,000	89,000
Employer contributions		11,524,000	11,524,000
Allocation of 142,000 shares of ABC common stock	4,637,000	--	4,637,000
Total additions	15,253,000	28,818,000	44,071,000
Deductions:			
Interest expense		5,683,000	5,683,000
Allocation of 142,000 shares of ABC common stock		4,637,000	4,637,000
Distributions to participants	4,586,000		4,586,000
Total deductions	4,586,000	10,320,000	14,906,000
Net increase	10,667,000	18,498,000	29,165,000
Net assets (deficit) available for benefits beginning of year	24,949,000	(26,505,000)	(1,556,000)
Net assets available for benefits end of year	$35,616,000	$ (8,007,000)	$27,609,000

ABC Company Employee Stock Ownership Plan
Notes to Financial Statements
Years Ended December 31, 20X1 and 20X0

1. **Description of Plan**

   The following brief description of the ABC Company Employee Stock Ownership Plan (the "Plan") is provided for general information purposes only. Participants should refer to the Plan document for more complete information.

   a. **General**--The Plan is a noncontributory leveraged employee stock ownership plan extended to all eligible employees of ABC Company (the "Company"). An employee may become a participant in the Plan upon completion of 1,000 hours of service within a consecutive twelve-month period. The Company's Board of Directors and the plan administrator control and manage the operation and administration of the Plan. A committee of employees appointed by the Board of Directors serves as the Plan's trustee. The Plan is subject to the provisions of the Employee Retirement Income Security Act of 1974 (ERISA).

   b. **Allocation of shares and distributions**

      The Plan purchased Company common shares using the proceeds of a bank borrowing (see Note 6) guaranteed by the Company and holds the stock in a trust established under the Plan. The borrowing is to be repaid over a period of ten years by fully deductible Company contributions to the trust fund. As the

Plan makes each payment of principal, an appropriate percentage of stock will be allocated to eligible employees' accounts in accordance with applicable regulations under the Code. Shares vest fully upon allocation.

The borrowing is collateralized by the unallocated shares of stock and is guaranteed by the Company. The lender has no rights against shares once they are allocated under the ESOP.

Accordingly, the financial statements of the Plan for the years 20X1 and 20X0 present separately the assets and liabilities and changes therein pertaining to

(1) The accounts of employees with vested rights in allocated stock (Allocated) and
(2) Stock not yet allocated to employees (Unallocated). No distributions from the Plan will be made until a participant retires, dies (in which case, payment shall be made to his or her beneficiary or, if none, his or her legal representatives), or otherwise terminates employment with the Company and its participating subsidiaries. Distributions are made in cash or, if a participant elects, in the form of Company common shares plus cash for any fractional shares.

Each participant is entitled to exercise voting rights attributable to the shares allocated to his or her account and is notified by the trustee prior to the time that such rights are to be exercised. The trustee is permitted to vote any share for which instructions have not been given by a participant.

2. **Summary of significant accounting policies**

a. **Use of estimates and risks**--The preparation of financial statements in conformity with generally accepted accounting principles requires Plan management to make estimates and assumptions that affect the reported amounts of assets and liabilities and disclosure of contingent assets and liabilities at the date of the financial statements and the reported amounts of revenues and expenses during the reporting period. Actual results could differ from those estimates.

Investment securities, in general, are exposed to various risks, such as interest rate, credit, and overall market volatility.

Due to the level of risk associated with certain investment securities, it is reasonably possible that changes in the values of investment securities will occur in the near term and that such changes could materially affect the amounts reported in the statements of net assets available for plan benefits.

b. **Investment valuation and income recognition**--The common shares of the Company are valued at fair value on December 31, 20X1 and 20X0. Fair value is determined by monthly independent appraisals. Distributions are made in cash or if a participant elects, in the form of company stock. Distributions are valued and payable to requesting participants at the end of each month. Dividend income is accrued on the ex-dividend date. Purchases and sales of securities are recorded on a trade-date basis. Realized gains and losses from security transactions are reported on the average cost method.

c. **Expenses**--Expenses of the Plan are paid by the Company as provided in the Plan document.

3. **Plan termination**

Although it has not expressed any intention to do so, the Company has the right under the Plan to discontinue its contributions at any time and to terminate the Plan subject to the provisions set forth in the Plan document and ERISA. Should the Plan be terminated, the assets of the Plan would be distributed to the participants based on their individual account balances, as determined under the Plan provisions.

4. **Tax status**

The Internal Revenue Service has determined and informed the Company by a letter dated June 30, 20X0, that the Plan and related trust are designed in accordance with the applicable sections of the Internal Revenue Code (IRC). The Plan has been amended since receiving the determination letter. However, the Company believes that the Plan currently is designed and being operated in compliance with the applicable requirements of the IRC and that, therefore, the Plan continues to qualify under Section 401(a) and the related trust continues to be tax exempt as of December 31, 20X1. Therefore, no provision for income taxes has been included in the Plan's financial statements.

5. **Benefits payable**

As of December 31, 20X1, net assets available for benefits included benefits due to participants who have withdrawn from participation in the Plan of $20,000. There were no benefits payable at December 31, 20X0.

6. **Loan payable**

In 20X0, the plan entered into a $80,000,000 term loan agreement with a bank. The proceeds of the loan were used to purchase the Company's common stock. Unallocated shares are collateral for the loan along with a $5 million line of credit maintained by the Company. The agreement provides for the loan to be repaid over ten years. The scheduled amortization of the loan for the next five years and thereafter is as follows:

20X2	$6,500,000
20X3	7,000,000
20X4	7,500,000
20X5	8,000,000
20X6	8,500,000
Thereafter	$31,470,000

The loan bears interest at the prime rate of the lender. For 20X1 and 20X0, the loan interest rate averaged 7.34% and 5.12%, respectively.

7. **Employer contributions**

The Company is obligated to make contributions in cash to the plan which, when aggregated with the plan's dividends and interest earnings, equal the amount necessary to enable the plan to make its regularly scheduled payments of principal and interest due on its term loan.

8. **Changes in the plan**

The plan was not amended during 20X1 or 20X0.

9. **Party-in-interest transactions**

The Plan has not considered Company contributions to the Plan or benefits paid by the Plan for participants as party-in-interest transactions.

10. **Investments**

The Plan's investments are presented in the following table as of December 31, 20X1 and 20X0:

	20X1		*20X0*	
	Allocated	*Unallocated*	*Allocated*	*Unallocated*
Number of shares	1,069,000	1,759,000	1,074,000	2,055,000
Cost	$27,014,000	$74,456,000	$29,910,000	$80,000,000
Market	$34,890,000	$57,430,000	$24,568,000	$47,015,000

11. **Reconciliation to Form 5500**

The following is a reconciliation of the net assets available for benefits and the benefits paid to participants per the financial statements to the Form 5500 as of and for the year ended December 31, 20X1:

Net assets available for benefits per the financial statements	$27,609,000
Withdrawals currently payable per Form 5500	20,000
Net assets available for benefits per Form 5500	$27,589,000
Withdrawals paid per the financial statements	$ 4,586,000
Amounts currently payable at December 31, 20X1	20,000
Withdrawals paid to participants per Form 5500	$ 4,606,000

HEALTH AND WELFARE PLANS

The following section includes examples of financial statements for health and welfare plans, including a defined benefit health and welfare plan, a supplemental unemployment benefit plan, vacation benefit plan, and a 401(h) plan. The following financial statements have been prepared in accordance with the provisions of AICPA SOP 92-6, *Accounting and Reporting by Health and Welfare Benefit Plans.*

- Example A--Defined benefit health and welfare plan
- Example B--Supplemental unemployment benefit plan
- Example C--Vacation benefit plan
- Example D--401(h) plan

Example A: Defined Benefit Health and Welfare Plan

ABC Company Health Plan
Statements of Net Assets Available for Benefits
December 31, 20X1 and 20X0

	20X1	*20X0*
Assets		
Investments:		
DEF Bank Equity Fund	$1,700,000	$ 900,000
DEF Money Market Fund	300,000	100,000
Total investments	2,000,000	1,000,000
Receivables:		
Employer contributions receivable	100,000	50,000
Interest income receivable	25,000	15,000
Total receivables	125,000	65,000
Total assets	2,125,000	1,065,000

Liabilities		
Administrative expenses payable	25,000	20,000
Net assets available for benefits	$2,100,000	$1,045,000

See notes to financial statements.

ABC Company Health Plan
Statement of Changes in Net Assets Available for Benefits
Year Ended December 31, 20X1

Additions:	
Net appreciation in fair value of investments	$190,000
Interest income	50,000
Total investment income	240,000
Contributions:	
Participant contributions	600,000
Employer contributions--net	600,000
Total contributions	1,200,000
Total additions	1,440,000
Deductions:	
Benefit payments	300,000
Administrative expenses	85,000
Total deductions	385,000
Net increase	1,055,000
Net assets available for benefits, beginning of year	1,045,000
Net assets available for benefits, end of year	$2,100,000

See notes to financial statements.

ABC Company Health Plan
Statements of Plan Benefit Obligations
December 31, 20X1 and 20X0

	20X1	*20X0*
Amounts currently payable to or for participants, beneficiaries, and dependents--Claims payable	$150,000	$140,000
Other obligations for current benefit coverage, at present value of estimated amounts:		
Claims incurred but not reported	40,000	30,000
Total obligations other than post retirement benefit obligations	190,000	170,000
Postretirement benefit obligations:		
Retirees	2,500,000	2,000,000
Fully eligible active participants	1,300,000	1,500,000
Participants not yet eligible	1,500,000	1,700,000
Total	5,300,000	5,200,000
Plan's total benefit obligations	$5,490,000	$5,370,000

See notes to financial statements.

NOTE: According to the provisions of SOP 92-6, in many instances combining claims currently payable and claims incurred but not reported is allowable. See paragraph .41 of SOP 92-6.

ABC Company Health Plan
Statement of Changes in Plan Benefit Obligations
Year Ended December 31, 20X1

Amounts currently payable to or for participants, beneficiaries, and dependents:	
Balance at beginning of year	$ 140,000
Claims reported and approved	310,000
Claims paid	(300,000)
Balance at end of year	$ 150,000
Other obligations for current benefit coverage, at present value of estimated amounts:	
Balance at beginning of year	30,000
Net change in claims incurred but not reported	10,000
Balance at end of year	40,000
Total obligations for current benefit coverage	190,000
Postretirement benefit obligations:	
Balance at beginning of year	5,200,000
Decrease during year attributed to:	
Benefits earned	500,000
Plan amendments	(400,000)
Total	5,300,000
Plan's total benefit obligations	$5,490,000

See notes to financial statements.

NOTE: If the claims currently payable and claims incurred but not reported are combined in one line on the Statement of Plan Benefit Obligations, then the amounts may also be combined on the Statement of Changes in Plan Benefit Obligations. The "balance at the beginning of the year" would combine the opening balance for each type of claim and a separate line item would report the net change in claims incurred but not reported, the actual claims reported and approved, and the actual claims paid during the year. The "balance at the end of the year" would combine the ending liability balance for each type of claim.

ABC Company Health Plan
Notes to Financial Statements
Years Ended December 31, 20X1 and 20X0

1. **Description of Plan**

   a. **General**--The following brief description of the ABC Company Health Plan (the "Plan") is provided for general information purposes only. Participants should refer to the Plan document for additional information.

      The Plan provides various health care benefits for current and retired employees of ABC Company (the "Company"). The Company's Employee Benefit Committee and the Plan Administrator control and manage the operation and administration of the Plan. DEF Bank serves as the trustee of the Plan and manages the Plan's investment assets. The Plan is subject to the provisions of the Employee Retirement Income Security Act of 1974 (ERISA).

   b. **Benefits**--The principal benefits provided under the Plan include medical, dental, vision, prescription drug, mental health, and chemical dependency benefits. Benefit payments are processed by third-party administrators. The third-party administrators process claims submitted by participants and determine the benefits to be paid based on the provisions of the Plan. Participants are responsible for the payment of copays, the amount of which varies depending upon the nature of the medical service provided. Benefits are paid directly to participants, or applicable medical providers, from disbursing accounts maintained by the third-party administrators or from the Plan's bank account. The Company instructs DEF Bank to transfer funds from the trust to reimburse the various disbursing accounts.

c. **Eligibility**--Substantially all salaried and hourly employees who have completed 1000 hours of service with the Company are eligible to participate in the Plan. Dependent coverage also becomes available to eligible employees. Retired employees who satisfy the definition of a retiree, as stated in the Plan document, qualify for all of the benefits provided under the Plan.

d. **Contributions**--The Company funds the Plan for benefit claims submitted by active and retired participants to the third-party administrators which are in excess of participant contributions.

2. **Summary of significant accounting policies**

a. **Investments**--Investments consist of an investment in the DEF Bank Equity Fund, which is presented at fair value based upon the fair value of the underlying investments of the equity fund and an investment in the DEF Money Market fund, which is presented at fair value.

b. **Expenses**--The Plan's expenses are paid by either the Plan or the Company, as provided by the Plan document.

3. **Benefit obligations**

a. **Postretirement benefits**--The postretirement benefit obligation represents the actuarial present value of those estimated future benefits that are attributed to employee service rendered to December 31, 20X1 and 20X0. Postretirement benefits include future benefits to be paid to or for (1) currently retired or terminated employees and their beneficiaries and dependents and (2) active employees and their beneficiaries and dependents after retirement from service with the Company. Prior to an active employee's full eligibility date, the postretirement benefit obligation is the portion of the expected postretirement benefit obligation that is attributed to that employee's service rendered to the valuation date.

The actuarial present value of the expected postretirement benefit obligation is determined by an actuary and is the amount that results from applying actuarial assumptions to historical claims cost data to estimate future annual incurred claims costs per participant, and to adjust such estimates for the time value of money (through discounts for interest) and the probability of payment (by means of decrements such as those for death, disability, withdrawal, or retirement) between the valuation date and the expected date of payment.

For measurement purposes, health care cost trend rates were assumed to be 7% for 20X2 and to gradually decrease to 5% in the year 2012 and remain at that level thereafter. All of the assumptions in the 20X1 valuation are the same as in the previous valuation. The following were other significant assumptions used in the valuations as of December 31, 20X1, and 20X0:

- Retirement rates vary by age and service for various groups of employees and divisional locations.

- Mortality assumptions were primarily based on the UP-1984 Mortality Table with certain modifications made for various groups.

The foregoing assumptions are based on the presumption that the Plan will continue. Were the Plan to terminate, different actuarial assumptions, and other factors might be applicable in determining the actuarial present value of the postretirement benefit obligations.

The Plan's deficiency of net assets over benefit obligations at December 31, 20X1, and 20X0 relates primarily to the postretirement benefit obligation, the funding of which is not entirely covered by the contribution rate provided by the current funding vehicle. It is expected that the deficiency will be funded through future increases in the contribution rates from the Company.

The weighted-average health care cost trend rate assumption has a significant effect on the amounts reported in the accompanying financial statements. If the assumed rate increased by one percentage point in each year, it would increase the obligations as of December 31, 20X1 and 20X0, by $1,000,000 and $2,000,000, respectively.

b. **Other benefit obligations**--Benefit claims currently payable include the Plan's liability for claims incurred as of December 31, 20X1 and 20X0, but not reported, and the Plan's liability for claims reported as of December 31, 20X1 and 20X0, but not yet processed. The Plan's liability for claims incurred but not reported is estimated by the third-party administrators utilizing actuarial methods which take into consideration prior claim experience and the expected time period from the date such claims are incurred to the date that the related claims are submitted and paid.

4. **Use of estimates and risks**

The preparation of financial statements in conformity with generally accepted accounting principles requires Plan management to make estimates and assumptions that affect the reported amounts of assets, liabilities, benefit obligations, and disclosure of contingent assets and liabilities at the date of the financial statements. Actual results could differ from those estimates.

The Plan utilizes, through participation in the DEF Equity Fund, various investment instruments including short-term investments, US government securities, corporate debt instruments, corporate stocks, pooled separate accounts, and common/collective trust accounts. Investment securities, in general, are exposed to various risks, such as interest rate, credit, and overall market volatility. Due to the level of risk associated with certain investment securities, it is reasonably possible that changes in the values of investment securities will occur in the near term and that such changes could materially affect the amounts reported in the statements of net assets available for plan benefits.

5. **Tax status**

The Internal Revenue Service has determined and informed the Company by a letter dated June 30, 20X0, that the Plan and related trust are designed in accordance with applicable sections of the Internal Revenue Code (IRC). The Plan has been amended since receiving the determination letter. However, the Company believes that the Plan currently is designed and being operated in compliance with the applicable requirements of the IRC and that, therefore, the Plan continues to qualify under Section 401(a) and the related trust continues to be tax-exempt as of December 31, 20X1. Therefore, no provision for income taxes has been included in the Plan's financial statements.

6. **Plan termination**

The Plan may be amended at any time and in any manner by the Company. Although the Company intends to continue the Plan indefinitely, it reserves the right to terminate all or part of the Plan at any time and cancel all or part of the coverage and benefits under the Plan for current and future employees or retirees. In no event shall the Company cause any portion of the Plan's assets to be used for purposes other than for the exclusive benefit of participants and their beneficiaries nor may any portion of the Plan's assets become the property of the Company.

7. **Changes in the plan**

Effective June 1, 20X1, the Company introduced medical plan changes made to the cost-sharing arrangement between the Company and the employees through increases in employee deductibles, coinsurance, and out-of-pocket maximums for the indemnity plans. These changes increased the contributions which will be required to be made by participants of the Plan. This amendment decreased the plan's postretirement benefit obligations by $400,000. This amount is reflected in the plan's statement of changes in benefit obligations for the year ended December 31, 20X1.

Example B: Supplemental Unemployment Benefit Plan

The following section provides an example of a supplemental unemployment benefit plan set of financial statements.

ABC Company
Supplemental Unemployment Benefit Plan
Statements of Net Assets Available for Benefits
December 31, 20X1 and 20X0

	20X1	*20X0*
Assets		
US treasury obligations	$150,000	$100,000
Cash	1,000	2,000
Income receivable	2,000	1,000
Total assets	153,000	103,000
Liabilities		
Administrative expenses payable	3,000	2,500
Net assets available for benefits	$150,000	$100,500

See notes to financial statements.

ABC Company
Supplemental Unemployment Benefit Plan
Statement of Changes in Net Assets Available for Benefits
Year Ended December 31, 20X2

Additions:	
Employer contributions	$90,000
Interest income	8,000
Total additions	98,000
Deductions:	
Benefit payments	40,000
Administrative expenses	8,500
Total deductions	48,500

Net increase	49,500
Net assets available for benefits, beginning of year	100,500
Net assets available for benefits, end of year	$150,000

See notes to financial statements.

ABC Company
Supplemental Unemployment Benefit Plan
Statements of Benefit Obligations
December 31, 20X1 and 20X0

	20X1	*20X0*
Benefit obligations payable to or for participants beneficiaries and dependents:		
Benefits currently payable	$ 50,000	$ 40,000
Long-term benefits payable	570,000	550,000
Plan's total benefit obligations	$620,000	$590,000

See notes to financial statements.

ABC Company
Supplemental Unemployment Benefit Plan
Statement of Changes in Benefit Obligations
Year Ended December 31, 20X1

Benefit obligations:	
Beginning of year	$590,000
Benefits earned	70,000
Claims paid	(40,000)
Plan's total benefit obligations	$620,000

See notes to financial statements.

ABC Company
Supplemental Unemployment Benefit Plan
Notes to Financial Statements
Years Ended December 31, 20X1 and 20X0

1. **Description of Plan**

a. **General**--The ABC Company Supplemental Unemployment Benefit Plan (the "Plan") is a welfare benefit plan for factory employees of ABC Company (the "Company") covered by a collective bargaining agreement between the Company and the United Steel Workers of America (the "Union"). The Plan provides benefits to covered employees who are provided less than thirty-six hours of work per week.

b. **Participation**--All Company employees who belong to the Union and have been employed by the Company for at least two years participate in the Plan.

c. **Administration**--A trustee appointed by the Company maintains a fund to receive and invest contributions made by the Company and to pay benefits and expenses of the Plan. Under that Plan and trust agreement, XYZ Bank (the "trustee") invests contributions and trust assets in obligations issued or guaranteed by the United States Government or other appropriate securities approved by the Company.

d. **Contributions, funding, and benefits**--The Company contributes to the fund $.05 per hour worked by each Plan participant based upon a formula provided in the collective bargaining agreement. Any contributions required by the formula are determined monthly and paid to the Plan in the subsequent month. Plan benefits are based upon eligible employees' hourly earnings and state unemployment benefits. The Plan provides for the payment of weekly or short-week supplemental unemployment benefits. The benefits payable are reduced by any state unemployment benefits or any other compensation received. The amount of full-or short-week benefit is determined according to a formula contained in the Plan and, depending upon length of service, may continue for up to fifty-two weeks. Benefits paid for any week for which the employee received state unemployment benefits are limited to $85 plus an additional $2.50 for each dependent up to a maximum of four dependents. Benefits paid for all other weeks are limited to $108 plus an additional $2.50 for each dependent up to a maximum of four dependents.

e. **Termination priorities**--The Plan assets remaining upon termination will be used to pay trustee expenses and benefits to eligible participants on layoff in the order in which they were laid off and cannot revert to the Plan sponsor.

2. **Summary of significant accounting policies**

a. **Basis of accounting**--The accounting records of the Plan are maintained on the accrual basis.

b. **Investments and investment income**--Investments are stated at quoted market value. Purchases and sales of securities are recorded as of the settlement date. Investment income is recorded on the accrual basis.

c. **Expenses**--Expenses are paid by the Plan in accordance with the provisions of the Plan document.

3. **Use of estimates and risks**

The preparation of the financial statements in conformity with generally accepted accounting principles requires Plan management to make estimates and assumptions that affect the reported amounts of Plan assets, liabilities, and benefit obligations and the disclosure of contingent assets and liabilities at the date of the financial statements. Actual results could differ from those estimates.

The Plan utilizes investment instruments including US government securities that, in general, are exposed to various risks, such as interest rate, credit, and overall market volatility. Due to the level of risk associated with certain investment securities, it is reasonably possible that changes in the values of investment securities will occur in the near term and that such changes could materially affect the amounts reported in the statements of net assets available for plan benefits.

4. **Tax status**

The Internal Revenue Service has determined and informed the Company by a letter dated June 30, 20X0, that the Plan and related trust are designed in accordance with applicable sections of the Internal Revenue Code (IRC). The Plan has been amended since receiving the determination letter. However, the Company believes that the Plan currently is designed and being operated in compliance with the applicable requirements of the IRC and that, therefore, the Plan continues to qualify under Section 401(a) and the related trust continues to be tax exempt as of December 31, 20X1. Therefore, no provision for income taxes has been included in the Plan's financial statements.

5. **Party-in-interest transactions**

   The Plan has not considered Company contributions to the Plan or benefits accrued for or paid by the Plan for participants as party-in-interest transactions.

6. **Changes in the plan**

   The Plan was not amended during 20X1 or 20X0.

Example C: Vacation Benefit Plan

This section provides an example of a set of financial statements for a vacation benefit plan.

ABC Company
Vacation Benefit Plan
Statements of Net Assets Available for Benefits
December 31, 20X1 and 20X0

	20X1	*20X0*
Assets		
US treasury obligations	$500,000	$400,000
Certificates of deposit	427,500	250,000
Total assets and net assets available for benefits	$927,500	$650,000

See notes to financial statements.

ABC Company
Vacation Benefit Plan
Statement of Changes in Net Assets Available for Benefits
Year Ended December 31, 20X1

Additions:	
Interest income	$ 20,000
Employer contributions	800,000
Total additions	820,000
Deductions:	
Payments for vacation benefits	542,500
Net increase	277,500
Net assets available for benefits, beginning of year	650,000
Net assets available for benefits, end of year	$927,500

See notes to financial statements.

ABC Company
Vacation Benefit Plan
Statements of Benefit Obligations
December 31, 20X1 and 20X0

	20X1	*20X0*
Amounts currently payable to or for participants, beneficiaries and dependents:		
Vacation benefits payable	$775,000	$530,000
Plan's total benefit obligations	$775,000	$530,000

See notes to financial statements.

ABC Company
Vacation Benefit Plan
Statement of Changes in Benefit Obligations
Year Ended December 31, 20X1

Benefit obligations currently payable to participants, beneficiaries and dependents:	
Beginning of year	$530,000
Vacation benefits earned	787,500
Vacation benefits paid	(542,500)
Plan's total benefit obligation, end of year	$775,000

See notes to financial statements.

ABC Company
Vacation Benefit Plan
Notes to Financial Statements
Years Ended December 31, 20X1 and 20X0

1. **Description of Plan**

   a. **General**--The following description of the ABC Company Vacation Benefit Plan (the "Plan") provides only general information. Participants should refer to the Plan document for a more complete description of the Plan's provisions.

   b. **Participation**--The Plan covers all employees of the ABC Company (the "Company") who have completed one year of service with the Company and have attained the age of twenty-one.

   c. **Contributions and benefits**--The Company contributes to the Plan $.50 for each hour worked by Plan participants. Vacation benefits are paid to participants when the participants elect to take vacation time.

2. **Summary of accounting policies**

   a. **Use of estimates and risks**--The preparation of the financial statements in conformity with generally accepted accounting principles requires Plan management to make estimates and assumptions that affect the reported amounts of Plan assets, liabilities, and benefit obligations at the date of the financial statements and the disclosure of contingent assets and liabilities. Actual results could differ from those estimates.

      The Plan utilizes investment instruments including US government securities and certificates of deposit. Investment securities, in general, are exposed to various risks, such as interest rate, credit, and overall market volatility. Due to the level of risk associated with certain investment securities, it is reasonably possible, that changes in the values of investment securities will occur in the near term and that such changes could materially affect the amounts reported in the statements of net assets available for plan benefits.

   b. **Valuation of investments**--Investments are valued at fair value as of the end of the plan year based upon quoted market prices.

   c. **Expenses**--Expenses of the Plan are paid by the Company as provided by the Plan document.

3. **Tax status**

The trust is established under the Plan to hold the Plan's assets is qualified pursuant to the appropriate section of the Internal Revenue Code, and, accordingly, the trust's net investment income is exempt from income taxes. The trust has obtained a favorable tax determination letter from the Internal Revenue Service and the Company believes that the trust continues to qualify and to operate as designed.

Example D: 401(h) Plan

The following provides an example of the financial statements for a 401(h) health and welfare plan. The example is exerpted from the AICPA's *Audit of Employee Benefits Plans*. The footnotes to the plan's financial statements provide only those footnotes which are unique to a 401(h) plan.

C&H Company Welfare Benefit Plan
Statement of Changes in Net Assets Available for Plan Benefits
Year Ended December 31, 20X1

Additions:	
Contributions:	
Employer contributions	$15,000,000
Employee contributions	3,000,000
Total contributions	18,000,000
Investment income:	
Net appreciation in fair value of investments	300,000
Interest	500,000
Dividends	50,000
Total investment income	850,000
Less investment expense	15,000
Net investment income	835,000
Net increase in 401(h) account	106,000
Total additions	18,941,000
Deductions:	
Benefits paid directly to participants:	
Health care	16,000,000
Disability and death	770,000
Total benefits paid	16,770,000
Administrative expenses	180,000
Total deductions	16,950,000
Net increase during the year	1,991,000
Net assets available for benefits, beginning of year	7,566,000
Net assets available for benefits, end of year	$ 9,557,000

The accompanying notes are an integral part of the financial statements.

C&H Welfare Benefit Plan
Statement of Benefit Obligations

	December 31, 20X1 and 20X0	
Amounts currently payable to or for participants, beneficiaries, and dependents:		
Health claims payable	$ 1,100,000	$ 975,000
Death and disability benefits payable	100,000	75,000
Total amounts currently payable	1,200,000	1,050,000

	December 31, 20X1	and 20X0
Other obligations for current benefit coverage, at present value of estimated amounts:		
Claims incurred but not reported	425,000	390,000
Long-term disability benefits	925,000	610,000
Total other obligations for current benefit coverage	1,350,000	1,000,000
Total obligations other than postretirement benefit obligations	2,550,000	2,050,000
Postretirement benefit obligations:		
Current retirees	3,900,000	3,500,000
Other participants fully eligible for benefits	2,100,000	2,000,000
Other participants not yet fully eligible for benefits	5,000,000	4,165,000
Total postretirement benefit obligations	11,000,000	9,665,000
Plan's total benefit obligations	$13,550,000	$11,715,000

The accompanying notes are an integral part of the financial statements.

C&H Company Welfare Benefit Plan
Statement of Changes in Benefit Obligations
Year Ended December 31, 20X1

Amounts currently payable to or for participants, beneficiaries, and dependents:	
Balance, beginning of year	$ 1,050,000
Claims reported and approved for payment	16,930,000
Claims paid (including disability)	(16,770,000)
Claims paid through 401(h) account	(10,000)
Balance, end of year	1,200,000
Other obligations for current benefit coverage, at present value of estimated amounts:	
Balance, beginning of year	1,000,000
Net change during year:	
Long-term disability benefits	315,000
Other	35,000
Balance, end of year	1,350,000
Total obligations other than postretirement benefit obligations	2,550,000
Postretirement benefit obligations:	
Balance, beginning of year	9,665,000
Increase (decrease) during the year attributable to:	
Benefits earned and other changes	1,250,000
Plan amendment	(175,000)
Changes in actuarial assumptions	260,000
Balance, end of year	11,000,000
Plan's total benefit obligations, end of year	$13,550,000

The accompanying notes are an integral part of the financial statements.

Notes To Financial Statements

A. **401(h) Account**

Effective January 1, 19X0, the C&H Company's defined benefit pension plan was amended to include a medical-benefit component in addition to normal retirement benefits to fund a portion of the postretirement obligations for retirees and their beneficiaries in accordance with Section 401(h) of the Internal Revenue Code (IRC). A separate account has been established and maintained in the defined benefit pension plan for such contributions. In accordance with IRC Section 401(h), the

Plan's investments in the 401(h) account may not be used for, or diverted to, any purpose other than providing health benefits for retirees and their beneficiaries. The related obligations for health benefits are not included in the [defined benefit pension plan's] obligations in the statement of accumulated plan benefits but are reported as obligations in the financial statements of the C&H health and welfare benefit plan.

E. **401(h) Account**

A portion of the Plan's obligations are funded through contributions to the Company's defined benefit pension plan in accordance with IRC Section 401(h). The following table presents the components of the net assets available for such obligations and the related changes in net assets available.

Net Assets Available for Postretirement Health and Welfare Benefits in 401(h) Account

	December 31,	
	20X1	*20X0*
Investments at fair value:		
US government securities	$ 140,000	$150,000
Money market fund	900,000	800,000
	1,040,000	950,000
Cash	20,000	10,000
Employer's contribution receivable[2]	20,000	15,000
Accrued interest	7,000	6,000
Total assets	1,087,000	981,000
Accrued administrative expenses	(15,000)	(15,000)
Net assets available	$1,072,000	$966,000

[2] *A receivable from the employer must meet the requirements of paragraph 10 of FASB Statement No. 35,* ***Accounting and Reporting by Defined Benefit Pension Plans****.*

Changes in Net Assets in 401(h) Account For the Year Ended December 31, 20X1

Net appreciation in fair value of investments:	
US government securities	$ 10,800
Interest	80,200
	91,000
Employer contributions	40,000
Health and welfare benefits paid to retirees	(10,000)
Administrative expenses	(15,000)
Net increase in net assets available	$106,000

H. **Reconciliation of Financial Statements to Form 5500[3]**

The following is a reconciliation of net assets available for benefits per the financial statements to Form 5500:

Net assets available for benefits per the financial statements	$9,557,000
Claims payable	(1,200,000)
Net assets held in defined benefit plan-401(h) account	(1,072,000)
Net assets available for benefits per Form 5500	$7,285,000

The following is a reconciliation of claims paid per the financial statements and net investment income related to the changes in the investments of the 401(h) assets to Form 5500:

Claims paid per the financial statements	$16,770,000
Add: Amounts payable at December 31, 20X1	1,200,000
Less: Amounts payable at December 31, 20X0	(1,050,000)
Claims paid per Form 5500	$16,920,000
Net investment income per the financial statements	835,000
Less: Net investment income related to the changes in the investments of the 401(h) assets	91,000
Net investment income per Form 5500	$ 744,000

[3] *The reconciliation of amounts reported in plan financial statements to amounts reported in Form 5500 is required by ERISA.*

MULTIEMPLOYER PLAN

The following provides an example of a set of financial statements for a defined benefit multiemployer-sponsored pension plan.

Local 25 IBEW Pension Plan
Statements of Net Assets Available for Benefits
December 31, 20X1, and 20X0

	20X1	*20X0*
Assets		
Investments:		
Investment in guaranteed insurance contracts	$ 750,000	$500,000
Investment in mutual funds	500,000	350,000
Total investments	1,250,000	850,000
Employers' contributions receivable--net of allowance for doubtful accounts of $50,000 and $20,000 at December 31, 20X1, and 20X0, respectively	200,000	100,000
Total assets	1,450,000	950,000
Liabilities		
Administrative expenses payable	10,000	8,000
Net assets available for benefits	$1,440,000	$942,000

See notes to financial statements.

Local 25 IBEW Pension Plan
Statement of Changes in Net Assets Available for Benefits
Year Ended December 31, 20X1

Additions:	
Net appreciation in fair value of investments	$ 80,000
Interest income	70,000
Total investment income	150,000
Employers' contributions	658,000
Total additions	808,000

Deductions:	
Benefit payments	255,000
Administrative expenses	55,000
Total deductions	310,000
Net increase	498,000
Net assets available for benefits, beginning of year	942,000
Net assets available for benefits, end of year	$1,440,000

See notes to financial statements.

Local 25 IBEW Pension Plan
Notes to Financial Statements
Years Ended December 31, 20X1 and 20X0

1. **Description of Plan**

The following brief description of the Local 25 IBEW Pension Plan (the "Plan") is provided for general information purposes only. Participants should refer to the Plan document for more complete information.

a. **General**--The Plan was established under an agreement between the Local 25 IBEW Labor Union and the Contractors' Association (the "Employers"). The Plan is a noncontributory defined benefit plan which provides for retirement, early retirement, and disability benefits covering all members of the IBEW 25 labor union (the "Union") employed under the terms of the collective bargaining agreement with the members of the Contractors' Association. XYZ Bank serves as the trustee of the Plan, and together with several investment managers, manages the Plan's investments. The Plan is subject to the provisions of the Employee Retirement Income Security Act of 1974 (ERISA).

b. **Pension benefits**--Participants become fully vested after five years of vesting service, as defined by the Plan. There is no partial vesting of benefits. Benefits are payable in the form of a joint-and-survivor annuity or single-life annuity. The amount of benefits payable upon retirement is contingent upon the number of years of service and the benefit rate in effect at the time of retirement.

2. **Summary of significant accounting policies**

a. **Basis of accounting**--The financial statements of the Plan are prepared on the accrual basis of accounting.

b. **Valuation of investments**--The Plan's interest in the mutual fund represents its investment in the XYZ Bank Mutual Fund. The Plan's investment in the mutual fund is presented at fair value, which has been determined based on the fair value of the underlying investments of the mutual fund. The Plan's insurance contract with HK Insurance Company is valued at fair value by discounting the related cash flows based on current yields of similar instruments with similar maturities. Purchases and sales of securities are recorded on a trade-date basis.

c. **Expenses of the Plan**--Expenses of the Plan are paid by the Plan in accordance with the provisions of the Plan document.

3. **Actuarial present value of accumulated plan benefits**

Accumulated plan benefits are those future periodic payments, including lump-sum distributions, that are attributable under the Plan's provisions to the service employees have rendered. Accumulated plan benefits include benefits expected to be paid to (1) retired or terminated employees or their beneficiaries, (2) beneficiaries of employees who have died, and (3) present employees or their beneficiaries. The actuarial present value of accumulated plan benefits has been determined by an independent actuary, and is an amount which results from applying actuarial assumptions to adjust the accumulated plan benefits to reflect the time value of money (through discounts for interest) and the probability of payment (by means of decrements such as for death, disability, withdrawal, or retirement) between the actuarial valuation date and the expected date of payment. The effect of Plan amendments on accumulated plan benefits is recognized in the year in which such amendments are effective.

The more significant assumptions underlying the actuarial computations as of December 31, 20X1 and 20X0, are as follows:

Retirement	*Investment Return*	*Mortality*
Average retirement age--65	8% per annum, compounded annually	1983 Group Annuity Mortality Table

The foregoing actuarial assumptions are based on the presumption that the Plan will continue. Were the Plan to terminate, different actuarial assumptions and other factors might be applicable in determining the actuarial present value of accumulated plan benefits.

During 20X1 certain amendments to the plan became effective which increased accumulated plan benefits by $220,000. See Note 10 for additional information.

At December 31, 20X1, the actuarial present value of accumulated plan benefits was as follows:

Vested Benefits:	
Participants currently receiving benefit payments	$1,500,000
Other participants	500,000
Total vested benefits	2,000,000
Nonvested benefits	300,000
Total actuarial present value of accumulated plan benefits	$2,300,000

The changes in the actuarial present value of accumulated plan benefits for the year ended December 31, 20X1, are as follows:

Actuarial present value of accumulated plan benefits, beginning of year	$1,800,000
Increase (decrease) during the year attributable to:	
Increase in interest due to decrease in the discount period	144,000
Benefits accumulated--net	391,000
Benefits paid	(255,000)
Plan amendments	220,000
Net increase	500,000
Actuarial present value of accumulated plan benefits, end of year	$2,300,000

4. **Use of estimates**

The preparation of financial statements in conformity with generally accepted accounting principles requires management to make estimates and assumptions that affect the reported amounts of assets, liabilities, accumulated plan benefit information, and disclosure of contingent assets and liabilities at the date of the financial statements. Actual results could differ from those estimates.

5. **Concentration and credit risk**

The plan utilizes, through participation in mutual funds and other investments, various investment instruments, including short-term investments, US government securities, corporate debt instruments, corporate stocks, and insurance contracts. Investment securities, in general, are exposed to various risks, such as interest rate, credit, and overall market volatility. Due to the level of risk associated with certain investment securities, it is reasonably possible that changes in the values of investment securities will occur in the near term and that such changes could materially affect the amounts reported in the statements of net assets available for plan benefits.

The Plan's participants are primarily members of a labor organization employed by construction contractors in the electrical industry. In the event of a construction reduction, a significant decline in contributors could occur, and the amount of contributions to the Plan could materially decrease. Contribution accounts receivables from employers could be impaired.

6. **Funding policy**

Contributions to provide benefits under the Plan are made solely by the employers. The funding policy is to make cash contributions to the Plan in amounts computed by the Plan's actuary using the unit credit actuarial cost method. This method and the actuarial assumptions referred to above have been designed to provide sufficient funds to pay benefits as they become payable under the Plan. The employers met the minimum funding requirements of ERISA in both 20X1 and 20X0.

7. **Plan termination**

In the event the Plan is terminated, the net assets of the Plan will be allocated for payment of Plan benefits to the participants in an order of priority determined in accordance with ERISA, applicable regulations thereunder and the Plan document.

Certain benefits under the Plan are insured by the Pension Benefit Guaranty Corporation (PBGC) if the Plan terminates. Generally, the PBGC guarantees most vested normal age retirement benefits, early retirement benefits, and certain disability and survivor's pensions. However, the PBGC does not guarantee all types of benefits under the Plan, and the amount of benefit protection is subject to certain limitations. Vested benefits under the Plan are guaranteed at the level in effect on the date of the Plan's termination, subject to a statutory ceiling on the amount of an individual's monthly benefit.

Whether all participants receive their benefits, should the Plan be terminated at some future time, will depend on the sufficiency, at that time, of the Plan's net assets to provide those benefits, the priority of those benefits to be paid, and the level and type of benefits guaranteed by the PBGC at that time. Some benefits may be fully or partially provided for by the then-existing assets and the PBGC guaranty while other benefits may not be provided for at all.

8. **Tax status**

The Internal Revenue Service has determined and informed the employers by a letter dated June 30, 20X0, the Plan and related trust are designed in accordance with applicable sections of the Internal Revenue Code (IRC). The Plan has been amended since receiving the determination letter.

However, the Employers believe that the Plan currently is designed and being operated in compliance with the applicable requirements of the IRC and that, therefore, the Plan continues to qualify under Section 401(a) and the related trust continues to be tax-exempt as of December 31, 20X1. Therefore, no provision for income taxes has been included in the Plan's financial statements.

9. **Party-in-interest transactions**

   The Plan has not considered Company contributions to the Plan or benefits accrued for or paid by the Plan for participants as party-in-interest transactions.

10. **Plan amendments**

    Effective July 1, 20X1, the Plan was amended to provide for an increase in the monthly benefits payable to participants retiring on or after July 1, 20X1, from $20 per year of credited service to $25 per year of credited service. This amendment increased accumulated plan by $220,000. This has been reflected in the accumulated plan benefits as of December 31, 20X1.

ADDITIONAL FINANCIAL STATEMENT DISCLOSURES

The purpose of this section is to provide examples of footnote disclosures which represent some of the more unusual situations that may be encountered during the audit of an employee benefit plan.

Going Concern Situation

The following footnote disclosure would be appropriate in circumstances where the plan sponsor is facing a going-concern situation, and there is no anticipated impact upon the plan at this time.

> The Plan's financial statements for the year ended December 31, 20X2, have been prepared assuming that the Plan and the Company will continue as a going concern. The Company has incurred significant losses over the past several years primarily due to increased competition. The extent of these losses raises substantial doubt as to the going concern of the Company. The Company has made all required contributions to the Plan and has no intent to terminate the Plan. These financial statements do not include any adjustments that might result from the outcome of this uncertainty.

Funding Deficiencies

The following footnote disclosure would be appropriate in circumstances where a defined benefit pension plan has failed to meet the ERISA minimum funding requirements during the plan year.

> Contributions to provide benefits under the Plan are made solely by the Company. The Company's funding policy is to make cash contributions to the Plan in amounts computed by the Plan's actuary using the entry age normal cost method. This method and the actuarial assumptions referred to above have been designed to provide sufficient funds to pay benefits as they become payable under the Plan. The Company has not met the minimum funding requirements of ERISA in 20X2. The Company plans to make additional contributions during 20X3 to satisfy the 20X2 funding requirements. The Company has received approval from the IRS to satisfy the 20X2 funding requirements during 20X3. The Company met the minimum funding requirements of ERISA in 19X1.

Tax Status

The following footnote disclosures provide examples of a tax status footnote: (a) where the plan administrator has not yet requested a determination letter for the plan (Example A) and (b) where the plan has entered into a Voluntary Compliance Program sponsored by either the IRS or DOL (Example B).

Example A

The Company has not yet requested a determination letter for the Plan. However, the Company believes that the Plan currently is designed and being operated in compliance with the applicable requirements of the IRC and that, therefore, the Plan continues to qualify under Section 401(a) and the related trust continues to be tax exempt as of December 31, 20X2. Therefore, no provision for income taxes has been included in the Plan's financial statements.

Example B

The IRS has determined and informed the Company by a letter dated June 30, 20X1, that the Plan and related trust are designed in accordance with applicable sections of the IRC. The Plan has been amended since receiving the determination letter.

The Plan was not timely amended to bring it into compliance with the requirements of the Tax Reform Act of 1986. The Company voluntarily requested to correct the defect under the Closing Agreement Program of the IRS. Under this program, the Company and the IRS entered into a signed closing agreement in which the IRS concluded that it will treat the Plan as having been amended for the purposes of the Tax Reform Act of 1986.

Prohibited Transactions

The following footnote disclosure provides an example of a prohibited transaction which the plan entered into during the plan year.

During 20X1, the Company failed to remit certain employee salary deferral contributions in the amount of approximately $50,000 to the trustee, DEF Bank, in accordance with the DOL's rules regarding the timeliness of depositing such employee contributions. The amounts were originally contributed by participants during April 20X1 and subsequently deposited with the trustee during August 20X1. The Company contributed an amount of $16,000 to the plan during 20X2, which represented the investment income that would have been earned by the participants had their contributions been deposited with the trustee on a timely basis.

Reconciliation of Financial Statements to the Form 5500

The following footnote disclosure provides an example of a situation when there are differences between the plan's financial statements and Form 5500 which require a reconciling footnote to be added to the plan's financial statements.

The following is a reconciliation of the net assets available for benefits and the benefits paid to participants per the financial statements to the Form 5500 as of and for the year ended December 31, 20X2:

Net assets available for benefits per the financial statements	$ 5,000,000
Withdrawals currently payable per the Form 5500	20,000
Net assets available for benefits per the Form 5500	$ 4,980,000
Withdrawals paid per the financial statements	$ 1,000,000
Amounts currently payable at December 31, 20X2	20,000
Withdrawals paid to participants per the Form 5500	$1,020,000

Plan Merger

The following footnote disclosure would be appropriate for a plan merger.

Effective December 31, 20X2, the Plan merged into the ABC Retirement Plan for Salaried Employees ("Salaried Plan"). Assets of approximately $3.5 million and accumulated plan benefit obligations of approximately $3.2 million were transferred to the Salaried Plan on December 31, 20X2. The benefits provided under the Salaried Plan are comparable to those provided under the Plan.

Plan Termination

The following footnote disclosure would be appropriate for a plan which has been terminated.

Effective January 1, 20X2, the Board of Directors approved the termination of the Plan. Benefits continued to accrued through March 1, 20X2. As of December 31, 20X2, the final distribution of plan assets to participants had been completed. The Company has introduced the ABC Company Savings Plan, with an effective date of January 1, 20X3, to replace the Plan.

APPENDIX

ACTUARIAL CONCEPTS, METHODS AND ASSUMPTIONS

Actuarial Valuation

The report which actuaries prepare to report the amounts to be used for funding purposes for a defined benefit pension plan is referred to as an **actuarial valuation**. A valuation is made as of a specific date and is used to *estimate* the cost of benefits to be paid over varying periods of time in the future. Actuarial valuations are also required for plans which have been terminated. The estimated cost is expressed in terms of the present value of the expected future benefit payments to each individual participant. The present value is that amount which, if invested at the date of the valuation at a stated rate of interest, would provide for benefits expected to become payable. The present value attributable to each participant is aggregated to calculate the total estimated cost or obligation. A valuation is considered an estimate because there are significant uncertainties concerning future events that will affect the amount of benefits ultimately paid. An employee could live longer/shorter, earn more/less, and retire earlier/later than assumed. Return on investments could vary from the discount rate assumed.

For a given defined benefit pension plan, the amount paid to a retiree is determined by the benefit formula specified in the plan document. Formulas differ from plan to plan. One of the most common types of benefit formulas for a defined benefit pension plan consists of years of service multiplied by the average salary in the last five years of employment. In collectively bargained plans, the formula is often years of service multiplied by a fixed dollar rate which is negotiated by the union.

Actuarial Methods

An actuarial method is a mathematical model used to estimate the cost of a plan. Actuarial methods can be "accrued" or "projected" cost methods. An accrued method is based on accumulated benefits of a participant at the valuation date, making no projections about the future earnings or employment patterns. A projected cost method incorporates assumptions about future earnings. However, all actuarial cost methods used for funding and accounting assume that no new employees will be added to the plan and that participants that terminate in the future will not be replaced. The pension obligation is therefore based on the existing number of participants for service rendered as of the valuation date. This is a significant assumption that will change over time. It is important to understand that an actuarial valuation is not dynamic; it is a snapshot of estimated costs based on service rendered to date.

Pension plan actuarial valuations are prepared for different purposes and may use different actuarial methods and assumptions. There may be as many as three different valuations performed annually for a single pension plan, which consist of the following:

1. One valuation is used to determine the funding requirement that is required by ERISA and the IRS. This valuation is the one used for purposes of the preparation of Schedule B of Form 5500. Schedule B of Form 5500 requires the following type of information to be provided:
   - Date of the actuarial valuation
   - Current value of assets
   - Actuarial value of assets for funding standard account
   - Contributions made to the plan during the year by employer(s) and employees
   - Actuarial cost method used
   - Actuarial assumptions used
   - Statement of the funding standard account for the current plan year

   With respect to the information previously listed, the plan auditor should be able to agree the information regarding the current value of plan assets, the information regarding current liabilities of the plan by type of participant, contributions made to the plan, the actuarial cost method, and actuarial assumptions to either the plan's financial statements or to the actuarial valuation received directly from the actuary.
2. A second valuation is used to determine the pension obligation and expense recorded in the **plan sponsor's** financial statements, following the guidance of Statement of Financial Accounting Standards 87 (SFAS 87).
3. A third valuation is used in determining the pension obligation recorded or disclosed in the financial statements of the plan itself, following the guidance of SFAS 35.

SFAS 87 and SFAS 35 both specify the use of certain actuarial cost methods; however, there are differences between the requirements of each of the standards. While IRS and ERISA regulations allow any "reasonable" valuation method be used, they do not allow the method that is required by SFAS 35 for plans where the benefit formula is based on compensation. The method that is required by SFAS 35 also is not allowable for SFAS 87 purposes (unless there is no salary component to the benefit formula). The method required by SFAS 87 is allowable for IRS/ERISA purposes for many plans. Other actuarial methods are permissible for funding purposes and include the entry age normal, frozen initial liability, and aggregate actuarial methods.

The use of three different valuation methodologies, and in some cases three different sets of assumptions for a single plan, is an indication that there can be a number of different ways to assess a plan's funding status and cost. Again, the valuations prepared for these three purposes are only a snapshot of estimated costs based on existing employees and their service to date; these valuations are not intended to predict the actual cash outflows the plan will experience in the future.

	Allowable for use in		
Actuarial Method	*Plan's financials*	*Plan Sponsor's financials*	*Funding*
Unit credit	x		*
Projected unit credit		x	x
Entry age normal			x
Frozen initial liability			x
Aggregate			x

* *Generally not allowed for funding if benefit formula is compensation-based.*

Actuarial method for SFAS 35 purposes (plan's financial statements). SFAS 35 requires that the accumulated plan benefits reported in the plan's financial statements be at their actuarial present value, defined as those future benefit payments that are attributable under the plan's provisions to employees' service rendered to the valuation date.

Measurement is primarily based on employees' history of pay and service and other appropriate factors as of that date. Future salary changes are not considered. Future years of service are considered only in determining employees' expected eligibility for particular types of benefits, for example, early retirement, death, and disability benefits. The discount rate equals the expected long-term rate of return for plan assets. The discount rate should be consistent with returns, which are realistically achievable on the types of assets held by the plan. To the extent that the discount rate is based on values of existing plan assets, the values used in determining assumed rates of return shall be the values presented in the plan's financial statements.

The "unit credit" actuarial method reflects these requirements and is typically used for SFAS 35 purposes. An example of a valuation for one participant in a plan using the unit credit method is as follows:

Assume that the

- Participant has ten years of service as of the valuation date
- Annual benefit formula is 1% of the employee's average final salary over the last five years of employment multiplied by the years of service
- Current age is forty
- Retirement age is sixty-five
- Long-term rate of return is 10%
- Employee will live for twenty years after retirement
- Average salary over the past five years is $50,000

The obligation relating to this employee is calculated as follows:

Annual benefit: ($50,000 average salary) x (.01) x (10 years of accumulated service) = $5,000/year

Monthly benefit: $5,000/12 = $417/month

Present value (PV) at retirement date of $5,000 annuity, paid monthly over 20 years, discounted at 10% = $43,536

PV at valuation date of the above present valued obligation over the 25 years to retirement, discounted at 10% = $4,018

Approximate obligation at valuation date for participant = $4,000

(The previous calculation does not incorporate a factor to apply the probability of turnover, disability, early retirement, or of the individual dying prior to retirement.)

This calculation is performed for each plan participant. Note that the assumptions of turnover, early retirement, and disability are applied to the aggregation of the plan's total accumulated plan benefits. The present value amounts are aggregated to determine the total present value of accumulated benefits (the amount disclosed in the financial statements of the plan).

This unit credit valuation method results in a cost attribution pattern where costs are low in the early and middle years of a participant's career and accelerate rapidly near retirement as salary and years of service increase.

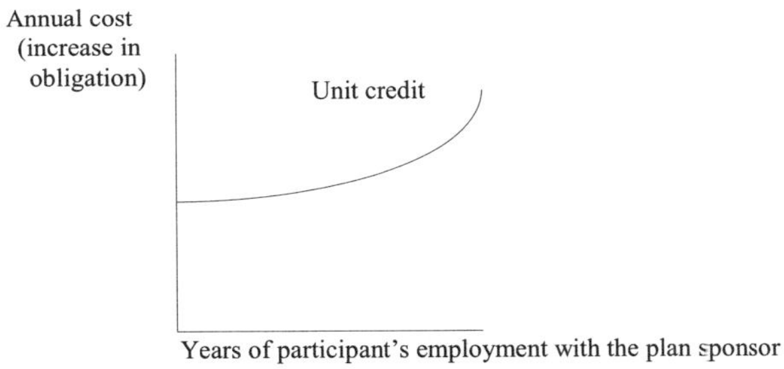

Actuarial method for SFAS 87 purposes (plan sponsor's financial statements). The SFAS 87 projected benefit obligation requires the valuation to include an assumption about future compensation levels for those plans basing benefits on compensation. The related accounting and disclosures of SFAS 87 also incorporate the effects of funding levels and anticipated return on plan assets. The "projected unit credit" method is used for a SFAS 87 valuation, which differs from the unit credit method by one important aspect; it incorporates expected salary levels over the period of the participant's employment. For a defined benefit pension plan which covers hourly employees, use of the unit credit method is acceptable. For such plans, the unit credit method yields the same results as the projected unit credit method.

Using the same assumptions as before, with the additional assumption that the participant's salary increases 3% per year (this rate is the gross rate increase, not net of inflation), we see that the obligation in year ten of employment is significantly larger than using the unit credit methodology (SFAS 35).

Assume

- Same assumptions as previous example, plus
- That the average salary of $50,000 increases 3% per year, or average salary over the five years preceding retirement of $105,000.

Annual benefit: ($105,000) x (.01) x (10 years of accumulated service) = $10,500/year

Monthly benefit: $10,500/12 = $875

PV at retirement date of $10,500, paid monthly over 20 years, discounted at 10% = $91,427

PV at valuation date of above present valued obligation over 25 years, discounted at 10% = $8,438

Approximate obligation at valuation date for participant = $8,400

The projected unit credit valuation method results in a cost attribution pattern where costs are more level throughout a participant's career.

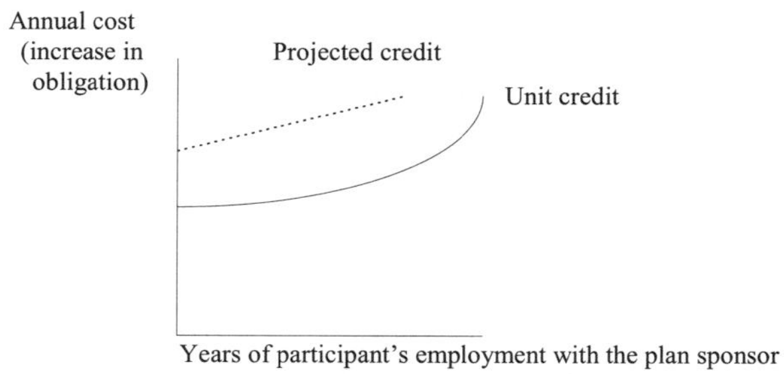

Actuarial methods for IRS and ERISA purposes (funding). IRS and ERISA regulations specify the rules for funding and require an annual actuarial valuation to determine the minimum that must be funded and the maximum contribution that is tax-deductible by the plan sponsor.

In general, a plan sponsor must contribute an amount equal to the "normal cost" attributable to the current year of an employee's service. However, the required contribution can be higher or lower than the normal cost, depending on how well-funded the plan is. If plan assets are greater than plan liabilities, then the contribution will be less than the normal cost and vice versa. Additionally, the Internal Revenue Code imposes an upper contribution limit by virtue of the "full funding limitation" rules above, which states that the contribution is not tax-deductible to the employer.

Generally, the plan's actuarial liability is determined by an actuarial valuation similar to that previously described for SFAS 35 and SFAS 87 purposes where it is the present value of benefits earned to the valuation date. As previously mentioned, a valuation method which incorporates future compensation increases must be used for plans that have benefit formulas that have a compensation component. The valuation may use different assumptions than those used for SFAS 35 and SFAS 87 purposes and must be opined by the actuary to be "reasonable."

A plan's actuarial assets are either at fair value or at market-related value. Market-related value is determined using a technique to smooth out severe swings in the year-to-year market values of plans.

The mechanism under ERISA for determining a plan's funding status is the "funding standard account." The funding standard account is an accumulation of charges and credits of actuarially determined items, contributions and special adjustments.

Among the charges to the funding standard account are

- The plan's normal cost
- The amortization of the following estimated costs as established by ERISA over a period which cannot exceed thirty years but also cannot be taken all in one year:
  - The unfunded actuarial liability
  - Increases in unfunded actuarial liabilities arising from plan amendments
  - Actuarial losses (e.g., actual mortality of participants later than the estimates originally used by the actuary)
  - Any increase in unfunded actuarial liability as a result of changes in actuarial assumptions (e.g., lower discount rate)

Credits to the funding standard account include

- Employer contributions paid plus contributions receivable at the end of the year if paid within a specified period of time
- The amortization of the following estimated costs as established by ERISA over a period which cannot exceed thirty years but also cannot be taken all in one year:
  - Actuarial gains, for example, resulting from higher turnover rates and lower average actual retirement age
  - Any decrease in unfunded actuarial liabilities resulting from changes in actuarial assumptions, such as an increase in the discount rate
  - Any decrease in unfunded actuarial liabilities resulting from plan amendments

The actuarial information and funding status is reported on Schedule B to IRS Form 5500, Annual Return/Report of Employee Benefit Plan.

Funding Status and PBGC Premiums

Title IV of ERISA established a program of termination insurance for defined benefit pension plans, which is administered by the Pension Benefit Guaranty Corporation (PGBC) under the jurisdiction of the Department of Labor. Defined benefit pension plans and some defined contribution pension plans, such as money purchase plans, are required to subscribe to this plan termination insurance. PBGC insurance premium rates are based on the number of participants (flat-rate portion) and the amount by which the plan's benefits are underfunded (variable-rate portion) based on the PBGC assumptions. PBGC assumptions are more conservative than SFAS 35, SFAS 87, and IRS/ERISA assumptions. Hence, plan liabilities on a PBGC basis are typically much higher. In general, the variable rate premium is .9%

of the unfunded PBGC liability. (Note that some exceptions apply to this general rule.) The basic fixed premium paid by single employers in 1999 is $9 per participant per year. The 1999 variable-rate charge is $9 per $1,000 of unfunded vested benefits. The premium rate for multiemployer plans is $2.60 per participant, per year.

Actuarial Assumptions

Actuarial valuations are based on both the methodology used (the actuarial method, as discussed above) and the assumptions about uncertainties about future events, or actuarial assumptions.

The significant assumptions in an actuarial valuation are: the interest return assumption, or discount rate; mortality rates; withdrawal rates; disability rates; and early and late retirement rates. Assumptions are suggested by the actuary, but must be approved by the plan sponsor who ultimately takes responsibility for the assumptions used by the actuary, except that the actuary must give an opinion that the assumptions used for determining the IRS and ERISA funding requirements are reasonable.

Interest return. The interest return assumption is used to discount future benefit payments. SFAS 35 valuations do not factor in the funding of the plan and thus use only one interest return assumption, which is the expected long-term rate of return for plan assets. The interest rate assumption has the most significant monetary impact in a pension valuation. If the interest rate changed by two percentage points in the examples above (which exclude certain other actuarial assumptions), the resulting obligations would change as follows:

Discount Rate	*Unit credit method*		*Projected credit method*	
	Annual benefit	*Obligation*	*Annual benefit*	*Obligation*
8%	$5,000/year	$7,300	$10,500/year	$15,400
10%	$5,000/year	$4,000	$10,500/year	$ 8,400
12%	$5,000/year	$2,250	$10,500/year	$ 4,700

Mortality and disability. The length of time an employee (and a spouse, if covered under a joint and survivor annuity option) will live affects the probability and timing of benefit payments. If an employee dies before becoming eligible for pension benefits, generally no payments are made unless the plan provides for a death benefit, which is fairly common. The total amount of pension benefits for an employee who reaches retirement is determined by how long s/he (and his/her spouse) live after retirement. Mortality tables based on experience studies are used in determining this probability.

There are several standard commonly used mortality tables, which are developed periodically by actuarial professional groups based on experience studies. A commonly used table is the "1983 Group Annuity Mortality Tables for males and females" (GAM). Because of a lag of a number of years between the time data collection occurs for the development of a table, the mortality rates do not incorporate the more recent increases in life expectancy.

Some plans develop their own mortality rates based on the specific experience of their plan participants. These are typically long-standing plans with a large number of participants in industries where mortality rates may differ from the standard rates.

Many pension plans also provide benefits to employees who become disabled while employed by the plan sponsor. Standard disability tables also are generally used to predict the rate of disability.

Retirement age. Most plans provide for a normal retirement age and early retirement with reduced benefits. Some plans may also permit early retirement under certain conditions such as company downsizings or restructurings, which may or may not result in a reduced benefit for the employee. Plans may also permit employees to work after the normal retirement age and continue to accrue service credits.

Withdrawal (turnover). In many plans, there is a vesting requirement whereby employees who leave the employment of the plan sponsor before completing the minimum period of service will not receive any pension benefits. The valuation should address the employees who leave the employment of the plan sponsor who are vested in their pension benefits but will not accrue future service. These individuals are still part of the plan and do affect the actuarial present value of accumulated plan benefits.

Future compensation levels. In plans whose benefit formulas contain a future compensation component, assumptions are made of future compensation increases due to increased experience of the employees and inflation. As previously mentioned, SFAS 35 valuations do not assume any change in compensation levels.

Social security benefits. In plans that incorporate the effect of social security benefits into the benefit formula (typically by reducing the pension benefit for a portion or all of the social security benefits), it is necessary to estimate future social security benefits. Generally this is done by assuming the social security benefit level in effect at the valuation date.

Actuarial Gains and Losses

Because the assumptions predict uncertain future events, those assumptions will differ from actual experience and will from time to time need to be "trued-up." The effects on the actuarially determined present value of accumulated plan benefits of deviations between actual experience and expected experience are called actuarial gains and losses. If experience has been favorable, the adjustments that result are actuarial gains; if experience has been unfavorable, the adjustments are actuarial losses. For example, when the actuary utilizes mortality tables to estimate the lifespan of plan participants, to the extent a participant lives longer than expected, resulting in more benefit payments to be made to the individual, that results in an actuarial loss. An actuarial gain would occur if a participant passes away earlier than estimated by the actuary.

Demographic Information Used in the Valuation

In making valuations, actuaries work with information provided by the plan sponsor. For each employee currently covered by the plan, former employees having vested rights and retired employees receiving benefits, the following demographic information is typically provided: employee name and identification number, date(s) of employment, retirement date, years of service, birth date (and spouse birth date), gender, and compensation history.

Dating of Actuarial Valuations

Actuarial valuations for pension plans are required each year, as separately required for use in the plan's financial statements (SFAS 35), the plan sponsor's financial statements (SFAS 87), and for funding purposes (IRS/ERISA). The measurement dates, or date as of which the plan obligation is measured, are shown in the table below.

Valuation used for	*Measurement date*
Plan's financial statements (SFAS 35)	Required as of the end **or** the beginning of the plan year. End of the year is considered "preferable."
Plan sponsor's financials (SFAS 87 and SFAS 106)	Required as of the date of the financial statements or, if used consistently from year to year, as of a date within three months prior to the date of the financial statements and rolled forward to year-end
Funding	Generally, as of the beginning of the year

For purposes of SFAS 35 valuations, in many cases, the valuations for accumulated plan benefits information presented as of the end of the plan year are actually dated January 1 as opposed to December 31 of the prior year. It is important to note that the plan's assets and obligations need to be presented as of the same date, and to the extent that the plan may have had plan amendments which became effective on January 1, such amendments should not be considered in the actuarial valuation; however, the effect of the amendment should be disclosed.

Measurement Issues Related to Retiree Health Benefits

A number of companies provide health benefits to their retired employees using a health and welfare employee benefit plan, commonly referred to as other postretirement employee benefits (OPEB). Benefits most commonly include medical care, prescription drugs, dental, and vision. Similar to pension plans, an actuarial valuation is used to estimate the obligation and is based on an actuarial method and assumptions about mortality, turnover, and discount rates. Unlike pension plans, there is usually no correlation between years of service and the amount of benefit provided by the plan.

A single OPEB actuarial valuation is typically used in both the plan's financial statements and in the plan sponsor's financial statements, and must follow the guidelines in SFAS 106, *Employers' Accounting for Postretirement Benefits Other Than Pensions,* and AICPA SOP 92-6, *Accounting and Reporting for Health and Welfare Plans*. The measurement date is the same as that required by SFAS 87 for pension plans, which is as of the date of the financial statements or, if used consistently from year to year, as of a date within three months prior to the date of the financial statements and rolled forward to the plan's year-end. As with other financial statement items requiring estimates, much of the information can be prepared as of an earlier date and projected forward.

The obligation estimate for an OPEB plan is more complicated than a pension calculation as benefits are often not provided as defined dollar amounts, but must be estimated using a number of additional assumptions. Additionally, the employee turnover assumption used in a pension valuation becomes more important to a retiree health benefit valuation because in most plans, participants do not receive benefits unless they actually retire from the employment of the plan sponsor itself and not a future employer. Retirement rate assumptions are also critical, as benefits paid prior to age 65 are usually fully subsidized (i.e., not reduced for early commencement as they are in a pension plan) and because benefits paid prior to age 65 also are not reduced by medicare coverage.

Those additional assumptions in the retiree health benefit estimate can include:

- Medical care cost trend rate. The total increase in the cost of providing medical services due to an increase in the cost of service, increased utilization of service, and advances in medicine and medical technology. The rate does not include increases due to the aging of the population. This assumption has the greatest impact on the obligation estimate. This rate is applied to base period per capita claims cost to estimate the per capita claims cost at each age during retirement. The rates are developed using past and present health care cost trends, developed from historical claims data, and consider estimates of health care inflation, changes in health care utilization and delivery patterns, technological advances, and changes in the health status of plan participants.
- Rate of pre-65 retirement. Individuals are eligible for Medicare benefits beginning at age 65. The extent of coordination of the medical plan with Medicare can influence utilization patterns of retirees and will significantly affect cost.
- Benefit plan design. The medical services covered by the employer and what cost the retiree will pay may change over time.
- Industry factors. The industry in which the retiree works may influence his or her lifestyle and type of illness or diseases experienced.
- Geographic location. Medical costs vary widely by areas of the country because of differing physician practice patterns and costs for the service provider.

- Retiree demographics and effects of aging. It is necessary to consider the differences in claim cost due to the age of the retiree, because individuals generally use more medical services as they age.
- Delivery system. The method of delivering the benefits or the type of medical plan used will influence the cost of providing the benefits.
- Effect of retiree coinsurance, copay arrangement, and deductibles. A reasonable estimate of coinsurance savings to the employer must be made, and the existence of copay arrangements and deductibles should also be considered.

OTHER ACTUARIAL CALCULATIONS

Health and Welfare Plans (Incurred But Not Reported Claims)

An actuarial estimate may also be used in benefit plan reporting for health and welfare plans which provide medical or dental benefits, to estimate the plan's liability for claims that had been incurred by the participants at the balance sheet date but not reported to the plan. This liability is commonly referred to as "incurred but not reported," or IBNR. Generally, historical claims data is used to estimate the lag between incurrence and reporting of a claim. The lag is then applied to a typical historical or expected claims amount for a period. For example, if the lag is estimated to be 1.5 months, and $1,000,000 of claims are paid in a typical month, the IBNR liability would be $1,500,000 at the balance sheet date. In addition, an estimate may also be required for catastrophic claims which may be incurred by participants. Historical catastrophic claim data would be used to estimate the lag between incurrence and reporting of a claim similar to other claims. Also, an actuarial valuation may be prepared to calculate the IBNR liability as well as any liability due to catastrophic claims.

Postemployment Benefits (SFAS 112)

As discussed in Chapter 9, Accounting, Auditing, and Reporting for Health and Welfare Plans, a health and welfare plan may be designed to provide postemployment benefits to participants. Such postemployment benefits may consist of the following: severance, salary continuation, disability-related benefits, job training and placement services, and continuation of benefits such as health care benefits and life insurance that may be provided by an employer to former or inactive employees after employment but before retirement. The liability for such benefits typically would be recorded in the financial statements, and an actuarial valuation may be required to estimate the employer's future liability to provide such benefits to participants. For further discussion of the accounting and reporting of postemployment benefits, see Chapter 9, Accounting, Auditing, and Reporting for Health and Welfare Plans.

GLOSSARY

*NOTE: Some of the following terms and definitions are excerpted from the AICPA audit and accounting guide, **Audits of Employee Benefits Plans.***

Accumulated plan benefits. Benefits that are attributable under the provisions of an employee benefit plan to employees' service rendered to the benefit information date.

Actuarial cost method. A recognized actuarial technique used for establishing the amount and incidence of employer contributions or accounting charges for pension cost under a pension plan.

Actuarial value of accumulated plan benefits. The amount as of a benefit information date that results from applying actuarial assumptions to the accumulated plan benefits, with the actuarial assumptions being used to adjust those amounts to reflect the time value of money (through discounts for interest) and the probability of payment (by means of decrements such as for death, disability, withdrawal, or retirement) between the benefit information date and the expected date of payment.

Allocated contract. A contract with an insurance company under which related payments to the insurance company are currently used to purchase immediate or deferred annuities for individual participants. These contracts are generally not included in the assets of an employee benefit plan.

Benefit information date. The date as of which the actuarial present value of accumulated plan benefits is presented.

Benefits. Payment to which participants may be entitled under an employee benefit plan, including pension benefits, disability benefits, death benefits, health benefits, child and dependent care benefits, and benefits due upon termination of employment.

Cash-or-deferred arrangement (section 401(k) plan or CODA). A plan that may be incorporated into a profit-sharing or stock bonus plan (a few pre-ERISA money purchase pension plans also incorporate cash-or-deferred arrangements). Under this arrangement, a participant is permitted to elect to receive amounts in cash or have them contributed to the plan as employer contributions on behalf of the participant.

Common or commingled trust (CCT). A trust for the collective investment and reinvestment of assets contributed from employee benefit plans. A CCT is maintained by more than one employer or a controlled group of corporations and is administered by a bank, trust company, or similar institution that is regulated, supervised, and subject to periodic examination by a state or federal agency.

Contract value. The value of an unallocated contract. This value is determined by the insurance company in accordance with the terms of the contract.

Contributions receivable. Amounts due as of the date of the financial statements. Amounts receivable include legal or contractual obligations and, for a single-employer plan, obligations resulting from a formal commitment.

Contributory plan. An employee benefit plan under which participants bear at least a portion of the cost of the plan.

Defined benefit pension plan. A pension plan that specifies a determinable pension benefit, usually based on such factors as age, years of service, and salary. A defined benefit pension plan may also include a plan that is funded pursuant to periodic agreements that specify a fixed rate of employer contributions (for example, a collectively bargained multiemployer plan).

Defined contribution plan. A plan that provides an individual account for each participant and provides benefits that are based on (1) amount contributed to the participant's account by the employer and/or employee, (2) investment experience, and (3) any forfeitures allocated to the account, less any administrative expenses charged to the plan.

Deposit administration contract (DA). A type of contract under which contributions are not currently used to purchase single-payment deferred annuities for individual participants. Payments to the insurance company that are intended to provide future benefits to present employees are credited to an account. For investment purposes, the monies in the account are commingled with other assets of the insurance company. The account is credited with interest at the rate which is specified in the contract. The account is reduced by the purchase price of annuities when participants retire and with any incidental benefits (death, disability, and withdrawals) which are paid directly from the account.

Discretionary trust. An arrangement in which the trustee has discretionary authority and control over investments and is authorized by the plan or its investment committee to make investment decisions.

DOL. The United States Department of Labor.

Employee. A person who has rendered or is presently rendering service.

Employee stock ownership plan (ESOP). A stock bonus plan that borrows money from, or on the guarantee of, a related party (party-in-interest) for the purpose of acquiring securities issued by the plan sponsor and that invests primarily in such securities (a leveraged ESOP). The term "employee stock ownership plan" is also generally applied to (1) nonleveraged stock bonus plans that satisfy various requirements and (2) profit-sharing plans (and certain pre-ERISA money purchase pension plans) that invest primarily in securities issued by the plan sponsor.

ERISA. The Employee Retirement Income Security Act of 1974.

Fair value. The amount that the plan could reasonably expect to receive for a plan investment in a current sale between a willing buyer and a willing seller.

FASB. The Financial Accounting Standards Board. The Financial Accounting Standards Board establishes accounting standards.

Form 5500. A form developed jointly by the IRS, DOL, and PBGC, which may be used to satisfy the annual reporting requirements of the IRC and Titles I and IV of ERISA.

Frozen plan. See **wasting trust.**

Full-scope audit. An audit of the financial statements of an employee benefit plan in accordance with generally accepted auditing standards.

Funding policy. The standards which dictate the amounts and timing of contributions by the employer(s), participants, and any other sources (for example, state subsidies or federal grants) to provide the benefits which are specified by the plan.

GAAP. Generally accepted accounting principles.

GAAS. Generally accepted auditing standards.

General account. An undivided fund maintained by an insurance company that, for investment purposes, commingles plan assets with other assets of the insurance company. In other words, funds held by an insurance company that are not maintained in a separate account are said to be held in its general account.

Guaranteed investment contract (GIC). A contract between an insurance company and a plan that provides for a guaranteed return on principal which is invested over a specified period of time.

Health and welfare benefit plan. A plan that provides (1) medical, dental, visual, psychiatric, or long-term health care; severance benefits; life insurance; accidental death or dismemberment benefits; (2) unemployment, disability, vacation or holiday benefits; and (3) apprenticeships, tuition assistance, day care, housing subsidies, or legal services benefits.

IBNR. Claims that are incurred by eligible participants but not yet reported to the plan.

IRC. The Internal Revenue Code.

IRS. The Internal Revenue Service.

Immediate participation guarantee contract (IPG). A type of contract under which contributions are not currently applied to the purchase of single-payment deferred annuities for individual participants. Payments to the insurance company that will be used to provide future benefits to current employees, plus its share of the insurance company's actual investment income, are credited to an account. The insurance company is then obligated to make lifetime benefit payments to retired employees.

Individual separate account. A separate account in which only one plan participates.

Insured plan. A plan that is funded through an insurance contract.

Investment fund option. An alternative investment option made available to participants in a defined contribution plan. The alternatives are usually pooled fund vehicles (e.g., registered investment companies or commingled funds) providing varying types of investments, such as equity funds or fixed-income funds. The participant can select among the various available alternatives and may periodically change the selection.

Limited-scope audit. Au audit in which ERISA allows the plan administrator to instruct the plan auditor not to perform any auditing procedures with respect to information prepared and certified by a bank or similar institution, or by an insurance carrier that is regulated, supervised, and subject to periodic examination by a state or federal agency, other than to compare the information provided with that which is presented in the financial statements.

Master trust. A combined trust account made up of assets of some or all of the employee benefit plans of a company that sponsors more than one plan or a group of corporations under common control. Each plan has an undivided interest in the assets of the trust, and ownership is represented by a calculation of proportionate dollar interest or by units of participation.

Money purchase pension plan. A defined contribution plan under which employer contributions are based on a fixed formula that is not related to profit.

Multiemployer plan. A plan in which more than one employer is required to contribute to the plan. The multiemployer plan is maintained pursuant to one or more collective bargaining agreements.

Multiple-employer plan. A plan in which more than one employer participates and includes only plans whose contributions from individual employers are available to pay benefits to all participants.

Named fiduciary. The individual responsible for the operation and administration of an employee benefit plan, including the naming of a plan administrator. The named fiduciary is usually an officer or other employee of the plan sponsor who reports to the plan sponsor's board of directors or trustees or management.

Net assets available for benefits. The difference between a plan's assets and its liabilities. For purposes of this definition, a plan's liabilities do not include participants' accumulated plan benefits.

Noncontributory plan. An employee benefit plan under which participants do not make contributions to the plan.

Nonvested benefit information. The actuarial present value of nonvested accumulated plan benefits.

Participant. Any employee or former employee, or any member or former member of a trade or other employee association (e.g., union), or the beneficiaries of those individuals, for whom there are accumulated plan benefits.

Party-in-interest. A fiduciary or employee of the plan, any person who provides services to the plan, an employer whose employees are covered by the plan, an employee association whose members are covered by the plan, a person who owns 50% or more of such an employer or employee association, or relatives of those persons previously listed.

PBGC. The Pension Benefit Guaranty Corporation.

Pension benefits. Periodic (usually monthly) payments made to a person who has retired from employment.

Plan administrator. The person or group of persons responsible for the content and issuance of a plan's financial statements in much the same way that management is responsible for the content and issuance of a business enterprise's financial statements.

Pooled separate account. A separate account in which several plans participate.

Profit-sharing plan. A defined contribution plan in which employer contributions to the plan are made on a discretionary basis or based on a fixed formula related to profits, compensation, or other factors.

Prohibited transaction. A transaction between a plan and a party in interest that is prohibited by ERISA.

PWBA. The Pension and Welfare Benefits Administration, a division of the US Department of Labor.

Reporting date. The date at which the information regarding the net assets available for benefits is presented.

Self-directed plan. A defined contribution plan in which the participant authorizes specific investment transactions, such as purchases and sales of specific common stocks and bonds. A self-directed plan does not provide predetermined investment fund options; participants may purchase or sell any common stock or bond which is available.

Self-funded plan. A plan funded through accumulated contributions and investment income.

Separate account. A special account established by an insurance company solely for the purpose of investing the assets of one or more plans. Funds in a separate account are not commingled with other assets or the insurance company for investment purposes.

Service. Periods of employment taken into consideration under an employee benefit plan.

Single-employer plan. A plan sponsored by one employer.

Sponsor. For a pension plan established or maintained by a single employer--the employer; for a plan established or maintained by an employee organization--the employee organization; in the case of a plan established or maintained jointly by two or more employers or by one or more employers and one or more employee organizations--the association, committee, joint board of trustees, or other group of representatives of the parties who have established or who maintain the pension plan.

Stock bonus plan. A defined contribution plan under which distributions are normally made in stock of the employer, unless the person receiving the distribution elects otherwise.

Target benefit plan. A form of money purchase plan under which the employer's annual contribution, on behalf of each participant, is the actuarially determined amount required to fund a target benefit established by a plan formula. The target benefit is usually based on compensation and length of service. For some target benefit plans, the substance of the plan may be to provide a defined benefit to its participants.

Third-party administrator (TPA). A party unrelated to the plan who contracts to be responsible for plan administration.

Thrift plan. A profit-sharing or stock bonus plan under which participants make after-tax employee contributions to the plan that are usually matched, in whole or in part, by employer contributions.

Unallocated contract. A contract with an insurance company under which related payments to the insurance company are accumulated in an unallocated fund to be used to meet benefit payments when employees retire. Benefits are provided either directly or through the purchase of annuities. Funds in an unallocated contract may also be withdrawn and otherwise invested. Unallocated contracts are included in the statement of net assets available for benefits of an employee benefit plan.

Unfunded plan. A plan whereby benefits are paid directly from the general assets of the employer or the employee organization that sponsors the plan.

Unit of participation. An undivided interest in the underlying assets of a trust.

Vested benefit information. The actuarial present value of vested accumulated plan benefits.

Vested benefits. Benefits that are not contingent on an employee's future service.

Wasting trust. A plan under which participants no longer accrue benefits but that will remain in existence as long as necessary to pay benefits that have already accrued.